THE TEUTONIC KNIGHTS

THE TEUTONIC KNIGHTS

A MILITARY HISTORY

William Urban

GREENHILL BOOKS, LONDON
MBI PUBLISHING COMPANY, MINNESOTA

The Teutonic Knights: A Military History

First published 2003
This edition published 2005 by Greenhill Books/Lionel Leventhal Ltd, Park House, 1 Russell Gardens,
London NW11 9NN
and
MBI Publishing Company
Galtier Plaza, Suite 200, 380 Jackson Street, St Paul MN 55101-3885, USA

British Library and Library of Congress Cataloguing-in Publication Data available

Hardback ISBN 1-85367-535-0
Paperback ISBN 1-85367-667-5

For more information on our books, please visit www.greenhillbooks.com, email
sales@greenhillbooks.com, or telephone us within the UK on 020 8458 6314. You can also write to us
at the above address.

Typeset by Servis Filmsetting Ltd, Manchester
Printed and bound in Great Britain by Creative Print and Design (Wales), Ebbw Vale

Contents

Maps

List of Illustrations

Endpapers: Crusaders in combat against eastern warriors.

Preface

My previous publications in Baltic history* have been of four kinds: translations with Jerry C. Smith of important chronicles; articles attempting to correct factual errors or present new interpretations of events in the crusades in Prussia and Livonia; summaries of the crusades for various encyclopaedias; and five detailed histories of individual crusading eras – the thirteenth centuries in Prussia and Livonia, the later crusades in those regions, and the decisive events connected with the battle at Tannenberg and its aftermath. This volume is, therefore, the culmination of almost forty years of research and writing. It is the first survey of the military history of the Teutonic Order in English and the first lengthy one in any language in almost a century.

There are many people that any author can reasonably thank for contributing to his or her work. I am no different. At the beginning was Archie Lewis, who persuaded me to work on a subject that few in the United States knew much about at the time – the Baltic frontier between Roman Catholicism, Russian Orthodoxy and paganism. The German-American Clubs and the Fulbright Commission financed a year in Hamburg, when I learned something about the subject and began to write. Several years later the Fulbright Commission gave me a grant to work at the Herder Institut in Marburg, a marvellous location for research that I subsequently visited many times. And so it went, right down to the publisher of my most recent books, John Rackauskas and the Lithuanian Research and Studies Center in Chicago. All along the way I have met interesting and helpful people, visited places I will never forget, and made life-long friends.

William Urban, 2003

* See Bibliography.

Introduction

Why a book on the military history of the Teutonic Knights now? Why not earlier? Good questions, and questions worth considering. One answer is that the best historians of the crusades have traditionally concentrated their attentions on the Holy Land; most medieval historians in recent decades have lacked much interest in military affairs; and amateur historians in the English-speaking world are not prepared to handle the many languages involved in studying Baltic and East Central European history. In addition, the Cold War made research in those regions difficult and, too often, also made people wonder if military history specialists were not politically suspect. Another good answer, perhaps more fundamental, is that the English-speaking public was generally unaware that there had been crusades in the Baltic, and, moreover, for many years also lost interest in the medieval efforts to recover Jerusalem. No demand, hence no response by authors and publishers.

However, public taste changes. Today books on the crusades are popular once again. Moreover, there is an interest in crusading activities on the periphery of Europe. Just as Chaucer's knight understood that there were crusading efforts in Spain, Prussia, Asia Minor and the Balkans equal to those in the Holy Land, or almost so, now modern scholars and the general public recognise this as well.

Nor does the Baltic seem as physically distant as it was only a few years ago. Tourists can now easily visit towns and castles built by the Teutonic Knights. Castle ruins are romantic, and ruins abound in what were once Prussia and Livonia. Poland has taken the lead in developing this theme: Malbork (Marienburg) is already a tourist centre, as is the battlefield of Grunwald (Tannenberg), with its disputed positioning of the opposing armies; and the historic centres of ancient towns such as Gdańsk (Danzig) have been restored. Latvia has Riga, Estonia the old city of Tallinn (Reval), completely surrounded by the original walls and towers, and Lithuania has the beautiful island castle at Trakai. People who have seen Eisenstein's inaccurate but thrilling movie *Alexander Nevsky* can visit the shores of the lake where the real battle was fought, on its frozen surface, on 5 April 1242.

There are two sites in Central Europe which are also worth seeing – Bad Mergentheim in Germany, north-east of Stuttgart, which was the seat of the grand master of the Teutonic Order after the secularisation of the Prussian lands; and Vienna, where the modern headquarters sit one block from St Stephan's cathedral. Both have attractive museums. There are also the order's many surviving convents, churches and castles in Germany, Austria, the Czech Republic and even Italy.

There is much history to be learned here, or perhaps re-learned: the Teutonic Knights were once powerful and respected in Central Europe, but their reputation has suffered in medieval and modern times at the hands of propagandists, nationalists, Protestants and secularists. This drumbeat of condemnation was, of course, to some degree earned, but was exaggerated by the accompanying suggestions that their enemies were pure in heart, mind, and action. These perceptions are now being rethought.

Similarly, our understanding of Europe is being revised in countless ways. The frontiers of medieval Christendom are remarkably similar to those of the modern European Union, and wars on the periphery represent challenges for modern statesmen. Chamberlain could abandon Czechoslovakia to Hitler as a place far distant, about which Englishmen knew little; but today newspaper readers in the English-speaking world can talk knowledgeably about European conflicts much farther away and more difficult to understand. Even so, those of us who experienced the difficulties of travelling in East Central Europe before 1989, and who try to describe our experiences to students and younger colleagues, already encounter faces as uncomprehending as when we attempt to explain the complexities of medieval life and politics.

Hitler, by the way, mistrusted Roman Catholics and hated nobles, so he had nothing good to say about the Teutonic Order. As a lower-class Austrian he disliked the Prussian Junkers too (who, in any case, mostly came from Brandenburg, not East Prussia, were almost all Protestants, and only very rarely had ancestors who were members of the military order). So for understanding the military history of the Teutonic Order, it is best for us to drop the Hollywood stereotypes until the next Indiana Jones fantasy comes along. The true stories about the Teutonic Knights are sufficiently interesting (exciting, controversial, etc) that we do not have to distort them, and modern politics already contain sufficient misleading stereotypes without digging back into medieval history for more.

It is my hope that this volume will further our understanding of a very important era in military history, of the complexities of medieval politics, to a certain extent of human behaviour in general, and of the ways that modern societies think about their past. I find narrative history relaxing, especially when it is removed from the constraints of nationalism and politics. So settle back, and take a moment to enjoy an armchair time-travel back to the Middle Ages, back to a time when men and women were neither better nor worse, perhaps, than today, just somewhat different.

1

The Military Orders

Missionaries and Armed Missions

The medieval Roman Catholic Church was often of two minds about the use of force to carry out its various missions in secular society. Firstly, one must forgive the sinner without forgetting the need to protect those who are sinned against. Therefore to forgive the repentant robber is one thing, to ignore robbery is another. Similarly, it was important to enjoin priests from taking up weapons and to encourage believers to resolve their personal disputes peacefully; but it was also necessary to support those secular rulers who were responsible for protecting the priests and their congregations from outside attack and domestic violence.

No one can pretend that medieval society was peaceful, or that piety equalled pacifism. Yet monasteries and nunneries provided secure moral and physical refuge from the turmoil of daily politics, and most Roman Catholics who approved of using force in defending the realm and in arresting criminals were aware of the New Testament injunctions against killing and violence. This stood in sharp contrast to the blatant worship of strength and cunning that was central to Scandinavian paganism; the Viking sagas gloried in their heroes' deeds in ways that Western epic poetry could hardly match. Yet even the most valiant Vikings came to understand, through stories such as the *Njal Saga*, that paganism was no foundation for a proper society; there had to be some underpinning for government other than rule by the strongest.

For the most part it was missionaries who persuaded the regional strongmen in Scandinavia that, for the good of their people and their own survival, they had to end the ancient way of life based on plunder and war. That is, before anything else, they had to become Christians. Once these newly baptised strongmen made themselves kings of Norway, Denmark and Sweden, they had clerical advice on how to collect taxes, enlist other powerful lords to serve them and enforce their edicts, and erect the foundations of a state government. Surprisingly quickly this brought an end to the Viking reign of terror across northern Europe.

To a lesser degree (or a greater, depending on one's point of view), the Western military response to the Northmen's raids aided in this conversion process. The development of feudal institutions created a warrior class in North-Western Europe that was better trained and equipped than Vikings were, with peasants who provided them with the means of buying weapons and horses, building castles and supplying garrisons. Also, as some Viking leaders took over Western lands it became in their interest to defend their new properties against relatives who still saw French, English, Scottish and Irish farmers as their natural prey.

Although many missionaries entered pagan lands without armed guards, they were courting martyrdom; and in truth, some of those priests and monks would have welcomed the opportunity to die for their faith and thereby earn a prominent place among the elect in heaven. But there were relatively few trained churchmen, and the rulers of Western states needed them at home even more than the Church needed martyrs. Consequently, many years before, when Irish priests first began to work among the pagan Germans, Frankish rulers sent armed guards to accompany them. This established the practice of sending along skilled warriors to protect the missionaries, a practice that ultimately lead to the crusade in Livonia. Such guards did not save St Boniface from Frisian assassins, but for other missionaries – those who did not insist on cutting down holy woods for lumber to build their churches – their presence was sufficient warning that open resistance would not be tolerated.

The combination of preaching even at the risk of the missionary's life, of encouraging non-Christian rulers to emulate successful Christian monarchs, and of threats to use force, was not a strategy that could work against Moslems. Although we do not remember the Islamic invasions of Europe – they lack the glamour and flair of the Northmen, and their ships were standard Mediterranean galleys – Moslems pushed into northern Spain, sacked many Italian cities, set up bases in the Alps, and regarded southern France as a good place to take a vacation.

Frankish volunteers in the Spanish wars against the Moors and Islamic volunteers from North Africa long predated the crusades. Similarly, Western mercenaries were fighting for the Byzantines against the Turks before Pope Urban II issued his call in late 1095 for the Franks to retake the Holy Land from an enemy of Christianity, which was oppressing believers and preventing pilgrims from worshipping at the holy places in and around Jerusalem.

Careful listeners caught papal references to the benefits that would accrue to local societies if all the riffraff and thugs put their energies and talents into fighting the enemies of Christendom rather than beating up on one another and on their innocent fellow-citizens. Just getting unruly nobles and their followers out of the country for a while would, he intimated, bring peace at home. This is an often-forgotten aspect of military service that is worth remembering – it was not long ago that Western judicial systems, faced with the problem of deciding what to do with wayward young males, gave them the choice of jail time or enlisting in the armed forces. It was hoped that a little discipline, a glimmering vision of having a larger purpose in life, and just growing up would change a juvenile delinquent into a useful citizen.

Finding a place to serve society effectively was one of the roles performed by monastic orders, but a life of celibacy and fasting, reading and hoeing, was not attractive to youths trained as warriors, who saw fast horses and sharp swords as more exciting than long prayers and hymns in Latin. The military orders, however, were just what the church doctors ordered – and they were accepting recruits even in years when no crusade was in sight.

The role of the Christian knight was not to spread the Gospel, but to protect those who had the calling and the training to do so. The Christian knight was not well educated (though he was far from being the ignorant lout so often decried), but he was usually conventionally pious and extraordinarily willing to put his life at risk and his money in the hands of strangers in the hope of accomplishing feats that brought him few, if any, material benefits. One may talk about the valuable products that merchants brought back from the east, but what real wealth existed in the shiploads of Palestinian earth that Pisans hauled home for their cemetery is beyond the grasp of the modern mind. That may be the most important point of all – that the mind of the medieval crusader is not always to be understood as equivalent to anything in mainstream modern post-industrial society. It can be understood, of course, to a certain degree, but only on its own terms.

✠

Lessons of the Early Crusades

The capture of Jerusalem by the Franks in the first crusade (1095–9) demonstrated the great strength of that combination of religious enthusiasm, military technology and expertise, growing population and economic vitality, and the new confidence of secular and ecclesiastical elites which characterised Western Europe by the end of the eleventh century. The floods of Western warriors that had set out on the great adventure had been reduced to a thin trickle of hungry, exhausted men by disease, desertion and death in battle by the time they reached the Holy Land. But those few survivors were still able to overwhelm some of the new and fragile Turkish states that ruled over sullen and angry Arabs, some of whom were Christians. Then, as was only partly anticipated, once the crusaders' immediate task was crowned with success most of the knights and clerics wanted to return home. Too few warriors remained to complete the conquest, and barely enough reinforcements arrived to hold what had been won. The peasants who had set out on the great pilgrimage to Jerusalem had been massacred not far from Constantinople, and the Italian merchant communities that had rejoiced at the opening of the eastern markets were soon quarrelling over the right to exploit them. It appeared that the crusader states would be short-lived phenomena, destined to survive only until the Turks found a leader who could organise local resources and imbue his followers with a religious passion equal to that of the Western newcomers.

In the ensuing decades each time a Turkish leader arose who dared attack the crusader kingdoms, the West could react only slowly, raising ponderous armies that arrived too late to be fully effective. It was clear to all that some new kind of military organisation was needed, one that could provide experienced knights as garrisons for isolated and endangered castles; which could gather supplies and treasures in Europe and transport them to the Holy Land to feed and equip those garrisons; that understood local conditions and could explain them to newly-arrived crusaders; and was not involved in the dynastic ambitions of the great families. The Westerners found this organisation in the military orders.

The first military order was the Knights Templar, probably founded in 1118 by a handful of visiting French knights whose religious fervour led them to leave their secular lives for one of worship and service to the Church. Technically the first Templars were probably closer to a lay confraternity than a monastic order, not unlike organisations one still finds in the Roman Catholic world today, performing useful services for their communities. King Baldwin II of Jerusalem gave them lodgings in his palace on the Dome of the Rock. Crusaders believed that this site was the location of Solomon's Temple; hence the new organisation became known as the Templars.

The Templars might have remained another obscure and short-lived noble confraternity had not the patriarch of Jerusalem enjoined them to employ their military talents in escorting pilgrims along a dangerous stretch of road from the coast to the holy city. For years the Templars performed their duties in remarkable obscurity and with only moderately notable success, but they took pride in their accomplishments; their grand masters later commemorated the early years of poverty by using a seal that depicted two knights riding on one horse (implying that they could not afford two mounts). In the course of time their talents and knowledge of the land won recognition, and rather than being undervalued their contributions to the defence of the Holy Land were somewhat exaggerated – this was good for recruiting new and more wealthy volunteers. By the 1130s the order was on its way to fame and prosperity. Recruits flooded in, usually bringing 'dowries' in the form of land and money that were necessary to support the order's dedicated warriors in the Holy Land.

The Knights of Saint John, better known as the Hospitallers, were the second military order. Their foundation was earlier than the Templars', however, dating to about 1080, and papal recognition came sooner, too, in about 1113, but they assumed a military function only in the 1130s. As their name implies, their original purpose was to provide medical services to pilgrims and crusaders.

There was considerable scepticism among traditional churchmen about permitting clerics to shed blood; the knights were merely friars, not priests, but they had taken vows and were therefore clerics. One of the oldest traditions of Christendom was non-resistance to evil – it took very little reflection for any Christian to remember that Christ had reproved Peter for raising his sword to defend his Lord from arrest and crucifixion. On the other hand, bishops and abbots had led armies since time immemorial, and numerous popes had blessed armies fighting enemies of the faith. St Bernard of Clairvaux (1090–1153), one of the dominant personalities of his time, provided the ultimate rationale for the military orders in a treatise entitled *De Laude Novae Militiae* ('In Praise of the New Knighthood'). He proclaimed, first, the importance of the holy places for reflection and inspiration. He wrote that such places were essential to the salvation of those pilgrims who travelled long distances and endured great hardships in order to pray at sites significant to the life of Christ and His saints. St Bernard attributed special significance to the Holy Sepulchre, Christ's tomb, a place where all pilgrims longed to pray. Then he made the obvious connection to the importance of crusaders maintaining access to those sites, a task that Turkish rulers were already making more difficult. Of course, dynastic politics in the kingdom of Jerusalem were not helping the situation; the patriarch of Jerusalem lacked the means to support a conventional force of knights or mercenaries; and not even St Bernard had been able to persuade secular rulers to work together during the Second Crusade (1147–8). The military orders were the obvious best means of carrying out St Bernard's perception of the crusaders' mission – to make the land and sea routes safe for pilgrims.

The military orders met practical, religious and psychological needs, and were perfectly suited to providing garrisons for the castles in the Holy Land during those long, boring and dangerous times between crusading expeditions. Eric Christensen, whose excellent book *The Northern Crusades* cannot be praised sufficiently, summarises this in a chapter entitled 'The Armed Monks: Ideology and Efficiency'.* Rulers learned that the military orders were willing to serve in places that secular knights would not, or could not. The military orders also responded to deeply felt needs of the human psyche – they reconciled the apparent contradictions between spiritual and earthly warfare. Christians did not have to remain passive when confronted by great evils; nor did they have to wait for a shift in public opinion or the presence of a great leader to raise an armed force. The military orders made the crusade an on-going operation, one that never ceased or rested.

The armament of the knights of the military orders always remained essentially that current in Western and Central Europe, reflecting minor changes generation by generation. In general each warrior wore mail armour, a helmet and greaves, carried a spear and shield, used a heavy sword with great effectiveness, and rode a large war-horse that was trained to charge into bodies of armed men or against oncoming horses. The only major concessions to climate were the wearing of a light surcoat that protected the mail from the direct rays of the sun, and avoiding travel in the heat of the day. The harsh climate of the Holy Land was, of course, a distinct shock to visitors from Northern Europe, who were often quickly prostrated from the heat and local diseases. This made the presence of the military orders all the more important, in that they could provide advice and example to the newcomers, which, if taken, would convert such newly-arrived crusaders into effective warriors rather than invalids or easy victims of Turkish fighting skills.

The contrast between the brute force of Western knights and the subtlety of the swift, lightly-armed Turkish and Arab warriors is part of what makes the crusades interesting from the intellectual point of view. There was never a question of two armies simply going at one another, with the stronger and more numerous prevailing. Instead, there was a complex interaction of strategy and tactics, each side possessing advantages and disadvantages, with the commanders weighing and calculating each move carefully before committing their forces to action. That is, weighing and calculating as much as was possible, always aware that the nature of warfare is to flout all plans and predictions. No general, no army, could forever impose order on the chaos of battle. Climate, geography, numbers, equipment and supplies all had their

---

* Eric Christensen, *The Northern Crusades* (Penguin, London and New York, 1998). Christensen is not only a solid scholar, but his pithy comments are often very witty as well.

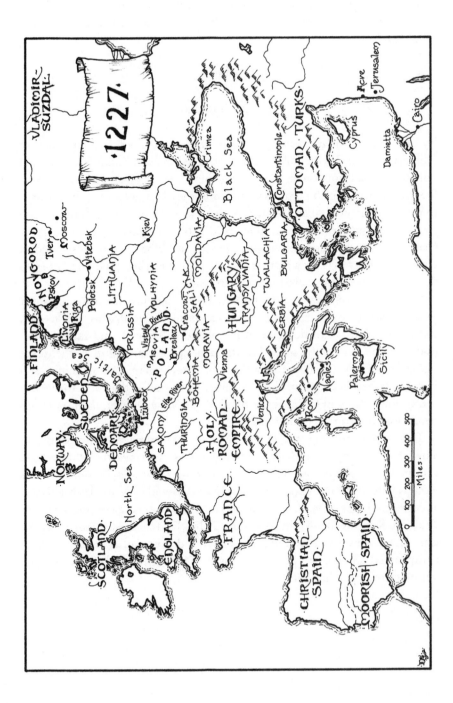

part in determining victory or defeat, but in the end much rested on individual and collective wills. Also, as both Christian and Moslem conceded, on the will of God.

✠

Other Crusades

By the mid-eleventh century it was well recognised that enemies of Christianity and Christendom existed outside the Holy Land. Spaniards and Portuguese had no trouble identifying their long struggle against Moslem foes as analogous to the crusades, and soon they had persuaded the Church to offer volunteers similar spiritual benefits as were promised to those who went to defend Jerusalem. Germans and Danes, inspired by St Bernard of Clairvaux, attacked ancient enemies east of the Elbe River. This Wendish Crusade of 1147 overran a bastion of Slavic paganism and piracy and opened the way for eastward migration and expansion.

Poles were soon aware of the potential of employing the crusading spirit in their own eastward and northward expansion. The Prussians, however, were more difficult to defeat than the Wends had been, and they had no leaders who could be persuaded of the benefits of conversion, as the dukes along the southern Baltic coastline in Mecklenburg, Pomerania and Pomerellia had been. Instead, after initial successes in the early thirteenth century, especially in Culm at the bend of the Vistula River, their garrisons fled before the pagan counterattacks.

Technically speaking, the Polish invasions of Prussia were not crusades. They had not been authorised by the popes nor preached throughout Europe by the clergy. But that was a technicality that the Teutonic Knights would correct when, in the late 1220s, Duke Conrad of Masovia and his relatives invited Grand Master Hermann von Salza to send a contingent of his Teutonic Knights to assist in defending Polish lands against Prussian paganism. There was never much thought given to defence, of course. The Poles had planned all along to conquer Prussia. They only needed a little help. Temporarily, they thought.

2

The Foundation of the Teutonic Order

The Third Crusade

Germans had expected the Third Crusade (1189–91) to be the most glorious triumph that Christian arms had ever achieved. The indomitable red-bearded Hohenstaufen emperor, Friedrich Barbarossa (1152–90), had brought his immense army intact across the Balkans and Asia Minor, had smashed the Turkish forces that had blocked the land route east from Constantinople for a century, and had crossed the difficult Cilician mountain passes leading into Syria, whence his forces could pass easily into the Holy Land. There he was expected to lead the combined armies of the Holy Roman Empire, France and England to recover the lost ports on the Mediterranean Sea, opening the way for trade and reinforcements, after which he would lead the Christian host on to the liberation of Jerusalem. Instead, he drowned in a small mountain stream. His vassals dispersed, some hurrying back to Germany because their presence was required at the election of Friedrich's successor, his son Heinrich VI; others because they anticipated a civil war in which they might lose their lands. Only a few great nobles and prelates honoured their vows by continuing their journey to Acre, which was under siege by crusader armies from France and England.

The newly-arrived Germans suffered terrible agonies from heat and disease in Acre, but their psychological torment may have equalled their physical ailments. Richard the Lionheart (1189–99), the English king who was winning immortal fame by feats of valour, hated the Hohenstaufen vassals who had driven his Welf brother-in-law, Heinrich the Lion (1156–80), into exile a few years before; and he missed few opportunities to insult or humiliate his supposed allies. Eventually Richard recovered Acre,

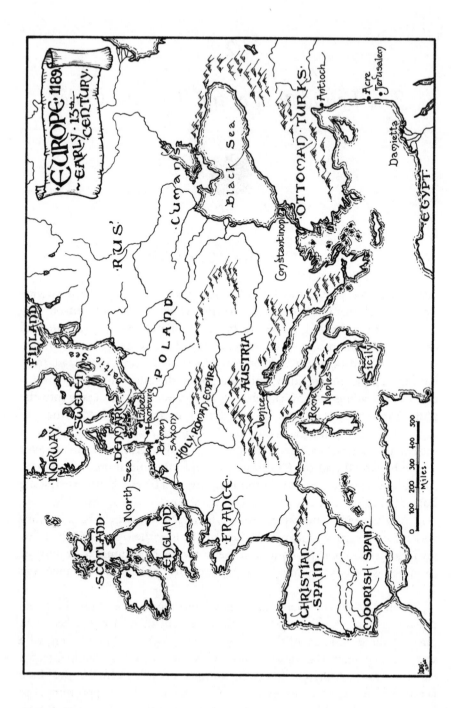

but he achieved little else. The French king, Phillip Augustus (1180–1223), furious at Richard's repeated insults, went home in anger, and most Germans left too, determined to get revenge on Richard at the first opportunity – as the duke of Austria later did, by turning him over to the new Hohenstaufen emperor for ransom. All German nobles and prelates looked back on this crusading episode with bitter disappointment. Reflecting on the high hopes with which they had set out, they felt that they had been betrayed by everyone – by the English, by the Byzantines, by the Welfs, and by one another. They had but one worthwhile accomplishment to show for all their suffering, or so they thought later: the foundation of the Teutonic Order.

✚

The Foundation Era 1190–8

The establishment of the Teutonic Order was an act of desperation – desperation based not on a lack of fighting men, but on ineffective medical care. The crusading army besieging Acre in 1190 had been more than decimated by illness. The soldiers from Northern Europe were not accustomed to the heat, the water, or the food, and the sanitary conditions were completely unsatisfactory. Unable to bury their dead properly, they threw the bodies into the moat opposite the Accursed Tower with the rubble they were using to fill the obstacle. The stink from the corpses hung over the camp like a fog. Once taken by fever, the soldiers died like flies, their agony made worse by the innumerable insects that buzzed around them or swarmed over their bodies. The regular hospital units were overburdened and, moreover, the Hospitallers favoured their own nationals, the French and English (a distinction that few could make easily at the time, since King Richard possessed half of France and lusted after the rest). The Germans were left to their own devices.

The situation was intolerable and it appeared that it would last indefinitely – the siege showed no sign of ending soon, and no German monarch was coming east to demand that his subjects be better cared for by the established hospitals. Consequently some middle-class crusaders from Bremen and Lübeck decided to found a hospital order that would care for the German sick. This initiative was warmly seconded by the most prominent of the German nobles, Duke Friedrich of Hohenstaufen. He wrote to his brother, Heinrich VI, and also won over the patriarch of Jerusalem, the Hospitallers and the Templars to the idea. When they asked Pope Celestine III to approve the new monastic order, he did so quickly. The brothers were to do hospital work like the Hospitallers and to live under the Templar rule. The new foundation was to be named the Order of the Hospital of St Mary of the Germans in Jerusalem. Its shorter, more popular name, the German Order, implied a connection with an older establishment, one practically defunct. Later the members of the order avoided mentioning this possible connection, lest they fall under the control of the Hospitallers, who held supervisory rights over the older German hospital. Nevertheless, the new order does not seem to have discouraged visitors and crusaders from believing that their organisation had a more ancient lineage. Everyone valued tradition and antiquity. Since many religious houses indulged in pious frauds to assert a claim to a more illustrious foundation, it is easy to understand that the members of this new hospital order were tempted to do the same.

In 1197, when the next German crusading army arrived in the Holy Land, it found the hospital flourishing and rendering invaluable service to its fellow-countrymen. Not only did the brothers care for the ill, but they provided hostels for the new arrivals, and money and food for those whose resources had become exhausted, or who had been robbed, or who had lost everything in battle. A significant contingent of the new army came from Bremen, a swiftly growing port city on the North Sea that would soon be a founding member of the Hanseatic League. Those burghers lavished gifts upon the hospital they had helped to establish. As the visitors observed the relatively large number of brothers who had been trained as knights but who had been converted to a religious life while on crusade, they concluded that the hospital order could take on military duties similar to those of the Templars and Hospitallers.

The narrow strip of land that formed the crusader kingdom in the Holy Land was protected by a string of castles, but these were so weakly garrisoned that Christian leaders feared a sudden Turkish onslaught might overrun them before relief could be brought from Europe. The local knights supported by fiefs were far too few for effective defence, and the Italian merchants (the only significant middle-class residents committed to the Western Church) were fully occupied by the need to patrol the sealanes against Moslem piracy or blockade; the most they could do was assist in garrisoning the seaports. Consequently the defence of the country had come to rely on the Templars and the Hospitallers, who had a formidable reputation as cruel and relentless warriors but whose numbers were insufficient to the task after the defeats which had led to the loss of Jerusalem in 1187. Moreover, the two orders frequently quarrelled with one another. The Germans who came to Acre in 1197 decided that their hospital order could provide garrisons for some frontier castles, and they requested Pope Celestine to reincorporate it as a military order. He agreed, issuing a new charter in 1198. The English-speaking world eventually came to call this German order the Teutonic Knights.*

Technically, the knights in this new military order were friars, not monks. That is, they lived in the world, not in a cloister. But that is merely a technicality, important in their era but hardly significant for ours. What is important is that their organisation was a recognised and respected part of the Roman Catholic Church, under the protection of the popes and with easy access to the papal court. This court, the curia, under papal supervision appointed officers to conduct the final hearings on all disputes involving members of the Church and assigned legates to conduct on-the-spot investigations of significant crises. In practice, of course, the pope and the curia were too busy to inquire closely into the daily practices of religious orders. Although they could react swiftly when reports of irregular practices came to their ears, it was more efficient to require each order to write out its rules and regulations, then periodically review its actual practices against the precepts of its founders.

✠

Laws and Customs

Because the character of the Teutonic Knights reflected its charter, its rules, its legislation, and that body of laws known as the customs, it is important to look at these documents in detail. They were written down in German so that every member could understand them easily, and they were short and clear, so that they could be easily memorised. Each member took vows of poverty, chastity, and obedience. From the moment the knights entered into the religious life as monks they owned nothing personally; everything was owned in common. In theory they were obliged to tend the sick and thus honour their original purpose for existence. To a certain extent this was compatible with their military duties and their religious devotions, but where it was not such hospital duties were passed on to a special non-noble branch of the membership. The knights attended services at regular intervals throughout the day and night. They were to wear clothes of a 'priestly colour' and cover them with a white mantle bearing a black cross that gave them an additional nickname, the Knights of the Cross.

---

* The reasons for this nomenclature are not particularly clear, although it may have something to do with the traditional insular unwillingness of Englishmen to take the time to tell *Deutsch* from Dutch. More likely there was a bit of modern intellectual snobbery involved – *Teutonic* was a more refined word than German, with its implications of fat old men sitting in a dark tavern, smoke spilling out of their long pipes, and tankards of beer on the tables.

Although there were members who were priests, hospital orderlies, and female nurses, the Hospital of St Mary of the Germans in Jerusalem was primarily a military order. Therefore its membership was largely made up of knights who required horses, weapons, and the equipment of war. Those items had to be maintained personally, so that armour would fit, the swords would be of the right weight and length, and the horse and rider accustomed to one another. Care was taken to avoid acquiring pride in these articles; the rules proscribed gold or silver ornaments or bright colours.

Each knight had to have supporting personnel, usually at a ratio of ten men-at-arms per knight. The men-at-arms were commoners and often members of the order at a lower level. Known as half-brothers, or grey-mantles (from the colour of their surcoats), these took on their duties either for a lengthy period or for life as each chose. They served as squires or sergeants, responsible respectively for providing the knight with a spare horse and new equipment when needed, and for fighting alongside him.*

The knights had to keep themselves in fighting trim, which would have been a serious problem if they had been strictly cloistered. They were permitted to hunt – an unusual privilege specifically conferred by the papacy – because hunting on horseback was the traditional method of training a knight and had the additional benefit of acquainting him with the local geography. To forbid hunting would have been impractical and also very unpopular among German knights who had grown up amid extensive forests still filled with dangerous beasts and plentiful game. The knights were permitted to hunt wolves, bears, boars, and lions with dogs, if they were doing it of necessity and not just to avoid boredom or for pleasure, and to hunt other beasts without dogs.

The rule warned the knights to avoid women. In the cloister that was no problem, but this was often difficult when travelling or on campaign. At times they had to stay in public hostels or accept hospitality, and it would have been very impolite to turn down a beaker of ale or mead when offered. Moreover, when recruiting members or on diplomatic business they often

---

* Men-at-arms fought in units of ten mounted warriors under the direction of a knight. Since these men traditionally followed a knight's flag, the unit was called a banner. Sometimes men-at-arms were equipped with heavy armour and rode a trained war-horse, but for scouting duties and raiding lighter equipment was more appropriate (and cheaper). In the Holy Land these men were called Turcopoles, and dressed for the hot climate – with light arms, less armour, and faster horses, like their Arab and Turkish foes. Later the Teutonic Order's men-at-arms were usually Germans, though, unlike the knights, they could be born in Prussia or Livonia. Advancement of a man-at-arms into the ranks of the knights was extremely rare. They ate and slept in their own barracks, but observed the same daily religious services as knights and priests.

resided in their host's castle or villa, because it was impractical to travel on to a neighbouring monastery and thereby miss the banquet, where business was usually conducted on an informal basis. Realising that their duties prevented the knights from living a life of retirement from the world, the rule simply warned them to shun such secular entertainments as weddings and plays, where the sexes mingled, where alcoholic beverages flowed freely into gaudy drinking cups, and where light amusement was all too enticing. They were explicitly warned to avoid speaking to women alone, and, above all, speaking to young women. As for kissing, the usual form of polite greeting among the noble class, they were forbidden to embrace even their mothers and sisters. Female nurses were permitted in the hospitals only when measures were taken to avoid any possibility of scandal.

Punishment for those brothers who violated the rules could be light, moderate, severe, or very severe. Those condemned to a year of punishment, for example, would have to sleep with the servants, wear unmarked clothing, eat bread and water three days of each week, and were deprived of the privilege of holy communion with their knightly brethren. That was a moderate punishment. For more severe infractions there were irons and the dungeons. Once the punishment was served, the culprit could be returned to duty (although barred from holding office in the order) or he could be expelled. For three offences only was there no possibility of forgiveness – cowardice in the face of the enemy, going over to the infidels, and sodomy. For the first two the offender was expelled from the order; for the last he was sentenced to life imprisonment or execution. The most common offences, always minor, were punished by whipping and deprivation of food.

✠

Officers

No medieval organisation – or even state – had a large officialdom. The Teutonic Knights were no exception. The chief officer was originally called the master, but once the order saw a need for executive officers in Germany, Prussia and Livonia, it seemed appropriate to designate them as masters and to call the officer superior to them the grand master; this was the customary title of the heads of the other military orders, and its use would signify a claim that the Teutonic Knights' own grand master was the equal of the leaders of the Templars and Hospitallers. Also, it emphasised the primary role of defending the Holy Land over demands by regional masters for access to the order's resources.

The grand master was elected by the grand chapter (or general chapter) to serve for his lifetime or until he resigned. The election process was formal and complex. The second-in-command to the late grand master set a date and a location for a meeting of all the nearby knights who could be spared from their duties and also summoned representatives from the more distant provinces. When the high officers and representatives were assembled, he recommended a knight to serve as first elector. If the members approved of his choice, that knight then nominated a second elector, and the members either voiced their approval or required him to submit other names until agreement was reached. The two then chose another, and the members expressed their will until eight knights, one priest, and four members from the lower ranks had been selected as an election panel. This electoral college then took an oath to do its duty, without prejudice or previous commitment, to select the best man available for the vacant office. In closed session the first elector made the initial recommendation to the panel. If that nominee did not win a majority of the votes, then the others in turn proposed names until a choice had been made. When the college announced its decision to the chapter, the priests broke into *Te Deum Laudamus* and escorted the new master to the altar to take his oath of office.

The grand master was primarily a diplomat and overseer. Election ennobled him far beyond the status of his birth. He met with the important nobles and churchmen of the areas where the order was active and carried on an extensive correspondence with the more distant potentates and prelates, including the emperor and the pope. He also travelled widely, visiting the various convents of the order, inspecting discipline, and seeing that the order's resources were being properly managed.

The grand master appointed the officials who served as his inner council. The grand master, the grand commander of the forces in the Holy Land, and the treasurer, were each responsible for one of the three keys to the giant chest that kept the treasury of the order. This responsibility underlined the limits on the authority which was entrusted to any one individual, whatever his office. Important decisions were always made by a group, often by the grand master and his subordinate officials, but also often including the membership assembled as a grand chapter.

The treasurer was responsible for monetary affairs. Although the knights had taken oaths of poverty, the Teutonic Order could not survive without food, clothing, weapons, good horses, and the services of artisans, teamsters, and sea captains that often only money could buy. In theory only the chief officers were supposed to know the financial status of the organisation, but those who attended the grand chapter were given sufficient information to make responsible plans for building castles, churches, and hospitals, and embarking on military campaigns, and they passed on their information to fellow knights and priests.

The grand commander was responsible for day-to-day supervision of activities that were not directly related to warfare. He directed the minor officials in their functions, supervised the treasurer in collecting and dispersing funds, conducted correspondence, and kept records. His duties were obviously much the same as those of the grand master, although on a lesser scale, and he commanded the order's forces in the Holy Land when the grand master was absent. There were also regional commanders in the Holy Roman Empire (Austria, Franconia, and so forth), and local castellans who presided over the many convents and hospitals.

The marshal was responsible for military preparation. His title, which originally referred to a keeper of horses, indicates how important the equipping and training of the cavalry was to battlefield success, and he gave more time to that duty than to his other responsibilities. In theory the master of the robes and the commander of the hospital were subordinate to him, but in practice they were essentially self-sufficient. It is perhaps better to think of the titles as honorific rather than as the equivalent of heads of modern bureaucracies. Together they formed an experienced inner council that the grand master could rely on for advice and counsel.

Business involving the order's subjects, trading partners, and other rulers was conducted in a court atmosphere, the grand master hearing requests, listening to arguments, and making responses after decisions had been reached. The decisions were carefully recorded and filed away. Eventually the archives of the order encompassed hundreds of thousands of documents. The most important were kept by the grand master's scribes for easy reference; others were stored in local convents.

Few of the members had reason to interest themselves in the details of administration. The priests had their own duties to perform. The sergeants (or men-at-arms) were limited to minor responsibilities of little prestige, such as managing small estates and caring for equipment. Few of the knights had sufficient intelligence and experience to hold high office or were of sufficiently high birth to be given responsibility without having proven themselves beforehand. Noble birth was almost essential to advancement. Nobles were assumed to have inherited ability in the same way that war-horses inherited strength and courage; and because they had important relatives and experience in court life, they could win advantages for the order that mere ability and piety could never achieve. Not all 'nobles' were equally noble, and few ordinary knights were of truly noble birth – German knights were often descendants of burghers, gentry, and even the so-called 'serf knights' or *ministeriales*, whose growing importance never quite erased the memory of their distant lowly origins. The number of knightly members from prominent families was always small, and a few of them were directed to the monastic life only because they lacked the qualities necessary to survive outside a cloister.

Whatever stain remained on one's reputation from being of *ministeriale* birth, or even of burgher origin, largely vanished in the ceremony of induction. The sacrifices were great, not just in the vows which were taken, but in the 30–60 Marks which had to be contributed as 'dowry', often in the form of land. This was no paltry sum, but relatives undoubtedly contributed willingly because membership not only enhanced the family prestige, but promised them likely financial and political profit as well. In addition, if the knight was bankrupt, joining the Teutonic Order expunged his debts.

Daily activities for the knights were scrupulously planned along lines that can still be recognised in most armies today – keep the soldier busy, keep him out of trouble. The greatest difference between a Teutonic Knight and a modern soldier was not in weapons and equipment, but in the former's total commitment to a dual calling. Being a friar as well as a warrior, he was expected to attend the short but regular services at the times specified by the Church and endure a discipline that would be beyond bearing in any modern military organisation – because it was a lifelong obligation. Poverty, chastity and obedience were real sacrifices made by real men.

✙

Religious Life

The total commitment to a religious as well as a military life was emphasised to the knight when he applied for membership. After he had passed the preliminary interrogations, he was brought before a chapter and asked:

> The brethren have heard your request and wish to know if any of these things apply to you. The first is whether you have taken an oath to any other order, if you are betrothed to a woman, if you are another man's serf, if you owe money to anyone or have debts to pay that might affect the order, or if you are in bad health. If any of these is so, and you do not admit it, when it becomes known you may be expelled from the brotherhood.

The recruit then took the following oath: 'I promise the chastity of my body, and poverty, and obedience to God, Holy Mary, and you, to the Master of the Teutonic Order, and your successors, according to the rules and practices of the Order, obedience unto death'.

Because there are historians who say that the order was a political organisation with little or no religious meaning, it is important to remember that the Teutonic Knights differed little from any other religious order that did not require its members to withdraw from the world but sought to improve it. By the same standards we would have to assume that the papacy was no more than a political organisation (although the activities of some popes of this era tempt one to that conclusion, the assumption would be incorrect). But there was a mixture of religious and secular ideas and interests that cannot be blithely separated without making a caricature of the Teutonic Order. The corporate prayer included in the *Statutes*, though written at a slightly later date, illustrates this amalgam of ideals better than a long dissertation:

Brothers, beseech our Lord God, that he comfort Holy Christianity with His Grace, and His Peace, and protect it from all evil. Pray to Our God for our spiritual father, the Pope, and for the Empire and for all our leaders and prelates of Christianity, lay and ecclesiastical, that God use them in His service. And also for all spiritual and lay judges, that they may give Holy Christianity peace and such good justice that God's Judgement will not come over them.

Pray for our Order in which God has assembled us, that the Lord will give us Grace, Purity, a Spiritual Life, and that he take away all that is found in us or other Orders that is unworthy of praise and opposed to His Commandments.

Pray for our Grand Master and all the regional commanders, who govern our lands and people, and for all the brothers who exercise office in our Order, that they act in their office of the Order in such a way as not to depart from God.

Pray for the brothers who hold no office, that they may use their time purposefully and zealously in worship, so that those who hold office and they themselves may be useful and pious.

Pray for those who are fallen in deadly sin, that God may help them back into his Grace and that they may escape eternal punishment.

Pray for the lands that lie near the pagans, that God may come to their aid with his Counsel and Power, that belief in God and Love can be spread there, so that they can withstand all their enemies.

Pray for those who are friends and associates of the Order, and also for those who do good actions or who seek to do them, that God may reward them.

Pray for all those who have left us inheritances or gifts that neither in life nor in death does God allow them to depart from Him. Especially pray for Duke Friedrich of Swabia and King Heinrich his brother, who was

Emperor, and for the honourable burghers of Lübeck and Bremen, who founded our Order. Remember also Duke Leopold of Austria, Duke Conrad of Masovia, and Duke Sambor of Pomerellia . . . Remember also our dead brothers and sisters . . . Let each remember the soul of his father, his mother, his brothers and sisters. Pray for all believers, that God may give them eternal peace. May they rest in peace. Amen.

Understanding the religious idealism of the Teutonic Order is fundamental to comprehending the ways it carried out its mission. It was an important aspect to all the military orders, as important as radical Protestantism was to Cromwell's Roundheads, or communion in both kinds to a Czech Hussite. If the narrative sources do not dwell upon this religiosity, it is no surprise. No author has yet been able to make an endless round of prayer, contemplation, and corporate worship into interesting reading. But the order's chroniclers constantly referred to the piety of individuals and of convents, even to the point of disturbing their narratives. It should be borne in mind that even medieval historians had a good sense of what made a good story, and they knew that dramatic events captured the ears of their audience. The Old Testament was dearer to their heart than was the New – and that, perhaps, is the key to the religious thought of the military orders.

The total involvement of the individual in a religious life is not often found today, and many find it difficult to believe that people once seriously considered it normal behaviour. Therefore some people living today regard those who are deeply religious in the medieval sense as freaks or hypocrites. We easily accept contradictions in our own behaviour but demand a consistency from medieval man that makes him either a saint or a brutal impostor. The knights and priests born between 1180 and 1500 were neither. They were complex personalities who had varying reasons for entering a religious life, but certainly almost all of them saw themselves as part of a divine plan that made order out of chaos and gave reason to their lives. Whatever else they might do in this world made little sense when compared to the vast span of eternity that lay ahead in the death that waits inevitably for each one of us. To them any other behaviour, particularly any behaviour that ignored the fate of one's immortal soul, was foolish and dangerous.

Firm in the belief that they had chosen the right path, the knights followed it, convinced that destiny had really given them no choice. Success or failure, victory or defeat, were incidental and in the hands of God. Pride in their achievements, they knew, would bring swift retribution in the form of battlefield defeat but would not slow the divine plan for an instant. Their duty lay in acceptance and obedience – and, fortunately for them, the divine voice usually told them what they wanted to hear.

✠

Warrior Monks

The accuracy of the foregoing passages notwithstanding, life in a convent of Teutonic Knights was not dull. To be sure, northern winters were long and dark, just as summers in the Holy Land were long and hot, but there was always much to do. As Voltaire remarked at the conclusion of *Candide*, work is the cure for poverty, vice and boredom. Without much question, the ultra-catholic priests and officers of the Teutonic Order would have agreed with that deist's analysis of the human condition.

Knights had duties in the order's convents. The head of each convent had a title we can translate as castellan or commander, and he supervised all other officers. Some officers were important, such as the treasurer, who may or may not have been able to account for incomes and expenditures personally but who supervised men of burgher ancestry who understood the process. Most offices were minor, such as supervising the fields and horses, but each provided a means of determining which knights were responsible and easy to work with, who exercised good judgement, and who was to be passed over when promotions were discussed.

There was a good deal of drinking every day, and even more during feast days and when visitors were present. The knights liked their beer and wine, especially the varieties from home. On the other hand, there were many fast days, and letters to the pope requesting exemptions from strict fasting for officers who were ill or aged demonstrate that they took these customary limitations seriously.

Hunting was a passionate characteristic of the noble classes in general, and the Teutonic Knights were no exception. Later, when many of their castles lay in forests or on the edge of wildernesses, they were quite willing to enter into treaties with their enemies that provided hunters protection from ambush or attack. They maintained packs of dogs for chasing stags and aurochs, and they hired local warriors as guides in war, who – since only relatively few days of any year could be spent fighting – were most commonly employed as huntsmen.

They learned the local languages. They probably did not attain the fluency and accuracy of modern scholars, but knights serving on the Lithuanian frontier had no trouble understanding pleas from what they believed were Polish women who had escaped their captors. Any knight working with native militia had better be able to give the basic commands, even when the natives were supposed to know the German words, and any knight on the road had better know the words for inn, food and beer. Fluency was especially important for those officers of the order, called advocates, who lived among the native Baltic peoples and trained their military units.

Most knights entered the order as youths. Usually second or subsequent sons, they found service in a military order a useful and honourable career. Even if they did not win fame and high office, they knew that they would be cared for if injured and when they reached old age. Most importantly, they believed that they would ultimately be rewarded by the favour of Lady Mary and Her son, their Lord and Master. A few years of sacrifice would be rewarded with life everlasting. Martyrdom guaranteed this goal even for those who personally fell short of perfection in observing the vows of poverty, chastity and obedience.

Not all the knights were saints. Not by a long bow-shot. A few were even repentant criminals. Medieval society had few alternatives to either forgiving criminals or executing them. Whippings, of course, were suitable to the lower classes, and a few individuals could be dumped at the bottom of a well, to dig out earth and stone until water was struck or their sentence was finished. But in general, incarceration was not practical. It was much better, society reasoned, to send repentant criminals to a convent where they could spend their days in rounds of prayer, work and sleep. Thus they might save their immortal souls while performing socially useful tasks. The Teutonic Knights were only one of many orders which accepted the services of individuals accused of crime. This did not mean that these former outcasts from society were allowed to achieve high status or hold office, but their willingness to fight on a distant and dangerous frontier expunged the stain of crime from their family name.

It might be more accurate to think of the Teutonic Knights as similar to a modern professional athletic team. Their commitment to physical fitness, their dedication to their calling, their pride in their accomplishments, their earthy sense of humour, their excesses in celebration – all this separates them from ordinary men as much as does the passage of time.

In sum, if the knights and their brethren were not saints, neither were they evil incarnate. They reflected the characteristics of the noble society of their era, and the more one studies their enemies, the less one is likely to stereotype them as unusually arrogant or land-hungry, much less evil.

3

War in the Holy Land

The Holy Land

We know little about the first decades of the Teutonic Knights' history. The most important event was a land transaction in 1200, when King Almarich II of Jerusalem sold them a small territory north of Acre. In addition to that and to their hospital in that port city, they had a few scattered holdings along the coast at Jaffa, Ascalon, and Gaza, and a few estates on Cyprus. Only later, after the acquisition of the Joscelin legacy, did the Teutonic Knights have a significant territorial base in the Holy Land; and even that was challenged by a twenty-four year lawsuit. The suspicion and jealousy of the established military orders, combined with their prestige and power, made it difficult for a new organisation to fasten a foot firmly in the soil of Palestine.

So small were the Teutonic Knights' possessions and so insignificant were their military contributions in the early years that we know nothing more about the first three masters than their names. They must have earned a good reputation among the crusaders and made a number of valuable friends, because the order was able to expand rapidly after Hermann von Salza was elected master in 1210. This man, brilliant as he was, could have done little if his predecessors had not handed on to him an efficient and respected organisation, with strong discipline, and a larger number of knights than were needed to protect their estates around Acre.

✚

Hermann von Salza

Hermann von Salza was an empire-builder of the stamp of a Henry Ford or a John D. Rockefeller, who saw opportunities where others saw only problems, and who knew how to work within an existing system to create a new type of empire, using the ability and capital of other men to achieve goals that no one else had dreamed of trying. Because he did this, the history of the Teutonic Knights really begins not with the Third Crusade, but with Hermann's election in 1210.

Hermann von Salza was the offspring of a Thuringian *ministeriale* family – that is, they were considered knights, but were not quite nobles; generations back some commoner ancestor had improved his rank through courage, competence and loyalty, but his red blood had failed to turn sufficiently blue. In an era when worldly success depended upon good marriages and relatives high in the church, Hermann's parents were neither wealthy nor of high birth. Consequently he could not expect to advance far if he followed his father's career as a secular knight. For *ministeriales* the most that could be hoped for was to acquire another office or two and make a slightly better marriage; to choose a religious life and become a prior, or perhaps a minor bishop or abbot; or to emigrate to the east, where Polish dukes welcomed capable warriors and administrators. Hermann von Salza joined these roads to build his order a highway to fame. In joining the Teutonic Knights he combined the military and the religious careers – and later he would send his military order to east-central Europe.

It was fortunate that he chose a small military order, because he could not have attained high office in one of the older or more prestigious orders. Although his amiable personality and diplomatic talents would have made an impression anywhere, they would have been insufficient to overcome the handicap of his *ministeriale* birth. However, within the Teutonic Order's small membership his abilities stood out prominently, and he was elected master at an early age, probably while in his thirties. He was one of those rare people who inspire instant trust in their honesty and ability – if he had not had that characteristic he could not have become the confidant of pope and emperor, much less have served as a mediator in bitter disputes between seemingly irreconcilable enemies.

There was little in his early career to suggest his later prominence. He probably attended the Fourth Lateran Council in 1215, but certainly did not speak publicly; he accompanied the young emperor, Friedrich II (1194–1250), to Nuremberg in December 1216; and he made arrangements to send a small body of knights to defend the frontiers of the kingdom of Hungary against nomadic Cuman raiders. This obscurity evolved into fame during the Fifth Crusade.

Hermann von Salza joined the expedition that set out in 1217 from Cyprus to Damietta, the Egyptian port that protected the rich Nile delta and the route to Cairo. This crusade promised to be that decisive success which had eluded crusaders for so long. This was partly because the target – Egypt – was vulnerable, and partly because so many of the expedition's knights were furnished by the military orders. As a result there was initial agreement about the strategy and tactics that had been lacking in recent efforts, especially during the ill-fated Fourth Crusade which had been diverted against Constantinople – to the everlasting harm and embarrassment of Christendom. Even so, the lack of a single, dominant leader was a major weakness of the crusader forces. Hermann stood out among the grand masters less because of his ability or the number of knights under his direct command than because the Germans who contributed so much money and so many men to the expedition looked to him for advice and leadership. Hermann used the opportunity wisely to obtain privileges and donations for his order.

Hermann von Salza served personally at Damietta. For two years the Christian and Moslem worlds fought desperately, each side bringing up reinforcements from farther and farther away, until it seemed that there would be no one left to call upon. At last the fortress fell, and the crusaders proceeded up the Nile toward Cairo. That offensive ultimately proved unsuccessful. Though everyone called upon the emperor to come to their aid, Friedrich II found plausible reasons to delay his departure. As negotiations dragged on, one by one the crusaders returned home. Though the Christian leaders could have obtained access to Jerusalem in return for surrendering Damietta, the papal legate stubbornly refused to settle for anything less than total victory. Discovering prophecies of a mythic King David and Prester John, tying them together with rumours of a great king threatening the Moslem rear (perhaps Genghis Khan, whose Mongol hordes were overrunning all his neighbours' territories), and promising an easy victory over the disorganised Egyptians, he persuaded the grand masters of the Templars, the Hospitallers, and the Teutonic Knights to undertake a final offensive in 1221 that became trapped in the waterways of the Delta. The result was a total defeat, the loss of almost the entire army and the city of Damietta. Hermann was among the prisoners. He was soon ransomed, but he had reason to conclude that his order's future did not lie solely in the Holy Land.

Although many blamed the disaster on Friedrich II, who had not honoured his vow to bring an army to Egypt, Hermann von Salza was not among their number. Hermann was a Hohenstaufen loyalist, at least as far as his obligations to the Church allowed. He was in Germany in 1223 and 1224 on imperial business, negotiating for the release of the Danish king, Waldemar II, who had been kidnapped by Count Heinrich of Schwerin, an event that was drawing all the northern states toward civil war. Hermann, who undoubtedly knew the count from the Fifth Crusade, arranged for the king's ransom. Part of this complicated agreement was a promise from the

Danish monarch that he would participate in Friedrich II's forthcoming campaign. Although the emperor had not gone to Damietta when the pope pleaded with him to save the crusaders, now Friedrich II was soliciting volunteers for an expedition that would revenge all previous defeats. As a prominent imperial spokesman Hermann was able to establish the Teutonic Knights in the public mind as the guiding force of the German crusading movement. Although he had earlier sent a few knights to defend the Carpathian passes into Hungary from nomadic raiders, he did not wish to become distracted by intrigues there or by an intriguing proposal from Duke Conrad of Masovia (1187–1247) to send troops to protect the northern borders of Poland against attacks by pagan Prussians.

Hermann von Salza felt the new urgency to support the crusade in the Holy Land fully and without hesitation. The Fifth Crusade had barely failed in its attack on Egypt, but it had failed, and he understood that imperial interests would not have been advanced by Friedrich abandoning Italy to his enemies at that critical moment. Now Sicily had been pacified. More importantly, the emperor had arranged to wed the heiress of the kingdom of Jerusalem, whose lands would come into his hands only if he went to the Holy Land and took possession. When the emperor announced that he would fulfil his crusading vow in 1226 or 1227, the membership of the Teutonic Knights realised that if they provided a large contingent of knights for the imperial crusade they stood to benefit from Friedrich's gratitude.* In the matter of crusading no man stood closer to the emperor, either as friend or counsellor, than Hermann von Salza, who knew that Friedrich rewarded his friends as much for what they might do for him in the future as for their past loyalty and service. Therefore Hermann made it clear that the emperor could anticipate full co-operation from the Teutonic Knights. The membership of the order, however, was looking forward to sharing in a great victory over Christendom's Islamic foes, and they were not interested in diverting significant resources into another Eastern European fiasco.

✠

The Holy Land

The imperial fleet that sailed from Brindisi in 1227 returned to port immediately because an epidemic had claimed the life of Count Louis of

---

* As a symbol of his friendship the emperor issued the Golden Bull of Rimini in 1226, granting the order extensive lands and privileges in Prussia should the Teutonic Knights choose to accept the invitation from Duke Conrad of Masovia to send knights there.

Thuringia (Thüringen) and stricken many other crusaders. Although the emperor was excommunicated by Pope Gregory IX for failing to press on to the Holy Land, Friedrich II did not hurry to Rome to seek a reconciliation – he knew the aged pope too well to believe that this could be obtained except at an exorbitant cost. Instead, he re-embarked his troops as soon as they were healthy, apparently not caring that the papal condemnation would give his enemies in the Holy Land the excuse they needed to refuse him aid. Friedrich miscalculated. His failure to resolve the dispute with the pope quickly doomed his crusade to failure. Everywhere he met a sullen reception, and practically every noble and cleric in the Holy Land declined to participate in any campaign led by an excommunicate. Under these circumstances Friedrich was drawn even closer to the Teutonic Order than would have been the case. Because Hermann von Salza's order remained loyal and assisted him in every way, he gave its members special consideration in Jerusalem after the city was recovered through the ensuing peace treaty, and he gave them the toll receipts from Acre.

As long as he remained in the Holy Land with his army, the emperor could do much as he pleased, but he could not remain there long. Grand Master Hermann, realising this, avoided antagonising the local nobles or the other military orders. In that way he saved his order from the reprisals that followed when Friedrich II left Acre in 1229 under a shower of rotten fruit and vegetables; and he arranged for a speedy removal of the excommunication which had been placed on the order for its support of Friedrich's crusade. Still, all was not well in the Holy Land – wherever the imperial garrisons were small or isolated, they were attacked by the Christian nobles and prelates who were angry about Friedrich's failure to help them in the past, about his policies in Sicily, and about his quarrel with the pope, considering him nothing more than an atheistic fortune-hunter.

Hermann von Salza accompanied the unfortunate emperor back to Italy and helped to reconcile him with Pope Gregory IX. He had given up all hope of establishing his order permanently and solely in the Holy Land. Quickly he sent off the first contingent of knights to Prussia. His estimate of the situation in the Holy Land proved correct. By 1231 most of the imperial garrisons were expelled, and it was only a matter of thirteen more years until Jerusalem was recaptured by the Moslems. After that the Christians in the Holy Land stood on the defensive, awaiting the inevitable attack that would deprive them of their last footholds.

The Teutonic Knights did not give up their interest in the Mediterranean – far from it. Their knights were more necessary for providing a garrison for Acre than ever before. But Acre was a port city, hot, humid, and crowded, not a suitable place to live year in and year out. Knights flourished in the countryside, where the climate was healthier and there were opportunities to ride and to hunt, where there were fields and fodder for the horses; in addition knights needed a dependable supply of locally grown food and wine. In 1220 they had purchased a run-down castle in Galilee from the Hennenberg family, and now they began to repair it, using the tolls from Acre to finance the work. They named the huge fortress Montfort, probably deriving both the name and the architecture from a castle their members had built in Transylvania; its German name was Starkenberg (Strong Mountain), and, indeed, it was sited in a location that was very difficult to assault. However, compared to other crusader castles it was not a formidable defensive post, and was probably more valued for its handsome guest house and remarkable view over the wooded hills on one side and the Acre plain on the other than for its contribution to the defence of the Holy Land. The surrounding lands were the richest in northern Galilee, and the order added to them in 1234 and 1249, but the castle was too far away for the garrison to protect the farmers from raiders. Crusaders assisted in enlarging the fortifications in 1227, and Friedrich II contributed money in 1228. A second castle was built three miles to the south, again perched on a rocky ridge. The architecture of both structures was thoroughly German, with little influence from the neighbouring castles: a massive keep dominated, with towers connected by a strong curtain wall.

The real weakness of crusader castles in the Holy Land was the inability to protect the surrounding farming communities that provided food and labour. Once Moslem armies had carried off or killed the local people, and burned their settlements, the castles became isolated islands in a deserted land. Without hay or pastures, the knights could not maintain their horses properly, and without horses they were ineffective as warriors.

Although the Teutonic Knights lost Montfort in 1271, they kept a considerable force in Acre until 1291, when the combined forces of all the military orders were driven from that last stronghold too. The grand master withdrew to Venice, where he could continue to direct the crusade against the Moslems. Only in 1309 did he move to Prussia and abandon the war in the East.

One of the enduring controversies inside the Teutonic Order was whether resources should be concentrated on defending the Holy Land, or used in the Baltic, or nourished to provide services in the Holy Roman Empire. Throughout the thirteenth century the knights in the Holy Land jealously guarded their pre-eminence, denouncing grand masters who spent too much time 'abroad' (outside the Holy Land) or who wavered from loyalty to the Hohenstaufen cause; soon enough the German master, Prussian master, and Livonian master were eloquently championing the interests of their regions too. One grand master after another endured criticism and frustration in attempting to reconcile the demands of regional power blocs and to avoid the scandal of schism. This office was not one to be held by the thin-skinned or impatient.

Only slowly, therefore, did the Teutonic Knights shift their attention and resources away from the Holy Land to the new crusades in the Baltic. Jerusalem long remained their primary commitment, both actively and financially, and only the loss of Acre in 1291 caused them to reluctantly and slowly abandon all hope of regaining the holy city. The military order had goals that were more important than either lands or power, but one cannot separate motives easily or neatly. Religious idealism, superstition, ambition and duties combined in complex ways to prevent the knights from seeing clearly that their duties were best performed against the pagans of north-eastern Europe.

4

The Transylvanian Experiment

Defending Hungary against Pagan Attack

As happens often in human affairs, it was chance that led the Teutonic Knights to consider making a change in their life's mission. A common acquaintance introduced Hermann von Salza to the king of Hungary, and within a short time the grand master committed his order to its first great venture in Eastern Europe. The central figure in this affair was Count Hermann of Thuringia, the overlord of the Salza family. The Salzas had been loyal vassals who had probably named Hermann in honour of their power-ful patron, who was famous for his brilliant court, where he encouraged poetry and chivalry. The count's ancestors were noted crusaders – his father had been on the Third Crusade and he himself had been present when the Teutonic Order was transformed from a hospital order into a military one. It is quite possible that Hermann von Salza had accompanied him on that crusade and had joined the Teutonic Knights at that time. Certainly Count Hermann had followed Hermann von Salza's career with much interest. At the time that the news would have found its way back to the Thuringian court that Hermann von Salza had been elected master of the Teutonic Order, Count Hermann was negotiating with Andrew II of Hungary (1205–35) to win the hand of four-year-old Princess Elisabeth for his son Louis. The king had long contemplated a crusade to the Holy Land, a subject that fascinated him and Count Hermann alike, but he could not leave Hungary while it was endangered by the increasingly strong attacks of the pagan Cumans.

The Hungarian kingdom extended over the vast plain that lay south of the Carpathian mountains and stretched across the Danube River to the hills that bounded the kingdom of Serbia. In its south-eastern part the steep

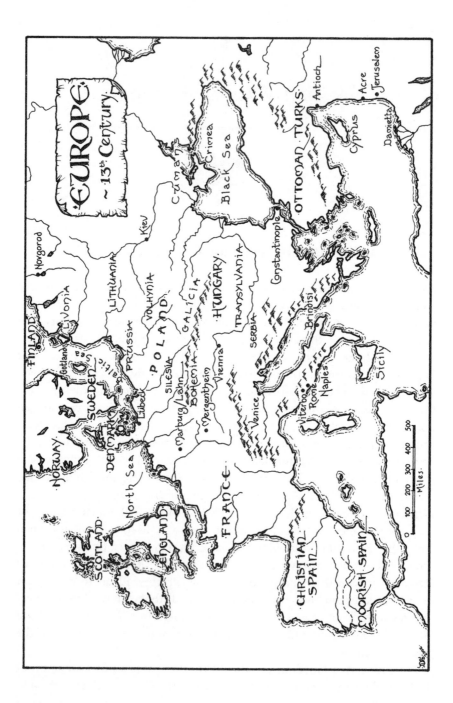

EUROPE
~ 13th Century.

Novgorod

FINLAND

LIVONIA

Gotland

LITHUANIA

Kiev

Cuman?

Crimea

Black Sea

OTTOMAN TURKS

Antioch

Acre

Cyprus

Jerusalem

Damietta

Constantinople

VOLHYNIA

GALICIA

HUNGARY

TRANSYLVANIA

SERBIA

Brindisi

SWEDEN

Baltic Sea

PRUSSIA

POLAND

SILESIA

BOHEMIA

Vienna

Venice

Sicily

NORWAY

DENMARK

Lübeck

Marburg/Lahn

Mergentheim

Naples

Rome

Viterbo

North Sea

SCOTLAND

ENGLAND

FRANCE

CHRISTIAN SPAIN

MOORISH SPAIN

0 100 200 300 400 500
Miles.

mountain chain became less formidable and dissolved into rolling, forested hill country variously called Transylvania or Siebenbürgen (seven fortresses). This wild region was never fully settled by the Hungarians, who were themselves descendants of nomads and therefore preferred the plain, and it was but sparsely populated by the descendants of the Roman settlers of Dacia. The passes served less for commerce than to lead the Cumans from the coastal plain into Hungary. King Andrew had tried to stem the invasions by planting vassals in the region, but these either lacked a sufficient number of warriors to hold the land securely or preferred a safe and easy life in the interior. When Andrew mentioned this problem to Count Hermann or his emissaries, he was most likely told that a military order such as the Teutonic Knights could protect this endangered frontier, making it possible for the king to go on crusade with a free mind. Although there were other ways that Andrew could have heard of Hermann von Salza and his order – his queen was from the Tyrol, an early base of the order – it seems more than a coincidence that the king invited the Teutonic Knights to come to Transylvania only shortly after signing the marriage contract with Hermann of Thuringia.

The king promised lands in the endangered region and immunities from taxes and duties; this implied that the military order could bring in settlers and maintain itself from their rents and labour without having to share its hard-won early revenues with the monarch. In effect, Andrew was presenting them that part of Transylvania called the Burzenland. He kept the right to coin money and a claim to half of any gold or silver that might be discovered, but he renounced his claims to taxes and tolls, and his authority to establish markets and exercise justice. This appeared to be a generous offer, and because the officers of the military order had little experience in such affairs, Hermann von Salza accepted the invitation on the assumption that the king's goodwill would continue into the future.

Almost immediately a contingent of knights, accompanied by peasant volunteers from Germany, entered the unsettled region and built a series of wood-and-earth forts; the peasants then established their farms and villages, providing the taxes and labour necessary to support these military outposts. Such settlements by religious orders were very common in this era, and the ethnic origin of the peasants generally meant little to the nobles and clerics who profited from their presence. The peasants soon began to harvest reasonably abundant crops, making it easy to attract yet more immigrant farmers from Germany. Only after these tasks had been accomplished did it become apparent that the king's offer was terribly vague and unspecific. By that time, however, little could be done to change it, because he was absent on the Fifth Crusade.

Andrew had sailed to the Holy Land in 1217 with a large army, accompanied by Hermann von Salza and a force of Teutonic Knights. Finding the crusaders in Cyprus idle, without much hope of mounting an offensive toward Jerusalem, the king and Hermann von Salza had called all the crusader leaders together and proposed to attack Egypt. If they could capture Cairo, which seemed weakly defended, they could exchange that city for Jerusalem and the surrounding fortresses. First, however, they had to capture Damietta. When that siege did not succeed as quickly as hoped, King Andrew returned home overland, making a truce with the Turks in Asia Minor to permit him safe-passage back to Hungary.

Meanwhile, the contingent of Teutonic Knights in Transylvania had not been content to act the part of quiet vassals, defending the frontier in a static manner. They were ambitious and aggressive, pressing outward against the Cumans, and they found it easy to occupy new territories, because the nomads had no permanent settlements that might provide centres of resistance. By 1220 the Teutonic Knights had built five castles, some in stone, and given them names that were later passed on to castles in Prussia. Marienburg, Schwarzenburg, Rosenau, and Kreuzburg were grouped around Kronstadt at a distance of twenty miles from one another. These became bases for expansion into the practically unpopulated Cuman lands, an expansion that went forward with such surprising speed that the Hungarian nobles and clergy who previously had shown little interest in the region became jealous and suspicious.

If the Teutonic Knights had been given another decade, they would probably have pushed down the Danube River valley to occupy all the territories down to the Black Sea; this would have relieved the pressure that the nomadic Cumans had long exerted on Hungary and the Latin kingdom of Constantinople. Garrisoning castles in the lower Danubian basin, they could have reopened the land route to Constantinople that had been unsafe for crusaders in recent decades. But the Teutonic Knights were too successful too quickly. The Hungarian nobles began to have doubts that the Cumans were still a danger. They could remember that those wild horsemen had beaten the Byzantines and the Latin king of Constantinople, and had even invaded their own country. But that was in the past. Now it seemed that even a handful of foreign knights could drive them away. The Hungarian nobles did not understand the special organisation and dedication that made it possible for a military order to succeed where they had failed. For their part, the Teutonic Knights ignored the rights of the local bishop and refused to share their conquests with important nobles who had previously held claims on the region.

It was only natural that the Teutonic Knights did not wish to surrender what had been won or built by their efforts and with their money, particularly when they would need every parcel of land and every village to provide the resources in food, taxes, and infantry necessary for future campaigns toward the Black Sea. But in addition their leaders may not have possessed the diplomatic skills of Hermann von Salza, who knew how to make friends and allay the suspicions of potential enemies; moreover, being far away in the Holy Land and Egypt, Hermann was not even in a position to offer advice. Consequently the Teutonic Knights in Transylvania operated with considerable autonomy, and they did not make many friends.

The result was a conflict of ambitions and bitter jealousy. As the Hungarian nobles came to see it, King Andrew had unwisely invited in a group of interlopers who were making themselves so secure in their border principality that the king himself would soon not be able to control them. They accused the order of overstepping its duty to defend the border and of planning to become a kingdom within the kingdom.

Even if Hermann von Salza had not been at Damietta, it is unlikely that he could have done much about these developments. If the pope was unable to persuade distant and quarrelsome nobles to support the crusading movement, what chance did a minor noble in charge of a minor military order have?

Andrew returned home to a kingdom bitter about the losses and expenses of his crusade. His reputation had diminished badly, and the country had suffered in the absence of firm government. In 1222 the nobility extorted from him a document called the Golden Bull, which was very similar to the *Magna Carta* that English barons had extorted from their own unlucky king only a few years before. Even so, when the nobility demanded that he take back his grants to the Teutonic Order, he refused. He examined the complaints, concluded that the order had indeed exceeded its mandate, and agreed that changes should be made in the charters; but he ended by issuing a new charter more extensive in its terms than the first. He allowed the Teutonic Knights to build castles in stone; and, although his grant forbade them to recruit Hungarian or Romanian settlers, he implicitly approved their having brought in German peasants. Hermann von Salza had doubtless used his influence with Pope Honorius III (1216–27) and Count Louis of Thuringia to strengthen the royal resolve on this issue, but he could not affect the attitude of the Hungarian nobility; nor could he win over the heir apparent, Prince Bela, who had thrown in his lot with them. These continued their complaints against the Teutonic Order and supported the local bishop in his ambition to subordinate the order to his rule.

Hermann von Salza reasoned that his order need not anticipate trouble as long as King Andrew was alive, but that he could expect great difficulties once Prince Bela mounted the throne. This could be avoided, perhaps, if the order could loosen its ties to the crown. When he returned to Italy he spoke to Honorius III about the problem, and subsequently the pope took the order's lands in Transylvania under papal protection. In effect, the Burzenland became a fief of the Holy See.

This action was a fatal mistake. In place of trouble at some future date, Hermann von Salza had to deal with it at once. Andrew ordered the Teutonic Knights to leave Hungary immediately. Not even he was willing to see a valuable province lost, stolen from his kingdom by legal chicanery. The pope intervened as best he could, and Hermann von Salza tried to explain that the act had been misinterpreted, but it was of no use. The Hungarian nobles had their issue, and now the king stood with them. When the Teutonic Knights unwisely refused to leave without a further hearing, Prince Bela was authorised to lead an armed force against them. The order was driven ignominiously from its lands and expelled from the kingdom. Only the peasantry remained, forming an important German settlement until 1945, when their descendants were expelled by the Rumanian government.

The Hungarians did not replace the Teutonic Order with adequate garrisons or follow up on the attacks on the Cumans, thereby enabling the steppe warriors to recover their self-confidence and their strength. Soon the Cumans were again a danger to the kingdom.

The Hungarian debacle shook the confidence of the Teutonic Order badly. Many men had given their lives, and much money had been collected with great difficulty to build the fortifications and make the new settlements secure. These efforts were all wasted. The order's reputation was besmirched. In the recent past many gifts had come from the emperor and the princes – estates in Bari, Palermo and Prague. How many potential donors would consider the stories they heard and then make their donations elsewhere? The answer was not at all certain, although the example of the Tyrolean count of Lengmoos was encouraging – in the midst of the controversy he had joined the order and brought all his lands with him as a gift. Such a knight, reared in the art of the Alpine plateau where German chivalry and poetry flourished a short way from rich and vibrant Italian cities, was a living example of the problem the Teutonic Order faced. It could thrive in Germanic regions, winning recruits and donations from idealistic nobles and burghers, but it had no reason to operate in those areas. To have a purpose for existence the Teutonic Knights had to fight infidels or pagans, and those could be found only on the borders of non-German states. Unfortunately, the nobles and people of those states often had little in common with the members of the Teutonic Order; therefore, hostility rather than sympathy was their natural attitude toward the crusaders once the immediate danger had passed.

✠

The Mongol Storm blows in from the East

Already by the time the Hungarian king had expelled the Teutonic Order from the ramparts of the Carpathians, he could hardly have failed to hear reports of the 1223 battle on the Kalka River in south-east Rus'.* But it was another fifteen years before the full extent of his error became apparent. The Mongols had won their first battle, then returned home; but in 1237–9 it became clear that they were in Rus' to stay.† In the meantime the Polish and Hungarian kings had been expanding into Galicia and Volhynia, the most westerly Rus'ian states. Rumours that the Mongols planned to mount an offensive against Poland and Hungary spread quickly, based partly on Tatar warnings and partly on the assumption that the grand khan was determined to rule over all Rus' and every steppe tribe. However inaccurate or misleading these accounts may have been, they were indicative of a massive shift in the balance of power. King Bela of Hungary (1235–70) had hoped to profit from this confusion, but his gains were only temporary.

The Cumans, under pressure from the grand khan to pay tribute and contribute warriors to his armies, withdrew into Hungary, where they remained an important and disruptive element for the rest of the century. Pagan nomads, they had little in common with the Christian nobles and peasants of the Danubian basin. But they were sufficiently like the Mongols to be seen as potential competitors for dominance in southern Rus'. Therefore, the grand khan ordered Batu, a grandson of Genghis Khan, to eliminate them. Doing this would not be easy, however, because first he

---

* Rus' is the name Western historians use for medieval Russia, with its centre in Kiev but its authority widely scattered among the descendants of the early grand princes. This usage minimises confusion with the very different Russian state that formed in the sixteenth century, with its centre in Moscow.

† By 'Mongol' scholars generally mean the empire of the grand khan, with its centre in Mongolia, from which the khanate's wars against China, Persia and the Near East could be directed most effectively. By 'Tatar' we refer to the lesser khans living in the west, from Turkestan to Kazan. By 'Golden Horde' we mean the westernmost Tatars, with their centre at Sarai on the lower Volga. Some lived as far west as the Crimea. In practice, these names are used interchangeably.

had to crush Rus'ian resistance in Galicia – and he could anticipate meeting Polish and Hungarian forces there, too – then penetrate through the fortified passes of the Carpathian mountains. The khan, ever resourceful, decided upon a bold strategy that would put a second army in the rear of the royal forces at the passes: he would send a swiftly moving cavalry force across Galicia and Poland, then press through the mountains at the gap west of Cracow, thunder through Moravia, Slovakia and Austria, making a counter-clockwise sweep along the base of the mountains, and enter Hungary from the rear. As it turned out, this distracting invasion was not necessary – King Bela could not persuade his nobles to follow orders, so the high passes were inadequately defended. The Tatars overwhelmed the royal army in the summer of 1241 and chased the king all the way to the Adriatic coast.*

It is not recorded whether Bela repented of his having expelled the Teutonic Order from the Carpathian mountain passes, but he probably did not. Bela never had many doubts about his own abilities, and he generally managed to foist blame for his failures onto others. On this occasion it was convenient to blame the Poles, for not having defended Galicia properly. In fact, this was not completely inaccurate.

When the Mongols had first invaded Galicia that spring, Conrad of Masovia had led the Polish armies east and won an engagement near Sandomir. Although his forces slew the Mongol general, the victory was hardly decisive – his own forces, dismayed at their heavy casualties, had allowed thousands of their opponents to escape when they could have destroyed them; some of his units, in fact, had been routed by their Tatar opponents. Certainly few Poles were eager to fight the invaders again soon, and in any case, the warriors had performed their military duties for the season. The second invasion, probably spearheaded by a new Mongol-Turkish army, consequently caught the Masovian and Volhynian dukes by surprise. There was no possibility of meeting the invader in Galicia, nor even of intercepting him on the frontier. As each Piast duke concentrated on defending his own ancestral lands, the Mongols pressed on toward Cracow, then into Silesia. Near Liegnitz the Tatar cavalry crushed the army of the duke of Silesia, who may have been supported by units of Teutonic Knights. The Tatars then turned around and rode through Moravia and then into Hungary, to join with the victorious forces that had routed Bela's army.

---

* Nora Berend, *At the Gate of Christendom: Jews, Muslims and 'Pagans' in Medieval Hungary, c.1000–c.1300* (Cambridge University Press, 2001); Norman Davies, *God's Playground: A History of Poland in two volumes* (Columbia, New York, 1982).

✠

The Mongol Impact on East Central Europe

The Tatar presence in East Central Europe did not last long. The khan withdrew from Hungary in 1243 upon hearing news of the grand khan's death: he would need every warrior to support his cause during the election of the latter's successor. The Christians emerged from their hiding places or came back from exile to find empty and devastated lands, but no sign of the enemy. The Mongols had come and gone like some biblical plague, perhaps to return without warning to once again punish the people for their sins. It did not occur to many that their principal sin was political disunity, and those with sufficient wisdom to recognise this saw no practical way to correct the fault.

Rus' lay prostrate. Only one state, Novgorod, remained independent, and its fate was uncertain. Those familiar with the brilliant movie by Sergei Eisenstein, *Alexander Nevsky*, with Prokofiev's magnificent score, might remember the opening scene, where a Mongol tax collector is exacting tribute and slaves. In the movie Alexander Nevsky stands up proudly to his dangerous Asiatic visitor; in real life he served in the Tatar armies and was ultimately murdered by the khan.

The Polish lands had been ravaged terribly. The power of the king was negligible for years thereafter, and none of the once powerful Piast dukes were able to provide national leadership. This not only made it almost impossible to defend Galicia against nomad raiders, but also hindered Masovia's ability to prosecute its ongoing campaigns against the pagans in Prussia. In fact, it was the pagans who were soon on the offensive, carrying away Polish captives to be sold in the slave markets of the East.

The consequences for Hungary were even more profound. So many Hungarian peasants had perished that several regions could be repopulated only by attracting immigrants from surrounding lands. Although the ethnic origin of these peasants was not important immediately, the presence of Rumanian, Serbian, Slovakian, and German peoples on the Hungarian plain would eventually become a serious obstacle to creating a national identity.

The most important beneficiary of the situation was the Teutonic Order. Only a military order had access to reinforcements, supplies, and a dependable source of immigrant peasants and merchants, volunteers for combat, and pious donations to aid the struggle against the enemies of Christendom. Moreover, to the extent that the Teutonic Order could pin down Prussians and Lithuanians in the defence of their own lands, this would relieve Hungary and Poland from fear of devastating raids. Therefore, for many years the German crusaders' presence in Prussia was very welcome.

✠

Conflict between the Pope and the Emperor

The confrontation between Friedrich II and the popes grew worse each year until the emperor's death in 1250. The principal victim of the conflict was the Holy Roman Empire, which was fragmented, left leaderless for half a century, and remained permanently weakened. Through these years of desperate struggle the membership of the Teutonic Order was badly divided over whether to give primary loyalty to the emperor or the pope, but in the end somehow managed to prevent becoming permanently identified with either camp. For the rest of the century the grand masters were close friends and allies of the popes; in the next century they tended to favor the emperors, but the contests of those decades were between weak opponents, not strong ones. In these years the Church declined in power and reputation, while the Holy Roman Empire recovered slightly during the reign of Charles IV.

The orientation of the Teutonic Order reflected these larger trends: in the thirteenth century, the primary interest was in defending the Holy Land; in the fourteenth century it was prosecuting the war in Prussia.

Meanwhile, local families in Germany and Bohemia became very important as supporters of the Teutonic Knights, contributing sons and money to the military order generation after generation. This provided the Teutonic Knights with hospitals, churches, and estates that not only produced significant revenues, but brought in knights, priests and men-at-arms for membership and recruited volunteers for the crusading expeditions.

5

The War against Paganism in Prussia

Pagan Prussia

Prussia was never a part or a province of the kingdom of Poland, although Polish culture had made some inroads among the nearest tribe, that which had pushed west into Culm. Perhaps only the Danes could put forward any claim to be the lawful overlords of any of the Prussians, and that claim was very weak indeed, although in the early thirteenth century King Waldemar II was on the way toward giving it substance by making expeditions into Samland – that prominent peninsula bounded by the *Frisches Haff* (Freshwater Bay) and the *Kurisches Haff* (Kurland Bay) – and other coastal provinces. Waldemar's kidnapping by Count Heinrich of Schwerin in 1223 brought a sudden end to those prospects.

Duke Conrad of Masovia had a claim on the southern borderlands of Prussia because he was their closest Catholic neighbour, save only for Duke Sventopełk of Pomerellia (1212–66), whose lands lay on the western bank of the Vistula River. Conrad and Sventopełk were thus best situated to revive the Polish crusades of the mid-twelfth century that had failed to conquer and convert the pagans in Prussia. Although Duke Conrad tried to move down the east bank of the Vistula, he never succeeded in doing more than occupying briefly the territory of Culm, which was, like his own provinces just upriver (Płock and Dobrin), so much a battlefield that some areas were depopulated.

The Prussians were ethnically and linguistically different from the Poles, Scandinavians, and Rus'ians. They were neither Germanic nor Slavic. Like their neighbours to the east – the Lithuanians and some of the tribes of Livonia – they were Balts, descendants of Indo-Europeans who had not migrated elsewhere during the great movements of peoples and had held onto their own languages and customs with relatively little change over the centuries.

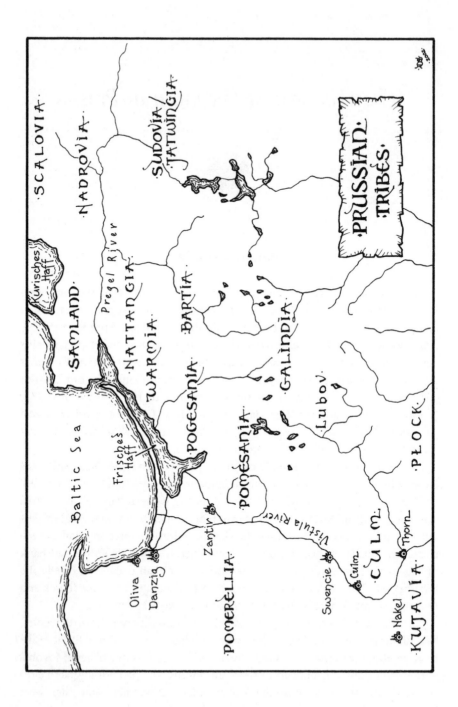

Prussian was part of a language group which included Lithuanian and Latvian, as well as the tongues of several smaller peoples such at the Jatwingians and Semgallians. This language group had once extended from Moscow to the Baltic Sea, but as prehistory became history the pressure of Slavic newcomers caused its domains to shrink drastically. Modern studies of the language that concentrate on the retention of native words in spite of centuries of intrusion and influence by larger language families reveal much about the speakers' pre-Christian culture. Words relating to three important economic activities – bees, horses, and wagons – demonstrate that Baltic culture was far from primitive (though, undoubtedly, the lack of population limited the extent to which the Prussians could specialise or maximise their potential for producing wealth). But the study of other areas of activity illustrates that Prussian society was failing to keep pace with its neighbours' progress in economic and governmental development. Institutions associated with feudalism were almost completely lacking. Consequently the Prussians had few prospects of unifying in ways that were necessary for an effective national defence, for promoting agriculture and commerce, and for sharing in the wider European culture.

The Prussian lands extended along the Baltic coast from the Nemunas (Memel) River in the north-east to the Vistula River in the south-west, and bordered Lithuania, Rus'ian Volhynia, Masovia, and Pomerellia. This meant that their neighbours spoke four different languages. Prussia was divided into eleven districts, each representing a major tribe: Culm, Pomesania, Pogesania, Warmia, Nattangia, Samland, Nadrovia, Scalovia, Sudovia, Galindia, and Bartia. According to the fourteenth-century chronicler Peter von Dusburg, one of the Teutonic Order's most knowledgeable writers, the most powerful tribes were the Samlanders, who could raise 4,000 cavalry and 40,000 infantry, and the Sudovians, who had 6,000 horsemen and 'an almost innumerable multitude of other warriors'. He estimated that the other tribes had about 2,000 horsemen each and an appropriate number of infantry, except for Culm and Galindia, which were largely depopulated – particularly Galindia, an interior province usually described as a wilderness. Galindia's terrain was so rugged and wooded and filled with so many lakes and rivers that all armies avoided crossing it. Modern estimates place the total Prussian population at approximately 170,000, a figure considerably smaller than Peter von Dusburg's calculation. Although not as numerous as their Lithuanian or Livonian neighbours, the Prussians were settled more densely on the land and were better organised. There were numerous forts that served as refuges for the people in wartime, and although these were not comparable to Western castles of the first rank they served their purpose effectively.

Peter von Dusburg described Prussian paganism thus:

The Prussians had no knowledge of God. Because they were primitive, they could not understand Him by reasoning, and because they had no letters, they could not learn of Him through the Scriptures. They appeared to be primitive beyond measure and marvelled greatly that anyone could make his thoughts known to another by writing. Because they did not know God, they took erroneously all creations for gods, such as the sun, the moon, and the stars, thunder, birds, and even animals and so on right down to the toads. They had forests, fields, and sacred waters in which no one was allowed to cut down trees, plough, or fish. In the midst of that perverse nation, apparently in Nadrovia, in a place called Romow, which owed its name to Rome, dwelt a man named Criwe, whom they honoured as a pope, since just as the pope rules over all the faithful of the Church, so he ruled over not only this one people, but also over the Lithuanians and the many nations of Livonia. Such was his authority that not only he himself or others of his blood, but even his messengers sent with a staff or other sign who crossed the boundaries of the infidel nations were held in great reverence by the rulers, the nobles, and the common people. He guarded, according to the old writings, an eternal fire. The Prussians believed in life after death, but not as they should believe. They believed that one, if he were noble or base, rich or poor, powerful or weak in this life, so also would he be after the resurrection into the future life. And that required the nobles to take with them in death their arms, horses, servants and maids, clothes, hunting dogs and hawks, and everything else pertaining to a warrior. With lesser people were burned the things pertaining to their work. They believed that the burned things were resurrected with them and would be used by them. With each death the following devil's game occurred: when the relatives of the deceased came to the pope Criwe and asked if on such-and-such a day or night he had seen someone going by his house; then Criwe described without hesitation the appearance of the deceased according to his clothes and weapons, his horse and retinue, and predicted, so as to strengthen his augury, that the deceased left such-and-such a sign on his house with a spear or other such tool. After a victory they bring their gods an offering, and from the booty won in the victory they give a third to Criwe, who burns it.*

* Much scholarly ink has been spilled over the nature of Baltic paganism. Recent opinions range from Marija Gimbutas, *The Balts* (Thames & Hudson, London, 1963) and Algirdas Greimas, *Of Gods and Men: Studies in Lithuanian Mythology* (Indiana University Press, 1992), who see a complete pantheon of gods and spirits, to Endre Bojtár, *Foreword to the Past: A Cultural History of the Baltic People* (Central European University Press, Budapest, 2000), who argues that the deities and most of Baltic folklore are nineteenth-century inventions, similar, perhaps, to currently fashionable neo-paganism and the goddess cult. The oldest descriptions of pagan practices were collected in their original languages by Wilhelm Mannhardt, *Letto-Prussische Götterlehre* (Lettisch-Literärische Gesellschaft, Riga, 1863).

While Peter von Dusburg was fascinated by the thought of a pagan anti-pope, it is obvious from other sources that Prussian religion was far from a mirror image of Christianity that worshipped the dark lord, Satan, and his ilk. It was rather a development of that Indo-European nature worship that is familiar to us through Greek, Roman, Celtic, and Germanic mythology. There was a strong element of Scandinavian religious thought that was probably introduced during those centuries when the Vikings exercised a loose authority over the region; and also some Christian ideas that had come in recently from Orthodox Rus' and Roman Catholic Europe. Western missionaries had visited Prussia since the tenth century, although without making many converts.

The customs of the Prussians were like those of their Baltic neighbours, the Livonian and Lithuanian tribes. The dominant class was the warrior nobility, who lived from booty, hunting, and the produce of their slaves. The free men lived by a combination of hunting and farming that gave them experience in the use of arms and a sense of tribal territory. There were a few priests, some artisans and merchants, and agricultural slaves. The clans organised civic life, raised armies, and regulated justice. Thus one's place in society was determined largely by the condition of one's birth.

The Prussians had been long known for hospitality and friendliness, but recent attacks by Scandinavians and Poles had caused that to change. Similarly, the simple nature worship of the past was evolving to resemble Christianity in its emphasis on powerful personal deities such as Perkunas, who had some attributes of a warrior god.

Unlike the Kurs (Curonians or Courlanders) and the Estonians, Prussians do not seem to have participated in piracy. Although they had slowly expanded their territories to the west, toward the Vistula River valley, that area might have been largely depopulated by Viking slave raids previous to their arrival. There is little evidence of their raiding their neighbours for cattle or slaves as was common in Livonia and Lithuania; but on the other hand there is almost no evidence of any kind for the politics or warfare of these years.* The Sudovians certainly were aggressive, but their lands abutted

---

* One can hardly take a firm stand on nothing, but nationalists of all types rarely hesitate to put their feet down wherever they believe a solid foundation should exist. And other than the experts in the less well-known languages of the region, past and present, who would know to what degree their accounts are reliable? Abundant records exist for later centuries, when Poles, Germans and papal legates were writing letters, reports and treaties, and chroniclers were composing works of surprising quality. In the nineteenth century well-trained histori-ans began to compose competent histories of this era and to publish edited editions of primary sources. Alas, some political histories were little more than polemics, but in the late twentieth century scholars had begun to overcome some of their most obvious political biases, at least to the extent of recognising alternative interpretations of events.

the Lithuanians, an even more aggressive people, and they may have learned the military arts solely in order to protect themselves. This made their military situation significantly different from that of other Prussian tribes. Similarly, the warlike tribesmen in Culm and Pogesania were possibly only reacting to Polish and Pomerellian pressure.

✠

Prussian Disunity

Clan government was rough and ready, and status and power were probably more important to securing 'justice' than having a just grievance was. In this the Prussians may have been no more deficient than the Poles and Germans, whose systems of justice still relied on individual power and the support of relatives and dependants. Clans protected their members from injury by the threat of taking revenge against enemies. If a clan lost a member in a fight, his relatives would kill the murderer – or, more likely, one of his kinfolk. For lesser crimes they would demand compensation. The tribal council was responsible for resolving disputes, and since the council was composed of the elders of the clans, its decisions were generally respected. The council met at intervals to discuss justice, common action, and to celebrate religious festivals. It had some authority to discipline unruly clans, but apparently exercised it only rarely.

Prussian mores were as strange to those who wrote about them as Christian customs were to the Prussians. Drunkenness was the national pastime, as it was for their Slavic neighbours, for Scandinavians, and for Germans. There were parties for marriages, deaths, births, religious festivals, and to honour visitors. The host passed a bowl brimming with an alcoholic beverage among his guests, the womenfolk, the sons and daughters, and even the servants, until everyone was in a stupor. It was an act that demonstrated mutual trust and friendship. As alcoholic beverages they knew only mead, made from honey, and kumiss, made from mare's or cow's milk. Because infant females were often killed soon after birth, Prussian women were scarce, and the fathers could demand a high bride price for the sale of their daughters. Nevertheless, polygamy was practised, and a prominent noble was expected to have several wives and concubines. That made it necessary to raid neighbouring lands in order to bring back women as prisoners. This combination of bride purchases and slave-catching probably lowered the status of women in Prussian society. On the other hand, it might have enhanced the role of native wives. There is evidence that women sometimes were important at all levels of society, but they did not assert this importance overtly.

The local markets could hardly be called mercantile centres, nor the villages towns, but the Prussians were not completely isolated from the commercial world. There was one important natural resource – amber. Known to Romans, Babylonians and ancient Egyptians for its lustre and smoothness, amber had been sought by foreign merchants time out of mind. In any form, rough or polished, this petrified tree sap made attractive jewellery, and the wood chips and insects trapped in the glowing material made it more interesting than common jewels. Also, amber could be found in only a few areas of the world, but no matter where it washed up on the shore, it was of a quality inferior to the Baltic product; as a result, Prussian amber had the attraction of being rare, mysterious and expensive.

There is a wealth of anecdotes about Prussian life. The nobles bathed regularly in sauna-like buildings, but the commoners avoided the practice altogether. Some people thought white horses unlucky, and others black horses. The Prussians had no calendar; whenever they wished to call a meeting, they sent around a stick with notches cut in it to signify the number of days remaining before the assembly. The Germans noticed that they had no spices for their foods and no soft beds. Their houses were scattered in the woods, surrounded by their fields, never too far from the refuge provided by a log fort. It was a primitive civilisation, but it was far from that of the so-called noble savage; the primitive and warlike nature of the people, combined with their impenetrable forests and swamps, made it possible for them to remain independent and to practice their peculiar customs long after their Polish and Rus'ian neighbours had adopted Christianity and become great kingdoms.

The size of the Prussian territorial unit, the tribe, was limited principally by the ability of the clan-based government to provide defence for its members. The main strongholds were the centres of tribal activities and the safest refuges in time of need. The smaller forts of the individual clans were sufficient to shelter people from minor raids, but unless reinforced would quickly fall to large invasion forces; as a result, such small forts were usually abandoned in times of great danger, the people hurrying to hiding places in the forests. Of course, abandoning homes, crops, and livestock was a highly undesirable course of action. If the clan fort was too far from other clans to receive prompt help, the clan might find it necessary to surrender or to move to a safer location; if the clan was numerous enough to be self-sustaining, it could evolve into a new tribe. The clans do not appear to have had any requirements for marriage inside or outside the group, or to have had any function other than religious and military. The individual nobles and elders do not appear to have been limited greatly by clan responsibilities.

Prussian Military Traditions

Independent action was such a characteristic of the people that an early traveller, Ibrahim ibn Jacob, noted that in warfare the individual warrior would not wait for his friends to help him but would rush into combat, swinging his sword until he was overwhelmed. This berserk courage was apparently limited to the nobility, because the general evidence is that the ordinary fighting man slipped off into the woods when confronted by greater numbers, leaving his fellows to fend for themselves, but surviving to fight another day. In this they were much like the general run of humanity.

The armament of the average warrior was extremely poor, so much so that he must be considered practically unarmed. The clubs and stones that the average militiaman used effectively in ambushes and in defending forts did not give him the confidence to fight pitched battles where the enemy had horses, armour, and swords. That was left to the nobles, who served as light cavalry with sword, spear, helmet, and mail coat. This equipment was less heavy than a western knight's outfit but was well suited to the swampy, wooded lowlands and the rough, wooded hills of their native land. Most likely the Prussian nobles would not have adopted western weapons even if they had been more easily available.

Prussian nobles were in many ways like nobles elsewhere. They lived by hunting and warfare and on the labour of their slaves. The women and children they captured on raids served as household help and as concubines, but often they treated them as human merchandise in the regional slave markets. There is some evidence of a trade route south through Poland, and no one would be surprised if many captives were sold down the Rus'ian rivers, the traditional slave route to the Turks and Byzantines. Although this eastern traffic was long past its heyday and was being interrupted by nomad incursions into southern Russia, it was still profitable. Men were of little use as prisoners or slaves unless they could be sold immediately, because they could escape too easily while performing agricultural work in the small forest clearings. Children were even less valuable, because it was expensive to raise a child to adulthood just to work in the fields. Women were more suitable in every sense for the primitive farming in grain crops and for gathering food in the woods.

Prussian nobles did not work, but lived by their own set of traditions that distinguished them from the commoners. The nobles in Germany and Poland did not work either, but they did not live by the labour of slaves or the income derived from the sale of prisoners taken in warfare. The tradition of slave-catching and the concept of honour that lay behind the successful Prussian social/religious system were cited by Christians in Poland and Pomerellia as the main reasons for their making war on the pagans in Prussia. A cynical modern observer might suggest that Christian rulers' eagerness to expand their domains was considerably more important. No matter. Either way it appears that religion *per se* was not the most significant cause of the wars between the Christians and pagans along the Vistula River. Religion became important later, of course, for all parties. The Prussians, certainly, once provoked, were not content to remain at home and practice their rites in peace, but were compelled by their evolving customs to continue their raids on Christian neighbours long after they had taken revenge for the initial outrages. Clearly, it was this increasingly aggressive activity over the years, whether it started as raw war-lust or as a reaction to Polish invasions, that eventually brought not just the Poles and Pomerellians but also Germans from the distant Holy Roman Empire to make war against them.

✠

Efforts to bring Christianity to Prussia

The oft-raised issue of Prussian independence and Prussian freedom meant something very different to the warriors of thirteenth-century Prussia than to the nineteenth-century liberals who praised them for their resistance to foreign invaders. The issue is a false one because the Christians had little choice but to defend themselves; there was no living with such a barbarous system. Moreover, the modern concept of nationalism does not track well onto medieval concepts of ethnic identity. Nevertheless, the issue is sometimes still raised, often in the context of imperialism and neo-imperialism, with Western nations almost always in the wrong.* There were philosophers in the thirteenth century, like Roger Bacon, who discussed the same questions that bother us today. There is no doubt that informal debates took place between the elders and priests of the Prussian clans and the trained dialecticians of the Church when the missionaries sought to convert the tribesmen.

---

* Modern historians have sought to identify the Teutonic Knights as the spearhead of the medieval *Drang nach Osten* (the German push to the East); with imperial Germany's expansionist plans; and with Nazism. In the Cold War period a crude hostility to all Slavs was attributed to the entire West. In reality this important medieval migration is better associated with the peaceful settlement of German knights and peasants in eastern lands (as in the legend of the Pied Piper of Hamelin) by invitation. Across Europe landowners and clergymen were opening forests and swamps to farming and herding; Polish peasants and gentry were on the move eastward; and Jews and German artisans and merchants were creating towns.

On the one hand there was praise for the traditional values and free choice, for martial virtue and no taxation; on the other, condemnation of gross superstition, ignorance, and barbaric habits. The churchmen who prized freedom of the mind and spirit did their best to persuade the simple but shrewd rural folk that what they had to offer in the way of civilisation and salvation was worth the sacrifice of ancient, warlike ways – and they failed. The churchmen had to overcome too many obstacles: their own minds were not as open as they thought; they brought with them concepts favourable to serfdom; their promotion of feudal government alienated the local nobility; they seemed to be the forerunners of foreign rulers; and they did not speak the Prussian language very well. But Prussian paganism owed its survival to more than just the failure of the missionaries. At its root was a flourishing military culture.

Military success had bred brutal and ambitious nobles who profited from the slave raids into Christian lands. Though approached by peaceful missionaries, they refused to stop their attacks, and occasionally killed those bold and uncompromising visitors. Before Prussian nobles would accept Christianity they had to be shown that the God of Victory favoured the other side. After that the missionaries could slowly introduce the changes that would break the traditions supporting the pagan philosophy.

The Prussians had not always enjoyed complete independence. Each generation had been obliged to defend its freedom and way of life. The Vikings had been the most successful in subjugating parts of Prussia and had come and gone so easily that the Prussians came to regard all strangers as hostile. The first missionaries to the region, Adalbert of Prague (997) and Bruno of Querfurt (1009), met martyr deaths; and the Prussians' hostility toward Christians, expressed in their raids, caused the Polish king Boleslaw III (1146–73) to lead crusades against them. The archbishops of Gniezno promoted the cult of St Wenceslas, depicting on the bronze doors of their cathedral his martyrdom by the Prussians. So it was that while the people of nearby Mecklenburg and Pomerania were being converted to Christianity by the Wendish Crusade, only the Prussians and the people living to their east and north-east held true to the old religions, and even there the Christians made strong inroads – between 1194 and 1206 many inhabitants of Culm were made into Christians by a combination of persuasion, self-interest, and raw force. The Poles were becoming stronger and moving closer. Some pagan Prussians must have known that time was running out.

In 1206 the abbot of the Polish Cistercian monastery at Lekno went to Prussia to negotiate for the release of some prisoners taken in recent raids. To his surprise he met a friendly reception, so friendly that he came to believe that he could make numerous converts to his faith if he remained there permanently. He wrote to Pope Innocent III to ask permission to conduct a mission supported by the other Cistercian abbeys in Poland. The pope responded:

> Commending his pious request, we give permission for him to preach the gospel to them and act as Christ's messenger, calling upon God to convert them to Christ. And since the harvest will be great, one worker will not be sufficient. Therefore, by apostolic authority we allow him to take brothers of the Cistercian Order with him, and others who want to join in the work of ministry, to preach the gospel and baptise those who accept the word of God . . .

The abbot's zeal was further fired by reports brought from Livonia by monks who had spoken to Theodoric, the Cistercian monk responsible for the success of the mission organised by the bishop of Riga. If Theodoric and his fellow-monks could convert pagans in Livonia and Estonia, why could he not do the same in Prussia?

Complicating the peaceful conversion were the periodic efforts of Polish kings and dukes to expand their rule. While this eastward push was often successful, in Prussia it did little beyond disrupt the missionary effort and bring about pagan retaliation. However, deploring past mistakes was not an option open to the Christian rulers. As the Piast dukes, especially Conrad of Masovia and his bishops and abbots, watched their subjects being carried off and sold to slave traders from the Moslem and Orthodox worlds, they had to act. Unable to defend their frontiers alone, they called on the military orders for help. The Teutonic Order was among those willing to talk about providing help.[*]

✠

The Teutonic Knights enter Prussia

The first small force of Teutonic Knights to enter Prussia was commanded by Conrad von Landsberg, a native of nearby Meissen who was familiar with Polish geography and customs. His tiny army came with the intention of establishing a foothold in the lands that Duke Conrad of Masovia and Bishop Christian had promised them. Grand Master Hermann von Salza had needed every knight and man-at-arms for Friedrich II's crusade, but he understood that he could not allow the Prussian invitation to remain totally unanswered.

[*] Conrad created his own military order, the Dobriners, which he hoped to control fully; it was later wiped out fighting in Volhynia. The Templars and Hospitallers accepted estates in Pomerellia and Poland, but their contributions to later military expeditions were too small to be significant.

He was aware that competitors – the Dobriner Order, the Templars, and the Hospitallers – could expand in this direction too; and he understood that the duke might change his mind. Medieval rulers – like modern ones – had short attention spans and often reversed their decisions with little warning or reason.

In all likelihood Conrad von Landsberg gathered up his handful of knights from convents in Central Germany, probably taking only new recruits and perhaps a few warriors who were too ill or injured to join the grand master when the fleet sailed for the Holy Land. There were only seven knights, accompanied by seventy to a hundred squires and sergeants, and servants to bake bread, malt beer, wash clothes, and keep the horses and equipment in order. Since it was a partly cloistered order, and also a hospital order, there were priests and doctors with them too. All were male, and attendance at the eight religious services held each day was a major function that took up much of their time. They were well-armed, well-equipped, and very well-trained, but no one thought them supermen. Outwardly they were ordinary knights; inwardly they were dedicated monks.

Conrad von Landsberg did not dare to enter directly into Culm, at the strategic bend of the Vistula River, but stayed on the south bank, in Masovia, where Duke Conrad had built a small castle on a hill opposite the future location of Thorn (Toruń). With black humour the German crusaders named it Vogelsang (bird's song). The chronicler Nicholas von Jeroschin explained: 'There sang many a wounded man, not as the nightingale sings, but with the sorrowful song that the swan sings as he is killed.'

This small force of Teutonic Knights could not have held out against a large army of Prussians, but the district had already been partly depopulated in earlier Polish invasions, and some of the local natives were Christians with ties to Duke Conrad and Bishop Christian. Therefore the number of pagans in Culm was not large, and those who were there had no reason to consider the newly arrived warriors a serious menace. That was a mistake. Once Conrad von Landsberg had completed his castle/convent, he sent his knights across the Vistula River to cut down the nearest pagan warriors, to burn their fields and villages, and to destroy their crops. He offered peace only on the condition that the people became Christians.

✠

William of Modena

At this time a papal legate, Bishop William of Modena, was in Prussia. This Italian prelate was well acquainted with Baltic affairs, having previously served in Livonia and Estonia. He had just come from Denmark, where he

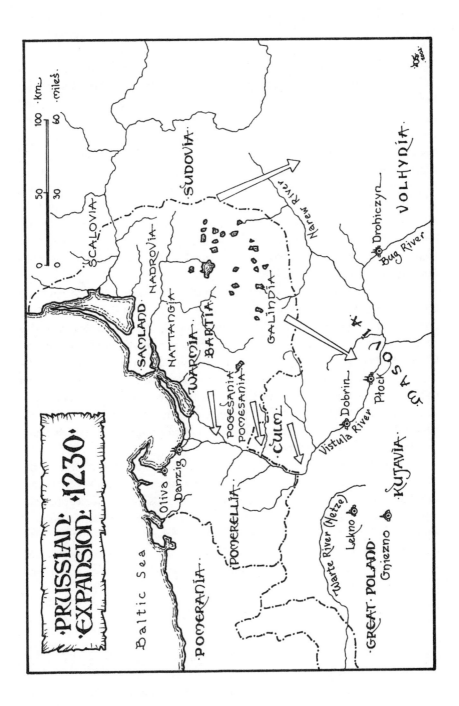

·PRUSSIAN·EXPANSION· ·1230·

Baltic Sea

POMERANIA·

POMERELLIA·

Oliva

Danzig

SAMLAND

NADROVIA·

NATTANGIA·

WARMIA·

BARTIA·

POGESANIA·

POMESANIA·

CULM·

SCALOVIA·

SUDOVIA·

GALINDIA·

Narew River

Bug River

Drohiczyn

VOLHYDIA·

MASO

Vistula River

Dobrin

Plock

KUJAVIA·

Warte River (Netze)

Lekno

Gniezno

·GREAT·POLAND·

km.

miles.

100

60

50

30

0

0

had been discussing the disordered affairs of the Livonian Crusade with King Waldemar II. Thence he had sailed to Prussia, and was present from the late autumn of 1228 (or early spring of 1229) until shortly before January 1230, when he seems to have been in Italy, conferring with Hermann von Salza.

Information about the legate's activity is scanty. He translated a grammar book into the Prussian language so that the natives could learn to read, and he made a few converts, apparently among the Pomesanians and Pogesanians north of Culm. It is very likely that the new converts mentioned in papal documents of 1231 and 1232, whom the Teutonic Knights were warned against disturbing, refer to those Prussian Christians, and not to the crusaders in Livonia as some modern historians have assumed. William of Modena was always very concerned about the well-being of converts. He feared that ill-treatment would cause them to believe that all Christians were hypocrites and tyrants, whereas Christianity should bring a greater amount of peace, justice, and fairness than existed before, in addition to the benefits of spiritual consolation and eternal life.

William of Modena was also determined to co-ordinate the crusading efforts of regional powers which might otherwise spend more time and effort frustrating one another than in prosecuting the holy war. It is at this time, in January 1230, that documents from Count Conrad and Bishop Christian were obtained (or recreated, or falsified), an action that complicated immensely subsequent efforts to understand what had been promised to the Teutonic Order and when the promises were made. Later generations, unable to call up the dead for personal testimony, relied on their instincts, basing their judgements more upon their current political interests than any determination to find the truth.

Whatever success William of Modena had, it fell short of discouraging the Teutonic Knights from continuing their attacks on settlements in Culm. Until this time the Teutonic Knights had raided across the great river but had not tried to establish themselves there. This was the era of reconnaissance. Quite literally, that meant getting to know the land and the people. The handful of knights and sergeants were learning the language, the customs, and the military tactics of their opponents, preparing for the day when reinforcements would arrive.

✠

Hermann Balk

In 1230 reinforcements under the command of Master Hermann Balk rode into Vogelsang. A capable warrior who was to lead the crusade in Prussia and Livonia for many years, Balk was a reasonable, conciliatory man in every respect except one – when dealing with pagans or infidels, he had no tolerance, patience, or mercy. Among Christians of any kind – German, Polish, Prussian – he seems to have been respected and trusted. The traditions he established were upheld in their essentials for the rest of the century, right down to the master's seal depicting the flight of the Holy Family into Egypt. Perhaps symbolising Balk's pre-eminence, his was the only master's seal to bear his name. All others were anonymous.

Hermann von Salza had been able to send this party of knights because he was at last free from his extraordinary commitments in the Holy Land. Although he now had greater responsibilities there than before the imperial crusade, a truce was in effect and the usual number of troops was not required. If enlistments remained at the present high level, he could expect to send more troops to Prussia every year without diminishing the garrisons around Acre. Moreover, there was still some small hope that the Teutonic Order would be able to return to Hungary, a move that would limit the involvement in Prussia. Pope Gregory IX was writing to King Bela, asking him to return the confiscated lands. But Hermann von Salza was a realist. While he did not expect to get the Transylvanian lands back, he knew that God had strange ways – kings changed their minds, they got into unexpected troubles, and they died. Hermann von Salza was ready to go back to Hungary if God should put the opportunity before him again.

Prussia was a different matter, exciting in its possibilities and challenging in its difficulties, but much preparation and hard work would be necessary and time would pass before results could be expected. The grand master could not send in more than a handful of knights until supplies were built up to feed more troops, and until castles were constructed to protect and house them. It was a matter of careful administration to send just the right number of men at the right time and thereby make the best use of the slender resources that Hermann von Salza had available for his operations everywhere – in the Holy Land and Armenia, in Italy, and in Germany. Prussia came last in his estimation.

Hermann Balk went first to the problem that had so bothered the leaders of the order for two years – the grant by which Duke Conrad had given them lands for their maintenance. Culm was occupied by the enemy, so the Prussian master would somehow have to find his own means of financing the campaigns to subdue the pagans. This was understandable. What he could not agree to was that after Culm was occupied it would still belong to Bishop Christian and Duke Conrad. In short, what was in it for the Teutonic Knights, who would presumably have to remain in Culm to defend it from the other Prussians? Balk, therefore, went to the duke and bishop and apparently confronted them with the story of the order's Hungarian debacle. He had brought an army and was ready to use it to protect them, their lands, and their subjects, but the duke and his bishop had to be ready to pay the price. He requested (politely surely, but certainly firmly) a grant of sovereignty more similar to that granted by the emperor in the Golden Bull of Rimini in 1226 than that which they had proposed. What he got has been the subject of dispute between German and Polish historians ever since, but whatever the exact terms, the grant was sufficient to satisfy him, the grand master, and the grand chapter meetings that discussed it.

Relatively quickly crusader armies composed of Germans, Poles, Pomerellians and native militias overran the western Prussian tribes. As many as 10,000 men took the cross in the summer of 1233, perhaps inspired by the opportunity to see a piece of the true cross, and built the fortress at Marienwerder in the middle of Pomesania, on a tributary of the Vistula, about half-way between Thorn and the sea; that winter those crusaders who had stayed were joined by Dukes Sventopełk and Sambor of Pomerellia for an invasion of Pogesania. When the pagans came out in a phalanx to meet the crusaders on the frozen surface of the Sirgune River, they were quickly panicked by the appearance of the Pomerellian cavalry in their rear; the effort to flee became a massacre.

The count of Meissen was important in the great offensive of 1236–7. First he built large sailing ships, then sank the small pagan vessels that came out to challenge him, and finally he transported his men downstream to strike in the enemy's rear. The Pogesanian militia came out to fight, but fled after hearing the count's men blowing horns (presumably in their rear). Clearly, the Prussians were in no mood to stand up to heavy cavalry, flights of crossbow quarrels, and disciplined infantry. Western methods of making war swept the Prussians from level battlefields. It was harder to find the pagans in the woods and swamps, especially in the summer, but in winter – a season of war in which the crusaders came to specialise – they could be easily traced back to their lairs.

Each year small crusader armies came to Prussia, and each year the result was the same – an expansion of the order's conquests. Many of these volunteers were Polish, and everyone involved in this crusade understood that without the steadfast support of the Piast and Pomerellian dukes the volunteers who came from Germany could have done little besides provide garrisons for the castles already constructed. Why, then, if the Poles were doing so much of the fighting, were the Teutonic Knights so important?

The answer is that Polish and Pomerellian crusaders went home or stayed home. At first they were only gone from the onset of bad weather in the fall until the long days of the short summer began, but within a few years their active contributions went permanently missing – Duke Conrad had troubles on his other frontiers, Duke Sventopełk was quarrelling with his brothers, and eventually all the Piasts of Poland were feuding. None of these feudal lords, nor their bishops, had the resources to provide an occupation force – that became the role of the Teutonic Knights here just as it had been in the Holy Land. Celibate knights, pledged to poverty and obedience, were willing to serve through the wet seasons and the long cold winter nights. Secular knights who preferred a hot drink and a warm woman (or the other way around) were not eager to patrol dark paths in the forest or endure the freezing winds atop a lookout tower above lonely ramparts.

To assist in occupying the newly conquered territories, the Teutonic Knights settled secular knights on vacant lands in Culm, recruiting most of them from Poland; and in these early years they attracted burghers from Germany to found one new town a year, guaranteeing their rights in the Charter of Culm (1233). These immigrants were not numerous, though they would become so by the end of the thirteenth century, and were even more plentiful in the fourteenth. A large part of the fighting force, however, was composed of Prussian militiamen and nobles, the former serving as infantry, the latter as cavalry (often referred to – though slightly inaccurately – as 'native knights').*

Whenever crusading forces were available, the Teutonic Knights, who were now experts on local topography and native customs, led the German and Polish knights, together with the allied Prussian cavalry and militiamen, down the Vistula River and along the coastline, capturing one fortress after another. There were distractions – in 1237 the Teutonic Knights incorporated a local military order, the Swordbrothers (see next chapter), and thereby took on additional responsibilities in Livonia that required diverting men and material to the north; then Pope Gregory IX excommunicated Emperor Friedrich II, precipitating a long and costly struggle that tore Germany apart; the Mongol onslaught of 1241–2 devastated Galicia-Volhynia, Hungary, and Poland, temporarily making it impossible for those powerful states to provide military assistance in the crusades; and in the 1240s Sventopełk of Pomerellia joined rebellious Prussians in an effort to drive the Teutonic Knights out of lands he wanted to make his own. This last conflict, the First Prussian Insurrection, was a close-run affair, but at last

---

* Native nobles rarely had sufficient income to allow them to function full-time as warriors and administrators. Nor did the Teutonic Order want to disperse its potential incomes by creating a class of secular knights. The masters gave away few fiefs, and most of those were small grants in Culm, given to Polish knights. The masters appointed members of the Teutonic Order to train and lead the native troops. Known as advocates, these lived with their charges, so they were usually fluent in Prussian and understood their customs well.

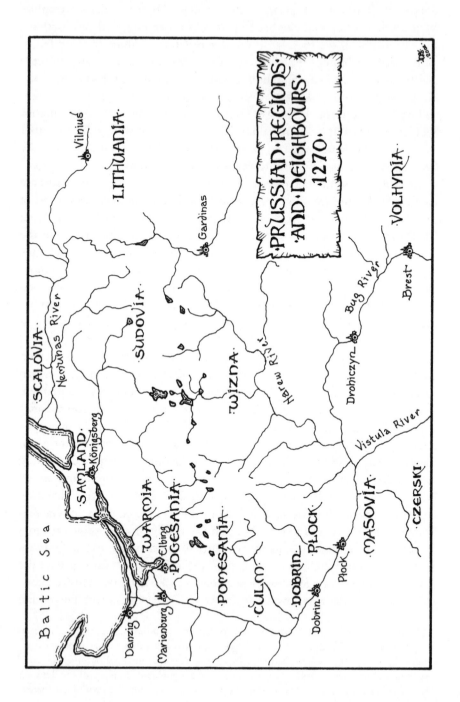

Sventopełk was forced to make peace, then forced again to surrender. Afterward the Prussian tribes negotiated a surrender that guaranteed them considerable autonomy in the conduct of their daily lives.

Meanwhile the Livonian branch of the order was also making headway in its offensives south from Riga. It seemed on the verge of a significant victory in 1250 when Mindaugas of Lithuania accepted Roman Christianity, thus removing the justification for attacking his lands. Although some critics of the Teutonic Order see the knights as nothing more than land-hungry robbers, in this instance they gave up an opportunity to seize territories in order to make one of Christendom's greatest foes into a strong ally.* Shortly thereafter Prussian resistance began to collapse, too – in 1256 King Ottokar II of Bohemia, the most powerful single ruler in the Holy Roman Empire, led to Samland an army so powerful that the local natives realised resistance was futile. Shortly afterward, in 1257, the Samogitians asked for a two-year truce to consider their options. The crusaders granted this request, confident that self-interest would induce their foes to make a formal acceptance of the true faith. For a moment it appeared that Christendom had triumphed totally in the Baltic region.

The crusaders' enthusiasm for peaceful conversions should give pause to those who cannot manage to disassociate the medieval mind from modern ideologies such as nationalism and racism, or who prefer to believe that the Germans were out to depopulate the entire region and resettle it. But it is unlikely that the Teutonic Knights will be judged by the most consistent of their statements and actions, for they, like most human organisations, exhibited over time a wide range of behaviours; if one always assumes the worst of them and the best from their foes, one can see them as evil, indeed; and that is the way that many historians, particularly those who judge the past as essentially part of the twentieth century, have written about these German warriors.

The crusading position began to come apart in 1259, when the Samogitians chose to fight for their pagan faith and traditional customs (which included raiding Christian settlements). They inflicted annihilating defeats upon Prussian and Livonian armies, forced Mindaugas to recant his conversion, and persuaded native peoples to the north and west to rise in revolt against their German masters. Soon Lithuanian armies were penetrating into Livonia, Prussia, Volhynia and Poland. Pagan victories seemed to confirm the rightness of the pagan religion. Holy War was now truly a contest of faiths, not merely a struggle between rulers as to who would rule.

---

* Mindaugas did promise the Livonian master Samogitia, but he could do this easily, since the Samogitians did not recognise him as their ruler anyway.

This time the Teutonic Knights were more or less on their own. Neither German nor Polish crusaders came in great numbers, much less Bohemian monarchs and prelates. Moreover, the Holy Land became once again the centre of crusading energies, and the Teutonic Knights, like other military-religious orders, gave that region priority. The war in Prussia became a contest of border raids, sieges and surprises, and patrolling the wilderness to prevent the eastern Prussians and Lithuanians from coming through the depopulated Galindian forests and swamps to attack isolated settlements. Poles and Germans worked together to close the gap and eventually they were joined by Volhynians in carrying the war to the common enemy.

✠

Pagan and Orthodox Enemies

The fifteen years of this Second Prussian Insurrection (1260–75) had been difficult ones, as Peter von Dusburg reminded his readers:

> There was hardly a time in which there was enough bread to eat, and one, two, or more times they had to ride to battle and drive the enemy away. And so, they acted as did those Jews who wanted to rebuild the holy city of Jerusalem when threatened by enemies, in that half of them worked and the others stayed on guard from dawn till dusk. With one hand they worked, and in the other they held a sword.

The worst years of the insurrection were over by 1273, the year that the bishop of Olmütz (Olomouc), a Czech prelate with excellent access to information about Poland, Galicia and Hungary, wrote a memorial for Pope Gregory X reminding him that the entire eastern part of Europe was still threatened by pagans, heretics and 'schismatics' (members of the Orthodox church):

> There are four realms in this region – Hungary, Rus', Lithuania, and Prussia. There are imminent dangers to the Christians in the kingdom of Hungary. First, because the Cumans are there, where they are not only aliens, but attack the kingdom and, among other customs, kill the very young and very old and take the youths and maidens captive and teach them their evil rites, and such is their power that they multiply, and, there-fore, Hungary is certainly in danger from them, and the neighbouring lands, too. And in that kingdom there are heretics and schismatics who have fled from other lands. The very Queen of Hungary is a Cuman,

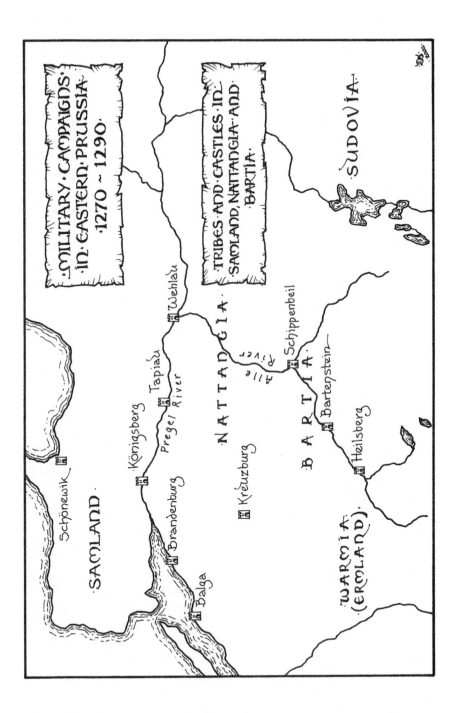

MILITARY·CAMPAIGNS·
IN·EASTERN·PRUSSIA·
·1270 ~ 1290·

TRIBES·AND·CASTLES·IN·
SAMLAND, NATTADGIA·AND·
·BARTIA·

SUDOVIA·

SAMLAND·

Schönewik

Königsberg

Tapiau

Pregel River

Brandenburg

Balga

Wehlau

NATTADGIA·

Kreuzburg

Alle River

Schippenbeil

BARTIA·

Bartenstein

Heilsberg

WARMIA·
(ERMLAND)·

whose parents were and are pagans. Two daughters of the Hungarian king have been married to schismatic Rus'ians . . . The Rus'ians are schismatics and servants of the Mongols. The Lithuanians and Prussians are pagans who devastate many bishoprics in Poland. These are the closest to us.

There were great dangers still, and not far away. The surrender of the Nattangians, Warmians and Bartians made the Teutonic Knights responsible for protecting these new 'converts'; this could be done only by striking deeper into the interior of the country against the remaining pagans, the Sudovians, and their Lithuanian allies. Moreover, the Teutonic Knights had to fight alone. Ottokar of Bohemia was now fighting Rudolf von Habsburg for possession of Austria and the throne, and until the decisive battle in 1278 the king needed his supporters to provide all the military aid they could – Brandenburg, Bavaria, Cracow, Silesia, Thuringia and Meissen all sent knights to Bohemia. As a result, although all of these rulers were traditional allies of the Teutonic Order, often men who had been on crusade themselves, each was too deeply involved in the struggle for empire to send help to Prussia in this moment of direst need.

✚

War along the Frontier

The Sudovians were not an easy enemy for the crusaders to fight. First of all, they were good warriors and fairly numerous; secondly, their lands lay far to the east, in the midst of seemingly impenetrable swamps and forests. It was easier to find a great aurochs, that huge ox-like beast already on the verge of extinction, than to locate Sudovians hiding in the woods. Nor was it much easier to spot a Sudovian raiding party before it struck without warning at isolated settlements and garrisons.

The first Sudovian attacks came even as the Nattangians and Bartians were surrendering. The Sudovians fell on the construction party that was rebuilding Bartenstein, a strategic point on the Alle River in central Bartia, and killed all the men there, then burned the uncompleted structure. That was a hard blow to the Teutonic Knights. Bartenstein was to be the anchor of their defensive line facing the wilderness. The Sudovians, led by an intrepid leader named Scumand, were then able to raid freely among the disorganised and defenceless tribes that had so recently been their allies.

By terrorising the Nattangians and Bartians, however, the Sudovians drove those tribes, willy-nilly, into the arms of the Teutonic Order. Much as those tribesmen may have sympathised with the Sudovians, they were unwilling to see their families perish in Scumand's frightening raids. Without a castle base from which to operate, the Teutonic Knights could do little to help them; therefore, it was up to the natives to protect themselves. At first the warriors who had survived the insurrection lacked confidence and leadership, and until 1274 they did little but hide in their forts. Then a stout-hearted matron – a relative of Herkus Monte, the most famous leader of an earlier Prussian rebellion – began to berate her sons, accusing them of being unable either to defend themselves or their people. Stung by her accusations, they gathered the warriors from several forts and fought a pitched battle against the Sudovians, killing 2,000 of the raiders. This cleared the country of most of the border ruffians and made it possible for the Teutonic Knights to rebuild Bartenstein. When Prussian natives in their own self-interest brought their formidable military skills to the service of the Teutonic Knights the balance of power tipped in favour of the Christians. The episode also proves that the Nattangians had hardly been exterminated or even reduced hopelessly in numbers.

New leaders were now heading the military order, and with them came new strategies and new tactics. Grand Master Anno von Sangerhausen had gone from Prussia to the Holy Land in 1266 and remained there until the conclusion of peace with Sultan Baibars in 1272; then he had returned to Germany to recruit those crusaders from Thuringia and Meissen who brought the war in Nattangia to a conclusion; shortly after returning from Prussia to Germany again, he died. The grand chapter that met in July of 1273 chose as his successor Hartmann von Heldrungen, a man of advanced years who as a youth had known Grand Master Conrad, Duke of Thuringia, who had witnessed personally the union with the Swordbrothers, and who had visited Prussia in 1255. Following tradition, Grand Master Hartmann went to Italy and took ship for the Holy Land, where the knights outside Prussia and Livonia still saw their chief duty – the defence of Acre until that day when a new crusading force would come to liberate Jerusalem again. Hartmann, however, soon returned to Germany. There simply was not enough room in the order's convent in Acre to house the number of officers and knights who were available for duty. Some of them had to be sent back to Europe, subject to immediate recall.

That same grand chapter meeting also confirmed the election of Conrad von Thierberg as Prussian master. Conrad, a Frank by birth, had served most of his career in Prussia as castellan of Zantir and Christburg, strongholds in the north-west. From 1269 on he had been acting-master on several occasions. Now that he held office in his own right he called on his younger brother to be marshal. Because they shared the same first as well as last name they were known as Conrad the elder and Conrad the younger.

The grand chapter had instructed Master Conrad to attack east from Königsberg up the Pregel River and drive a wedge between the Sudovians and the Nadrovians. The assembly of knights hoped that this would facilitate the conquest of the Nadrovians; from their lands they could use the Nemunas to operate against the southern flank of the Samogitians. Also, the new castles on the Pregel could be easily supplied by ship, and they would protect traffic moving toward the Alle River. Moreover, in contrast to the recent past, the grand chapter apparently sent enough knights and men-at-arms to make the effort successful.

Master Conrad opened the campaign by sending the advocate of Samland, Theodoric, with his native militia against two large log forts on the Pregel River. Both were taken, and the Samlanders found so many horses, cattle, and other booty in them that they could barely carry their loot or drive the animals home. Next he sent Theodoric by boat with a force of Teutonic Knights and 150 sergeants and many native infantry to a more distant castle. As soon as the advocate had placed his archers in position, he directed the native militiamen to make the assault with storm ladders. Too late, the Nadrovians tried to surrender; the attack had proceeded too far to call back the troops, so the slaughter encompassed most of the warriors inside the walls. A few pagans managed to make themselves understood and were spared to be taken away for resettlement with the women and children, but not many. The victors then burned the fort and departed.

Once the border forts were cleared away, Master Conrad led the army into the interior of Nadrovia. He plundered the nearby districts before besieging the main fortress, a stronghold protected by 200 well-armed men. His assault was similar to others directed against native log and earth forts, and the outcome was similar too: after hard fighting Master Conrad's troops captured it, slaying most of the garrison. Not long afterward the rest of the Nadrovians surrendered. An order chronicler summarised this victory:

> There were many glorious deeds done against the Nadrovians which are not written in this book because it would be tedious to describe them one by one. But the Nadrovians had a large, strong army at that time and many castles. Nevertheless, they put aside their hate and surrendered to the brothers, except for a few who went to Lithuania. And to the present day that part of Nadrovia remains a wilderness.

In accordance with plans made many years before, the Teutonic Knights proceeded to advance north-east. Nadrovia now served as the base for attacks on Scalovia on the lower Nemunas, beyond which lay Samogitia. The leaders of the crusade had long desired to crush the stubborn and courageous resistance of the Samogitians, whose attacks on Kurland were obstructing communication with Livonia; currently the Prussian master could safely send messages, men and supplies only by sea, and then only in the summer. The strategy was clear. Just as the Prussian master's advance into Scalovia had become possible only because earlier victories had eliminated all dangerous threats to his flank, now he was eliminating the danger to his current flank, with the ultimate goal being to make secure the border regions of Kurland and Livonia. Ultimately, just as the Nadrovians now served as crusader auxiliaries, not enemies, so the Scalovians would soon assist against the Samogitians and, if all went as planned, the Samogitians would eventually assist in fighting the Lithuanians.

The Lithuanians understood this perfectly, and so they gave all the help they could to the endangered tribes on the frontier. Awkwardly, these reinforcements came only at those times when the common warriors were not needed for agricultural work, and all warriors disliked the boring duties involved in regional defence. So the most logical employment of these forces was in attacking Livonia and Prussia, thus tying down the Christian forces to protect their porous frontiers. The Teutonic Knights, quite understandably, chose to tie down the pagan troops in the same way, by threatening to invade the highlands at all times of year, with minimal warning and maximum damage.

To reduce the Lithuanian ability to assist the Samogitians, the order's Livonian branch built a great castle at Dünaburg in 1274, effectively cutting the most direct route to Pskov and Novgorod. The Lithuanian grand prince, Traidenis (?–1281/2), is supposed to have referred to it as 'built in the middle of his heart'. He besieged the log and earth castle for four weeks, using every man and every weapon at his disposal. But he could neither take the fortress nor stop the devastating raids by its garrison. Soon a vast uninhabited zone existed in the region between Dünaburg and the highlands.

The first offensive opened a secure shoreline route to Memel (Klaipėda), the crusader castle at the mouth of the Kurland bay that had been built in 1252 with the help of crusaders from Lübeck. Thence it was an easy ride north along the coast to Kurland or down the narrow, sandy peninsula to Prussia. To widen the land corridor and prepare the way for raids directly into central Samogitia, Master Conrad's strategy was not that of direct assault, pushing east from Memel, but a flank movement up the Nemunas River. The Westerners were thereby able to use their technological advantages in transport and siege equipment and avoid the difficult problems of campaigning in the great forests and swamps of the interior.

The first objective was the Scalovian fortress at Ragnit, which stood on a tall hill overlooking the great river. An impressive bastion, it had resisted

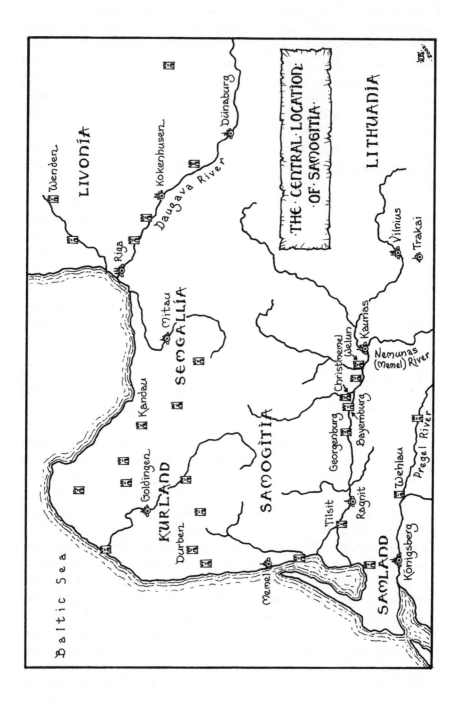

THE · CENTRAL · LOCATION · OF · SAMOGITIA ·

Baltic Sea

LIVONIA

Wenden

Kokenhusen

Dünaburg

Daugava River

Riga

Mitau

SEMGALLIA

Kandau

Goldingen

KURLAND

Durben

SAMOGITIA

Memel

Tilsit

Ragnit

Georgenburg

Bayernburg

Welun

Christmemel

Kaunas

Nemunas
(Memel) River

Vilnius

Trakai

LITHUANIA

Wehlau

Pregel River

SAMLAND

Königsberg

many attacks over the decades, including one by a strong Rus'ian army. The log and earth fortifications could not be easily stormed, and there was a pond within the walls that provided water and fish for the garrison in case of siege. The natives considered it impregnable.

In 1275 Master Conrad sent Theodoric of Samland by ship to Ragnit with a thousand men. The advocate debarked his men and equipment and moved them up the hill. When everyone was in place he ordered the troops to attack. The defenders massed their men along the rampart to resist the scaling attempt, providing a target that the crusader archers could hardly miss. After unrelenting missile fire forced the defenders back off the ramparts, the crusaders mounted ladders, poured over the wall and began the usual slaughter. The victors levelled the fortifications by fire and demolition. Then, in a campaign lasting only one additional day, Theodoric captured the fortress at Romige on the other side of the river.

The Scalovians did not leave those deeds unavenged, but sailed down to Labiau, on the coast of the bay north of Königsberg, and attacked early one morning while the guards slept. They butchered the people and burned the castle. Master Conrad felt obliged to retaliate in turn. He called up his knights and native troops, then raided those parts of Scalovia that were nearest. Nicholas von Jeroschin wrote:

> They murdered so many of the unbaptised that many drowned in their own blood. They captured men and women in their hideouts and brought them back. And while they were there, preparing to retreat . . . the Scalovian chief, Stone God, brought a great army of his subjects together and pursued the brothers' army. When the Master heard of this, he sent a strong force off to one side and it remained hidden until the Scalovians came up to attack him. Then the brothers sprang out of the ambush, cut down many, and drove the rest into flight.

By now many Scalovian nobles were sending messengers to the Teutonic Knights with offers to surrender on terms. It was a difficult task even for the officers experienced in border warfare and knowledgeable in the language and customs of the enemy to tell which offers were genuine and which were lures to bring small bodies of crusaders to destruction. More than once the neighbouring Kurs had asked for garrisons for their border castles and had then ambushed the company that was sent. Now that the Scalovian nobles were making the same request, the Teutonic Knights responded cautiously.

There were many minor combats which even the order's chroniclers found too repetitive to record, but the result was the same as in Nadrovia – the majority of the Scalovians surrendered and a minority left their homes for

Lithuania. In places, and especially along the frontier, which had been depopulated a great wilderness grew up. But the pagans, led by Scumand's Sudovians, struck back ferociously, raiding as far west as Culm. They even besieged the bishop's castle at Schönsee in 1273. Such attacks prompted the Teutonic Knights to replace ageing wooden fortifications with stone-walled castles.

Some Prussians fled to Traidenis, who proposed settling them on the border of Volhynia, probably at Gardinas (Grodno). This came to the attention of the Galician-Volhynian duke, who then ordered a new frontier settlement built at Kamenec on a tributary of the Bug River to protect his lands from attacks coming out of Gardinas and to solidify his control of the trade route north of the Pripet marshes, from Pinsk to Brest and on to Drohiczyn.

There is little doubt that Master Conrad would have attacked Samogitia next if circumstances had permitted. That land of strong pagans lay just to the north, and raids could be co-ordinated with the order's Livonian branch. But Master Conrad was not able to move north. He was required to turn his attention to Pogesania, where the Third Prussian Insurrection had begun.

✠

The Third Prussian Insurrection 1275–83

The uprising seems to have been provoked by Scumand, whose recent raids had been so devastating that the order's chief castellan in Pogesania had been sacked in 1276 and replaced by a more daring official. Perhaps angered by subsequent defeats that several of his smaller raiding parties suffered that year, Scumand asked the Lithuanians to help him. They agreed, and in 1277 he led them and 4,000 of his own tribesmen through the wilderness into Culm, where he captured one small castle on the Ossa River, then passed by Rehden, Marienwerder, Zantir, and Christburg, burning all the villages near them and the small forts that lay along his route. Peter von Dusburg described a pitiful scene, one confirmed by the Polish chronicler, Długosz:

> They drove home an indescribable amount of booty and Christians, who were set to eternal serfdom. May God have pity on them! What lamentation there was, when friend wept with friend and people were separated, and it was a trial when children were taken from mothers who were still carefully nursing them; and when daughters were taken from mothers as the pagans parcelled out the prisoners among themselves and handled them shamefully. Oh, how horrible it was, and what a terrible sight some were when their friends saw them. No one could look on their plight without crying.

Meanwhile, Lithuanian armies following the wilderness paths from Gardinas down the Narew River into Masovia were continuing west, plundering Polish villages and crossing the Vistula River into Kujavia. This was the very situation that had brought the Teutonic Knights into Prussia in the first place – the Piast dukes' inability to protect the northern frontiers of Poland. It was not just that the raids were terrible, because the crusader raids were terrible too, and probably some of these people had been recent victims of the latest campaign of the Teutonic Knights, resettled in these supposedly safe regions; but the fate that awaited the Polish prisoners was believed to be much worse.

Although the Christian raids lacked none of the initial terror and fright-fulness, there was a somewhat different attitude between Christians and pagans. The Christians resettled most of their prisoners as farm labourers, often as serfs; in short, many such captives continued life much as before. The Christians ransomed some captives and exchanged others, but they rarely sold them on the international slave market. The pagans, being more economi-cally backward, needed fewer serfs and therefore often sold their prisoners into foreign slavery, used them in human sacrifices, or made them into con-cubines and household slaves. According to the crusaders, prisoners taken by the barbarians were no longer treated as human beings, but rather like human cattle. We know of uprisings among the prisoners, throwing themselves unarmed on the backs of their captors when the pagans halted the slow progress of the line of captives in order to face a pursuing column of Teutonic Knights and militiamen. Desperate times, desperate measures.

Presumably both sides recognised that some of their prisoners had been taken captive previously, and, acknowledging that these captives had been unwillingly in enemy hands, allowed those unfortunates to return to their own people. In meetings held before combat to discuss tactics and the divi-sion of the booty, native tribesmen insisted that released captives not count as their share of the loot, should the army succeed in overhauling and destroying a raiding party.

Both sides must have made efforts to provide relief for the victims of raids. However, not even the Teutonic Knights and the bishops were rich enough to provide new homes and lands for every family made destitute, nor had they the bureaucracy to keep detailed records such as would be necessary to reunite scattered families or establish proof of identity, past services, and so forth. This had to be done by personal knowledge and memory, and all the inefficiency which that entails. The Teutonic Knights often resettled their captives in villages under their ancestral leadership and allowed them to retain their arms. Although this policy was often successful in winning over many natives, it worked best when the war was going well for the crusaders. When military operations went wrong, it was a different story. These tribesmen still had the capacity to organise and to fight; and since both nobles and commoners had reasons to revolt, all they needed was encouragement and some prospect of success. When Scumand demonstrated that the Teutonic Knights were impotent to protect their more secure provinces, even the Pogesanians rebelled. The uprising in this long pacified district north of Culm came an as a nasty surprise to the Prussian master.

The rebels had an immediate and surprising local success. Under the leadership of a Bartian chief they captured the castellans of Elbing and Christburg, probably by a ruse. This Bartian noble, who earned a reputation for cruelty far above the other rebel leaders, hanged a priest and killed a squire in an attempt to terrorise his prisoners; he probably would have caused the officers to perish, too, if a loyal native had not freed them from their chains and helped them to escape.

That the rebellion failed to spread was partly due to the caution that tempered native hatred and partly to the work of Theodoric, the advocate of Samland, who hurried back from Germany when he heard the news. As the probably biased report of Dusburg put it:

> The Samlanders loved him, and he brought them all together, spoke to all the people, and won them away from the evil error that they had already begun through the devil's activity. And when this was made known to the Nattangians and Warmians, they turned away from their first evil acts and took a powerful oath that they would remain loyal to the brothers.

There was only one execution, that of a polygamist whose wives testified against him. Because the frightened Teutonic Knights saw a self-confessed conspirator in any native who continued pagan practices such as having plural wives or cremating the dead, there must have been great opportunities for individuals to turn in personal enemies as traitors. But there was no persecution that we know of. Perhaps there was a deliberate policy of turning a blind eye toward the native sins at this moment. The execution of the bigamist proved that the order would not tolerate open disobedience, but also that the master would not seek out secret sins. More repression might have caused other nobles to revolt while they still could. (Who might have a secret concubine? Did ancient oaths not come to lips anymore?) The master certainly did not want to encourage other tribes to join the Pogesanian rebels. This was a policy of which Machiavelli would have approved. On the other hand, the Pogesanians who had already taken up arms gave the Prussian master no alternative to crushing them by force. Conrad von Thierberg led an army there in the summer of 1277 and returned in the autumn, killing and capturing, and resettling so many of the people that vast stretches of land remained empty thereafter. Many Pogesanians abandoned their homes, fled through Galindia and Sudovia, and were eventually given homes by the Lithuanian grand prince around Gardinas, where they resumed their fight against the Teutonic Knights. The grand prince, by putting confirmed enemies of the crusaders at that dangerous and important place, demonstrated that he, too, was a shrewd politician.

Master Conrad presumably settled the Pogesanian captives around his new castle at Marienburg, where he could watch them more carefully. He had begun this castle to supersede Zantir, an outdated fort on the Vistula estuary, as the order's regional centre. In the next century it became the seat of the grand master and one of the largest and finest castles in the world, but at the moment it was simply a stronghold that formed a rough triangle with Elbing and Christburg, enabling the order to watch the former rebels more closely. Like other castles being built at this time and later, it was constructed of brick. There was practically no stone in coastal Prussia, and it was too expensive to import except for use in architectural features such as lintels and capitals. As soon as a brick industry had been developed, all important buildings in Prussia, whether castles, churches, storehouses, or palatial homes, were built of that sturdy material.

Following the Third Prussian Insurrection, the Teutonic Knights took the Sudovian problem more seriously. Although the tribe had been battered by the Teutonic Knights, the Volhynians, and the Poles, and even by the Nattangians in recent years, it was clearly still dangerous and capable of carrying the war deep into the order's territories. When Lithuanians came to their aid, the Sudovians were particularly fearsome – but that was only on the offensive, since Lithuania was too far away to assist in repelling attacks unless reliable information gave the anticipated date of a raid. Nobody could afford to have troops sit around and wait for invaders to appear. Alone, the Sudovians were not strong enough to turn back incursions from the German, Rus'ian, and Polish armies.

In the first major raid the crusaders scored an outstanding success, gathering up cattle, horses, and captives in tremendous numbers. Then, as they retreated, they laid an ambush for the 3,000 angry Sudovians who pursued them. At the cost of six men the Christians killed many of the pagan warriors who clumsily fell into the trap, and routed the rest.

There were defeats as well as triumphs, though some could be seen as moral victories. A Polish chronicler wrote this in 1279:

In this year the House of the Teutonic Order fought against the Lithuanians. Two knights of the Order were captured by the Lithuanians, who suspended one from a large tree, then placed his war-horse beneath him and built a huge fire with the intent of cremating them both. But as the horse was being consumed the heavens opened up and a great light descended on the crusader and dispersed the fire in all directions. Then the light ascended into the heavens with the body of the crusader, not leaving behind a vestige or sign of him. Then the watching Lithuanians saw a beautiful maiden ascend into heaven. Believing this to be magic rather than an act of divine goodness, they wanted to suspend the crusader's associate. This time they built a huge fire of logs. But God did not leave his knight helpless: immediately the heavens opened up and a giant white bird such as no one had ever seen flew down into the midst of the flames and carried the body of the knight back into heaven. The watching pagans cried, 'Truly powerful is the God of the Christians who thus protects his followers'.

✠

Problems in Poland and Pomerellia

The Poles rendered some indirect help in these conflicts, but not as much as they could have had they been united. The Piast dukes had first been fascinated by the fast-changing situation in the Holy Roman Empire, where Rudolf von Habsburg had killed King Ottokar in battle in 1278, and then they watched the Habsburg emperor wrestle with Duke Otto of Brandenburg for influence in Bohemia and Silesia. The Piast dukes were also jealous of one another. After years of dividing the kingdom into smaller and smaller duchies for the many heirs, there had been a sudden series of consolidations. Several dukes died without direct heirs, and their relatives quarrelled over the inheritances. Kujavia was divided among five brothers, but three were childless as of that date, and the family stood united against all outsiders. Silesia was cut into four pieces, each so under foreign domination that the dukes were unimportant outside their tiny possessions. Following the death of Boleslaw the Pious (1226–79) there was a struggle for his Cracovian duchy; the eldest son of Casimir of Kujavia (1211–67), Leszek the Black (1240–88), was the victor.

The Lithuanians and Sudovians had meanwhile taken the offensive in 1277 and 1278, ravaging vast regions of Volhynia. This lasted until the terrible famine of 1279 brought the pagans to Volhynia to beg for grain. When the grain was sent down the Bug River and up the Narew River, Conrad of Masovia-Czerski (Warsaw) set an ambush, stole the grain, and destroyed the ships.

Duke Leszek took seriously his obligation to defend the eastern frontier of Poland. Although he did nothing so dramatic as the 1273 invasion of Sudovia that had persuaded the tribes to pay tribute, he defeated an army of Rus'ians and Lithuanians that the Mongols had sent into Sandomir in 1280, and he was personally present to guard against Sudovian and Lithuanian raids in Masovia and Volhynia; in one pursuit of Prussians across the Narew's swamps he learned the raiders' hiding place from the howl of dogs who had recognised their owners – this allowed him to rescue all the captives without the loss of a single man. The other Piast dukes, however, did nothing beyond watch one another for signs of ambition or illness; they were unwilling to leave their provinces to fight against the pagans for fear their lands would be attacked in their absence. Leszek the Black did what he could to defend his lands against attacks from the east, but he had little authority in the west, where the bulk of the Polish population and wealth was located.

This situation fed anti-German sentiment in Poland; patriots found it easier to blame foreigners than themselves for their nation's difficulties. While this sentiment was mainly directed against the rulers of Bohemia and Brandenburg, who were rightly suspected of seeking their own aggrandisement from Polish troubles, the Piasts and their nobles and knights were suspicious of everyone; without making the Teutonic Knights prominent among their list of dangerous neighbours, they did not exclude them from that number. The political tensions created a climate of distrust of all things foreign, so that eventually Poles saw dangers everywhere. Strong states and confident cultures do not fear for themselves. But Poland at this time was weak and, except for Leszek's energy in the east, leaderless.

Just as the Piast dynasty seemed to be dying out, so was the line of Pomerellian dukes. Dukes Sambor (1204–78) and Racibor (?–1275/6) had no male children, and they hated their nephew Mestwin (duke 1266–94) so much that they tried to deprive him of his inheritance by every means possible. Duke Racibor willed most of his lands to the Teutonic Knights and other religious bodies, and Sambor did the same. Duke Mestwin was able to nullify Racibor's bequests by seizing his lands and then defending them against the claims of the Brandenburg dukes, but Sambor was able to deliver Mewe – a key position near the Vistula – to the Teutonic Knights, establishing them firmly on the left bank of the great river. This was a safer area for settling immigrants than in Prussia. Consequently Mewe quickly developed into a valuable German-speaking possession.

Mestwin had no surviving male children and had taken a vow of chastity, so the dynasty would end with his death. He could live with that prospect, but he still wanted to prevent the duchy, or even Mewe, from falling into the possession of his bitterest enemies, the Teutonic Knights. Much better to give it all to Piast relatives, as he did in a will dated 1282.

The Teutonic Knights must have given considerable thought to this, as they sat around their tables, eating and discussing politics among themselves and with their many visitors; but they apparently did nothing about it except talk. Talk and diplomacy. Their duty was the crusade, not the acquisition of Christian lands. Although the crusade could be carried on better if the order had more resources, demanding the lands willed to them by Racibor would have involved war with Poland. Crusaders were not supposed to make war on Christians (though the example of crusaders in the Holy Land demonstrated that they could); but, more important, the Prussian master could not afford to alienate powerful rulers in their rear. For now little could be done about Pomerellia. The Teutonic Knights had to concentrate on the war in the east.

War in Sudovia was principally a contest of small war-parties. The Teutonic Knights lacked the troops for large-scale offensives after 1279, because a serious defeat in Livonia required the master to send his reserves to that endangered front. The Livonian master had perished, and when Master Conrad von Thierberg died of natural causes later that same year Grand Master Hartmann von Heldrungen and the grand chapter that met in Marburg saw an opportunity to combine the command of the two regions so as to co-ordinate attacks on rebellious Semgallia and unconquered Samogitia. Those operations were to be given top priority again. That meant that only nuisance raids were to be conducted against the Sudovians. The new master, Conrad von Feuchtwangen, hurried to the Baltic. His experience in the Holy Land had persuaded him that the order's future was in its wars against pagans, not against Moslems; and he saw clearly that this future was in danger too. His was not an easy task. The enemy seemed to be everywhere and nowhere. He could smash almost any force he could locate, but locating the foe was not easy.

When Prussians attacked a mill in Elbing where the local populace had taken refuge, they behaved with such bad faith that in the future Christians would be unwilling to surrender. When the master led an army into Warmia to capture the fort that became the future site of Heilsberg, the Prussians struck back in Culm, capturing castles and burning villages. Vast areas became a no-man's-land, and neither side had the strength at the moment to occupy and settle the wilderness.

Nor was there any help to be had from the Poles, who had been so helpful in past campaigns by fighting in Volhynia, a land now almost completely in disorder. The Lithuanians, who were beginning to think of the southern Rus'ian lands as already theirs, committed so many resources to this many-sided struggle for hegemony that they had few men available to assist the Sudovians. The complexity of this desperate war on the frontier can be seen in 1280, when Lev of Galicia made an arrangement with the Tatar khan to borrow steppe warriors for an attack on Cracow. While the southern Piasts met the invaders, dukes Leszek and Casimir of Masovia attacked Lev's rear, leading their men into Volhynia. The lesson was that Poles had to watch their south-eastern steppe frontier before taking care of the north-eastern forest frontier.

Of course, what was true for Poles was equally so for Lithuanians – the big prizes were in Rus', not in the Prussian forests. Lithuanian ambitions to occupy Volhynia left the last independent Prussian pagans vulnerable to small-scale raids by their relatives who were now subjects of the Teutonic Order. While the crusaders' attacks in these years did not merit being called offensive operations, they wore the pagans down.

✠

Guerrilla Warfare

Conrad von Feuchtwangen had never been in the Baltic region before, and, as it turned out, he did not like the country or the weather. Nevertheless, he performed his duties responsibly and won everyone's respect by his thoughtful plans for breaking the military stalemate. The knights were espe-cially pleased by the large number of reinforcements he had brought with him from Germany, though they must have been puzzled about his not sending them immediately into combat. Instead, he reviewed the situation, asking for advice lest he make serious errors out of ignorance; then he called a chapter meeting in Elbing. After all the castellans were assembled, he explained the new strategy that he had been ordered to implement – to first end the rebellions in Livonia, then deal with Prussian problems. His officers were sceptical at first, but in the end they, too, concluded that Prussia was in no serious danger. The delegates then approved sending the reinforcements overland to Livonia. Until more troops arrived, Master Conrad would limit operations in Prussia to those of a guerrilla nature.

Among the prominent figures in this border warfare with Sudovia was Martin von Golin. He was called a 'freebooter' even by the Christian chron-iclers, who usually reserved such terms for the pagans. Alternatively, he was known as a *helde* (hero) or a *latrunculos* (a bold thief). He was no longer a young man.

This Martin attacked a certain village in Sudovia with four Germans and eleven Prussians, killing or capturing the people. And on the long return trip he came to a place where he sat eating with his friends, resting fearlessly after their labours, when the enemy burst among them. They killed his four German comrades while the others fled, leaving there all their arms and food. The Sudovians rejoiced greatly over this. Meanwhile, Martin angrily circled in the woods and brought together his surviving comrades. Since they had lost all their weapons, he slipped among the enemy while they slept and stole their swords, shields, and spears; and when he had them, he went to his hidden companions, and they quietly killed all those they found, except one who tried to flee, and Martin killed him. Then they took up their original booty and the arms and other things that the pagans had brought with them and returned home.

There were a few large-scale raids led by Marshal Conrad the Younger, among which was a particularly devastating one in the winter of 1280 that penetrated over the ice to regions that no Christian army had ever reached before. By that time there was a new master in Prussia, Mangold von Sternberg. In early 1280 Conrad von Feuchtwangen had concluded that the idea of uniting the command of Livonia and Prussia was not a good one, at least not under his leadership. He petitioned to be relieved of his duties and was refused permission. Then he left authority in Prussia to Master Mangold and sailed to Livonia with a force of thirty knights. There he directed operations in Semgallia for a while, then again requested permission to leave his uncomfortable northern post. This time his plea was heeded, and the command was again temporarily united under Master Mangold.

At first Mangold was no more able to press the war on the Sudovian front than his predecessor. The Lithuanians and Sudovians invaded Samland in such force that they raided freely for ten days, burning every settlement and farmhouse that lay outside fortified walls. Even so, the crusaders were making significant gains, particularly in the guerrilla war inside Sudovia, where individual nobles were surrendering one after another. The master ordered these men and their families baptised, then issued them grants guaranteeing them the same rights to hold lands and serfs and be immune from taxes that the native Prussian knights had.

The order's strategy was clearly wearing the Sudovians down. In February 1281 Mangold penetrated to the fortress inhabited by Scumand and killed 150 men and women. The operation was not a total success, since Scumand was able to ambush a party of raiders that had branched off from the main force, and killed an almost legendary warrior, the commander of Tapiau, but it was becoming clear that the Teutonic Order could capture almost any fort it decided to commit its resources to taking, while the Prussians remained master only of the forests. That was not a winning strategy for Scumand, however courageous and skilful he might be in guerrilla operations.

We know more about Scumand than we do about other Prussian war chiefs because he captured a young knight who lived to tell of his adventure, leaving us one of the few eyewitness accounts of life among the Sudovians. Peter von Dusburg retold it in these words:

This brother Louis von Leibenzelle was born of noble family and was trained in arms from youth . . . and when he fell into the hands of the foe, he was brought in bonds to Scumand and told that he had been selected to fight against an opponent equal to him. Scumand meant this to be humorous and kept Louis near him. One day it happened that Scumand went to a carouse, where the noble Sudovians assembled, as was the custom, and took Louis with him in a friendly way even though he was a prisoner. And in the drinking there arose such a quarrel that a mighty noble, a Sudovian, angered Louis with his sharp words that he was using in an insulting and threatening way. So Louis spoke to Scumand, 'Did you bring me here with the intention of having him use such evil words, so he can insult me and threaten me?' And Scumand said, 'You shall see that I am sorry that he is bothering you. If you have the courage to revenge your wrong, I will stand by you no matter what.' And when he heard this, Louis pulled out his sword in anger and cut down that Sudovian in front of them all, so that he died. Later Louis was cut free from his bonds by a youth who was a member of Scumand's retinue and led away to the brothers.

Not long afterward Leszek the Black led an immense army into Sudovia and Lithuania. Within a few weeks he defeated two pagan armies, thrashing each so soundly that the Polish frontier was not menaced for several years thereafter. In that same year, 1282, Scumand and his followers abandoned their ancestral land and withdrew into Lithuanian-occupied Rus', probably to nearby Black Russia, but perhaps as far away as Pinsk or Minsk.

The conclusion of the Sudovian war was not far off once Scumand had withdrawn from it; and it seems only just that, at that moment, command in Prussia was given to Conrad von Thierberg the Younger, who had served as marshal throughout the long struggle. When a grand chapter was called in Acre to elect a successor to Hartmann von Heldrungen, the last of the long Thuringian 'dynasty' that had dominated the Teutonic Order, Master Mangold had sailed to the Holy Land to cast his vote, then had died at sea on his return. The new grand master was a Swiss, Burchard von Schwanden, who had never been to the Baltic region. Wanting an experienced man in command in Prussia, he inquired of the membership for advice, and hearing good reports about Conrad von Thierberg the Younger presented his name to the grand chapter, which approved.

✠

The End of the Crusade in Prussia

The Prussian Crusade came to an end in the summer of 1283. When Master Conrad led a large army into the enemy heartland, he found few Sudovians offering resistance. Louis von Leibenzelle arranged for the peaceful surrender of the 1,600 people in the clan that had befriended him, after which these 'converts' were sent west with all their belongings and given new lands upon which to live. The next day Master Conrad besieged the last important stronghold and forced its garrison to surrender.

Master Conrad, knowing that he lacked the resources to protect such a vast area from Lithuanian or Rus'ian attack, and that he would soon have to commit his troops to the war against the Samogitians, moved the remaining Sudovians from their homeland to other parts of Prussia, some to Pogesania and some to Samland. Even Scumand, now an old and tired warrior, surrendered. He was forgiven his past hostility and given lands in the vicinity of Balga, where, according to Christian witnesses, he died a pious death a few years later. A giant figure to contemporaries, admired by Christians and pagans alike, the description of Scumand's valiant deeds was passed down to future generations largely in the chronicles composed by priests of the Teutonic Order. History may be written by the victors, but it is not always one-sided.

Sudovia was left unpopulated. The people disappeared from history as an organised entity, and the country became a heavily wooded desert, part of the great wilderness that separated Prussia, Masovia, and northern Volhynia from Lithuania. This wilderness had existed before, but as the rulers on all sides built log forts on its edges as bases for scouts and raiders, they soon eradicated whatever settlements remained in the forests and eroded the populated areas around the others' castles. The *Grosse Wildnis* grew into a formidable barrier.

The Teutonic Knights had too few resources to conduct an effective holy war across this wilderness; moreover, the disorders in Poland and Pomerellia threatened their lifeline to Germany, potentially making the route unsafe for crusaders. For Master Conrad securing the rear took priority over further advances to the east. Later, in 1308, when the opportunity came to occupy Danzig and Pomerellia, the Prussian master took it. The result was several decades of conflict with Poland, during which the Lithuanian grand princes consolidated their hold over several nearby Rus'ian states and staked a claim to Galicia-Volhynia. When serious military expeditions against the pagans were once again possible, both sides were much stronger and self-confident than before.

6

The Crusade in Livonia

Paganism and Orthodoxy

To the north, on the eastern shores of the Baltic Sea, there was a crusade already three decades old when the Teutonic Order arrived in Prussia. In the course of time this Livonian crusade shifted its emphasis from an armed struggle against paganism to an aggressive/defensive war with Orthodoxy. This conflict – or, better said, series of conflicts – illustrates well the complexity of the human mind, the ways that individuals and groups can hold multiple goals dearly and from time to time subordinate one goal to another or discard old policies to make room for new endeavours.

Many of the crusaders who participated in the first armed invasions of Livonia before 1200 were merchants from Gotland who wanted to eliminate pirate and robber bases, and it is unlikely that any of them had a thought about Orthodoxy being involved in their little war. They were angry about recent raids by Estonian and Kurish (Courlander) freebooters on what is today southern Sweden, and of attacks on merchant ships making their way to Novgorod via the Gulf of Finland. A century later, the merchants were still concerned with the safety of maritime and overland commerce, but by then the robbers were often under the protection of Rus'ian states which had guaranteed safe-passage to western merchants. Some of these Rus'ian states, in fact, were by 1300 governed by Lithuanian princes whose anti-crusader policies found considerable support among the populace of their cities.

Prior to 1200, before the arrival of Germans and Scandinavians in Livonia, Orthodox princes had exercised a loose sovereignty over the pagan tribes there – very loose over the Livs on the coast, who were too far away to reach conveniently, and none at all over the even more distant Kurs and maritime Estonians. In contrast, the princes could easily send troops to collect tribute from the Letts along the Daugava (Düna, Dvina), the Estonians closest to Pskov, and the Chud people living on the eastern shores of the Gulf of Finland. These armies, however, then quickly returned home, leaving no governors or churchmen to represent their authority until the next payment of tribute was due. Efforts at conversion were minimal. Apparently bitter experience with pagans to the north of Kievan Rus' and on the steppe had persuaded rulers and churchmen alike that little good would come of forceful measures; moreover, they seem to have concluded that even peaceful conversions would only result in a bastardised form of Christianity appearing, one that might even be dangerous to the true believers at home.

If the Rus'ians considered pagans bad, they believed that Roman Catholics were worse; they believed that the doctrine proclaiming the pope the head of the Church was a very dangerous heresy indeed. Consequently the princes and merchants of the northern cities watched the approach of Western churchmen with horror. Thus, since the northern Rus'ian states had both secular and theological reasons to oppose the German efforts to conquer Livonia, they made periodic efforts to drive the crusaders out. Sometimes Novgorod, Pskov and Polotsk sent armies, sometimes they encouraged and armed rebels, but most often they let the practical need to trade with German merchants determine their policies. It would be a mistake to view German-Rus'ian relations as either eternally hostile or dependably friendly.

The pagans in Livonia had one primary goal – to remain independent. To this end they played one great power off against another, sometimes very skilfully. To imagine the tribal elders as helpless witnesses of their own destruction is a mistake. The pagans' second goal was to use the great powers to destroy or cripple traditional rivals; this was a difficult balancing act, because one's ally could easily become one's master. Thus revenge and ambition were important in the decisions of the weaker groups to become allies with the crusaders, and in the determination of traditionally dominant regional powers to fight for the *status quo*. As the native peoples fought out ancient rivalries, they did so according to particularly brutal rules.

✠

Missionaries and Crusaders

The twelfth century saw many efforts to expand the boundaries of the Roman Catholic world other than by means of crusades in the Holy Land, Spain and Portugal, and the West's periodic quarrels with the Byzantines. Usually this was by missionary efforts into pagan lands, and, when the missionaries failed, by the application of economic pressure and force of arms. Most often, in cases where warfare was involved, theology took fourth place to dynastic ambitions, individual greed, and the rooting out of dens of pagan pirates and raiders. As a result, popular support for holy war in the Holy Roman Empire and Scandinavia varied according to the goals that potential volunteers and donors perceived. Vassals had to serve when summoned by the lords, of course, and relatives usually helped in outfitting and covering the travel expenses of those who wished to take the cross, especially if the total cost was reasonable; mercenaries were always eager for work, if the assignment did not appear *too* dangerous. Moreover, people who would have preferred to fulfil crusading vows in the Holy Land would calculate the risks to their health and lives, the time and money involved, and whether or not there was a serious military effort under way at the time; this usually worked in favour of crusading in the Baltic region. Lastly, some German nobles went on crusade to escape periodic civil wars; thus, civil unrest in the Holy Roman Empire sometimes hurt recruiting efforts for crusades, and sometimes it helped.

In short, motives for taking the cross were diverse, and more often than not secular motives were mixed in with idealism and religious enthusiasm. The medieval public, and those nobles and clerics whose interests were not being served, were as good at detecting hypocrisy as their modern equivalents; even then one tended to believe what one wanted to believe. Missionary efforts, in contrast, were generally endorsed enthusiastically. Although the cleric who sponsored the effort to preach the gospel might well be suspected of seeking fame and an enlargement of his diocese, the benefits would be widely shared and the risks would be few. Those who donated money would be honoured and perhaps saved in the afterlife, while those who went among the pagans would anticipate achieving either fame and honour or earning martyrdom.

Although the missions in the Baltic are usually remembered as German efforts, there were Swedish and Danish missionaries as well. In fact, the Scandinavian churchmen were well in advance of German monks until the merchant community in Visby, on the island of Gotland, opened the Livonian market at the mouth of the Daugava River in the late twelfth century. When the German merchants went to the Daugava, they were accompanied by their own priests. In 1180, one of them – Meinhard, an Augustinian friar – remained with the local tribe, the Livs (whence Livonia), as a missionary.

We have Meinhard's story, and the history of the next fifty years of the mission, from one of the finest chroniclers of the Middle Ages, Henry of Livonia, who wrote a stirring account of the heroic efforts of missionaries and crusaders to overcome pagan scepticism and resistance. The careful reader can also note the chronicler's comments about the Christians' many personal and group failings.*

Meinhard had sufficient success for the pope to name him bishop of Üxküll, the island where he had his small church; moreover, his success was sufficient to raise the ire of the pagan priests, who curtailed Meinhard's activities significantly, fearing that the missionaries would soon be followed by foreign troops. The priests' fears were not entirely groundless. The Livs and their neighbours upstream, the Letts, had already been visited by Rus'ian officials, collecting tribute for their distant lord, and their folklore undoubtedly contained stories of Viking raiders and travellers. Primitive societies often have widely divergent ways of dealing with strangers – sometimes both great hospitality toward guests and a suspicion that foreign visitors were generally up to no good.

Meinhard had built two fortifications to protect his small flock against Lithuanian raids, and had hired mercenary troops as garrisons. The earlier failure of the Germans to send volunteers to protect the small mission can be partly attributed to the conflict between Welf and Hohenstaufen parties for possession of the imperial title, the conflict worsening after the 1198 death of Heinrich VI. It was in the midst of this uproar that the mission to Livonia was changed into a crusading venture; it was partly to escape that conflict that numerous knights and clerics later took the cross to fight the pagans in Livonia, because by doing so their immunity as crusaders would protect their persons and property from seizure by whichever party was dominant at that moment.

So, with little help from his homeland, Meinhard had built – on the natives' promise to pay the tithe and taxes – two small stone castles. When it came time to pay the workmen and the mercenary soldiers, however, many natives refused to honour their commitment. Moreover, they then mocked their impoverished bishop for his gullibility. Meinhard seems to have accepted this with Christian fortitude, but since he died soon afterward we cannot be sure what he would have done next. Certainly his successors were less forgiving and patient.

In 1197, before the archbishop of Hamburg-Bremen left on crusade to the Holy Land he invested Berthold, the Cistercian abbot of Loccum, as

---

* *The Chronicle of Henry of Livonia* (trans. James A. Brundage, University of Wisconsin Press, Madison, 1961). This lively, intelligent account of the period 1180–1227 ranks as one of the better medieval chronicles. Apparently written for the benefit of William of Modena, the papal legate who arrived in Riga in 1225, it is more thorough and more reflective than all but a very few contemporary works.

bishop of Üxküll. The younger son of a *ministeriale* family which had colonised the swamps along the Elbe River, Berthold was familiar with many of the noble families of Saxony and the complexities of local politics.

Berthold first tried to make friends with the local tribal chieftains, entertaining them and distributing gifts, but his frightening experience at the consecration of a cemetery changed his approach. Pagans set fire to his fortified church, sought to kill him as he fled to his ship, and then pursued him downriver. Berthold went to Gotland, then to Saxony, where he wrote a detailed letter to the pope asking for permission to lead an army against the heathens. When the pope granted his request for 'remission of sins to all those who should take the cross and arm themselves against the perfidious Livonians', Berthold criss-crossed the North German countryside, preaching the crusade.

He returned to Livonia in July of 1198 with an army of Saxons and Gotland merchants. The Livs gathered their forces opposite the Christians, and, though they were unwilling to submit to mass baptism, they offered to allow Berthold to stay in the land and to compel his parishioners to remain faithful; but they would allow him only to persuade others to believe in Christ, not to force them to accept the new faith. This was not sufficient for Berthold. When the natives refused his demand for hostages and killed several German foragers, he ordered an attack. His army was not large, but it was well equipped. He not only had heavy cavalry – armoured knights on war-horses which easily overthrew the small Baltic ponies that failed to move out of their relentless path – but he also had infantry armed with crossbows, pikes, billhooks, and halberds, who were protected by iron armour and leather garments. By comparison the Liv militiamen were practically unarmed. Moreover, they were not particularly numerous, and their military tradition was one of perceiving a predictable defeat and evading its consequences. As the Western proverb puts it, discretion was the better part of valour.

Ironically, almost the only Christian casualty was Berthold himself. Although his Saxon knights quickly routed the pagans, Berthold's horse bolted, carrying him into the enemy's ranks among the sand dunes, where he was cut down before rescuers could reach him. After taking a terrible revenge for his death, the crusaders left small garrisons in the castles and sailed home. However, the size of these garrisons was insufficient to impress the pagans, who symbolically washed off their baptisms and sent them down the Daugava after the departing crusaders. They then besieged the castles, so that the monks were unable to go into the fields and tend their crops. When the Livonians warned that any priest who remained in the land past Easter would be killed, the frightened clergy fled back to Saxony.

The third bishop, Albert von Buxhoevden, brought a large army from Saxony, forced the Livs to become Christians, and founded a city on the Daugava at Riga. Within a few years the crusade he organised would overwhelm the Letts, push into Estonian territory to the north and east, and occupy the lightly settled areas south of the Daugava and along the coastline to the south.

Although adequate numbers of crusaders came almost every summer to protect the Christian outpost and even undertake offensive operations, it was clear that they were insufficient to conquer the pagans of the interior; and such crusaders contributed little to the defence of the country through the long winters. Bishop Albert's first thoughts were to make the foremost native elders into a knightly class. This was only partly successful, because so few of them had sufficient income to equip themselves properly. Caupo and a few elders were important in Livonia – Caupo even travelled to Rome to meet the pope – and the 'Kurish Kings' were prominent locally for many years. Albert's second plan was to grant tax fiefs to his relatives and friends; he gave this small number of German knights a share of the episcopal income rather than expecting them to live from the produce of their fields.* Some of the Germans married native noblewomen; and in time some of the native knights were absorbed into their number. But the number of German knights was small, and the bishop could not give out more tax fiefs without jeopardising his own slender income and that of his canons. His third plan was to create a new military order, the Swordbrothers. The Swordbrothers provided the garrisons that protected the conquests through the long winters and the military expertise that transformed visiting summertime contingents into more effective warriors.

Consequently thirteenth-century crusading armies operating in Livonia were composed of diverse forces: the Swordbrothers, the vassals of the various bishops, the militia of Riga and other towns, native militias, and visiting crusaders. Native troops were sometimes organised in uniformed infantry bodies, fighting under their own banner; such groups would take turns serving in the border castles, watching for enemy incursions; in battle they usually served on the wings (with the tribes sometimes being kept far apart, lest they mistake one another for the enemy or decide to fight out ancient rivalries right in the middle of a battle). When the prospect for victory seemed good, they fought well, but whenever the tide of battle turned against them, they fled hurriedly, leaving the heavily-armoured

---

* There were no serfs in Livonia in these early days, though there were a few slaves – prisoners taken in raids upon pagan lands. Serfdom became widespread only in the fifteenth century.

Germans in the lurch. Native light cavalry served as scouts and raiders; relatively unsupervised, they had more opportunities for loot, rape and murder than did the slower-moving knights and infantry. Many of the summer volunteers from Germany were middle class merchants who had the money to equip themselves as mounted warriors. All in all, the Livonian crusade differed significantly from crusades in the Holy Land or even Prussia.

After Bishop Albert moved his church to Riga, that city became an important mercantile centre, with Rus'ian traders coming down the Daugava to sell their wax and furs, and Germans sailing upriver as far as Polotsk with their cloth and iron. This brought an additional complication to his policies. The Orthodox Christian church held sway in the lightly settled forests of northern Rus'. These princes' titles were grander than their present wealth, but their lands were broad, the fields and forests rich, the mercantile cities along the great rivers prosperous, and they were proud that their isolation kept them from the temptations and corruptions of the Roman Catholic world. Individually the Rus'ian dukes of Pskov, Novgorod, and Polotsk attempted to drive Bishop Albert out of Livonia, claiming to be coming to the aid of their subjects. Only the Swordbrothers saved the bishop in these crises, as well as saving his hide* from the king of Denmark, who wanted to make himself master of the entire Baltic coastline. However, the Swordbrothers refused to be vassals. They claimed their allegiance was to the pope and to the emperor.

In time Bishop Albert gave one-third of the conquered lands to the Swordbrothers, but he did so grudgingly and made repeated efforts to assert his authority over them. When these quarrels grew so heated as to endanger the crusade, the pope sent a papal legate, William of Modena, to resolve the differences. In the end the bishop had to recognise the Swordbrothers' autonomy, then give much of his remaining lands to four subordinate prelates, two abbots, and his canons; then, once he had endowed his relatives with estates, there was little left to support a sizeable episcopal army. Nor could Bishop Albert rely solely upon the native militias, though they were very willing to join in the fight against traditional rivals. He needed advocates – experienced warriors who knew the native languages and customs – to train the militia in Western tactics and lead them in battle; but only the Swordbrothers had knights willing to live among the natives, and only the Swordbrothers would perform this task at a reasonable price (poverty, chastity and obedience had little lure for ambitious secular knights). Thus the Swordbrothers, whose military contingents were indispensable

---

* A *hide* was the amount of land needed to support one family. This varied according to locality, from as little as 60 acres to as many as 240; most commonly it was 120 acres.

when crusading armies were not present, and who could provide knights to organise the native forces, became the leaders of the crusade in Livonia.

If the Swordbrother organisation had great strengths, it also had weaknesses. Foremost of these was its need for more convents in Germany. This lack of local contacts made sustained recruiting drives difficult and hindered efforts to solicit contributions among the faithful; also, incomes from estates would have eased the order's chronic financial crisis. Secondly, the Swordbrothers' revenues from Livonian taxes and their own estates were insufficient to hire enough mercenaries to supplement properly the numbers of knights and men-at-arms. This perennial financial crisis drove them to expand their holdings in the hope of increasing the number of 'converts' who would pay tribute and provide the warriors needed to make their armies more equal to those of their enemies. This resulted in conflicts with the king of Denmark over Estonia; with the Lithuanians, the most important pagans to the south; and with the Rus'ians, especially those in Novgorod.

✠

The End of the Swordbrothers

The military disaster experienced by the Swordbrothers in 1236 was far from unexpected. For several years the order had realised that its manpower was insufficient to accomplish the tasks that lay before it. It dared not further overburden the natives, who had suffered significant losses in lives, cattle and property during the conquest. Consequently, its officers believed that the best way to increase the revenue needed to support its knights, mercenaries and priests was by obtaining property in Germany. Acquiring manors and hospitals in the Holy Roman Empire, of course, could not be done instantly, and certainly not without a powerful patron. In 1231 Master Volquin had sought to resolve the economic and political crisis by uniting his order with the Teutonic Knights. He had hoped that the superior resources of the 'German Order' would provide the men and money needed to defend Livonia, that its discipline would reinvigorate the Swordbrother convents, and that its good offices with Pope Gregory would resolve the conflicts with the bishop of Riga. Even more importantly, there was a terrible row with the papal officer appointed by William of Modena to serve in his absence, who seems to have seen this assignment as a step toward a great career in the Church.

The grand chapter of the Teutonic Order that met in Marburg chose not to act on the Swordbrother proposal, but the idea was far from impractical.

In the interchanges of experience and ideas that took place at their frequent meetings at the papal and imperial courts, the Teutonic Knights probably learned more than they taught. The Swordbrothers had the greater experience in the Baltic, having been there for two and a half decades before the Teutonic Knights sent their first permanent unit to the region.

Hermann von Salza sent two castellans from Germany to inspect the situation in Livonia. They spent the winter of 1235–6 there and reported their findings to the annual assembly that must have taken place shortly after Friedrich II and the grand master had attended the canonisation of St Elisabeth in Marburg. The report was so negative that there could have been little discussion. In addition to the political problems previously mentioned, they found that convent life among the Swordbrothers was far below the standards of the Teutonic Order, and that the Swordbrothers demanded such autonomy within any future united order that reforming their convents would be impossible.

The Swordbrothers came to their downfall soon afterwards. Their greed and ruthlessness made them vulnerable to accusations before the pope, and they were cut off from the money and the crusaders needed to survive. Desperate for some way out of his situation, Master Volquin led his armies into the pagan regions to the south. A reconciliation with the papacy arranged by William of Modena came too late.

The Swordbrother Order might have survived its financial crisis if Volquin had avoided unnecessary risks. Unfortunately for him, a party of crusaders from Holstein arrived late in the season in 1236 and, despite the lack of adequate numbers to guarantee success, they demanded to be led into battle. Master Volquin, not wanting to disappoint his guests, reluctantly undertook a raid into Samogitia, that part of Lithuania that lay between Livonia and Prussia. Perhaps earlier expeditions into Lithuania had been no less risky, but this time fate collected its due. Volquin led the crusaders across the Saule River (Šiauliai), where they attacked Samogitian settlements. Resistance was insignificant, because the native warriors chose to abandon their homes in favour of ambushing the raiders at the Saule River crossing on their way north. When the retreating crusader force reached the ford, they found it blocked by a small number of resolute pagan warriors. Volquin ordered the crusaders to dismount and wade across the stream. He warned that unless they hurried, it would soon be even more difficult to fight their way across, because the pagans would be reinforced. The Holstein knights, however, refused to fight on foot. Volquin could not impose his will on the visitors, and the crusaders made camp for the night. The next day, when the crusaders splashed across the stream, they discovered that the leading highlands chieftain, Mindaugas, had either led or sent a large body of men to fight alongside the Samogitians. In the ensuing combat Volquin and half his Swordbrothers perished, together with most of the crusaders. The native militias scattered early in the battle; unencumbered by heavy armour, most native warriors found ways to cross the river and flee north while the Lithuanians were preoccupied.

✠

Lithuania

In retrospect we can see that the prospect of occupying the borderlands next to Lithuania had been too tempting for the Swordbrothers. The Lithuanians had appeared to be so much like other native peoples that the crusaders probably did not consider them capable of united resistance. Like the Prussians, the Lithuanians had a single language and a single culture, and they were divided into perhaps as many as twenty different groups led by clan elders, but that was a misleading comparison for several reasons. First, there were actually only two major groupings, the highlanders (Aukštaitija) and the lowlanders (Žemaitija, or Samogitia) north of the Nemunas River. Second, one family had already made itself supreme in the highlands, that of Mindaugas, whose primacy can be dated approximately from the time of the victory over Volquin. He soon bore the coveted title grand prince. Third, the Lithuanians had a long tradition of co-operation in mounting terrifying raids on their neighbours. This was a tradition that any warlord could build upon, and Mindaugas was no ordinary warlord – he was a gifted, if cruel, upstart, who knew how to climb to the top on the ruins of collapsing states.

The crusaders and the Mongols had taught the Lithuanians one lesson – that national unity was necessary for independence. That was an easy concept to understand, but only Mindaugas grasped its corollary: that national unity can be attained only through a 'modernising' autocracy. He was soon crushing domestic dissent and leading his former rivals' armies through burning villages in Livonia, Rus', Volhynia, and Płock. One could say that 'a family that preys together, stays together'.

Other than by its militarism, which was not a pagan monopoly, Lithuania was not a threat to either Orthodox Rus' or Roman Catholic Poland. Its priests did not proselytise, and their belief system was hardly more superstitious than contemporary Roman Catholicism as practised at the local level – crusaders often believed in astrology, magic, and witchcraft. Some Western practices were based on aspects of the pre-Christian religions found throughout Europe, while others were approved by the wisest and best educated philosophers and churchmen (Friedrich II, a ruler so secular-minded that his enemies perceived him as the tool of the Anti-Christ, if not the archdemon himself, was a patron of astrology). The pagans rarely practised human sacrifice, though they occasionally burned alive a highly regarded enemy prisoner. Polygamy was already rare. Their ferocity in warfare is hard to distinguish from that practised by the Christians, other than in their preference for hit-and-run raids over slugging it out on a battlefield; all sides saw the civilian population as a legitimate wartime target. In short, since the princes and boyars would not have to modify their daily lives too much, the missionaries had reason to believe that the pagan leaders were willing to become Christians if the price was right.

At the moment the Lithuanians hardly deserved to be considered in crusader plans. Their proto-state in the highlands was far away, only half-organised, and, it was believed, would probably disintegrate long before a crusader army again approached its frontiers. Mindaugas was to prove such calculations false. He would take advantage of the political crisis in Rus' to enrich his followers by attacking the weakened states there, and by enriching the warrior class he made himself deserving of the title grand prince. Within a few years Lithuania would be a recognised state.

The lesson in this was clear. The papacy had great powers, and could not be defied even when it was wrong. The Swordbrothers had relied on the emperor's help and he had failed them. In the years that lay ahead the pope and the emperor would quarrel again, and the Teutonic Knights, who succeeded the Swordbrothers in Livonia, found it necessary to assess and reassess the position they would take in each of these disputes. This occasioned bitter disputes within the Teutonic Order, but in the end its members chose to be as neutral as they could and maintain at least an appearance of friendship toward both of their benefactors and lords.

A second lesson, well-remembered from the long wars that followed the Wendish Crusade (1147), was that it is always easier to convert a people by working through a native lord – if you can find one, or create one able and willing to become a feudal lord, ruling over his newly Christianised people with the aid of foreign arms and the assistance of foreign advisors. An astute native lord, using the Church against his rapacious neighbours, could make himself independent and relatively powerful. That was perfectly acceptable to most Christians, who knew that marriage alliances could gain land more surely and with less expense and risk than warfare entailed. It was a solution also thoroughly acceptable to the knights of the Teutonic Order, as long as it did not cost them lands already occupied at great cost in blood and treasure.

A third lesson was not lost either, at least not in this generation: the Swordbrothers would not have been in trouble if they had not coveted Estonia. The Teutonic Order carefully avoided territorial disputes with their powerful Christian neighbours whenever they could. That did not mean that they gave in easily whenever a duke claimed a territory or a new tax, but it did mean that they avoided warfare by calling upon neutral parties, particularly papal legates, to judge matters, and binding themselves to follow whatever decision was rendered. This averted many a potential test of arms.

✠

The Teutonic Knights

Grand Master Hermann von Salza was in Vienna with the emperor when he heard the news of the Swordbrothers' defeat, but his business was taking him south, into Italy, not north to Marburg in Germany where a special chapter meeting was ready to discuss the Swordbrothers' desperate call for help. He sent the two Swordbrother messengers to speak to the grand chapter, which debated the request without being able to reach a decision. At last the chapter referred the matter back to Hermann von Salza at the next chapter meeting in Vienna, an assembly which must have been spectacular, with both Hermann von Salza and Hermann Balk in attendance, and the emperor Friedrich II in the city. Still unable to reach a decision, the grand chapter sent the delegation on to Gregory IX, who was then in Viterbo, a papal retreat in the hill country north of Rome. There Hermann von Salza and the Swordbrothers presented a petition to the pope, asking that the Swordbrother Order and all their lands be incorporated into the Teutonic Knights. The pope withdrew into a private conference with the grand master, after which he summoned the two Swordbrothers and a few witnesses. Ordering the Swordbrothers to kneel, he released them from all their previous oaths, explained briefly what the rule of the Teutonic Order was, and asked if they vowed to keep it. When they said yes, his servants took their mantles off and laid new white ones with a black cross over their shoulders. They and all their brethren were now members of the Teutonic Knights.

The two messengers were so astonished at the speed of the ceremony that they could barely wait to ask the grand master about the conditions they had set for union with the Teutonic Knights. When they were told that the union had been made without conditions, and that Estonia would have to be returned to Denmark, they were bitter. Despite their disappointment, the knights honoured their vow of obedience. A papal document announcing the act of union was issued on 12 May 1237:

Because we hold nothing higher than the spreading of the Catholic faith, we hope that the pious request of the master and the brothers will have the desired effect, that the Lord will have the Brothers of the Hospital find courageous people in Livonia . . . and so we have decided that the master and the brothers and all their possessions shall be united with that order.

The next day Gregory IX wrote to his legate in the Baltic, William of Modena, to open negotiations between King Waldemar and the Teutonic Knights for the resolution of the dispute over Estonia. In June there was a chapter meeting in Marburg at which the assembled representatives voted to send sixty knights (about 650 men) to Livonia immediately, and to make Hermann Balk responsible for governing the region. Hermann raised his knights from the North German convents; these were men who understood the Low German language spoken by the Swordbrothers and most secular knights and burghers in Livonia. With 500 Marks contributed by the emperor he outfitted his men and shipped them from Lübeck to Riga before the onset of winter weather closed the seas.

The reinforcements saved the Livonian Crusade. Hermann Balk distributed the knights among the castles so that they would learn about the countryside, the natives, and the enemy. In 1238, at Stensby, he returned Estonia to King Waldemar, winning him as an ally for the Teutonic Order.

This brusque dismissal of the Swordbrothers' most significant achievement confirmed the worst fears of the surviving knights of that order. They withdrew from the reformed convents in the south of Livonia to those on the Rus'ian frontier and made life so difficult for Hermann Balk that after he sailed for Denmark he hurried to Italy to speak with Hermann von Salza and Gregory IX about the knights' refusal to recognise his authority. He got practically no hearing, however, because the dispute between emperor and pope had become so serious that they could not be persuaded to look into problems on a distant and inconsequential frontier. Shortly afterward Hermann von Salza died in Salerno. This was a crippling blow to the moderates in both church and state who had hoped against hope, if not for a peaceful resolution of the problem, then perhaps a delay in the deadly confrontation that would allow God time to work a miracle. Hermann was one of that handful of men who, with divine inspiration, might have been capable of such a feat.

✚

Conflict with Novgorod

Even before Herman Balk's arrival in Livonia, the crusade there was taking an unexpected turn: a combination of events suddenly made the entire Orthodox world seem vulnerable to conversion.

Orthodoxy had been on the defensive ever since the later decades of the eleventh century, when the Turks had suddenly invaded Asia Minor and crushed the Byzantine army. In fact, it was the near collapse of the Byzantine empire that had provoked the call for help that ultimately became the First Crusade. Although the resultant crusader armies had smashed the Turkish forces sufficiently to relieve the immediate pressure on Constantinople, they had moved on toward Jerusalem rather than eliminating the nearest Moslem threat altogether. In time the Turks recovered and became even stronger, while during the same period Byzantines and Westerners became ever more suspicious of one another. This mutual fear and resentment ultimately combined with internal turmoil in the Byzantine state to result in the Fourth Crusade being diverted from Egypt against Constantinople. From 1205 to 1261 Constantinople was ruled by Roman Catholics, and several of Byzantium's most important island possessions were seized by Italian city-states.

Rus' was the next Orthodox state to be hit by an onslaught of eastern horsemen. This time it was the Mongols, sent west by Genghis Khan. Although their principal goal was the conquest of Turkestan, one army went after the steppe peoples south of Kievan Rus'. The Rus'ian princes led their armies of mounted infantry onto the steppe in 1223, only to be overwhelmed by the unexpected tactics of the new enemy – sudden rushes and retreats, showers of arrows, and then the final deadly encirclement. Fortunately for the surviving princes, the Mongol army withdrew to the east as silently and mysteriously as it had come. The death of Genghis Khan in 1227 might have persuaded some princes that the danger was past, but there is little evidence that they were well informed on Mongolian affairs, and the new grand khan was very ambitious. The Mongols returned in 1237 with new fury, and this time they did not go home at the end of the campaigning season; by 1240 they had conquered every Rus'ian state except Novgorod. Orthodoxy was reeling. Rus'ians sent appeals for help to their Western neighbours, Poland and Hungary, to the pope, and even to the pagans in Lithuania. Only Mindaugas of Lithuania offered help, and that was under stiff conditions – he would respect the Orthodox religion as long as the Rus'ian merchants and boyars paid well for his services. They paid. It was the beginning of the great expansion that would eventually make the grand duchy of Lithuania into the largest state in Europe.

At this moment Livonian crusaders moved against Novgorod – a town so wealthy and powerful that it was called Lord Novgorod the Great. Compared to the cities of Byzantium and the Moslem world, this was a considerable exaggeration. To anyone who knew Constantinople, Samarkand, or even Venice, every northern city was small and poor. Still, to those who had only seen Lübeck or Kiev, Novgorod was impressive enough. Although Eisenstein's inspired movie, *Alexander Nevsky*, places the Teutonic Knights at the centre of this attack, apparently the order had little to do with the ensuing 'Battle on the Ice' at all. Instead, the attacking army comprised a loose coalition of forces brought together by the papal legate, William of Modena, who had returned west before any fighting actually started. He seems to have believed that if a crusade against Novgorod could be mounted successfully, it would overthrow the last Rus'ian citadel of Orthodoxy and thus reunite Christendom; if the attack was a failure, it would rid the region of some malcontents.

The malcontents were mostly German knights. Some were former Swordbrothers, unresigned to the fate ordained by the papacy. Some were secular knights who had settled in Estonia at the invitation of an earlier papal legate or the Swordbrothers who on one hand feared that King Waldemar might confiscate their estates and on the other lusted for larger holdings. But there was also King Eric XI of Sweden (1222–50), whose forces were moving east along the northern coast of the Gulf of Finland, subduing the local tribes and threatening to extend royal authority over the entire region that supplied the finest furs to the European trade. Lastly, there were crusaders. Most likely some of these were from North German cities, burghers who knew Novgorod and would have liked to dictate more favourable conditions of trade.

At first all went well. In early 1240 the Swedes occupied the mouth of the Neva River, the waterway flowing from Lake Ladoga, whence ships could continue sailing up the Volkhov River to Novgorod. Meanwhile, crusaders from Livonia moved across the Narva River; others attacked Pskov. The Swedish invasion, led by Karl Birger and a Finnish prelate, Bishop Thomas, threatened to prevent the Rus'ians from purchasing Western grain. (Novgorod was dependent on food supplies from the West as long as southern Rus' was in Mongol hands.) Since the merchants from Lübeck and Visby would not voluntarily sacrifice their commerce for royal benefit, the only way a Swedish blockade could be imposed was by controlling the river mouths. The Novgorod merchants, understanding the seriousness of the threat, called back their young duke, Alexander, who had just left the quarrelsome city, and pleaded with him to drive the Swedes away from their lifeline to the West. Alexander swallowed his anger and brought his skilled archers to Novgorod. A Rus'ian chronicler in Novgorod recounted the ensuing events thus:

> The [Swedes] came with their [ruler] and with their bishops, and halted on the Neva at the mouth of the Izhera, wishing to take possession of

Ladoga, or in one word, of Novgorod, and the whole Novgorod province. But again the most kind and merciful God, lover of men, preserved and protected us from the foreigners since they laboured in vain without the command of God. For the news came to Novgorod that the [Swedes] were going toward Ladoga, and [Prince Alexander] with the men of Novgorod and of Ladoga did not delay at all; he went against them and defeated them by the power of St Sophia and the prayers of our Sovereign Lady the Holy Mother of God and eternally Virgin Mary on the 15th day of July [1240] . . . And there was a great slaughter of [Swedes].*

Novgorod was saved from Swedish economic blackmail by this battle on the Neva, and Novgorod's duke, Alexander, was thereafter known by the sobriquet derived from his victory: Alexander Nevsky.

Bishop Thomas resigned in 1245, certain that he had failed in his life's mission of converting the Finns and Karelians. But he was too pessimistic. Four years later Earl Birger led what Swedes called 'the Second Crusade' to the region around modern Helsinki. In subsequent years Swedish immigration to this 'New Land' reached significant proportions and permanently changed the ethnic composition of the region. In future years some Swedish fishermen would find their way across the gulf to Estonia, where they established themselves in small villages along the coast.

✠

The Battle on the Ice

The Livonian threat to Novgorod was more dangerous than the Swedish one had been. A combined force of former Swordbrothers, petty knights from Estonia, Danes under princes Canute and Abel, Germans under the bishop of Dorpat, Hermann von Buxhoevden (Bishop Albert's brother), and Rus'ians under Prince Jaroslav (then in exile from Pskov) pushed into Novgorodian territory from the west. In September 1240 this army captured Isborg (Izborsk) and smashed a relief force from Pskov. After a week's siege of Pskov, they obtained its surrender on terms. Apparently relying upon allies inside the city (probably friends of Prince Jaroslav who gave their children as hostages) the crusaders placed a garrison of two knights and their retinues in the citadel – probably thirty to fifty men in all. The crusader leaders

---

* *Chronicle of Novgorod, 1016–1471* (trans. Robert Michell and Nevil Forbes, Camden Society 3rd series XV, London, 1914). This is not the easiest text to read, but it conveys vividly the flavour of the Orthodox faith.

must have spent the winter dreaming about the likelihood of closing Novgorod's trade routes in the next campaign, especially after hearing the news that Duke Alexander had quarrelled with the burghers of Novgorod, who favoured peace with the Germans (probably because they considered trade with the West to be essential to the city's survival), and had withdrawn to distant Perejaslavl, where his father Jaroslav ruled.

When Waldemar II of Denmark died in March and his sons remained home in case civil war erupted, the former Swordbrothers saw in this succession crisis not the loss of an ally but rather an opportunity to reclaim Estonia for themselves. They had already been conspiring with Danish vassals in Estonia who were willing to violate the 1238 Treaty of Stensby and simultaneously attempt the conquest of Novgorod. The records are too sparse to tell us absolutely to what extent former Swordbrothers were providing the leadership and men for this attack on Novgorod, acting without official permission and without the money and reinforcements the Teutonic Knights could have provided, but one of the ringleaders of the coup against Master Volquin that had forced him to occupy Estonia against his will seems to have been prominent among the leaders of the invasion.

Before April 1241 an army of Teutonic Knights, former Swordbrothers, Danish vassals, and native Estonians had occupied the Karelian lands east of Narva. From the castle they constructed at Kopore, they made daring raids to the south-east, at one time approaching within twenty miles of Novgorod, and they drove away so many horses that farmers were unable to plough their fields for the coming year.

These successes made the allies so confident of victory that they sent Bishop Heinrich of Oesel-Wiek hurrying to Rome with a request that Pope Gregory name him bishop of the regions to be conquered. Probably they had in mind an offer of Western military aid against the Mongols in return for Orthodox acceptance of church union under Roman leadership. Certainly, there were Rus'ians in Pskov and other cities who had indicated their willingness to agree to these terms, just as the Rus'ian dukes in Galicia were doing at that very moment (while the Mongol hordes were storming through their lands). And clearly, it was the military support from Pskov which made the attacks on Novgorod so devastating, since the Westerners could not have mustered sufficiently numerous warriors on their own to overawe Novgorodian resistance. The pope, too, signalled his approval by ordering the archbishop of Lund and his suffragan bishops to call upon their people 'like Moses to buckle a sword upon his thigh . . . and put on the armour of the Lord' to defend the converts in Estonia.

The presence of the papal legate, William of Modena, cannot be determined for the period between February 1241 and February 1242. In the years 1239 and 1240 he had been in Prussia, Lübeck and Denmark, attempting to reconcile every dispute which might interfere with the prosecution of the crusade. Knowing his itinerary for the missing year would answer the critical question: was William in Estonia organising the offensive against Novgorod or was he in Germany, Bohemia and Poland attempting to coordinate a common defensive strategy against the oncoming Mongols?

Similarly, the activities of the Livonian master, Dietrich von Grüningen, cannot be absolutely determined. He was one of the knights who had entered the order with Conrad of Thuringia in 1234 and had actually been named Livonian master in 1237 before it was apparently decided that he needed more experience – experience he certainly got in later years. He was Hermann Balk's successor in 1238, but was absent during the critical months of 1241 when plans were made for the attack on Novgorod. He returned some time in 1242, probably after the seas opened that summer. He remained in Livonia till 1245–6, when he took over the duties of the German master temporarily, and was then named Prussian master. Andreas von Felben was acting-master in Dietrich's absence. Since his later career was to be brilliant, we may conclude that he performed his duties effectively in 1241–2. It is unlikely that his name was connected with the failed enterprise in Rus'.

Certainly, the Teutonic Knights in Prussia were concerned about the Mongol threat. Even though a legend concerning the Prussian master, Poppo, has been repeatedly demonstrated to be false, popular historians continue to revive the story that he met his death at the battle of Liegnitz under a hail of Tatar arrows. The kernel of truth to this myth is based on the order's responsibility to defend Christendom against all its armed foes, and perhaps Poppo had been present at the battle and wounded. Direct evidence is lacking. Poppo did die at Liegnitz and was buried there, but that was many years later, when he was visiting his wife's convent.

In any event, the current moment was not a good one for Andreas to risk Livonian knights who might be needed elsewhere. Andreas was aware also that the knights most eager to attack Novgorod were rebels who were determined to annul the Treaty of Stensby and plunge his order into war with Denmark. Perhaps the temporary nature of his authority, that of acting-master, limited his confidence to offer bold leadership. Whatever his reasons, Andreas does not seem to have been committed to the crusade after the spring of 1241.

More importantly, Andreas von Felben had a more pressing problem to deal with than assisting crusaders in an attack on Novgorod. That was to subdue an uprising on Oesel, which he accomplished that winter by leading an army across the ice and overawing the rebels. The peace treaty survives, providing us with valuable insight into the crusaders' demands on their subjects. First of all, anyone performing pagan ceremonies was to be fined and whipped. Second, farmers were to convey their taxes by ship either to Riga or the bishop. Third, anyone who was guilty of infanticide was to be fined, and the mother was to be taken to the cemetery nine successive Sundays, stripped, and whipped. Fourth, once a year, at the time the taxes were paid, the advocate would hold court, rendering justice as advised by the elders of the land. Lastly, murderers were to pay a *wergild* of ten marks for homicides committed on strangers or among themselves, a heavy penalty which could be paid only with the help of one's clansmen. In short, the treaty dealt with a variety of concerns – religious, financial and social – which presumably were not covered by existing agreements. The treaty also demonstrates that the Oeselian Estonians were by no means powerless serfs. A master does not sign a formal treaty requiring the presence of priests, friars, vassals, his marshal and numerous knights and *multorum aliorum fidelium, Theutonicorum et Estonum*, unless the *seniores de Estonibus Maritimae et alii quam plures* were men of power and substance.

Meanwhile, Duke Alexander had been invited to return to Novgorod. The abased citizens, now persuaded that they could not fight the German-Pskov forces alone, apparently conceded all the points over which they had quarrelled. Late in 1241 Alexander overwhelmed the German-Danish garrisons east of Narva. Significantly, he spared the Westerners for ransom but hanged the Estonians as rebels and traitors. He thus demonstrated his limited aim: to retain control of the vital border territories. He had no intention of driving the crusaders into the sea; his attention was directed more to the south – where the Mongols held sway – than to the west. His intent was merely to guarantee that he would not be attacked from the rear while he was engaged with the Tatars. His move against the Western garrison in Pskov on 5 March 1242 was described by a German chronicler in these terms:

> He marched toward Pskov with many troops. He arrived there with a mighty force of many Russians to free the Pskovians and these latter heartily rejoiced. When he saw the Germans he did not hesitate long. They drove away the two Brothers, removed them from their advocacy and routed their servants. The Germans fled . . . If Pskov had been defended, Christianity would be benefited until the end of the world. It is a mistake to conquer a fair land and fail to occupy it well . . . The king of Novgorod then returned home.*

* *The Livonian Rhymed Chronicle* (trans. Jerry C. Smith and William Urban, new and expanded second edition, Lithuanian Research and Studies Center, Chicago, 2001). A naïve, lively, informative narrative.

The corresponding account in the *Chronicle of Novgorod* is very short: 'Prince Alexander occupied all the roads right up to [Pskov], seized the Germans and the Chud men, and having bound them in chains, sent them to be imprisoned in Novgorod'.

Alexander led a relatively small force into the diocese of Dorpat, only to turn back after Bishop Hermann's men routed his scouts at a bridge. Perhaps a small number of Teutonic Knights joined in the pursuit of Alexander's retreating forces, making the order's total contribution more respectable. The Orthodox and Catholic armies then met at Lake Peipus – the famous Battle on the Ice. Neither army was large. The Westerners had perhaps 2,000 men, the Russians perhaps 6,000, but these numbers were, in effect, balanced by the superior armament of the crusaders

The battle has become undeservedly famous, having been endowed – for twentieth-century political considerations – with much more significance than it merited in itself, through Sergei Eisenstein's 1938 film *Alexander Nevsky*, and the stirring music of Sergei Prokoviev. Indeed, although this movie is a reasonably accurate portrayal of some aspects of the battle, especially the costumes and tactics, and gives us an impressive sense of the drama of medieval combat, other aspects are pure propaganda. Certainly the ancestors of today's Estonians and Latvians were not dwarfs, as the movie suggests, nor were they serfs. Master Andreas was in Riga, and thus could not have been taken prisoner by Alexander himself and ransomed for soap. The Russian forces were mainly professionals, not pre-Lenin Communist peasants and workers facing the equivalent of German armoured columns; the Germans were not proto-Nazis, blonde giants who burned babies alive. In short, many scenes in *Alexander Nevsky* tell us much more about the Soviet Union just before Hitler's invasion than about medieval history. On the other hand, it is just possible that the crusaders did possess a portable organ – Henry of Livonia had mentioned an incident in an earlier combat in which the playing of a musical instrument caused the two armies to stop fighting momentarily to listen in wonder, and records from the end of the century list organs among the religious objects destroyed by Lithuanian pagans. Certainly Lake Peipus is far enough inland that the last days of cold weather might have preserved sufficient ice along the shores to support the weight of men on horseback.

Spring had not yet come on 5 April as the crusader army proceeded across the lake or, more likely, along the shore to meet the Russian forces that were massed in a solid body. Although some of the fighting probably took place on the ice, it is unlikely that the cavalry forces ventured onto it in significant numbers. The heavily armed Western knights formed the spearhead of a column followed by light cavalry and foot soldiers, which charged into the

Russian infantry. *The Livonian Rhymed Chronicle* summarised the battle tersely:

> The [Russians] had many archers, and the battle began with their bold assault on the king's men [Danes]. The brothers' banners were soon flying in the midst of the archers, and swords were heard cutting helmets apart. Many from both sides fell dead on the grass. Then the Brothers' army was completely surrounded, for the Russians had so many troops that there were easily sixty men for every one German knight. The Brothers fought well enough, but they were nonetheless cut down. Some of those from Dorpat escaped from the battle, and it was their salvation that they fled. Twenty brothers lay dead and six were captured.*

The battle, of course, had repercussions beyond the Livonian-Rus'ian border region: revolts broke out in Kurland and Prussia which threatened to involve the Teutonic Knights on so many fronts that they could not cope with their enemies. Alexander Nevsky, however, had no interest in destroying the crusader states in Livonia. First of all, the former Swordbrothers and Teutonic Knights who were represented at the battle lost only half as many knights as had perished at Saule. When one considers that these would be quickly reinforced by troops that the master held in reserve, the Teutonic Order remained a formidable foe; moreover, the crusaders would be fighting on the defensive in well-constructed wooden forts, and Alexander Nevsky had not equipped his forces for sieges. Moreover, the Mongol threat was so immediate that the prince could not afford to postpone attending to it. Consequently he offered generous terms to the Roman Christians, which the crusaders immediately accepted: Novgorod withdrew from Pskov and other border territories, Alexander freed his prisoners, and the Germans released their hostages. Three years later Alexander defeated a Lithuanian effort to exploit Novgorod's weakened condition. In the end, however, like the other Russian princes, he acknowledged the authority of the Golden Horde and performed military service for the Mongol khan. For the next twenty years there was no war between Rus'ians and Germans.

It had been a dangerous moment for Novgorod, but perhaps less dangerous than is sometimes thought. If Novgorod had been occupied by the Westerners, the Rus'ian state might indeed have shared the fate of Byzantium after the Fourth Crusade, to be dominated temporarily by foreigners, perhaps so permanently lamed in political and economic terms that it would be unable to ward off the more dangerous enemy advancing from

* Quoted in David Nicolle, *Lake Peipus 1242: The Battle on the Ice* (Osprey, London, 1996).

the East. Nevertheless, it is difficult to imagine the crusaders permanently suppressing Russian culture, the Russian Orthodox Church, and the Russian nobility. If the Golden Horde could not do this, could the Westerners, whose capacity vis-à-vis the Mongols' pales into insignificance? It is easy to exaggerate the importance of the Battle on the Ice. In the short term, it was more important for the crusaders, in that it put an end to the eastward drive of the armed mission; in the long term it gave Russians a memory of a glorious victory over formidable foes, a victory that stood out so brightly because of its rarity.

Victory, if the outcome had been reversed, would have given new life to the tensions in Livonia and Estonia. Those Teutonic Knights who had been former Swordbrothers and wholeheartedly supported the attack might have incurred new obligations that the Teutonic Knights as a whole would have to meet. Although the survivors of the former Swordbrother Order would continue to complain that they had not been properly supported ('The bishop . . . had brought along too few people, and the brothers' army was also too small'), they had no choice other than to submit to Master Dietrich. Only one of their knights appears later in Livonian records, and he only after the lapse of many years. At least one of their surviving leaders was sent to the Holy Land. Were other former Swordbrothers among those Teutonic Knights there who left the order in 1245 to join the Templars? We do not know. Even Andreas von Felben left the country temporarily, being stationed in his native Netherlands in 1243. Defeat seems to have provided Master Dietrich with the opportunity for a thorough housecleaning, a task he performed with such efficiency that in 1246 he was elected Prussian master, then eight years later German master.

✠

Dorpat and Novgorod

The 1240s and 1250s were, on the whole, decades of crusader successes in the Baltic. Most importantly, the bearers of the cross had persuaded Mindaugas of Lithuania that the Christian god was militarily superior to the pagan deities. In 1252 he was crowned king of Lithuania by a German bishop in the presence of the Livonian master. Although Mindaugas changed his habits not in the least and does not seem to have permitted missionaries to preach the Gospel through the countryside, the Westerners did not press him on these matters. One can conclude equally well that the Teutonic Knights were callous representatives of *Realpolitik*, more eager to take their share of lands and peoples than to insist on baptisms and changes in behaviour; or that they were understanding of the need to move slowly in this circumstance, not allowing theological fanatics to upset the traditional rhythm of native life. In 1257 the crusaders from Livonia and Prussia even forced the Samogitians to grant a two-year truce, during which missionaries and merchants would be allowed into the country to ply their trades.

The Teutonic Order had achieved these successes in spite of the newest archbishop of Riga, Albert Suerbeer, who never missed an opportunity to harass his enemies. Suerbeer's ambitions were no secret – he believed that the Church should direct the crusades, and that he was the proper local representative of the Church.

This era of peaceful conversion came to an end in 1259, when the Samogitian priests persuaded their people to pick up the sword again. Twice, in quick succession, pagan forces destroyed crusader armies from Prussia and Livonia. Revolts then broke out in Livonia and Prussia, and Samogitian armies invaded those lands to assist the rebels. The Samogitians then warned Mindaugas to join them or else. Mindaugas, always practical and shrewd, declared himself a believer in the pagan war gods, and led his forces into Livonia. Rus'ian forces then invaded Estonia as part of Mindaugas' grand strategy. Unfortunately for him, communication difficulties made it impossible to co-ordinate the movements of two widely separated armies, and each withdrew quickly after failing to locate the other. The Teutonic Knights and the bishops thus survived the most dangerous threat in their short history.

Had Mindaugas lived, the crusaders still might have been hard pressed to maintain their position. However, he was murdered in 1263 in a personal dispute. When his son emerged from his monastery to claim the throne, Lithuania was plunged into civil war. One of the conspirators, Prince Daumantas (Dovmont), fled to Pskov, where he made himself duke and twice in 1266–7 attacked Polotsk, the Rus'ian city that sat across the trade routes from Novgorod to Lithuania and from Riga into the Rus'ian interior. Each time this prince came so close to success that the crusaders began to fear for Christianity's survival in Lithuania (and soon afterward it did die out). In addition, Daumantas was raiding Estonia. To protect this endangered region, the Livonian Order had constructed a great castle at Weissenstein in Estonia, to anchor the defence of the province of Jerwen, and sent out calls for the crusaders who would be needed to strike a blow at Pskov that would perhaps eliminate the threat altogether. Consequently Master Otto was ready for the invasion which occurred in 1267, and although the enemy commanders quarrelled so heatedly that their forces wandered around almost aimlessly before attempting a brief and pointless siege of Wesenburg (Rakvere, the Danish stronghold built in 1252 to control strategic road junctions), it was clear that the Rus'ians would be back. What the Livonian master did not anticipate was that Albert Suerbeer, the archbishop of Riga, would plot to seize power while the Livonian master was preoccupied with the defence of the frontiers.

Among the crusaders who sailed to Livonia in 1267 was Count Gunzelin of Schwerin, a resourceful and dangerous man, though not a powerful lord. He had been active, but unsuccessful, in the numerous feuds in his region. For two decades he had quarrelled with his neighbours, and each time emerged weaker than before. However, his defeats were less likely due to lack of courage or ability than to a lack of financial and military resources. He had fought in the Danish wars in the 1250s, joined in a feud concerning the Mecklenburg inheritance, and served as a Welf partisan in the feuds of the early 1260s – all the while gaining but little for his efforts. Married to a member of the house of Mecklenburg, he stood to profit from the chaotic situation that followed the death of Duke Johann of Parchim, but he was eventually defeated by his opponent, young Duke Heinrich. It was at this time that he took the cross for Livonia, perhaps due to the lure of adventure and religion, perhaps in keeping with family tradition; or perhaps it was demanded by Heinrich, whose family traditions included crusading (one brother was Poppo, the former Prussian master) and who did not want to leave on crusade himself as long as his potential enemies remained home.

Or perhaps he even planned to resettle in the East. After all, Schwerin was not an old state – a little more than a century before, it had lain on the other side of the long-disputed frontier between Christendom and paganism – and, just as a mixed population of Germans and Slavs now lived there peacefully, Gunzelin's family was now thoroughly intermingled with the Slavic dynasties which had once dominated the region. Consequently he was not likely to fear living among strange peoples or encountering new challenges. For many years Count Gunzelin had been gathering estates in Livonia by exchanging properties with the monastic orders – a medieval form of crop insurance – and he was undoubtedly well informed on conditions in the East. Moreover, at the moment his lands were occupied by the duke of Brandenburg and he had several children for whom he had to provide an inheritance. In short, he saw little future in Schwerin.

The crusaders must have landed in Livonia in the summer or autumn of 1267 in the expectation of waging a winter campaign near Novgorod. Master Otto, although occupied with Lithuanian attacks along the Daugava, had ordered thirty-four knights from Weissenstein, Leal, and Fellin to reinforce the bishop's troops in Dorpat. Large numbers of native militia were available, too, and the Danish vassals were willing to fight here rather than attempt to defend their own lands later without help. Among the numerous crusaders was Count Heinrich of Mecklenburg with his German and Slavic troops. But Gunzelin apparently spent little time in Estonia.

Gunzelin's ship would have brought him directly to Riga, where he met Albert Suerbeer, whom, it can be presumed, he had met previously during the archbishop's long stay in northern Germany. But only now did the two men discover that they could be of service to one another. Albert resented the autonomy of the Teutonic Knights and the fact that they had confiscated his lands and stirred up trouble even among his canons. Gunzelin was poor, but ambitious and warlike; doubtless, he was well aware that his grandfather had dared to kidnap King Waldemar II, and bring the Danish empire crashing down. It is not clear who made the proposal to attack the Teutonic Knights and divide their territories, but, on 21 December 1267, Gunzelin and Albert signed a pact to work to this end. The archbishop appointed the count advocate of all his lands, with the duty of reorganising his holdings and protecting them against all enemies, and he gave him all authority, all incomes, and all responsibilities associated with his holdings. It was understood that the count would be rewarded with generous grants of land in the captured territories if he succeeded in taking any from the Teutonic Knights or pagan tribes, but if he failed, the archbishop would not even pay his ransom, implicitly denying all responsibility for his actions. It was a risky venture for the count, but counts of Schwerin were not intimidated by heavy odds.

Gunzelin hoped to become a great landowner in Semgallia, Selonia, and northern Nalsen in the Lithuanian borderlands. He may have thought these lands south of the Daugava would be an easy prize, since they were not heavily populated to begin with and currently had no experienced lord with a large retinue to defend them. As Gunzelin prepared the archiepiscopal territories for war, he presumably visited the vassals, inspected the castles, and estimated how many native troops he could summon to join his attack. Then, after ascertaining how many mercenaries he would need to accomplish his mission, he set out for Gotland to recruit them. Meanwhile, Archbishop Suerbeer made contact with all the order's potential enemies. If he could find sufficient support abroad, his conspiracy might stand a good chance of overthrowing the Teutonic Knights in Livonia.

While all these plans were being set in motion, a large Rus'ian army, this time commanded by Duke Dmitri of Perejaslavl, the son of Alexander Nevsky, had invaded Estonia. The Rus'ians had not been sure what they would do at first – invade Lithuania through Polotsk, or cross the Narva into Wierland and then march on Reval, or go through the swamps toward Dorpat. The Western army, also very large (estimated by the chronicler at 30,000 men), gathered at Dorpat. The two forces collided in a pitched battle on 23 January 1268, near Maholm, then again on 28 February further east, on the banks of the Kegola River. *The Livonian Rhymed Chronicle* summarised:

> When the people who were supposed to be with the brothers had arrived, orders were given to place the natives on the left flank. That was to be held by them in the battle. A larger army of royal vassals of German birth was brought there, and they held the right flank. Then they charged honourably. The brothers and their men struck together. Bishop Alexander was killed. Two formations of Russians advanced upon him, but they were forced into a rout. Up and down the field the Russian army had to retreat . . . The brothers revenged the injuries they had suffered from the Russians over a long period. The field was wide and deep, and the Russian defeat a great one . . . Each German had to fight sixty Russians . . . Prince Dmitri was a hero, and with five thousand chosen Russians he entered into battle. The other army had fled. Now hear what happened. The brothers' flagbearers were opposed to him on a very bad stream. He saw the brothers' army there, and the brothers had many men there, as I now tell you. There were one hundred and sixty there and that had to suffice. There were also foot soldiers, who, standing before the bridge, conducted themselves like heroes. They had done very well, and there were about eighty of them. They did their duty by the brothers and thrust back the Russians so that they were dismayed . . . Many Russian wives mourned over their husbands' bodies when the battle was over. The Russians still hold that against the brothers, it is true. The feeling has lasted many years.

The account of the battle in the *Chronicle of Novgorod* is more coherent:

> When they reached the Kegola river they found a force of [Germans] in position, and it was like a forest to look at; for the whole land of the [Germans] had come together. But the men of Novgorod without any delay crossed the river to them, and began to range their forces; and the men of [Pskov] took stand on the right hand, and Dmitri, and Svjatoslav took stand also on the right higher up; and on the left stood Mikhail, and the men of Novgorod stood facing the iron troops opposite to the great wedge; and so they went against each other. And as they came together there was a terrible battle such as neither fathers nor grandfathers had seen . . . Now that the great encounter [had] taken place, and the laying down of the heads of good men for Saint Sophia, the merciful Lord speedily sent his mercy, not wishing utter death to the sinner; punishing us and again pardoning. He, turning away his wrath from us, and regarding us

with his merciful eye; by the power of the Honourable Cross and through the prayers of the Holy Mother of God our Sovereign Lady, the Immaculate Mary, and those of all the Saints, God helped [Prince] Dmitri and the men of Novgorod . . . They pursued them fighting, as far as the town, for seven verses along the three roads, so that not even a horse could make its way for the corpses. And so they turned back from the town, and perceived another large force in the shape of a great wedge which had struck into the Novgorod transport; and the men of Novgorod wished to strike them, but others said, 'It is already too near night; how if we fall into confusion and get beaten ourselves.' And so they stood together opposite each other awaiting daylight. And they, accursed transgressors of the Cross, fled, not waiting for the light.

It had been a confused combat between two huge armies. Apparently each had been victorious on different parts of the battlefield, and afterward the Germans withdrew to defend another river crossing. Each side was exhausted, and the Rus'ians soon withdrew to their own country.

The ultimate victors were the Mongols, who understood well how to divide their enemies and thereby increase their own power. In 1275 they collected a second hearth tax from all the Russian lands – this time without resistance. It was this Mongol Empire, stretching from Russia to Baghdad, to Peking and Hanoi, that Marco Polo described in his long visit which began in 1268.

Conflict between Roman Catholics and Orthodox hardly mattered for many years to come. Both sides understood that all the advantages stood with the defensive forces. Not only were there strong fortresses with garrisons committed to defending them to the last, but logistical difficulties made prolonged sieges impossible. The Germans who served in the Teutonic Order and who made up the clergy, secular knights, and burghers, were committed to fighting for their possessions. But equally opposed to the Rus'ian and Lithuanian invasions were the native peoples who had been the principal victims of raids in the past. Their motto seems to have been 'better the devil you know'.

✝

Native Life at the End of the Thirteenth Century

The charge that the Teutonic Knights were hindering the process of conversion lies at the root of every condemnation of the order's actions in Livonia and Prussia. On the one hand, an interpretation dating from the end of the thirteenth century (reinforced at the end of the nineteenth century, and widely accepted at the end of the twentieth) denounced all interference with native customs as Western colonialism and cultural imperialism; at the same time the adherents of this doctrine denounced the order's failure to spread Christianity and education among the Baltic peoples so as to raise them to the level of the Germans (as though this was not intruding significantly into traditional practices). The order's enemies assumed that a low-key approach, through native priests, would make an impression on their hearers through their ability to use the native language skilfully and through a morality higher than that possessed by second-rate foreigners. Perhaps they were right. However, that was not the choice the order had. Religious education and the hiring of priests was the duty of the archbishop and bishops, not the master and his officials. If the friar-brothers had attempted to teach religion, no pope would have hesitated to rebuke them severely. Moreover, every effort to persuade the bishops and their canons to become members of the Teutonic Order provoked howls of indignant protest.

Clearly, all efforts to preach the word of God among the Baltic peoples were less than fully effective. Moreover, the reasons for the failure were obvious even to contemporaries: the Church hesitated to trust the sons of pagan priests not to make heretical interpretations of Christianity which would endanger the souls of their congregations; chastity was not a native folkway, and the nearby presence of married Orthodox priests was a dangerous example; and, moreover, because the foreign-born prelates and their canons did not speak Estonian or Latvian, they could not be sure what native-born priests might be saying or doing. The Church lacked the funds to maintain clergy in the countryside and was unable to prevent the priests they recruited in Germany from drifting back to the cities where they could find work and, at the very least, find someone they could speak to other than an occasional merchant, the local noble, or some advocate – individuals with whom they had (or should have) little in common. Lastly, all people who have accepted Christianity relatively quickly have adapted local myths and adopted ancient practices into their understanding of the new faith. We may not worry today about Irish fairies and Croatian *vilija*, but the medieval church did. And so the Church resisted incorporating Baltic pagan beliefs – most importantly those connected with burial and the remembrance of the dead – into daily worship and seasonal observances.

The native peoples resisted Christian burial rites successfully in every part of Livonia. However, we may have information about this form of resistance rather than about other methods only because it was much easier for the church to observe burial practices than to investigate the breaking of fasts, the performance of secret ceremonies, and beliefs in superstitions different from those held by Germans. The women, in particular, were more stubborn in their resistance to change, perhaps because their lives were less affected by the new regime than was the world of men. Moreover, neither Teutonic Knights nor priests were supposed to spend time with women.

All that converts seemed to have understood was the need to repeat certain prayers, to respect the saints, and to add new superstitions to their already heterogeneous belief system. Understanding the role of the trinity in a monotheistic creed was probably as difficult then as it is today, and the Christians' moral codes seemed to have little connection, at times, with how ordinary Germans lived. The rulers probably did not know what was going on in the villages – the knights of the military order least of all, because they were supposed to be in the convent at prayers instead of mixing with the natives (drinking parties with men were acceptable, but not entertainments where women were present). What the natives wished to preserve was preserved musically, in songs the foreigners could not understand. This singing tradition (though not the songs) has endured through the ages to our present time – in 1988–91, when the Baltic states won their independence again, they did so not through terrorism or force, but by means of a 'Singing Revolution'.

The Teutonic Order's indirect approach to conversion was more successful in Prussia, where large numbers of German and Polish peasants speeded the process of cultural assimilation and eventual Germanisation. Even so, the question of how sincerely converted the natives had been was discussed through the centuries. Missionaries preached in vain, because they were too few in number and lacked sufficient command of the language to stir the Livonians' hearts. Christianity made inroads into native society only when the Reformation and Counter-Reformation reached the Baltic.

Contrary to what is widely believed, serfdom and slavery were not the immediate fate of the newly conquered peoples. Taxation and labour duties, yes, monogamy, and formal acknowledgement of adherence to Christianity, but in most other ways the native peoples were able to retain their traditional practices. The elders continued to administer local affairs, the warrior class came to look forward to the opportunities war provided for earning booty and prestige, and farming families had to perform perhaps no more than three days of required labour each year in the fields of their often distant lord. Without question, both secular and religious lords endeavoured to enlarge their estates, abused judicial privilege, and used little restraint in collecting taxes. Almost as certainly, some vassals defended these as rights they had inherited from their Estonian and Livonian mothers and grandmothers – widows or daughters of nobles slain in the wars of conquest, or, in the case of the von Ropp family, marriage into a prominent Rus'ian dynasty.

Livonia remained administratively divided. Consequently, the experiences of individual communities were probably quite diverse. Relatively few Germans settled on the order's lands, only a few more on the archbishop's. German influence hardly extended beyond the walls of the small communities clustered around the major castles or the coastal towns. In Estonia, however, where the bishops of Dorpat and Oesel-Wiek governed through landed vassals, and in the lands of the Danish monarch, German knights, merchants, and artisans were more numerous.

Unfortunately, it was only this handful of administrators and merchants who compiled the records and wrote the letters which comprise our most important historical sources from this period. When we reach the last lines of *The Rhymed Chronicle* and realise that our author has laid down his pen for good, we experience a loss almost as painful as the one we feel when we came to the end of *The Chronicle of Henry of Livonia*. The century of the Baltic Crusade concluded with the outbreak of a quarrel we must follow through lawyers' briefs and statements by the order's enemies at hearings conducted by papal legates, which, unfortunately, were boycotted by the Teutonic Knights, so that we never hear their version of events directly. The Rigans dared not give up their alliance with Lithuanian pagans, because that would have meant, in effect, their surrender to the Livonian master. For thirty years the Rigans would continue to fight desperately but vainly for their liberty. The crusade of the thirteenth century thus ended in civil conflict that would last many decades and would reappear late in the fifteenth century.

7

Territorial Rivalries with Poland

Pomerellia and Danzig

The strategic significance of Pomerellia (West Prussia) was, first, that it lay on the southern Baltic coast along the last stage of the sea route from Lübeck to Prussia, and, therefore, its rulers could aid or hinder commerce as they saw fit; and second, it provided an alternative land corridor for crusaders coming from the Holy Roman Empire. Some crusaders came by sea, especially those from England and Scotland. Sailing was the most comfortable way to travel, though it was expensive, and it was the only way for crusaders and merchants to reach Livonia. But most crusaders to Prussia came from Meissen, Thuringia, and Upper Saxony, and for them the direct route to Thorn, Culm, and Marienburg lay across Great Poland. Whenever that road was closed by the Polish king, they could reach Prussia only via Brandenburg, the Neumark, and Pomerellia.

For Poland, possession of Pomerellia would guarantee access to the Baltic Sea, an important consideration for the increasing volume of grain being shipped down the Vistula to the international market. Moreover, the king could station forces in the rear of the Teutonic Knights' possessions in East Prussia, within easy striking distance of important castles such as Marienburg and Elbing.

The economic importance of the city of Danzig to the two sides is less clear. The Teutonic Knights had other outlets for their grain and forest products, and Danzig was never to submit meekly to the order's wishes. The slaughter of citizens in an early uprising was as exaggerated (10,000 people, many more than the actual population) as it was widely publicised by the Polish king. Later the order's officers would have to negotiate with the wealthy and self-confident patricians who dominated politics in this

Hanseatic city, and they would rely on Danzig warships in their efforts to suppress piracy. The Piast monarchs of Poland valued the theoretical sovereignty over Danzig more than any immediate military or financial advantages they could have obtained. Claiming that the German-speaking citizens of Danzig were really Poles was good propaganda, and it was plausible because language was not yet a certain sign of political allegiance.

The real issue was power – if the Teutonic Knights held Pomerellia and Danzig, they could bring crusaders to Prussia no matter what the king's current policies were, and they could raise troops and taxes from that land to support their operations on the eastern frontier; if the Polish king held Pomerellia, he could reduce Prussia to a dependency. Since the military order considered possession of Pomerellia necessary for survival, the grand masters gave this issue their highest priority. For the king, in contrast, possessing Pomerellia had few advantages other than in bringing the Teutonic Order to heel; the number of knights and taxpayers in that land would increase his power and wealth only marginally. Therefore it was an issue which he could deal with later.

Had the Polish kingdom never suffered military disasters at the hands of the Mongols in the 1240s, Pomerellia would probably have ended up in Piast possession – not only by right of inheritance (and the Teutonic Order suffered in this way for its vow of celibacy), but because the Piast dukes would have been strong enough to force the Teutonic Order to share in the fruits of the holy war right from the beginning, before it was firmly established in East Prussia. At the minimum the Masovian dukes would have taken Culm and named favourably-inclined prelates for the four Prussian bishoprics, and it is unlikely that any ambitious dynasty of any nationality would have been able to refrain forever from attempting to extend its control over the rest of the order's lands. Since Duke Conrad and his heirs controlled the water routes in Masovia that led toward Lithuania and into Volhynia, they were committed to defending those lands against pagan attacks. Additional early commitments in Prussia would likely have involved them even more deeply in the future conflicts with Lithuania.

This was not Poland's destiny, however. Since the Polish kingdom suffered one defeat after another, all Poles could do was to bemoan the lost opportunities. All patriots could do was await the day when the kingdom reawakened, when king, important nobles, clergy, knights, and gentry could work together again for the good of the commonwealth and the good of Christendom. At the mid-point of the thirteenth century that seemed far away, but by the end of the century it seemed within reach.

✠

The Unification of Poland

The unification of the Polish kingdom did not come swiftly or easily. It came about, in fact, almost by accident, as branches of the widespread Piast dynasty ceased to produce sons. The line that held the duchy of Cracow (and the crown) ended with the death of Boleslaw the Pious in 1279. Leszek the Black, a grandson of Conrad of Masovia, became king. Leszek proved himself to be a capable leader by defeating Rus'ians in battle, then crushing the Sudovian Prussians in 1282, and finally using Hungarian and Cuman warriors to capture Cracow in 1285. He survived a devastating Mongol invasion in 1287, only to die without issue the following year. With him died the immediate hopes of restoring Polish power and prestige.

Henryk of Silesia moved quickly to claim Cracow. Although his relatives supported Boleslaw of Masovia, Henryk had the bigger army and was closer to Cracow, and therefore he held the southern part of the kingdom easily. But Henryk was not popular – culturally he was less Polish than German. Orphaned early in life, he had saved himself from his Silesian relatives only by asking Ottokar of Bohemia to act as his guardian. He had grown up at the Bohemian court and his army had formed a third of the Czech force that was defeated by Rudolf von Habsburg in 1278 at the decisive encounter in which King Ottokar lost his life; but Henryk did not hesitate to seek out the victor of that contest and swear allegiance to him. After returning to Silesia, he brought in more German settlers and made the German influence at his court more dominant than before. Many Poles were offended by this and feared that under Henryk Poland would become a mere appendage of the Holy Roman Empire. To judge from Henryk's will, however, this fear seems to have been exaggerated. When he died suddenly in 1290 in the midst of negotiations with the pope for his coronation, he left instructions to give Cracow to Przemysł of Great Poland, and Silesia to his cousin Henryk, with the intent that this latter territory would return to the crown later. Unfortunately, not everyone agreed to this formula. Ladislas the Short (Władysław Łotietek, 1261–1333) of Kujavia protested, and so did Wenceslas II (Vaclav, 1271–1305) of Bohemia, who began a contest for the throne that lasted, with interruptions, almost two decades.

The Czech king was far more powerful than his opponent and by 1292 had occupied all of southern Poland. The north was held by Przemysł, who was the heir of Mestwin of Pomerellia as well as of the dukes of Great Poland. Przemysł acted first on the idea of reviving the kingship by having himself crowned by the archbishop of Gniezno in 1295, but his reign was short – he was assassinated within a year, in what may have been a failed kidnapping. Although no guilty party was ever discovered, many suspected that the dukes of Brandenburg were behind the plot, the motive being possession of Pomerellia. After the confusion had quieted down, Ladislas the Short held the late king's lands and pretensions. In the meantime, the vassals of Pomerellia became the de facto rulers; the foremost of these was Swenza (Święca, Schwetz) of Danzig and Stolp and his son, Peter.

By this time it was clear to everyone that the reunification of the Polish kingdom was but a short time off. The Prussian masters had to think about what this would mean for them. Their relationship with the Piast dukes had varied considerably over the years, but in general it had been friendly and mutually helpful. Moreover, in many ways the Teutonic Order had helped bring about the favourable changes that were now occurring in the kingdom. By protecting the frontier from pagan attack, the Teutonic Knights had helped stabilise the country, so that the dukes could concentrate on badly needed internal reforms. By bringing a steady stream of crusaders across Silesia and Great Poland, they had helped stimulate the local economy; this aided in the development of a middle-class that paid taxes and provided services, thus encouraging further development of internal trade and manufactures. The roads and bridges were improved so that communication became easier and more dependable throughout the kingdom.

Following the example of those churchmen who had settled Germans on the land in Silesia, Pomerellia, and Prussia, the dukes began an internal colonisation of their own, using Polish as well as German peasants. More important, they relaxed the laws that kept most of the peasantry in bondage. The newly freed peasants worked harder and were more productive than serfs, and this had a good effect on the economy, which in turn raised the ducal incomes. The numerous Polish knights profited from this, too. However, as they developed a sense of their importance they expressed their growing self-confidence and ambition in a jingoistic patriotism that included strong anti-German sentiments. This naturally worried the leaders of the Teutonic Order, because such vocal hostility had to affect their relations with the Piast dukes.

All the forces that were moving in the direction of a national rebirth in Poland could be harnessed for use in various ways by anyone lucky and skilful enough to unify the country and crown himself its king. The Teutonic Knights would have been frightened by the prospect of having a powerful German prince as a neighbour, but the prospect of having an unpredictable and quarrelsome Piast on the throne must have been particularly unsettling. Especially if that Piast was Ladislas the Short. Well-known to the knights of the order, he, in turn, knew them well. Neither trusted the other, yet neither wanted to begin a feud.

Ladislas was a man of moods but of consistent policy. His abrasive personality often stood between him and his goals, but his perseverance and combativeness won the hearts of many of Poland's knights and gentry. For many years this was unimportant to the Prussian masters, since Ladislas' ambitions caused him to look south, not north. Involved in many intrigues over many years, he had relatively little to do with the Teutonic Order for long periods of time; this meant that he made few efforts to undermine the crusade in Prussia in those decades when the outcome was still in doubt. Considering this, and considering that Ladislas would probably not succeed in his ambitions, the Prussian masters resisted the temptation to mix into Polish affairs, although they could have been of great assistance to Ladislas' enemies.

Ladislas, in fact, relied on the Prussian masters to protect his most vulnerable lands from attack. When the Lithuanians saw that Ladislas had stripped Great Poland of knights to make war in Silesia, they attacked Kalish. This was a daringly deep raid into Poland, and unless Ladislas gave up his pretension to the crown, he had to rely on the Teutonic Order to halt another dangerous invasion. Similarly Ladislas employed the Teutonic Knights against his Brandenburg foes.

✠

Pomerellia Up for Grabs

While Ladislas the Short and Henryk of Silesia were contending for the crown in the south, the dukes of Brandenburg had moved into Pomerellia again, claiming that land for themselves. In the late 1260s Duke Mestwin had sought their aid against his brother and the Teutonic Knights. The price was Mestwin becoming a vassal of the ambitious dukes. The feudal relationship, however, was rarely a quiet one. There was a quarrel in 1272, during which the Brandenburgers had occupied most of the duchy, but after failing to capture Danzig the dukes had declared themselves satisfied with a settlement that confirmed their status as Mestwin's overlords. Later, when Mestwin willed his lands to his Piast relatives, the Brandenburg dukes were not strong enough to make valid their right to dispose of escheated lands. In 1295 Przemysł made a brief visit to Pomerellia but was able to heal only a few of the many angry feelings left by Mestwin's quarrels with the bishops, abbots, and vassals. Przemysł's death the following year brought renewed chaos to the north – his daughter, who inherited a claim to his lands, was married to Wenceslas II; this made the Bohemian monarch the leading candidate to be king of Poland, and Wenceslas immediately moved to occupy Cracow.

Meanwhile, Leszek the Black and Ladislas the Short each raised claims to Pomerellia, and Henryk of Silesia tried to seize Great Poland. It was under these dizzying circumstances that the Swenza family rose to prominence, and it was no surprise that they recognised Wenceslas II as king and worked closely with his Brandenburg supporters, just as they did with Wenceslas III during his short reign (1305–6).

There was no way for the Swenzas to foresee that in 1306 Ladislas the Short would become king, nor even to anticipate that his short visit to Pomerellia that year would be such a disaster – Ladislas, wanting to punish the Swenzas for their disloyalty (and perhaps confiscate their lands in order to pay his expenses), ordered their arrest on charges of treason. The frightened nobles appealed to Brandenburg, whose aged duke soon occupied all Pomerellia except Danzig, and in Danzig only the citadel held out. The town, with its many German merchants, surrendered without fighting.

As the siege continued, the royalist commander at Danzig twice asked Ladislas to come to his aid, but he was told that since no rescue could be expected, he should seek aid from the Teutonic Knights. He did so. That fateful request was to mark the end of the first great era of crusading in Prussia, the era when all the enemies of paganism customarily co-operated. Nobody seems to have foreseen that the quarrel between the Prussian master and the king would endure as long as it did, but in retrospect it seems so logical that some historians have viewed the ensuing events as premeditated aggression.

This suspicion is associated with the change in the order's leadership. Conrad Sack retired in early 1306 on grounds of health. His last campaign had been a winter attack on Gardinas – his men had clambered over the walls under the cover of a snowstorm and had overwhelmed the sleepy garrison, but they had been unable to take the keep. His successor, the well-born Sieghard von Schwarzburg, the castellan of Culm, resigned after only a few months. The electors then chose Heinrich von Plötzke, a notable warrior who had been sent to Prussia by the grand master only a few months before.

Master Sieghard had sent a garrison to join the embattled royalist Pomerellians in Danzig. There was nothing particularly notable about this. This action and the little that followed immediately from it were considered so insignificant at the time that the chroniclers, Peter von Dusburg and Nicholas von Jeroschin, did not interrupt their narratives to mention it. But it was an important step. From that moment on, the Teutonic Order was deeply enmeshed in the Pomerellian-Polish issues; afterward, the more Heinrich von Plötzke learned about Ladislas' plans for Pomerellia, the less willing he was to turn the province over to him.

✝

The Teutonic Knights take Danzig and Pomerellia

Heinrich von Plötzke, acting on Ladislas' request, drove the Brandenburg forces out of Danzig in September of 1308. The citizens apparently welcomed the new occupying force at first, but became very impatient when no movement could be discerned in returning authority to royal administrators. In November the citizens staged an abortive uprising in which considerable blood was spilled – most of it belonging to the German merchants and artisans who had settled the city and made it into a mercantile centre more important than Elbing or Thorn.

The Teutonic Knights faced an unpleasant choice after putting down the revolt – to evacuate the hostile city and give up any hope of being paid for their services, or to finish the job in such a way as to make negotiations with Ladislas easier. Heinrich chose the latter – he captured Dirschau and every other stronghold in possession of the Brandenburgers. Not long afterward he presented a bill for services rendered – 10,000 Marks. Ladislas was as lacking in money and tact as he was in stature, and he refused to pay. Also, there was an implication that he expected the order to serve him whenever he summoned it. The refusal to pay the order for its services was a mistake on Ladislas' part that set back Polish unification for many years and brought about the fateful confrontation of Poland and the Teutonic Order that was so bothersome to him and his successors.

Somehow the lesson of Riga, which the Teutonic Knights had made war against since 1298, was lost. Perhaps this was the result of pride. Ladislas probably could not imagine himself being treated like a mere archbishop of Riga. Perhaps, like many successful people, he had come to rely upon his remarkable luck and his demonstrated knack for escaping dangerous situations. He had not got as far as he had by deferring to powerful opponents or accepting meekly whatever happened. Like all successful Piasts, he relied on persuasion, personality, intimidation, and finally force, escalating the pressure as each stage failed to produce the desired results.

Master Heinrich announced that he would keep Pomerellia in his possession until the matter could be settled.* His diplomats contacted the Brandenburg dukes, who in 1309 sold their claims of sovereignty to the Teutonic Order. The price was 10,000 Marks. That was as good a claim to

---

* As it turned out, only World War Two seems to have provided a solution – a very brutal one, involving as it did the forced removal of most of the German-speaking population of East and West Prussia, including most descendants of the original Prussian population.

possess a land as most rulers had; there was, after all, no 'ethnic identity' to most states – one was subject to a ruler, who usually cared little what the language or ethnic background of the taxpayers or vassals was. To be sure, people were aware of ethnicity, but class status was more important. The crisis of 1307–10 committed the Teutonic Knights to holding Pomerellia permanently.

This was the Prussian master's answer to what he saw as a threat from a unified Polish kingdom. Heinrich would not allow Ladislas to misuse his knights and abuse their friendship, nor to insinuate a claim of sovereignty over them; instead, they would use the resources of West Prussia (as Pomerellia is best known in the English-speaking world) and the alliance of Brandenburg to defy him. With the taxes and warriors of West Prussia added to their own, and the supply lines to Germany guaranteed, the Teutonic Knights believed that they could defeat any Polish army sent against them. For many decades this was indeed the case.

The action was wrong and, worse – as the proverb goes – it was a mistake. But that was true only in retrospect. At the time and for many decades thereafter the Teutonic Knights thought that the entire process had been properly handled, that it was a stroke of genius. Master Heinrich could justify the act to himself, to his membership, and to most impartial European nobles. Certainly the order had acted to the letter of the law, which was more than many rulers did in expanding their territories. This was an era when the letter of the law was thought more important than the spirit, and the question of national ties was usually considered irrelevant – dynasties went from country to country, and provinces were won and lost, bought and sold, without any concern for the wishes of the inhabitants. The nationalism of the times was that of the knighthood more than of any other group, and at this moment the West Prussian knights and gentry looked upon Ladislas the Short as an oppressor. By all these accepted standards, the Teutonic Knights had acted responsibly and nobly. But here was a case that was soon to be outside accepted standards. The Polish knights and nobles did not acquiesce as expected; they stood behind Ladislas and his successors in demanding the 'return' of a province that had been only loosely connected to the historical kingdom through most of the thirteenth century. Polish national feeling made Pomerellia a test case of patriotism, and the general anti-German feelings of the time became centred on the Teutonic Order. As West Prussia became a point of contention, neither the Polish kingdom nor the Teutonic Knights were able to deal effectively with problems on their eastern frontiers.

Polish hostility would make it impossible for the Teutonic Knights to win the crusade against the Samogitian and Lithuanian pagans, but we might bear

in mind that even if the Teutonic Knights had foreseen the long-term implications of their action, they had no good alternative to the response they
made to Ladislas' short-term challenge. Moreover, Prussia was now becoming more central to the order's activities than before. Two decades after the
loss of Acre to the Saracens, the German convents had reluctantly concluded
that the chances of returning to the Holy Land were slim. They decided to
concentrate their resources on supporting the perpetual crusade against the
Baltic pagans.

It was in this context that the grand master, Siegfried von Feuchtwangen,
transferred his seat from Venice to Marienburg. First, this recognised that
long-term complaints from Prussia were valid. For many years the Prussian
knights had felt that their interests were being ignored by the distant grand
master, and the depth of their anger had become clear in a stormy grand
chapter meeting in Elbing in 1303, during which the Prussian and Livonian
delegates argued with the Venetian and German representatives over the res-
ignation of the grand master, Gottfried von Hohenlohe. The order was
almost in a state of schism until Gottfried's death eight years later. In those
years Siegfried von Feutchtwangen had not dared to cross the Alps even for
inspections or to recruit crusaders, lest he offend those knights who wanted
to wait for an expedition to the Holy Land. Secondly, the situation in Italy
was becoming perilous. In 1303 the king of France had arranged for the kidnapping of Pope Boniface VIII, and the next pope had moved to Avignon
where both he and the king of France believed he would be 'safer'. Four
years after royal agents had mishandled the holy father, they arrested the
entire membership of the Templars in France and put them on trial for
heresy. Those knights confessed to grotesque and improbable crimes, and
later many were burned at the stake and their possessions confiscated. In
early 1308 the king of England similarly arrested the Templars in his lands.

As Siegfried von Feuchtwangen watched this development, he concluded
that it would be prudent to reside in a somewhat safer locality – there were
no powerful friends of the Teutonic Knights ruling in Italy or Germany at
this moment, and the wealth of the order was a tempting prize for hard-
pressed rulers. Moreover, the grand master did not have historic ties to
Venice; that was merely a convenient place to monitor politics in the
Mediterranean. He saw no hope of organising a crusade large enough to re-
establish a foothold in the Holy Land in the next few years, and therefore
any knights stationed outside the Baltic would not be of much use to anyone.
If by a miracle the crusaders could return to the Holy Land, the Teutonic
Knights would join them, but meanwhile they would concentrate on the
war against the pagans. Siegfried von Feuchtwangen established permanent
residence at Marienburg in 1309, but it would be the next grand master, Karl

von Trier, who actually reasserted the authority of his office over all the regional officers, making the grand master once again the leader of all Teutonic Knights; by then the organisation had a firm grasp of what its goals were – the extirpation of militant paganism in the Baltic.

Siegfried von Feuchtwangen named new officers, giving them the more exalted titles formerly used in the Holy Land. He also appointed advocates to rural districts and established a convent of knights in Danzig. As prosperity returned, Danzig became the leading commercial centre in the Baltic. Rule by the Teutonic Knights was no longer seen by the patrician burghers and artisans as an oppressive despotism.

✠

King Ladislas of Poland

Up to 1320 the Teutonic Knights did not consider Ladislas a serious threat. They had no reason to see him as a military genius or even a particularly good administrator, and they knew that conflicts broke out wherever he appeared, creating military chaos that he was able to repress only with difficulty. They must have welcomed his attacks on relatives, since that practically guaranteed that the Masovian dukes would support the order politically and militarily.

The Polish clergy was initially divided over whether to recognise Ladislas, but that ended when the hostile bishop of Cracow went into exile. Later Ladislas obtained the support of the archbishop of Gniezno, the chief prelate of the kingdom. Still, it was not until 20 January 1320 that he was crowned king, and the coronation took place without prior papal blessing. This awkward by-product of the quarrel of the German emperor and the Avignon pope created problems in the short term, but long term it established the Polish monarchy as independent of papal politics. It also marked the rebirth of the Polish monarchy on a hereditary basis, father to son, rather than passing the crown among all surviving brothers before giving it to the eldest son of the eldest brother, as ancient practice dictated. Moreover, Ladislas, being from the north of the country, wanted to possess Pomerellia, whereas most competing Piasts were interested only in Silesia. Also, he was a stubborn, vengeful man who did not forget past slights such as those given by the Teutonic Knights.

By 1320 Ladislas had learned much from his many defeats. Most importantly he had finally understood that one should not start a war without some hope of winning. Since he had no hope of victory over the Teutonic Knights at that time, he concentrated on reorganising his state on a feudal basis; and his appeals to the pope laid the foundation for future legal challenges to the order's possession of West Prussia, Danzig, and Culm.

✠

King Ladislas and the Pagans

When the Rus'ian prince of Galicia and Volhynia died in 1323, Ladislas sought to have Boleslaw of Masovia inherit his territories, but Gediminas of Lithuania made it clear that no broad swathe of lands along his western and southern borders could be transferred to a Piast duke without his permission. Negotiations over this revealed that Poland and Lithuania perceived common interests; most importantly, they had enemies – Tatars on the steppes, Teutonic Knights along the northern coasts – that could be resisted effectively if they worked together. An alliance was arranged. Gediminas sent daughters to the Masovian dukes, and Ladislas' fifteen-year-old son, Casimir (1310–70), wedded Aldona, an appealing Lithuanian princess. Aldona bought joy again to a court that had been saddened by the deaths of Casimir's two elder brothers. She went about in the company of beautiful maidens and musicians, and for a while her young husband loved her deeply. Later, when Casimir began pursuing other women, he abandoned her to his mother's domestic tyranny.

Ladislas was by now a wily diplomat. In early 1326 he signed a truce with the Teutonic Order that seemed to repudiate his Lithuanian alliance. Without much question the grand master probably thought that he was dividing the order's enemies and diverting the king to a war against the Tatars – Ladislas had recently obtained a papal indulgence 'for the defence of the Catholic faith in war or battle in the kingdom of Poland or in any other Christian land or in areas adjacent to the abovementioned kingdom or near to it inhabited or possessed by schismatics, Tatars, or any other mixture of pagan nations'. But Ladislas' actual target was Brandenburg, whose dukes had been staunch supporters of crusading. In the spring he allowed fiercely pagan Lithuanians to cross his domains, to fall without warning on German villages and towns, ravaging districts that had never felt a military threat from pagans even during the most hard-fought campaigns of the thirteenth century.

A chronicler contemporary to these events expressed the crusaders' outrage at the devastation of churches, the desecration of the host, the murder of priests and burning of convents, and the torture of prisoners of both sexes. He claimed that those scenes horrified even the Poles who had accompanied the pagans. He reported incidents that have the ring of eye-witness accounts: of pagan warriors quarrelling so seriously over one beautiful girl that a leader stepped forward, cut her in two, and said, 'now she's worth nothing. Each can have the part that pleases him'; and the nun who begged for death rather than lose her virginity, and was dispatched by the sword of a co-operative pagan after appropriate prayers. The Teutonic Knights used the stories to inflame popular feeling against the pagans and their Polish allies. A rumour circulated that the Lithuanian leader, David of Gardinas, had been murdered by a Polish knight, and many wondered if the Polish alliance with Lithuania would be ended by this general fiasco.

The Teutonic Knights did not await the expiration of the truce to take revenge for Ladislas' attack on their ally. They drew up alliances with Piast princes that threatened Ladislas' very grip on the Polish crown, first with Henryk of Silesia, later with Boleslaw of Volhynia-Galicia. The first treaty fairly burned with angry words denouncing Ladislas, accusing him of breaking the peace, aiding pagans in ravaging Christian lands, and of being an inhuman tyrant. Later Duke Henryk and his brothers became lay members of the Teutonic Order.

The grand master was now Werner von Orseln, the former castellan of Ragnit and grand commander. Although he was an enthusiastic proponent of war against the pagans, there was little fighting during the next three years. This was not due to Ladislas' actions, but because the emperor-elect and the pope were at war, making it impossible to recruit crusaders from Germany.

The long history of the Holy Roman Empire is marked by recurring conflicts between emperor and pope. The particular quarrel of this era was different because neither party had sufficient real power to harm the other significantly; their feud was characterised by few actions stronger than harsh words and empty threats. In 1326, after the pope laid an interdict over Germany, suspending all church services, the grand master summoned representatives to a grand chapter in Marienburg to discuss the matter. The knights and priests voted to support the emperor, Louis IV of Wittelsbach, duke of Bavaria.

At this same meeting the delegates voted on a number of changes in the statutes. The principal innovation was to revise the form of worship service, but later generations remembered the meeting best for a subsequent forgery that gave the German master authority to remove an incompetent grand master.

✠

Wars on Several Fronts

Grand Master Werner's first campaign, in 1327, was to the south along both banks of the Vistula, a territory King Ladislas was holding in his effort to assert royal authority over his Masovian relatives. Werner first cleared Polish forces from Dobrin and Płock, then pushed on into Kujavia. When his attack on Brzesc failed, Werner proposed a truce. He may have thought that he had taught Ladislas a lesson. If so, he was mistaken. This conflict was only the beginning of a long war. Ladislas accepted the truce, but was only waiting for the proper moment to strike back hard at his opponents.

Not realising what he had taken on, Werner proceeded with plans to transfer his forces east for an advance into Samogitia. Replacing the garrison of Livonian knights in Memel with Prussian knights gave the Livonian master additional troops for his siege of Riga; also, it made it easier for the Prussian marshal to co-ordinate operations up the Nemunas River. Werner then struck across the wilderness toward Gardinas, the fortress protecting the water route westward across the swamps and lakes to the Narew River and then to the Bug River, the easiest way to travel from Masovia and Volhynia to Lithuania. He employed a clever stratagem to lure the enemy into a headlong pursuit, then ambushed the surprised pagans. The Teutonic Knights then burned an area around Gardinas thirty miles across. Some Lithuanian nobles, either concluding that Gediminas could no longer protect them or being his personal enemies, came to Prussia with their wives and children, accepted baptism, and served in the crusader armies.

About this time Werner lost the use of Christmemel as a forward base on the Nemunas River. Supposedly, warning of a portending disaster was observed a year before, when three knights saw a star moving east from the constellation Aquarius. Of course, there was no way to interpret this as a prediction that an earthslide would destroy Christmemel's defences. The foundation of the wooden fort gave way and some walls collapsed. Inspecting the damage, the grand master realised that he could not repair it immediately. Therefore, at the conclusion of a magnificent banquet he set fire to the ruins and abandoned the site temporarily.

✠

John of Bohemia joins the Conflict

King John of Bohemia (1296–1346) was an extraordinary man by any standard. Crowned at the age of fourteen, he was an inveterate traveller and campaigner who was embroiled in so many quarrels that contemporaries said, 'nothing without King John'. In his early thirties, he left the government of Bohemia to his vassals so that he could concentrate on foreign adventures. His most persistent ambition was to lead a crusade to the Holy Land. Unfortunately for him, it was impossible to raise a Christian army powerful enough to challenge the Turks, so he accepted Samogitia as a reasonable substitute. In the winter of 1328–9 he came to Prussia with a large number of Bohemian, German, and Polish nobles and knights. He was also accompanied by the French troubadour, Guillaume de Machaut, who was to compose a poetic description of John's exploits. Grand Master Werner called up an estimated 350 Teutonic Knights and 18,000 foot soldiers. The combined army was so large that the participants expected to deal the Samogitians a fatal blow similar to that landed by Ottokar II of Bohemia the previous century. John wanted a victory so spectacular that cities in Samogitia would be named after him, just as Königsberg had been named to honour Ottokar.*

The crusaders marched across frozen swamps and rivers to an inland castle, where their demonstration of power persuaded the garrison to ask for terms, which, in turn, provoked a dispute among the crusaders. Werner argued for resettling the garrison in Prussia; he compared the pagans to wolves who would soon take off for the woods and resume their evil ways. The chivalrous king from Bohemia, however, insisted that the pagans be given a courteous and honourable baptism, after which they be allowed to remain in possession of the castle. John prevailed. Soon priests had baptised 6,000 men, women, and children.

This generous policy might have been wise if the crusaders had gone on to occupy all Samogitia, but they did not have the opportunity. At that moment news arrived that Ladislas had invaded Culm on the same day that the crusaders had marched into the wilderness. The messenger had ridden five days to urge the grand master to send the army back to protect Prussia. Werner and John reluctantly turned back to Culm, arriving too late to catch Ladislas. Meanwhile, the newly baptised Samogitians rebelled.

John and Werner believed that it would be impossible to invade Samogitia again until the grand master had eliminated King Ladislas' threat to Culm. Moreover, they were concerned about the question of honour, which was easily as important as the strategic situation: they had to take revenge for Ladislas' violation of the truce. In addition they had to punish Ladislas of Masovia (d.1343), whom they now considered a vile traitor to the Christian cause. In March of 1329, Werner and John signed a formal treaty of alliance. John asserted his claims to the Polish throne by right of inheritance and marriage, a fact that became important when his queen sur-

---

* After World War Two it was renamed Kaliningrad by its Soviet conquerors to honour a Stalinist party hack. Most evidence of the German past that survived the fighting was destroyed, thus eliminating the visual reminders that Emmanuel Kant (1724–1804) and Johann Gottfried Herder (1744–1803) had lived there, along with the monuments built by the Teutonic Knights and the dukes of Prussia.

rendered her hereditary claims to West Prussia to the grand master. They then invaded Masovia and Kujavia, devastating vast areas on both sides of the Vistula River and forcing Ladislas to plead for a truce.

Before hostilities ended, John had made Ladislas of Masovia become his vassal, and the Teutonic Knights had occupied Dobrin, the province that protected the southern approach to Culm. A year later John sold his share of the conquered areas to Werner.

✝

Papal Intervention

One of the great issues that divided the Teutonic Order and the papacy was the payment of Peter's Pence, a tax that Poland and England paid directly into the papal coffers. In recent years Pope John XXII had attempted to require this payment from other nations. Meeting resistance, he needed an example; the Teutonic Knights seemed perfect – they owed him obedience, their West Prussian subjects paid Peter's Pence, and the military order was fabulously wealthy. However, the Teutonic Knights refused on the grounds that many of their possessions were in Germany and Italy, and therefore were immune from this tax; moreover, paying the tax would lend credence to Polish claims to overlordship of Prussia. John XXII, who had little patience with such quibbles, encouraged the order's foes to bring lawsuits against them; and he made it clear that he would be very understanding of the special needs of his friends and supporters. There was a change in papal policy in 1330, when the pope offered to forgive all past debts if Culm and West Prussia would pay Peter's Pence in the future. The provincial assembly accepted the offer, but the grand master did not.

The pope then ordered the grand master and his officers to come to Avignon to explain their behaviour, warning that if they failed to do so their privileges would be suspended, his legates' excommunication would be confirmed, and he would put the officers of the Teutonic Order on trial *in absentia*. The officers still did not attend. The pope had even less success with his commands that the Teutonic Knights join in military attacks on the emperor and his son, Louis of Brandenburg. The Teutonic Knights were unwilling to risk compromise. Not only did they believe that the emperor and his son were within their rights, but they feared that the emperor could order their German possessions confiscated and that Duke Louis, his son, could harass crusaders as they crossed Brandenburg.

If the grand masters were sceptical about papal offers to mediate their disputes with Poland, modern historians might also be sceptical about this pope's criticisms of the Teutonic Knights. Still, papal legates were figures who could safely pass from one court to another, and all parties recognised that whatever one thought of the pope's motives, the pope was still the pope, and the Church provided the only international order that Christendom possessed. More importantly, perhaps, both the king and the grand master needed a pause in hostilities and somebody had to arrange these. Consequently papal efforts to arrange truces were successful in 1330, 1332, and 1334; but hopes for a permanent peace were frustrated because the parties were so far apart that only the passage of time and the passing of the principal figures could remove the mutual mistrust. The truces brought a suspension of hostilities but nothing more.

✠

Victory in Livonia

The truces did permit Werner von Orseln to resume his campaign in Samogitia. In the winter of 1330 he welcomed a large group of Rhenish crusaders and led them into the hostile wilderness. He did not find any forts to besiege. The natives, having long since been forewarned of the crusaders' approach, had abandoned their villages and hidden in the woods. Consequently Werner's expedition achieved relatively little. However, the crusaders' offensive had distracted the Lithuanians' attention sufficiently that knights from Ragnit were able to slip past enemy outposts and raid Vilnius, deep in the interior of the highlands. Finding the watchmen asleep, they sacked and burned the suburbs of the city.

The war in Livonia ended that same year with the surrender of Riga. Although the burghers expected brutal treatment, they were offered such unexpectedly fair terms that a complete reconciliation resulted. For decades to come the burghers abandoned their interference in foreign policy and confined their interests to trade. The Livonian Knights were as close to the Lithuanian fortresses of Vilnius and Kaunas as were the Prussian Knights, and from Dünaburg they could raid regions inaccessible from Prussia. Within a short time they contributed an important reinforcement to the expeditions into Samogitia.

✠

War with Ladislas

In Ladislas' mind the situation was becoming intolerable. The crusaders were simply making too much progress. Urged on by Ladislas of Masovia to recapture Dobrin, he turned to his allies, the rulers of Lithuania and Hungary. Gediminas, eager to reopen the communication route to Poland, agreed to a joint campaign in the late summer; he would cross the wilderness at Wizna and meet Ladislas' army in Dobrin or Culm. Ladislas sought to make good his shortage of experienced knights by sending Prince Casimir to Hungary. In a triumph of personal diplomacy, Casimir persuaded his brother-in-law, Charles Robert, to send knights in the spring of 1331 to assist in fighting a common enemy, John of Bohemia.

Before the reinforcements arrived, however, the grand master sent a large army to a large castle that had harassed ships along the Vistula. The besiegers moved up stone-throwers and towers, working so quickly that after three days little remained of the castle walls. Assault followed assault, and finally the besiegers built a great fire, incinerating many defenders and driving others to attempt a hopeless sally. The Teutonic Knights went on to capture Brzesc and Nakel, two fortresses shielding northern Kujavia. The king despaired, having lacked sufficient troops to attempt a rescue.

At that moment Casimir arrived with the Hungarian reinforcements. The nineteen-year-old prince had been fascinated by the informal but courtly life at the Visegrad palace in Hungary. With his sister's approval and aid, the blond prince had begun an affair with one of the royal ladies-in-waiting, Clara of Zać. Had Casimir been an eligible bachelor or had the affair been more discrete, the story might have had a romantic ending. As it was, on 17 April the Croatian lady's father stormed into court, swinging his sword; he wounded the king, cut four fingers off the queen's right hand, and was barely frustrated in his efforts to kill the young princes, Andreas and Louis. Royal vengeance was swift: the assailant's body was quartered and the parts displayed throughout the countryside, his son was dragged to death behind a horse and the corpse given to dogs, and Clara was hounded from place to place. The Zać relatives were exiled from the kingdom. Even so, Casimir was urged to leave the country quickly, lest revenge be taken on him.

Once Casimir brought the Hungarian reinforcements, Ladislas was ready to strike. With large numbers of knights at his command, and many mercenaries as well, he decided not to waste his army in sieges of well-defended castles, but to invade Culm, join forces with Gediminas, and either force the grand master to a pitched battle or overwhelm the cities there. The campaign began well. In September he misled the grand master as to his intentions by invading West Prussia, then cleverly crossing to the east bank of the Vistula. The timing was wrong, however. He arrived too late to join the Lithuanians. Gediminas knew that his army was being shadowed by a small force of Teutonic Knights, and when Gediminas' scouts were unable to locate the Polish forces at the agreed time and place the grand prince had prudently gone home. Ladislas was thus in East Prussia with a superiority in troops, but his advantage was not so great as to allow him to besiege cities. Moreover, with the grand master's army so close he could not send out many foragers, which caused him to be short of fodder and provisions for his forces. The king did not want to make a humiliating retreat, but he could not stay in Culm indefinitely. Werner, in spite of having both the German and Livonian masters present, was unwilling to offer battle, but he did not want the Poles and Hungarians to continue ravaging his most valuable province. Consequently when someone suggested a truce, both Ladislas and Werner were eager to accept. Werner agreed to restore the Kujavian cities to the king after having razed the fortifications and castles and promised to give Dobrin back to Ladislas of Masovia.

✢

Werner's Assassination

A short time later Grand Master Werner met his death at the hands of an assassin. The circumstances provide some rare insights into the process of justice among the Teutonic Knights. It appears that the assassin, a knight from the convent at Memel, had been reprimanded for violent and unpredictable behaviour which had culminated with his threatening the castellan with a knife. He had come to Marienburg in hope of obtaining a pardon but had simply been ordered back to Memel. The disappointed knight left the audience room but not the castle. He had little to look forward to. Light punishment was a year in which one was forbidden to associate with one's fellow knights and was stripped of honourable clothing and made to subsist on bread and water three days of the week; his would have been a heavy punishment, probably including both imprisonment and irons. Lurking in the corridor until Werner went to Vespers, he stepped out and dealt the grand master two deadly wounds. Apparently having made no plans for escape, he was promptly captured by a notary.

The officers who judged the assassin ruled that he was insane and not responsible for his actions, but they were unsure about the punishment they could inflict. The statutes provided the death penalty for the crimes of apostasy, cowardice, and sodomy, but not for murder. Consequently they wrote to the papacy for instructions, and when the answer arrived they followed the wisdom of the pope: life imprisonment.

✠

Luther von Braunschweig

Werner's successor was Luther von Braunschweig, the youngest of the six sons of Duke Albrecht the Great. The other two youngest sons entered the Templars and the Hospitallers. Luther had become the order's master of the robes, with responsibility for settling German peasants in Prussia. He was very successful, recruiting many of the immigrants from his brothers' domains in what had once been called Lower Saxony. (It helped that pagan raiders rarely penetrated into the heart of Prussia now.) He maintained his family ties carefully, so that two nephews later joined the Teutonic Order.

Luther was a gifted poet who used his patronage to encourage religious and historical compositions relating to the Teutonic Order. While most of his own works have been lost, his *Life of Saint Barbara* has been preserved because of the close connection of this saint with the order's conquest of Prussia, and because Luther's own grandfather had been on crusade in 1242 when the knights captured the reliquary containing Barbara's head and enshrined it in Culm.

Luther linked poetry with successful wars in Poland and Samogitia. Consequently a special lustre attached itself to his gracious and noble personality, a lustre that was enhanced by his exalted birth. Four years sufficed to make his memory bright a century later, when grand masters were neither especially gifted nor much admired.

Luther was determined to press the war against Ladislas even if it meant suspending the crusade until he had struck the king such blows as would eliminate him as a threat to the order's rear. In this he depended upon John of Bohemia to pin down Ladislas in Silesia. Both princes claimed lordship over that province and, divided as it was among insignificant Piast princelings, Ladislas would not abandon Silesia to fight in the north. If he did, a victory for King John in Silesia was almost as good as a victory for the Teutonic Knights in Kujavia or Great Poland. War on Poland was beyond the resources of Prussia alone: the Poles were highly respected warriors, well armed, and fighting in defence of their homes. Therefore Luther hired mercenaries from Germany and Bohemia to augment his forces, accepted the services of rebel Polish nobles, and prepared to conduct warfare on the scale of a great prince. As operations commenced in July of 1331, English crusaders hastened to join the expedition. For them one fight was as good as another, and there would be more booty in Poland than in Samogitia.

The mercenary troops were commanded by Otto von Bergau, the son-in-law of the marshal of Bohemia, and a close friend of King John. He led

500 knights, who were not only well paid but also shared the spiritual privileges of crusaders, the most important being an indulgence remitting the sins of all those who participated in this holy work. However, their conduct and that of the Prussian army in general was anything but holy. Widespread reports of rape accompanied the usual lists of burnings, murders, and kidnappings. The worst aspects of the conduct of war in Samogitia combined with mercenary habits in general to wreak havoc throughout northern Masovia and Kujavia. The use of mercenaries disguised as crusaders was a propaganda disaster for the Teutonic Knights and was skilfully exploited by the Poles at later papal hearings.

Ladislas did not offer serious resistance. He left Casimir in charge of a small force while he lay in wait for the Bohemian king with most of his knights. His plan worked well enough. The crusader assault passed through Kujavia without achieving much of military significance. The king did not concern himself about the destruction of homes, churches, and mills, and the mistreatment of the commoners. In a war based on plundering, atrocities were common. What was important was that no castles were lost. Casimir had defended them well.

✠

The Battle of Plowce, 1331

Like all contemporary military figures, Luther understood that the destruction of property was an effective means of warfare against an obstinate enemy. His orders to do as much damage as possible were interpreted by the mercenaries, auxiliaries, and knights as a licence to terrorise and impoverish the king's taxpayers. However, his forces were not achieving any truly significant successes.

King John, for his part, had been frustrated in his attempt to crush his opponent. Therefore he proposed that he meet the grand master at Kalish in September and force a decisive battle. Luther, agreeing, sent Marshal Dietrich von Altenburg to lead the Prussian army to the rendezvous. Dietrich crossed Kujavia, sending his forces along several routes to plunder and burn, but did not find the Bohemians at Kalish. This was not unusual. Communications being poor, most joint ventures like this one failed because one party was unexpectedly delayed or could not come at all. John, as a matter of fact, had just returned from an expedition to Italy and was unable to start his march on time. Dietrich, seeing the Polish army beginning to come together from all directions and not knowing that John was only a few days march away, began a slow retreat, plundering along the way. He was thus moving away from John, who himself turned about when he heard of Dietrich's retreat. As Dietrich marched away, Ladislas and Casimir trailed behind with '40,000' men. The royal levy was numerous, but less well armed than the crusading host, and the king was therefore unwilling to offer battle. However, when Dietrich divided his force into three parties, Ladislas swept down on the weakest division at Plowce.

Marshal Dietrich did not realise that he was so heavily outnumbered. Over the past days his Polish scouts had misinformed him about the size of the royal levy, causing him to think he was facing a small force, and now a heavy fog hindered efforts at reconnaissance. Dietrich aligned his men under five banners and faced the royal array. The king likewise formed his army in five units. The battle was cruelly contested, unusually so in an era when major encounters were rare and brief. The decisive moment came when the horse carrying the marshal's banner was pierced by a spear, perhaps by Polish knights among the crusaders who changed sides without warning, creating disorder in the German and Bohemian ranks. The flagbearer had nailed the banner to his saddle, and once the steed fell, he could not raise it again. Consternation among the crusaders was great, because they could not see their commander, and Polish knights seemed to be everywhere. Soon the combat was over. Ladislas' men, having smashed three units of enemy cavalry, captured fifty-six brothers and held them prisoner in a trench. When the king arrived, he asked who they were. Told they were Teutonic Knights, he ordered the ordinary knights killed and the officers held for ransom.

Ladislas' action was based on his fear that the other two divisions of the Teutonic Knights were on the way. In fact, the castellan of Culm did arrive that afternoon and drove the exhausted Polish knights from the field, capturing 600 prisoners. Finding Marshal Dietrich chained to a wagon, he released him, then rode over to the area where the naked, dead knights lay piled high. Trembling, he climbed down from his horse, wept, and gave orders to slaughter everyone they had captured. The native Prussians tried to stop him, saying that they wanted to keep the captives to exchange for their own people who had been taken prisoner. Dietrich told them not to worry, that God would still give them many good prisoners that day, and he watched as they slaughtered the men in chains. Pressing the pursuit hard, he did take another hundred prisoners before nightfall, but Ladislas and Casimir rode even faster – they understood well the consequences of falling into the marshal's hands at this time. They had fought well and bravely, and they considered it no disgrace to flee when continuing the fight with broken and exhausted units would be useless. Possession of the battlefield was not as important as the victory they had already won.

When the fighting came to an end, all that remained was to bury the dead. The bishop of Kujavia sent men to put the corpses into mass graves, during which process his workers counted 4,187 bodies. Immediately thereafter he built a chapel where visitors could pray for the souls of those who had fallen. The battlefield became a pilgrimage site for patriotic Poles, a shameful memory for Germans. One crusader poet ended his history at this point in the narrative without describing the battle.

It was Easter of 1332 before Luther was ready to seek revenge, but by that time his preparations were awesome. He not only had many mercenaries, but he had also recruited crusaders, some of whom came from England to participate in this war. After two weeks of siege he captured Brzesc, then Inowrocław, and finally all of northern Kujavia. Ladislas struck back in August but without effect. Then he sued for a truce to last until mid-1333, by which time Ladislas was dead.

✠

Peace Talks

Casimir was hurriedly crowned in Gniezno before the pope could raise objections to the coronation. Trouble came not from the papacy, but from Casimir's mother, who was unwilling to relinquish her royal honours to Aldona, Casimir's popular Lithuanian wife. Casimir, however, was firm – this was a matter of a royal prerogative. Aldona was crowned beside him and his mother withdrew to a convent.

With Ladislas no longer a factor, Casimir was able to open peace talks. He and the grand master agreed to ask Charles Robert of Hungary and John of Bohemia to arbitrate their differences, the former being favourable to Polish interests, the latter to Prussian. It was at this time that Casimir displayed fully those diplomatic talents whereby he later earned the title 'the Great'. First, he shrewdly worked on the mutual jealousies of the Wittelsbachs in Brandenburg and the Luxemburgs in Bohemia, promising Louis of Brandenburg his young daughter in marriage. Then he broke up strong domestic resistance to his 'pro-German' policies. He did not find it difficult to persuade the capricious John of Bohemia to abandon his Silesian wars and take up new adventures.

In the autumn of 1335 Casimir, John, and Charles Robert met in Visegrad in Hungary, a magnificent palace overlooking the Danube, for one of the most famous conferences of the middle ages. For weeks they mixed memorable spectacle with hard negotiating. In November a delegation of the Teutonic Knights arrived to present demands that Casimir renounce his claims to West Prussia. Since Luther of Braunschweig had died on a journey to dedicate the new cathedral in Königsberg, this delegation had been sent

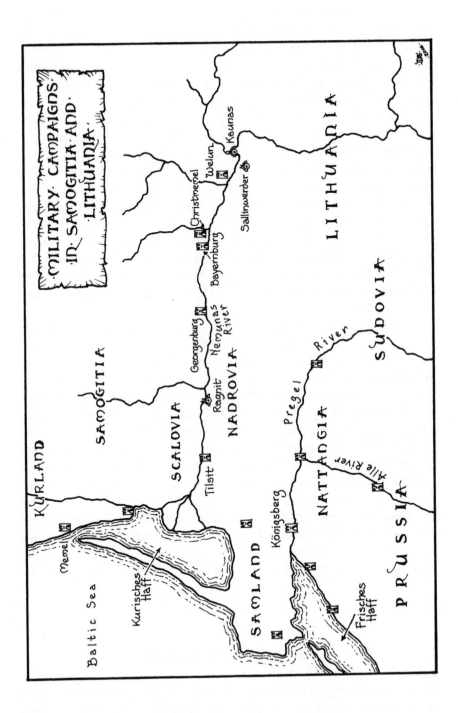

MILITARY CAMPAIGNS IN SAMOGITIA AND LITHUANIA

Baltic Sea

KURLAND

Memel

SAMOGITIA

Kurisches Haff

SCALOVIA

Tilsit

Georgenburg

Nemunas River

Ragnit

NADROVIA

Christmemel

Welun

Bayernburg

Kaunas

Sallinwerder

LITHUANIA

SUDOVIA

Pregel River

Königsberg

SAMLAND

NATTANGIA

Alle River

Frisches Haff

PRUSSIA

by the new grand master, Dietrich von Altenburg. Dietrich's Saxon ancestry was almost as illustrious as Luther's. A youngest son having to choose among the various careers available in the church, he selected one with a military order. Castellan at Ragnit, then advocate of Samland, and finally marshal, he was a capable commander with only one blot on his record, the battle at Plowce, and he wanted revenge for that defeat.

Neither side yielded much during the talks. Although the Teutonic Knights made significant concessions, exceeding their instructions, the mediators were unimaginative: they proposed a return to the *status quo ante bellum*. King John abandoned his claims to the Polish throne, thus invalidating his grants of West Prussia to the Teutonic Knights. Casimir, who wanted peace in the north so that he could concentrate on other frontiers, offered one significant two-edged concession: he offered to grant West Prussia to the grand master as a gift from the Polish crown, implying that the territory was still his to give away. This was at least a step toward an agreement. The two parties were ready to stop hostilities, but the talks went no further than Dietrich's promise to leave Kujavia and Casimir's promise to obtain his subjects' renunciation of West Prussia.

Casimir found he could not carry out his promises. First the dukes of Masovia advocated rejecting the settlement. Then Casimir's nobles refused to ratify the treaty, and finally the pope insisted that legatine rulings giving West Prussia and Culm to Poland be honoured. The grand master doubted that this had all happened without Casimir having exercised some influence. So he contacted King John, who revived certain Silesian issues that had been left unresolved. For the meantime, Dietrich garrisoned the castles in Kujavia, but he left the Polish administrators in place, since he had no plans to occupy that province permanently. In contrast, he garrisoned the castles in Dobrin and Płock more securely, since this was the best way to keep Polish raiders distant from Culm.

Although the crusading lords returning from Prussia in March of 1337 were entertained by Casimir (giving King John an opportunity to propose an end to the wars), it was not until after 1340, when Casimir's plans to lead his armies south-east toward Kiev were fully matured, that serious peace talks began.

✠

Samogitian Operations

Meanwhile, the pagans in Samogitia now had to defend themselves against attacks from the north as well as the east and south. The Livonian Knights were striking across the wilderness barrier from Memel, Goldingen, Mitau, Riga, and Dünaburg. This was a bitter war, with no quarter asked or given.

The ferocity of the campaigns can be seen in the fighting around a small castle not far from Kaunas. In February of 1336 Louis von Wittelsbach brought a crusading force from Brandenburg that included many Austrian and French knights, a force so large that over 200 ships were required to transport the equipment. Duke Louis expected that his siege of the earth and timber fort would be short and the 4,000 refugees and all the herds and personal possessions would soon be his, but when the pagans saw that the crusaders would soon storm the ramparts they lit a huge fire and began to throw all their possessions into the inferno, then strangled their wives and children and threw the corpses into the bonfire. They did this in the expectation that when they went to their equivalent of Valhalla, they would be accompanied by all their worldly goods and their families. The Christians' reaction to this was at first disbelief. Then, enraged at being robbed of their rightful booty, they recklessly began storming the fortifications, heedless of the costs incurred by failing to first break greater holes in the walls. The Christians prevailed by their superior numbers but not without heavy losses. The pagan chief, a heroic figure named Marger, smashed many heads before he saw that his own capture was imminent. At the last moment he fled down into a cellar where he had hidden his wife. Swinging his sword, he cut her into pieces and then thrust the weapon into his own belly. The crusaders were able to take few prisoners who could be made into serfs.

Louis von Wittelsbach then began construction on a castle on the Marienburg island near Welun, hoping to prepare the way for an even greater expedition the next year. When he realised that he would be unable to complete his task before his supplies were depleted, he burned the half-finished fort and retreated. During the next winter, in 1337, King John and Duke Heinrich of Bavaria appeared with forces from Bohemia, Silesia, Bavaria, the Palatinate, Thuringia, the Rhineland, Holland, and even Burgundy; and the Teutonic Knights came with the militias of Nattangia and Sambia. The weather was extraordinarily warm, so that boats could be used to transport the army up the Nemunas. After taking two forts near Welun, they built an earth and timber castle opposite the ruins of Christmemel and named it Bayerburg (Beierburg) in honour of the Bavarian duke. Bayerburg became a base for raids and a way station for larger expeditions headed for central Lithuania or north into Samogitia. Gediminas, knowing that he had to destroy this strategic castle or face dangerous attacks with little warning, besieged it for twenty-two days that June without success. As he retreated with heavy losses, the garrison sallied out to bear off the siege weapons and mount them on their own walls.

King John was not present at the conclusion of this expedition. He had caught a cold that settled in his eye and then became infected. The ailment became worse on his way home. He allowed a French doctor to treat him in Breslau (Wrocław), but became so angry at his bungling that he had the man drowned in the Oder River; in Prague he consulted an Arabian doctor, but without obtaining a cure. When the infection spread to the other eye, he was henceforth totally sightless. Blindness, however, far from dampening the king's chivalric ambitions, spurred him on to new deeds of valour. If anything, John's disability enhanced his reputation. Nor did it hinder him either in war or in diplomacy. Before he left Königsberg he borrowed 6,000 florins for expenses he would incur in negotiating with Casimir, and he worked at that task throughout his worst illness.

Casimir was ready for peace. Aldona had died in May after a long illness, without ever producing a son. Although Casimir had distracted himself with numerous love affairs, these would not provide the male heir his kingdom needed. War would distract him from the pressing business of arranging a marriage with some important family, and therefore he accepted a truce with the Teutonic Order. As it happened, Casimir was extremely unlucky in his married life. He had hoped to marry John's daughter, Margarete, but she died literally on the eve of the wedding in Prague. Casimir then hurried into an alliance with the unattractive heiress Adelheid of Hessen, whom he quickly sent into the country and refused to see again. Unable to obtain a divorce from the pope, it was obvious that the king would have no legitimate son.

The Teutonic Knights were unable to take advantage of Casimir's preoccupation in these years to mount a great expedition into Samogitia. Only small armies came to Prussia and those were hampered by bad weather. In the winter of 1339, for example, a count of the Palatinate led an attack on Welun, but after enduring extremely cold weather for four days he returned to Königsberg. Some Lithuanians were surrendering, accepting fiefs in Prussia; many more probably believed that the crusade would end soon, in a Christian victory.

✠

More Papal Investigations

Major expeditions were rare after 1340, partly because of events in the Holy Roman Empire, partly because substantial troops had to be stationed on the Polish front. The grand master accepted this as an unhappy but unavoidable fact. He could not make concessions to either the papacy or the Polish monarch, especially not when they seemed to be working together. When the legate's hearings were held in Warsaw in 1338 they followed the traditional course: the Poles brought forth a host of witnesses, while the Teutonic Knights boycotted the sessions. As before, the grand master asked the Dominicans, Franciscans, and Cistercians to write letters describing his order as a 'wall before the house of the Lord' and saying that the Teutonic Knights were given zealously to the performance of divine worship, proper habits, friendliness, observation of the rules of discipline, and so forth. But those letters were not to the point, and the hearings were.

The grand master said that the emperor, Louis IV, had forbidden him to answer any complaints raised before the pope, but that excuse carried more weight in Germany than in Avignon, where a former inquisitor sat on the papal throne. The result was that in 1339 a legate ordered the Teutonic Knights to return West Prussia, Culm, Kujavia, Dobrin, and Michelau to the Polish king, and to pay him 194,500 Marks in damages. This was an almost unimaginable sum.

Although the pope had summoned the grand master to Avignon to explain his conduct, he relented when Dietrich wrote that he was needed in the east to meet an imminent Tatar attack. The holy father urged the Teutonic Knights to continue their efforts to protect Christendom, and praised their 'defence of the house of Israel, religious enthusiasm, morals, strong enforcement of its rules, and its maintenance of the peace'. Thereafter it was easier for the pope to make additional concessions. His interest, in contrast to his predecessors, was in reforming clerical orders, not in destroying them. He realised that enforcement of the legate's verdict would have crippled the military order, and since he was committed to the crusade against the pagans he could not allow the principal bearer of the cross in the Baltic to be ruined. He therefore ordered a new commission to hold more hearings and urged the parties to compromise. Serious negotiations became possible after Dietrich von Altenburg died in 1342. Only when all the personalities had passed from the scene could new leaders seek an end to a conflict that no one could win.

✠

Peace with King Casimir

Relatively little is known about the early career of Ludolf König, who was elected grand master in June of 1342. A native of Lower Saxony who had been stationed in Prussia (a rarity in itself, because knights from the Low German language regions were generally assigned to Livonia), he had been master of the robes and grand commander. His policy of seeking peace with King Casimir was crowned with success within a year.

The 1343 Peace of Kalish was based on three propositions: firstly, the dukes of Masovia and Kujavia (who were possible heirs of Casimir, should he not produce a male heir) renounced all claims to West Prussia; secondly, Duke Bogusław of Pomerania, Casimir's son-in-law and therefore another likely heir, promised to see that the peace treaty was upheld no matter who inherited the throne; and thirdly, Casimir obtained from the cities and greater nobles of Poland oaths to maintain the peace and recognise the validity of the treaty. Ludolf, in his turn, promised to surrender Masovia and Kujavia.

Pomp and ceremony ended twenty years of war. Soon a chronicler could write, 'The pope finally lifted the interdict he had hung over Prussia.' The Peace of Kalish ended hostilities between the two greatest Roman Christian powers in North-East Europe. Although the peace was not to be permanent, it was as final as could be expected. There were no fundamental reasons for the parties to quarrel again. The Teutonic Knights wanted to move north-east against the Lithuanians, while King Casimir planned to advance south-east against the Tatars. The lands lying between them, Masovia and Kujavia, remained in the possession of minor Piast princes who were usually more or less neutral.

With this era of warfare behind them – an era that too many historians assume represents the entirety of the century, rather than three decades – the Teutonic Knights reopened the crusade against the Samogitians. This time they had no interference from the Franciscans, the order most sympathetic to heretical and non-Christian views. This was because about the time of Gediminas' death, 1340–1, two Franciscan friars were martyred in Vilnius. From that time until 1387 the Franciscans do not seem to have been in the Lithuanian capital.

Almost unnoticed, the Teutonic Knights had used the presence of the duke of Bavaria on crusade in 1337 to petition for an imperial grant of three small frontier territories.* That, in addition to the early grant from King Mindaugas in 1257, seemed to confirm the order's right to conquer Samogitia. Now all the grand master had to do was to attract a sufficient number of crusaders to assist his forces. He found that the way to do this was by making a greater appeal to the cult of chivalry.

---

* Some historians have interpreted this document as a grant of all of Russia and Lithuania. This is unlikely – the Teutonic Order was ambitious, but it was also extremely realistic.

✠

The Cult of Chivalry in Prussia

Popes Clement VI, Innocent IV, and Urban V restored some measure of public respect for the Church. They abandoned the long constitutional arguments over the imperial election and combated nepotism and corruption. Also, they gave more support to the crusades and ceased to harass the Teutonic Order about Riga and Danzig.

Within a short time Western crusaders were flocking to Prussia in greater numbers than to other contemporary crusades. The attraction was the opportunity to participate in elaborate feasts and hunts while simultaneously striking a blow against the enemies of Christ; and even that at reasonable cost and in relative comfort. In 1345 King John and his son, Charles of Moravia, appeared, accompanied by King Louis of Hungary, the duke of Bourbon, the counts of Holland, Schwarzenburg, and Holstein, and the Hohenzollern count of Nuremberg. Such an imposing collection of notables could not have been found anywhere else in Europe. While, strictly speaking, it is an exaggeration to say that Prussia became the showplace of the bored chivalry of Europe, for the period 1345–90 that judgement is not completely unfair.

This chivalry also represents a fundamentally new cast of characters. Within a short time William of Holland and John of Bohemia would be dead. When Charles of Moravia became king of Bohemia in 1346, and then Holy Roman emperor the following year, he would have no time for more crusading; nor could Louis leave his Hungarian domains again. In short, the next grand master would be forced to turn from recruiting a few great lords at intervals in favour of attracting many minor nobles for smaller annual forays. Chivalry was the device he used to lure them east.

✠

The Age of Chivalry

The Teutonic Knights had changed greatly in the four decades between 1310 and 1350. Fame and wealth, and greater contacts with the homeland, had made a profound impact on their way of life. They had the financial resources to live like lords at the very moment that chivalry was entering an era of extravagance and luxury beyond previous imagination. Moreover, competition with Casimir of Poland stirred them to win friends among the great lords of Europe, and the crusade in Samogitia required that they recruit widely among the lesser lords. Eventually they came to believe that their crusading goals could best be achieved if they put less stress on monkish values and more on chivalric ones. At this same moment they found in Winrich von Kniprode a leader who could bring all the strands of chivalry together. Consequently, the era from 1350 to 1400 became the spiritual and moral apex of the Baltic Crusades; but its hallmark was worldly display.

In contrast to the chivalric pageantry of France and England, this was a completely male activity. The Teutonic Knights had a few female members, but those were nuns who worked in the hospital and none, as far as we know, were of noble birth; thus they were completely unsuited to helping entertain at drinking bouts. The Teutonic Order's chivalry celebrated the virtues associated with war against the foes of Christ and Lady Mary.

Whereas the previous hundred years had seen great struggles and hard-won victories, the second half of the fourteenth century was an era of triumph, of public acclaim, and of international popularity. In part this reflected the failure of competing crusades – the Holy Land been lost, the Turks were overrunning Bulgaria and Serbia, and the Spanish *Reconquista* had been slowed by the Hundred Years' War. It was important that at least one crusade be successful, because holy war was an expression of the cult of chivalry that gave meaning to fourteenth-century noble society. Chivalry and crusading were not essential to good government or a prosperous economy, but they were important to nobles whose role in government, in economic life, and even in warfare, was declining. Chivalry was expensive and impractical, but that was one of its attractions: the new class of professionals could not afford to participate – they had to make their fortune before middle age caught up with them; minor nobles could not afford lavish gestures, nor could burghers who needed money for investments, and churchmen often advocated radically different moral and social values. Yet even these groups were attracted to a code emphasising generosity, service, honour, good manners, and gracious living. Everyone, in short, believed that society needed ideals, even unrealistic ones. Moreover, even the critics of chivalry agreed that it was necessary to defend Christendom against its enemies, and they understood that Western Christendom was better defended through victories rather than by defeats in battle. The Lithuanian *Reisen* offered both chivalry and victory, and for the many who were genuinely religious, the Church offered substantial spiritual rewards.

Perhaps this was all a reaction to the plague, that horrible flea-borne pestilence known today as the Black Death, which reduced the population of Europe by a third. As entire families perished, the heirs had more money to spend, and they were less inclined to save for the future. 'Eat, drink, and be merry,' was one common reaction; increased spirituality was another. The crusade to Prussia combined both.

Although the numbers of crusaders at this time never equalled those of earlier centuries, they were by no means a rare sight on the roads of Europe. It was no surprise for Chaucer's audience to read in the prologue to *The Canterbury Tales* the following lines:

A knight ther was, and that a worthy man
that from the time he first began
to riden out, he loved chevalrie,
trouthe and honour, fredom and curtesie.
Ful worthy was he in his lordes werre
and therto hadde he ridden, no man ferre,
as wel in cristendom as in hethenesse,
and ever honoured for his worthinesse.
At Alisandre he was whan it was wonne.
Ful often time he hadde the bord bigonne
above alle nations in Pruce.
In Lettowe hadde he reysed and in Ruce
no cristen man so often of his degree.

The *bord*, or table of honour, was well known (as was to be expected in the homeland of King Arthur), and while the greatest lords of chivalry were invited, the place of honour was not given on the basis of birth alone, but for courage in battle. Englishmen often saw the crusade as a religious pilgrimage on behalf of the Virgin Mary and St George. Knights on pilgrimage were a common sight in France, too, and in Germany. They were a special sort of pilgrim, for they did not come barefoot, practising poverty and humility, but with pomp and circumstance, and they were entertained not with prayer vigils and fasts, but with feasting and elaborate balls. The participants in this crusade were the epitome of chivalry, display, and pageant. Experienced veterans came to share the feasts and hunts, and to earn spiritual benefits that would offset mortal sins. Young squires flocked to Prussia, hoping to be dubbed a knight by a famous warrior, perhaps by a king or a duke.

✠

Chivalry in Prussian Literature

This chivalric spirit was celebrated in poetry and prose. In Prussia it had already stimulated an outpouring of literary creativity, especially between 1320 and 1345, when knights and priests composed religious and historical works of moderately high quality and significant local importance. Encouraged by two grand masters, Luther von Braunschweig and Dietrich von Altenberg, who were both authors themselves, Prussian writers produced lives of saints, translations of selected books of the Bible, and histories of the northern crusades. Composing in their native Middle High German dialects, the authors were more noted for the ambition of their poetry than for their success, but that was a shortcoming to be expected among men untrained in formal rhetoric, whose strength came more from passion and effort than from refined reflection. Although one can belittle the poetic achievement, it is more fitting to be astonished that there was any literature at all. Warfare is not usually compatible with refined literary tastes. How much easier it would have been to adopt the chivalric and spiritual creations of the homeland. Yet the fact remains that the Teutonic Order did not do so. It created a literature for its own needs.

The flowering of literary composition was brief. It had sprouted in the late thirteenth century, come to full flower before the middle of the next century, faded quickly, and died after the fateful events of 1410. Lists of the books kept in various convents and personal libraries suggest that the decline can be attributed to the authors having met the limited needs of the military order and not to an end of interest in literature. Few libraries in 1394 were large. The Marienburg collection of forty-one books in Latin and twelve in German was a respectable library for Northern Europe.

The general goal of these writers was to compose poems which encouraged readers and listeners to emulate the deeds of their predecessors. It was the customary practice in well-managed convents for everyone to eat together in silence, while one of the priests read aloud the lives of the saints, stories from the Bible, or the history of the order. Priority was given to the translation of books of the Old Testament (Judith, Esther, Esra, Nehemiah, David, Job, Macabees, and the histories) which were more suitable to a military tradition than was the New Testament. In fact, one could say without too much exaggeration that the medieval world often found the Old Testament more appealing than the New Testament. With no medieval group was this more true than with the Teutonic Order. Moses, Solomon, and David were men whom knights could understand. The rules of the judges were like those they followed every day. They easily grasped the essential elements of combat between the Lord's chosen people and their multitude of enemies.

The knights were less concerned with the New Testament. Although they were interested in Christ's message as it related to miracles, the Crucifixion, and the Last Judgement, knights could more easily imagine themselves at Armageddon. Appropriately, a prose version of the Apocalypse was among the first translations produced. Legends of the saints, especially tales of those martyred for the faith, were popular. They also celebrated a local saint, St Dorothea (d.1394 in Marienwerder) and recorded her miracles for the edification of posterity.

There was little effort to use the local literature outside the order itself. Education was the province of the bishops and canons. Priests obtained a master's degree in theology so as to qualify for advancement in the ranks of the canons and perhaps to become a bishop, and knights listened to popular epics and ballads. Humanistic education lay in the future; literature was studied as a guide to grammar, then abandoned as quickly as possible. Even so, over the years hundreds of ambitious young men from Prussia and Livonia went to study abroad, most going to Italy, where the universities were the best and most famous. Bologna attracted the largest number, although many later went to German universities established in the second half of the fourteenth century. The Teutonic Knights considered founding a university of their own in Culm, and in 1386 obtained papal permission to do so; however, they failed to follow through.

The most that can be said is that Prussia had its own backwater Scholastic Renaissance, impressive in its aspirations and accomplishments, but also very limited.

✦

Lady Mary

Noticeable by its absence was the love poetry that dominated the courts where the knights had spent their youth. That this could be suppressed so completely tells us much about the austerity of the Teutonic Knights' religious practices.

Historically the order had considered the Virgin Mary the ideal woman and had dedicated itself to her veneration. The full title of the order, it will be remembered, was the Hospital of St Mary of the Germans in Jerusalem. Thus the knights considered themselves warriors of Lady Mary. A modern literary historian found this such a strong trait that she remarked: 'It seemed, indeed, as though no Marienritter could envision a religious literary product without bringing Lady Mary into it'.

The significance of this devotion to the Virgin and a small host of other female saints (Barbara, Dorothea) is difficult to assess fully, but doubtless it was partly a sublimation of sexual drives into religious experience. The struggle to remain chaste was an unceasing one, a process that was aided by constant physical activity in the hunt and training for battle, simple food, a closely regulated daily life, attendance at church service day and night, fasts, watches, and the encouragement of personal piety connected with a devotion to the Virgin and the saints, figures that came to represent home, love, and the future life across the grave. Also, the worship of Lady Mary was the logical culmination of conventional romantic poetry, a poetry that exalted the virtues of women to the point that no mortal could live up to the model. This idealisation was easily transferred to the ultimate mother image, the mother of God. Lastly, there was the purely religious significance of the mother of God intervening to protect and save suffering mankind. The warriors of the Teutonic Order felt themselves to be suffering voluntarily on her behalf both in the austerity of their daily life and in their possible death on the battlefield.

In 1389 one Western author of crusader propaganda, Philippe de Mezières, wrote a description of the holy wars in the Baltic, using the device of a dream in which Divine Providence guided him throughout the world in the company of Queen Truth and the court ladies, Justice, Peace, and Mercy. As chivalrous literature it has some merit of its own, but its source of inspiration was France, not Prussia. It only indirectly reflected the knightly values of the Teutonic Order.

The Teutonic Knights liked secular literary works, but they favoured especially histories filled with battle, acts of valour, humorous incidents, and short reflections on God's justice and man's limited capacity to understand why He sometimes awarded victory and at other times defeat. Stories of warfare across the Samogitian frontier were detailed and explicit, offering lessons applicable to future combat.

The order's patronage of poets was generous. The Treasurer's Book at Marienburg (1399–1409) recorded numerous payments to jongleurs and fools, singers and orators, musicians and entertainers. Not only was the grand master of those years, Conrad von Jungingen, a patron of the arts, but he needed performers to entertain visitors and crusaders. However, the Treasurer's Book may reflect a later era's more secular court life better than a period fifty years earlier. Assuming its expenditures represented those of 1350 would be a questionable anachronism.

Numerous poems mention music, song, and dances. Women were not present at the entertainment provided by the order, despite a popular account by a much later historian who described Winrich von Kniprode as leading a lady into the ballroom for formal dancing. Dancing was an entertainment provided by the secular nobles and burghers in the cities where the crusaders stayed overnight on their journey to Königsberg. Troubadours were often provided by the guests themselves. Crusaders from famous courts brought their best musicians and singers to provide them with the means of increasing their own prestige while passing the long evenings of a northern winter in banquets and feasts. The internationally famed French poet, Guillaume de Machaut, was there. The Teutonic Knights had their own drummers, buglers, and pipers who played on every campaign. No intrusion into the wilderness was made without brass music and rolling drums; but that was military music, not professional entertainment. Lastly, there was music for the frequent prayers and masses. Choirs sang mass in the major convents, where order priests provided free schooling for burgher sons on the condition that they sing in religious services.

It would be well to remember that by modem standards the Teutonic Order was a pious organisation. That it combined this piety with a love of political intrigue, a delight in war, an enthusiasm for the hunt, and an enjoyment of good food and entertainment is an expression of the complexity of the mind, not its simplicity. If at various times one aspect of this complexity stands out among the documentary evidence above the others, that must be accepted with caution, because whim and luck have determined what evidence was written down and what has survived. However, the surviving literature indicates a deep religious feeling among the members of the order.

At the same time, there is evidence that a love of worldly display was becoming an increasingly dominant characteristic of the order. This evidenced itself less in the literature than in the architecture. The Teutonic Knights impressed their contemporaries more by their achievements in building than in any other way.

✠

Castles and Chivalry

The danger of serious pagan attacks in the heart of Prussia had passed by 1320, and the castles constructed over the next three decades are testimony to changing military needs. The simple square log and earth castles of the early period were replaced and enlarged, particularly in the living quarters, so that the convents became comfortable and convenient, suitable for guests as well as for the garrison. Impressive brick structures around a central court contained a dormitory, a chapel, a chapter room, a dining room, and often a small recreation area on the second floor; the private rooms of the commanding officer were generally located there as well. On the ground floor were work areas: a brewery, bakery, offices, equipment storage and repair, and the powder magazine. In the basements were storage areas, the kitchen, and the central heating plant.

The castles constructed before 1320 were designed for war and characterised by thick walls and high, stout towers. After 1350 the men who designed the castles (apparently clerics who had studied architecture) emphasised comfort and elegance. They had towers rising to a height of fifty-five metres, decorated capitals, carved archways, Gothic windows, and toilet and bathing facilities.

The showplace of Prussia was Marienburg. Karl von Trier had begun an expansion of the small rectangular castle about 1320 because the simple chapel, refectory, and dormitory were insufficient for the number of visitors who expected lodging there. His architects followed recent French designs, and later grand masters copied ideas from Avignon, where the popes were building a palace that was the wonder of the age. Karl's plan for Marienburg emphasised a central court surrounded by multi-storeyed red brick buildings. This high castle, as it was called, was fifty-two metres square, with machicolated walls and Gothic windows and doorways. The north gate was a monumental fourteen metres high, very suitable for ceremonial entrances but still practically unassailable. Around the courtyard was a two-storeyed walkway, covered for protection from the weather and decorated with columns and Gothic openings for a harmonious aesthetic effect. The buildings were four storeys high, topped with tile roofs, and so spaced that it seemed that building was piled atop building, each climbing further into the sky. In fact everywhere in the castle, inside and out, there was a successful effort to create the impression of monumentality: wall after wall, building after building, each topping the structures in front, all done in a dark red brick which gave a unity to the composition.

The low basement with broad arches created a number of large rooms for supplies, workshops, cells for a few prisoners, an iron-lined treasury vault, and the kitchen and furnace. Public offices were on the ground floor so as to be easily accessible for visitors and knights.

The convent was on the second floor, the north wing of which contained the large Mary Chapel and the chapter room. The chapel was entered through the highly decorated Golden Door (which was finished only in the fifteenth century). To provide more light for the large Gothic windows, the chapel jutted beyond the square outline of the castle. Thirty-eight metres long, ten wide, and more than fourteen high, the chapel was covered with a new form of arch: eight ribs stretched down from the boss to the corbels mounted half-way up the walls, creating a complicated and pleasing star pattern on the ceiling. Below the chapel of St Mary was the Chapel of St Anne, where the grand masters were buried.

In the chapter room, where important business was discussed, there was another striking innovation in arching, based on three narrow central pillars. The ribs formed a series of triangles, giving an air of spaciousness and ease to the room. Its pleasing proportions (2 x 2.5) further aided in setting a mood suitable for harmonious business and memorable receptions.

The architects enlarged the dormitories in the east and south wings, built day rooms, and constructed walkways to the toilets beyond the walls. The Priests' Tower soared high above the battlements, giving a magnificent view of the surrounding flat countryside and the rivers.

Winrich von Kniprode began the middle castle, a much larger but lower structure with a huge courtyard. As a visitor entered through the main gate, he saw the great refectory on the left, with a large kitchen, hospital, and rooms for guests. On the right, along the riverfront, he saw the palace of the grand master. Straight ahead was the wall and main gate of the high castle. The five-storeyed residence of the grand master was one of the most remarkable palatial homes of the Middle Ages. The Gothic decoration on the towers, built outward in successive rows of brick, with strong vertical lines in the windows and a peaked roof, caught every visitor's attention immediately. The interior, with its fantastic vaulting, lived up to the promise of the exterior. The large rooms had the feel of grace and comfort. The air of simplicity created by the plain brick and the austerity of the furnishings stood in stark contrast to the lavishness of the Gothic detail around the windows and doors; and the intricacy of the ribbing stood out all the more effectively for the puritan restraint found elsewhere.

The middle castle was no sooner completed than a lower castle was built. This addition was necessary to bring all the outbuildings inside the defensive system. Although the high and middle castles were intended to be defended separately, the whole formed a unit that was stronger than the sum of its parts. The town, which lay to the rear, had its own walls and towers, and the entire castle was protected by the river and extensive moats. The three castles covered more than eighteen hectares. The visitor approaching by water faced powerful walls extending to the narrow beach and set back just far enough that ships could not approach close enough for men to spring from the masts onto the walls. There was no true harbour, but there was a strongly fortified water gate at the landing place. The visitor coming by land passed through successive lines of defences, each more heavily defended than the last.

The very size and complexity of this bastion was useful for its effect on visiting crusaders and diplomats. The effectiveness of the whole fortification proved itself in 1410, when the castle was attacked for the first time and a few thousand men repulsed far larger numbers of Polish and Lithuanian besiegers.

Marienburg was designed for comfort. There were at least five separate bathhouses for the eighty knights, the grand master, the hospital, the servants, and the visitors. In each were hot rooms, steam rooms, and bathing tubs; and there were skilled attendants who knew how to bleed painlessly and to apply the hot towels considered essential to curing the colds so common in the wet northern climate. There were also nineteen wells lined with stone, and numerous toilet facilities. The central heating produced a room temperature of sixty-eight degrees in a modern test; probably the servants were able to do even better in the fourteenth century. There were covered walkways between all buildings so that no one needed to go into the rain or stand guard in discomfort.

As builder of this fortress, Winrich von Kniprode was able to associate his personality with it in ways that gave him fame far beyond the frontiers of the Holy Roman Empire. His successors improved upon the decoration and comfort, adding innovations as quickly as they heard of them.

✛

Chivalry and the Decorative Arts

The decorations of the palace, the chapels, and the cathedrals were not slavish copies of Italian and French models, but rather adaptations suitable to the climate and building materials available in Prussia. The lack of stone, for example, presented challenges to the sculptors who were to ornament the altars, walls, and doorways. The methods chosen were diverse: some artists applied stucco, others terracotta; a few imported limestone from Gotland; and some used linden wood. Unfortunately, few statues have survived the centuries in good condition. Moisture attacked the wood and frescoes relentlessly. Stucco and terracotta, on the other hand, have proven resistant to the damp climate. Mosaics provided interesting wall and floor decorations. Although puritan restraint discouraged portraying animals, plants, or objects, the tile floors were both aesthetically satisfying and easy to clean.

In the cathedrals and abbeys throughout Prussia there was a strong emphasis on wall painting not found in the convents of the knights. This may seem surprising, since three of the four bishoprics were staffed by priests of the order, who presumably shared the same artistic tastes as the designers of the convent chapels. However, there was an important difference. In the cathedrals one saw the strong influence of Italy, Avignon, and Bohemia, which the bishops and individual canons visited more frequently than did the knights and priests in the convents. They were apparently greatly impressed by what they saw, especially during the reign of Charles IV, when Italian artists were active in Bohemia. They wanted high-quality reproductions of

Bohemian triptychs and frescoes, altars and reliquaries. They imitated as best they could Charles' jewelled chapel at Karlstejn, with its motifs of King Arthur. They patronised artists from Cologne and other German cities as well. The Marienburg Treasurer's Book informs us that Grand Master Ulrich von Jungingen spent significant sums on sculptures, paintings, and illuminated manuscripts. Unfortunately only a few works of art of that time have survived, but if we dare extrapolate from those which did we conclude that the medieval holdings of the Prussian convents and churches must have been impressive. Where the quality was not so high, as was the case with a wall painting of a knight in a small church near Königsberg, the artist (or the patron) wrote: 'Cursed be he who criticises this painting!'

Painting was less important and therefore less innovative than architecture for several reasons. Firstly, the officers of the Teutonic Order were less interested in religious art than were their bishops. Secondly, the order was relatively puritan in its attitude toward decoration. Poverty was the first vow taken by the members, a pledge shared by the Franciscans and Dominicans, the two dominant orders in Prussia. The Cistercians, the major order in northern Poland, relied heavily upon whitewash to give a mood of simplicity and austerity to their churches. And thirdly, the cultural imperialism by which the grand masters hoped to impress visiting crusaders, neighbouring princes, and enemy chieftains was best accomplished through monumental castles, not with delicate paintings or graceful statuary (and even less with poetry and music). Painting and carving had to take a secondary role in the cultural life of the convents.

This emphasis on the military arts might have been even stronger had the rules of the order permitted tournaments. Although grand masters often ignored the letter of the rules, in this case they chose not to engage in the expensive and distracting pastime of jousting; tournaments would not have escaped papal notice, nor could they be justified as training for warfare, and would hardly enhance the reputation of the order should its best knights fall before the lances of French, English, or Polish warriors!

✠

Periodisation of Art and Architecture

The art and architecture of Prussia is simple to catalogue. There was the era 1300–50 that has been described above. A second distinct era lasted from 1400 to 1450, years of defeat and financial hardship for the Teutonic Order. Patronage in this later period came from the cities. Danzig became the cultural centre of all Prussia, followed by Thorn, Marienburg, Elbing, and

Königsberg. A third era, 1500–50, reflected the dominance of humanistically trained scholars and the Protestant Reformation. This was also the period that saw the loss of many Gothic treasures. Riots accompanying the abandonment of Roman Catholicism ended with many of the finest paintings and sculptures of the fourteenth century destroyed in bonfires.

Further losses of cultural treasures came in the Thirty Years' War, when Swedes carried away everything they liked, and during the wars of Frederick the Great and Napoleon. General neglect was perhaps even more destructive. Restoration efforts by nineteenth-century nationalists were often ill-conceived, telling us more about their artistic tastes than about the Middle Ages. Lastly, World War Two brought devastation to many castles, churches, and cities; much that survived was evacuated from Prussia and never returned. Happily, Polish restorers have made modern Danzig (Gdańsk) and Marienburg (Malbork) into tourist centres.

✙

Coinage an Expression of Chivalry

The art of the mintmaster made its first great strides during the reign of Winrich von Kniprode. Although the Teutonic Order had pursued a careful monetary policy for over a century, this had been confined to assuring that the various civic mints produced a uniform currency of 720 pence to the Mark. Many foreign pennies circulated in the cities, and only slowly did the order produce large quantities of its own *bracteats* (as the thin silver coins were called, a coin impressed so strongly on one side as to carry the pattern onto the reverse). Although we cannot determine the age or provenance of the majority of the *bracteats*, we know that mints existed in Culm, Thorn, Elbing, and other cities. Presumably those *bracteats* showing the order's cross on a shield reflected a deliberate effort to publicise the crusade. That seems to be part of Winrich von Kniprode's currency reform, which introduced the *Schilling* in about 1350. The *Schilling* was a large coin with the grand master's shield and his name on the face, and a crusader's cross on the reverse. A beautiful coin, minted twenty to the Mark, it was a propaganda triumph for the order, a visible reminder of the wealth of the state.

It comes as a surprise that the grand masters did not put their personal coats of arms on their coins, as the Livonian Masters did. That seems to be a concession to tradition, to avoid personal ostentation and sinful pride, and perhaps to emphasise the motto on the reverse, that each coin was 'money of the Teutonic Order in Prussia' and, therefore, could be relied upon.

✠

The Decline of Chivalry

Winrich von Kniprode lived at the right time to acquire a great international reputation. His era had honoured individual heroes such as the Black Prince, Bertrand du Guesclin, and Sir John Chandos, all of whom had served in the Hundred Years' War. Perhaps contemporaries had honoured those knights because there were so few heroes left. New tactics introduced during the fighting between England and France had made it more difficult to become famous, with archers and gunners shooting down potential champions at long distance. War had become a serious business where knights were actually killed rather than held for ransom, where low-born soldiers thirsted more for booty than for glory. Even in the tournament professionals were discouraging amateurs from participating. Developments in Italy were just as disturbing. Towns and princes were hiring mercenaries to fight their wars, and many noble knights became no better than military merchants peddling their wares and services; and, because mercenaries wanted to live to earn a salary later, they avoided pitched battles and refused to defend inadequate fortresses to the utmost. Where was the hero who spent carelessly, indulged in gay song and banquets, and entered light-heartedly into battle against heavy odds, with little thought of the morrow so long as glory could be earned now?

The medieval concept of chivalry was declining as the calendar approached 1400. Where it still flourished it was becoming exaggerated and unreal, a reflection of literature, not of life. It did not matter that chivalry had rarely existed outside the minds of a few kings and poets; it had remained real to nobles and commoners who honoured its ideals and aspirations. Those men had dreamt of a great crusade in which their deeds would extinguish everything that was shoddy and commonplace in their lives, and would leave behind stories of valour to be remembered for all time.

The best a crusader could do now was to make an armed pilgrimage to Spain or Prussia, where at least the spirit of the crusades was still alive. Even if the goal lacked the emotional impact or the religious importance of reconquering the Holy Sepulchre, there was at least some satisfaction in striking a blow against enemies of the cross and protecting endangered Christians from strange and powerful foes. The Spanish crusade had the advantage of being easily reached by knights from Italy, France, and the British Isles. But the Spanish hit-and-run tactics were uncongenial to northerners. The tragic fate of the Scots bearing the heart of Robert de Bruce against the Moors was well known. Advancing steadily, the Scots had found themselves abandoned by their allies and surrounded by a sea of Moslem light cavalry. This was a weighty argument in favour of campaigning in Prussia.

The Teutonic Knights were fortunate in the growing wealth and trade of Prussia. Policies to encourage immigration and trade were now paying handsomely in taxes and cheap produce. Winrich von Kniprode never lacked for money to build great castles, to fill banquet halls with furniture and food, or to hire the services of entertainers. He offered the visitor an opportunity to meet great men from all parts of Europe, even dukes and heirs to crowns. A young knight might make valuable friendships. Most of all, he would return home with exciting stories of men and deeds to enliven the long winter evenings for decades to come. If the forays into Samogitia were manhunts, they were hunts for armed men of exceptional skill and tenacity. It was an honour to fight and defeat such noteworthy and valiant foes. Lastly, Winrich offered young noblemen a way to serve God by defending Christians against barbaric foes who threatened Germans and native converts with death and slavery. This world was slowly passing away. A new and more practical society was emerging.

The chivalric tradition was not altogether for the good. As knights succumbed to secular temptations, grand masters issued repeated injunctions against modish dress, against long hair, and against riding around the countryside to hunt or frequent inns. Nevertheless, despite such efforts and in spite of the ban on private property and money, individual knights acquired fur coats, pointed hats, and buckled shoes. Some even decorated their scabbards and painted their shields. The knights' inability to maintain the outward traditions of their monastic calling was only a reflection of their inward failings.

Moreover, class traditions made the Teutonic Knights feel they were better than their subjects. As they behaved arrogantly toward their citizens (slighting their contributions to the crusade, raising new taxes, and quarrelling over the extent of their self-government), they slowly exhausted their moral capital and left behind a reputation for haughtiness and ambition. Among the nobles of the chivalric tradition, however, these very characteristics were proof of their superiority and worth. The Teutonic Knights were more concerned with the opinion of the visiting nobles. What their subjects thought, and what bourgeois historians of the future might write, were of little importance. Courage, prowess, and honour were all that really mattered.

✠

The International Crusade

Prussia was easy to reach by either land or sea, but it lay at sufficient distance to escape the turmoil of Western political struggles. Neither the Hundred

Years' War, the vicissitudes of the empire, the advance of the Turks, nor the troubles of the papacy disturbed it. It was an island of peace with a war on one coast (Samogitia), and it was winning that war with the help of the constant stream of crusaders from the West.

No longer was this just a German crusade, as it had been after the mid-thirteenth century when armies of Polish knights ceased to participate. Many Englishmen came, as did an Orsini duke from Naples and numerous French princes. Although the kings of Poland abstained, Poles from Silesia and Masovia came, as did Bohemians, some Hungarians, and a few Scots. It was indeed an international crusade.

The ceremony of knighthood lay near the heart of this crusading ardour. Each expedition into Samogitian forests and swamps was an opportunity for poor squires to win their spurs honourably and cheaply, and for rich nobles to earn respect by lavish hospitality and courage. The Austrian poet Peter von Suchenwirt described one expedition to seek knighthood in 1377. He concluded his narrative with this exhortation: 'One counsel I give to noble folk: he who will become a good knight, let him take as companion Lady Honour and St George. "Better knight than squire!" Let him bear that word in his heart, with will and with good deeds; so shall he defy slander, and his name shall be spoken with honour.'

Many squires took that admonition to heart. So did experienced campaigners. Prussia became a major showplace for fourteenth-century chivalry, visited by knights from Scotland, England, France, and Italy, men who had seen every monarch and tournament champion. Such knights came back for a second, third, and fourth crusade.

✠

International Popularity

Polish assertions that the Teutonic Order was evil in its intents, practices, and theology eventually lost credibility with mainstream churchmen and the Western public by the mid-1350s. Partly this was due to the hyperbole of the era, in which the slightest fault would be magnified into a chasm. But more importantly, it ran against the experience of eyewitnesses. Knights and prelates who had been in Prussia and Samogitia, who had seen holy war first-hand, who had met clerics and nobles while travelling across Germany and Poland, were able to make judgements for themselves. Their verdict was almost unanimously in favour of the crusaders.

The situation would be different in the 1400s. First of all, the crusade was effectively suspended from the 1390s on. Lithuania had been converted to

Christianity and tied closely to the Polish state; and Samogitia was occupied by the Teutonic Order. Secondly, the advance of the Turks into the Balkans diverted crusading energies in that direction; that was a field in which Polish participation was potentially important. Thirdly, the balance of power was slowly shifting, and Poland, despite finding it hard to believe that the long nightmare of disunity and weakness was at an end, emerged from the battle of Tannenberg (1410) as the dominant power of the region. Public opinion always respects power.

8

The Lithuanian Challenge

Lithuanian Expansion

In the mid-thirteenth century Teutonic Knights had brought about the conversion of a deadly enemy, Mindaugas, and crowned him as the first king of
Lithuania. They did this in the traditional manner for the region, by persuading him that it was to his advantage to have the crusaders as allies rather
than as enemies. With help from the Teutonic Knights – or, more to the
point, perhaps, without the Teutonic Knights striking into his territories
from the north and west – Mindaugas could expand his realm into Tatar-
threatened Rus'ian lands in a wide arc from his north-east to his south-west.

For Mindaugas, the only unpleasant aspect to the reversal of religious orientation – other than having to explain his change of heart to his priests and
boyars – was to have a few drops of water sprinkled on his head and having
to listen to an occasional strange ritual with exotic music. Being already
monogamous and not much impressed by any religious doctrine, pagan or
Christian, he changed his behaviour and attitudes very little. This scepticism
was not a good sign for the Teutonic Knights – conversions based solely on
Realpolitik are rooted in sandy soil, and in the early 1260s Mindaugas began
to see more disadvantages in being a Christian than advantages.
Consequently he returned to paganism with about as much enthusiasm as
he had embraced Catholicism – it seemed the best way to placate those
nobles who admired the way the Samogitian pagans were crushing crusader
armies. The change of heart saved Mindaugas only a short while, however,
his enemies assassinating him anyway, but his rejection of Roman
Catholicism altered the seemingly predetermined history of the Baltic
region. His successors were to remain pagan for more than a century, largely
because their important subjects believed that the native gods brought

victories in battle, but also because their Rus'ian subjects were more willing to tolerate pagans ruling over them temporarily than to accept Roman Catholic help. Gediminas (b.1257, grand prince 1316–41) was an eminently practical ruler, and so were his many descendants; perhaps nowhere else in Europe did a dynasty exist which operated more consistently by the rules of self-interest than did these talented and resourceful men. They were not about to put their Rus'ian policies at risk by conversion to Roman Catholicism, but they were quite willing to allow Western Christians to believe what they wanted – that only the Teutonic Order's aggressions stood between them and salvation.

The Lithuanian rulers were called grand princes, a term familiar to their Rus'ian subjects. But the theoretical title meant little. Most followers and retainers gave their loyalty to the Gediminid dynasty on the basis of family ties and the assurance of offices and rewards, not on the basis of ancient tradition or religion. Many Lithuanian nobles had undergone Orthodox baptism in order to placate the Rus'ians in the towns where they had been stationed as rulers and garrison commanders; many had married Christian women, Orthodox and Catholic alike. But others remained pagan. Without any doubt, paganism had some strong attractions, not the least of which was its assurance that Lithuania would continue to be ruled by a Lithuanian. Also, the adherence to paganism was the only way to guarantee that the independent-minded Samogitians would recognise a ruler from the central hill country of Lithuania – they would reject a weak Christian ruler as assuredly as they had rejected the powerful Mindaugas. Paganism was not a dying religion in Samogitia. To the contrary, it was held with all the fervour of un-educated and untravelled fundamentalists of any religion today.

When the pagans had returned to power they had burned the cathedral in Vilnius, covered its ruins with sand, and erected a shrine to Perkunas over it. This shrine to the thunder god probably had the same dramatic impact on the pagans as the Christian cathedral it replaced had made earlier. Traditionally, pagans conducted their ceremonies in the sacred forests, which perhaps explains why this masonry structure was left open to the sky with twelve steps leading up to a huge altar. There the priests may have placed a wooden statue of the god and maintained an eternal flame. This suggests an evolving paganism, a dynamic religion which adopted some of the more popular features of its competition.

The Gediminid princes prided themselves on being secular and tolerant for their day. They were superstitious, but they had no desire to force their paganism on others, or even to offer it to them. The grand princes allowed Franciscan friars to maintain a chapel in Vilnius for Roman Catholic merchants and emissaries, only once turning them into martyrs. Even more toleration was granted Orthodox churchmen – for the practical reason that many of their subjects were Orthodox. Some of their Tatar bodyguards were Moslems who lived in their own protected communities. The princes, therefore, followed a policy of nominal paganism that guaranteed extensive toleration of group traditions. This survived as late as World War Two in eastern and east central Europe, with governments negotiating with the leaders of minority groups who then enforced the laws and edicts issued from above.

This practicality should never mislead us into thinking that medieval group toleration is the same as modern tolerance for individual choices, or even that it is the same as Moslem toleration, which is too often only permission to live as second-class citizens. It was generous for its time, and that is surely praise enough.

✠

Crusader Efforts to Revitalise Holy War

Division in the crusader ranks brought an end to the string of successes that had marked the end of the thirteenth century. Once the Prussian master had control of the wilderness marking the frontiers with Lithuania and Masovia, once the Livonian master had conquered the Semgallians, each reverted to a defensive strategy. These were responses to local conditions: Poland was reuniting, Riga and the archbishop of Riga were becoming restive, and the papacy was in turmoil following the kidnapping of Boniface VIII and the transfer of the curia to Avignon. The Holy Roman Empire was insufficiently stable for the grand master to be able to establish the kind of close personal relationship that had existed with Ottokar of Bohemia. Intelligent powerful dukes and archbishops stayed at home to await the outcome of events.

As a result, the Teutonic Knights were unable to bring together the coalitions that had made victory possible only a few years before. The Rigans and the archbishop were now enemies, and the German nobles in Livonia as well as the native tribes were concerned about the civil war there. Crusaders from Germany and Poland had not come to Prussia for years. The Masovian and Galician-Volhynian dukes who had shared the rigours of the Sudovian campaign were not interested in fighting north of the Nemunas (Memel) River. As a result of all these developments, the Teutonic Knights were unable to make the show of force in the Samogitian wilderness that was necessary to suppress the pagans there who were supporting rebellions in Prussia and Livonia.

The Samogitians eventually threw in their lot with Duke Vytenis

(1295–1316). (They did so literally, since no decision was ever reached without a priest casting lots to ask advice from the gods.) Vytenis had been rampaging through Livonia. Now the united pagan armies struck the Christianised natives in Semgallia, Kurland, and Samland, and the leaders of the Teutonic Knights could do little to stop them. The problem became so serious that after 1300 every grand master had come north to investigate. Each had concluded that the problem was not military, but political. The solution was to remove the archbishop of Riga and his citizens from the enemy coalition. Knowing that this could be done better from Avignon than Marienburg, the grand masters had returned repeatedly to the Holy Roman Empire to confer with the leading political and ecclesiastical figures.

Meanwhile, patrols guarded the Prussian frontier against incursions, and minor raids across the wilderness kept some pagans at home to guard their villages and fields. The main base for Prussian patrols was at Ragnit, on the left bank of the Nemunas about sixty miles from the river's mouth and almost equidistant from Königsberg on the Pregel River and the castle at Memel, guarding the mouth of the Kurland bay and the coastal road to Livonia. Those three points formed a rough triangle defining the Christian presence in the river valley. Supported by another strong castle just down-river at Tilsit, the garrison at Ragnit had borne the brunt of the border war. For attacks across the wilderness, the castellan at Ragnit called on the advocates of Samland and Nattangia and their native militias. The method of warfare was to steal cattle, burn homes and crops, and kidnap everyone who did not hide or die in resisting capture. By the standards of the time this was not immoral. Instead, in an era when fortifications were almost impregnable and troops had to be paid in booty, wearing down the enemy was the only practical strategy. Moreover, the crusaders justified whatever brutal acts they and their subjects committed as necessary to achieve a worthy goal, the end of raids on Christian lands and the extirpation of paganism.

Similar patrols watched the paths along Livonia's southern and eastern frontiers from bases at Goldingen, Mitau, Dünaburg, Rositten, Marienhausen, and Neuhausen. The Livonian master had resettled the Semgallians to the north, around Mitau. Their lands reverted to forest and swamp, a desolate region patrolled by experienced and ruthless scouts from both sides. No one else entered the region. For the Livonian master to communicate with Prussia in the wintertime, he had to send riders across Kurland, then down the coast to Memel. Handing a message to one of the many captains who sailed from Livonian ports was risky because Riga was in revolt at this time, and merchants tended to stick together; in any case, the seas were only open in the summer.

Preachers of the crusades over the years had told Christians that the enemies of the cross were foes of both God and man. Therefore, pagans, Saracens, schismatics, and heretics had no right to exist. They were a danger to Christendom and had to be destroyed, like sheep when infected with disease, to save the healthy ones. Whatever doubts may have existed were quickly stilled by the Church. Churchmen declared that any war between Christians and infidels was a just war, a proper means of protecting and expanding Christendom. Citing St Augustine, they declared that the entire life of pagans was sinful, regardless of the goodness or evil of their actions, because everything they did was done without knowledge of the eternal truths of God. To be sure, pagans should not be forced to accept Christianity. They were to be permitted to survive, like the Jews, in hope that they or their descendants might eventually be converted and saved. In the meantime, pagans should not be permitted any role in society that might cause Christians to admire them. Therefore Christians should strip them of property and power, of pride and prestige. From this it followed that the Samogitian pagans had no right to an independent state, especially not one in which they persecuted Christians and hindered missionary activity. It was on the basis of that argument that the Emperor Frederick II had issued the Golden Bull of Rimini in 1226, giving Prussia and other pagan territories to the Teutonic Knights, and that Pope Alexander IV (1254–61) had awarded them everything they could conquer. Moreover, since pagans were dangerous enemies of Christendom, often raiding Poland, Prussia, and Livonia, popes had authorised a perpetual crusade and emperors had urged nobles and knights to take the cross against them. It was the pious duty of Christians everywhere to assist in the defeat of dangerous heathens. The Dominican friars, preachers of every crusade and members of the most prestigious order of the time, assured potential volunteers that once crusaders had cut down the enemies of God, then Christ himself would hurl their souls into hellfire.*

Still, it was easier to preach the crusade and recruit crusaders than it was to reach the Samogitians to kill them. The Samogitian branch of the Lithuanian people had immigrated into the lowlands north of the Nemunas River from the east and had not quite reached the coast. They lived in the valleys of the well-drained interior hill country, avoiding the mosquito-filled swamps and dense forests that formed a natural wilderness around them. This wilderness was almost untouched by humans, thanks to religious beliefs which incorporated forest gods and spirits into a wider pantheon, and thanks

---

* Christoph Maier, *Preaching the Crusade: Mendicant Friars and the Cross in the thirteenth century* (Cambridge University Press, 1994). Since bishops were often unable to support themselves in their Baltic dioceses, they travelled from one German bishopric to another, assisting fellow prelates in special celebrations, collecting pious donations, and preaching the crusade.

also to fear of attack from dangerous neighbours, which caused them to hew down giant trees across possible paths. This wilderness grew more dense after the arrival of the crusaders. Small raiding parties, often composed of native peoples who had suffered Lithuanian attacks for generations, annihilated isolated farmsteads, leaving few surviving settlements whose people could report incursions by larger parties of knights and native warriors; and the Samogitians, unlike the Lithuanians in the central highlands, lacked an effective system of taxation or military service that would support isolated castles as bases for scouts. Within a few years the western Samogitian communities vulnerable to attack from Memel and Kurland were abandoned and the tribesmen established new villages further inland. The unused fields soon became part of the forest. In time a vast wilderness up to ninety miles wide stretched along every frontier separating the Christian domains in Prussia and Livonia from Samogitia and Lithuania. Only a few paths led through it.

✠

Vytenis of Lithuania

By 1309 the Teutonic Knights had the situation in Livonia once more in hand. They had not defeated either the Rigans or Vytenis, but neither did they fear defeat. So secure was the situation that the Prussian master had been able to send his army into West Prussia, first to drive out the duke of Brandenburg, then to expel the Polish garrisons. By 1311 the master was ready to turn once again to Lithuania and strike at Gardinas (Grodno), a key position on the upper Nemunas that guarded the most direct routes along the waterways and paths to Volhynia and Masovia, or across the lake district to Prussia.

Vytenis was now a powerful lord. Called a king by his followers and the chroniclers of the Teutonic Knights, he was recognised only as a grand prince by the pope or emperor because they reserved royal titles for Christian princes. Vytenis had brought an end to assassination and civil war, and had sealed his power with victories in Livonia. He was a capable ruler and a wily commander. Often he would lead one army himself and send out others as diversions, so that the Teutonic Knights had to guess where the main blow would land; and, with so many routes to guard, they usually guessed wrong. Vytenis had Christian allies in the burghers and archbishop of Riga, and for their sake he occasionally made a pretext of seeking conversion. Franciscan friars at his courts in Vilnius and Trakai made his enquiries credible. Nevertheless, although he allowed his Rus'ian subjects and Roman Catholic visitors freedom of worship, he was a devout pagan; any hint of changing his religion would have increased the already great danger of assassination, and it would have stiffened Samogitian resistance to his claims to national leadership. Moreover, as a pagan, he personified the Christian fears of unpredictable and dangerous behaviour, of extraordinary cunning and deviousness. All these were qualities he must have had in abundance. He could not have ruled Lithuania without unfailing courage and a willingness to match wits and brutality with the worst of his enemies and the best of his friends. In barbaric splendour and simplicity he was a model pagan king, a worthy match for the crusaders.

The Teutonic Knights praised Vytenis' skill and courage, because they were proud to consider themselves more than a match for him. In 1311 they were given an opportunity to demonstrate their prowess. In February Vytenis made a raid into Samland and Nattangia, killing many Prussians and taking 500 captives. The crusaders knew from experience that it was almost impossible to ward off such attacks. The best that could be achieved was to organise a watch for incursions, so that the villagers could be warned to seek refuge and so the militia could hurry to its assembly points. As soon as the marshal was told of the raid, he hurried from Königsberg with his mobile forces and, gathering the militia, followed the raiders' path. He knew that raiding parties were most vulnerable immediately after the forces split up and separately returned to their homes, but he attacked while the pagans were feasting and dividing up the booty and prisoners. His victory was among the greatest of this era.

For their part, the Teutonic Order made at least one winter raid most years. Cavalry was very effective on the frozen rivers and swamps, and the Lithuanians were unable to hide in ambush in the snow as easily as among lush summer foliage. In the winter of 1311–12 six knights led 400 Nattangian militiamen through the Sudovian wilderness to Gardinas, taking a roundabout route through supposedly impassable swamps where they were lost for two days. The Lithuanians, who had patrolled all the usual paths carefully, had no warning when the Christians suddenly fell on them. The Prussians went on a rampage, burning, killing, collecting captives, and killing those who could not manage the difficult journey into exile. Then they escaped by the quickest route. Their terrible revenge for past sufferings inflamed the Lithuanians to an equally great hatred.

Nationalist historians of the modern era sometimes forget this mutual hostility of the native tribes. This desire to take revenge, to harm one's traditional foes, made it easy to raise armies, to organise raids, and to summon labourers for work on fortifications. It also led directly to terrible atrocities.

The attack on Gardinas was a direct challenge to Vytenis, whose prestige rested on his military victories and whose principal deity was a war god. In

April he pressed deep into Prussia, arriving without warning with a force estimated by a chronicler with the usual exaggeration at 8,000 men. Coming through the lake district during the period of thaw, he evaded patrols sent out by the Teutonic Knights and the dukes of Masovia, then swept up through Ermland to the castle at Braunsberg, yelling insults at the bishop on the ramparts and destroying every settlement along the coast. According to the Christian reports, he made churches a special target of his wrath, desecrating altars, tearing down crucifixes and trampling on them, handling and spitting on the consecrated wafers of the host, and then burning the buildings. In one day he carried away 1,200 captives, bound and fettered, and that evening he taunted them, asking: 'Where is your God? Why did he not help you, as our gods help us now and at other times?'

If that quote was accurate, Vytenis was rejoicing too soon. His forces were actually in very great danger. Ermland was far to the west. The deeper the penetration into the country, the more time the native militia had to assemble and the easier it was to catch up with the slow-moving, booty-laden raiders, whose path could easily be followed through the snow. At this moment the grand commander was gathering a large army at an assembly point along the route which Vytenis had to take out of the country.

Heinrich von Plötzke had dreamt of an opportunity like this for many of his fifty years. Now he had a force of eighty knights and thousands of militiamen in position to overtake the Lithuanian army. With luck he could destroy the invading force and perhaps kill or capture the king.

Vytenis was also a believer in fortune, but he understood that luck is a malleable commodity, one that can be moulded by the skilled hands of a courageous leader. When he saw the Christians approaching, he ordered his men to form a line of battle on a hill behind an improvised wall of hedges and trees. He must have thought that the Christians would hesitate to assault such a strong position, and that, if it came to a siege, he had the stolen cattle to feed his men, while the Christians could not have brought many supplies with them.

Heinrich recognised his enemy's strategy instantly. Although he would have preferred a battlefield where he could use his cavalry more effectively, he was willing to fight on foot. He ordered Gunther von Arnstein, the most heroic knight of his generation, to test the pagan defences. The probing attack failed, leaving behind forty to sixty dead, but Gunther had learned the location and strength of the enemy forces. When Heinrich heard Gunther's report, he ordered a general attack.

A crusader poet tells us that this was a moving scene: as the Christian warriors advanced into position there were cries from women and children, the returning shouts of their relatives in the militia, yells by desperate men ready for the furore of battle. The chronicle that related this scene may have been read aloud at mealtimes to teach proper attitudes to the knights and their men-at-arms. Such passages emphasising knightly deeds, courage, fairness, pity for the unfortunate, and service to the Church and Lady Mary, give us valuable insights into the mind of the crusading knight. Unfortunately, we lack a Lithuanian equivalent of this chronicle; the pagan tradition was oral, not written, and it has largely vanished.

When the entire force of Christians had formed their lines for the assault, Vytenis recognised the flags and banners of his opponents. Only then did he realise whom he was up against. Success in arms, he knew, was not a question of numbers, but of quality. The gay banners of the castellans and the grand commander's great black cross on a white field told knowledgeable pagans that they were facing the best the Teutonic Knights had. Consequently, as the attackers approached, the less bold Lithuanians (or, at least, the most discreet and prudent) began to seek their horses and ride hurriedly for home. Meanwhile, the captive women broke loose from their bonds and created confusion in the rear. Vytenis disappeared (and escaped), while thousands of his followers fell in the hand-to-hand fighting. The Christians took as booty 2,800 horses, thousands of spears and swords, reclaimed the booty and prisoners taken earlier, and took Vytenis' chamberlain captive. One chronicler wrote a hymn of victory: 'Oh, noble knights of God, God must honour you on earth and in heaven.' Heinrich commemorated the day by founding a nunnery at Thorn.

Despite what seemed to be an overwhelming victory, the battle made little impact on the general course of events because the Teutonic Knights lacked the forces to exploit it and because Vytenis had escaped. The grand prince regrouped his forces, encouraged his subjects to defend their forts resolutely, and ordered everyone to refrain from taking risks. Somewhat later, when a young castellan, Gerhard von Mansfeld, boldly rode into Lithuania, the pagans followed his small army back out of their country. Fearing an ambush, they refused his offer of formal battle, but they asked his name and warned him he would not live long if he continued to enter their country with so few men.

The fact was that significant advances could be made only by occupying key castles, and castles were difficult to capture. This was especially true in Lithuania, where the fortresses lay across a difficult wilderness, so that men, supplies, and siege engines had to be transported long distances. The easiest way to capture a castle was as ransom or by treason.

Treason worked best. As noted above, Heinrich had captured Vytenis' chamberlain, the castellan of Gardinas. If he held him for ransom, he could have demanded a small fortune or exchanged him for Lithuanian captives.

Instead, he listened to his promise to surrender Gardinas in return for his freedom. It was necessary to act quickly, however, so that he could explain his late return as the result of hiding in the woods or having lost his way. Moreover, there was no guarantee of obtaining a ransom, because Vytenis might conclude that this was a convenient excuse to eliminate a potential competitor and simply appoint a replacement. Therefore Heinrich released his prisoner on a promise to allow the crusaders to enter his castle by stealth and capture it. Not unexpectedly, the chamberlain did not keep his part of the bargain. Instead, he 'betrayed' the Christians by telling Vytenis of his bargain and arranging for an ambush of the Prussian forces near Gardinas.

Heinrich had not ignored the risks. He knew that the chamberlain might be a clever liar. We do not know what the chamberlain said to persuade the grand commander and his council, but we do know that treason was common in this era, that personal feuds were more important than clan loyalty, and that ambition often overrode personal loyalty. Moreover, the heathen code of honour emphasised keeping oaths, and Heinrich had undoubtedly extracted powerful oaths from his prisoner. For Heinrich's part, he was in a position to make handsome promises for the chamberlain's future, even to recognise him as a future ruler of Lithuania. In short, Heinrich had good reasons for trusting this pagan lord. But he had equally good reasons not to trust him too much.

Heinrich had brought his army almost to Gardinas when his scouts came upon an old man whom they put to torture until he revealed that Lithuanians were lurking near a river, waiting until half of the Christian army had crossed over before attacking. Heinrich spared the old man, as promised, and fled with his army back to safety.

Heinrich's next effort was in late May, when he called up 140 knights, a strong force of native knights and mounted militia, and 2,000 foot soldiers who probably followed a somewhat different route through the lakes, rivers, and swamps in small boats. As the mounted troops approached Gardinas through a thick forest, they came upon four scouts. Killing three, they captured the fourth and learned that nobody was aware of their approach. Quite the contrary. Vytenis was feeling so secure that he had sent the scouts as part of a group of fifty men to set up a hunting camp. Heinrich annihilated the advance force, then crossed the Nemunas River. Leaving twelve knights and the foot soldiers to guard the boats, he struck through the countryside, sparing neither age nor sex. The raiders took 700 prisoners, and of the dead they left behind 'only God knows the number'.

These victories made Heinrich von Plötzke a strong candidate to replace the deceased grand master, Siegfried von Feuchtwangen, but his bid for election failed, perhaps because of his controversial seizure of Danzig and West

Prussia, perhaps because of his domineering ways. In any case, he was unacceptable to the electors in Germany, who chose Karl von Trier as their new leader. Heinrich von Plötzke was given the consolation office of grand commander and, later, marshal.

✠

Karl von Trier targets Samogitia for attack

Karl von Trier was forty-six years old, relatively young to hold the highest office in the military order. However, Karl spoke fluent French, and his Latin was reputedly so good that even his enemies loved to hear him speak. Consequently, he was the ideal figure to deal with the French pope in Avignon. This was an important consideration, since the order was under investigation by papal officials. As a corollary to giving the papacy primary attention, Karl wanted to reduce the tempo of war against Lithuania. He also wanted to make peace with King Ladislas of Poland and to resolve the troubles in Livonia. These were not policies popular among the knights in Prussia. Karl's only chance to persuade them to accept his point of view was to go east and speak to them in person.

After completing a tour of Prussia, inspecting the order's resources and discussing various possible strategies, the new grand master ordered the attacks on Gardinas suspended. He had decided to concentrate all his forces against Samogitia in the hope of securing a shorter land route to Riga and putting an end to devastating pagan attacks on Kurland and Semgallia.

In April 1313 Karl von Trier loaded ships in Königsberg with supplies, war equipment, and men, and sent them to the Nemunas River via the Baltic Sea and the Kurland bay. Other forces he sent overland to Ragnit. Despite the misfortune of losing at sea four knights, 400 men, a vast amount of supplies, and building materials for a new castle, Karl marched his forces thirty miles upriver, where he built a bridge of boats across the stream. When the bridge was completed, priests led a great procession and held a festive mass before the workmen crossed over to build a great castle of logs and earth that Karl named Christmemel. It was to be the base for his attacks into the heart of Samogitia.

Not long afterward Heinrich attacked the castles farther upstream. He personally led the assault on Bisen, using a bridge of boats to bring siege weapons to bear, but without success. Meanwhile, the castellan of Ragnit sailed farther upriver to Welun. His plan was to assault the walls directly from a large warship, but a strong burst of wind drove his ship ashore as he approached the castle. Surprise was lost, and only after desperate fighting was the crew able to get the vessel back into midstream and return to Ragnit.

Vytenis was stirred into action by these attacks. He was especially worried about the large warship, because it threatened every riverside castle along the Nemunas. Therefore he ordered one of his vassals to destroy it as quickly as possible.

The Lithuanian commander ordered 100 cavalry to make their way to Ragnit, while 600 warriors went down the river in a hundred small boats. These forces were observed by scouts and lookouts, but they moved so quickly that they arrived at Ragnit ahead of all efforts to send a warning. The rest of the plan was not so easy to accomplish. Although the pagans found the great warship anchored in midstream with only four bowmen on board, the vessel was so huge that they could not scale the sides (especially while the archers were shooting them down one after the other). In fact, the attackers, who could not easily retreat upstream, might have been massacred if the archers had been reinforced. But at that critical moment the Lithuanian cavalry prevented a sortie from Ragnit. Soon thereafter the Lithuanians cut the anchor rope and the ship glided down the river, followed by the host of small boats. When the vessel ran aground, the Lithuanians were able to set it ablaze. The grand master did not replace the warship. Apparently he had concluded it was not as useful as hoped even in summer; and in winter such a large vessel would be icebound and probably crushed by the ice floes.

✚

Brutal Warfare

We know from other sources how brutal the campaigns of this era could be. Polish witnesses testifying to papal legates in 1320 and 1339 indicated that the warriors in the armies of the Teutonic Order practised torture, massacred prisoners, slaughtered innocent civilians, stripped women, abused clerics, and destroyed villages, fields, and churches. If that was happening in Christian Poland, one can imagine how badly they treated pagans in Samogitia.

Unfortunately for historians, the evidence at the papal hearings was seriously flawed: the Teutonic Knights boycotted the hearings. This offended the legates, who were further angered when the grand masters suggested that they lacked authority to override the order's past grants of immunity from harassment. Moreover, much of the evidence was hearsay, and some of the testimony was wildly exaggerated, a medieval characteristic that is the bane of the modem researcher. Many of the witnesses were certain to benefit from a decision against the order. On the other hand, some witnesses were men of position and experience, who had opportunity to know what had happened. Since the papal investigators heard each person's testimony privately, asking each witness a detailed list of questions, they had means of ascertaining the truth. The popes, hearing their legates reports of misdeeds and atrocities, summoned the high officials of the order to appear before them.

In their defence the officers of the Teutonic Knights denied some charges and explained that others were exaggerated or misrepresented. Their relationship with Poles, for example, was not uniformly bad. The bishop of Płock had given them the castellany of Michelau in return for an annual monetary payment. It was important to the bishop that the order's garrison would give some protection to the exposed frontiers of his diocese. The same fear of Lithuanian attack made the dukes of Masovia generally friendly. Moreover, the dukes in Pomerania and Silesia were seeking allies against Ladislas. Nor were the Poles without fault in the dispute. Years earlier the Council of Vienne had ordered the Polish bishops to pay a special crusading tax to support the operations of the Teutonic Order; the bishops never obeyed that resolution. Lastly, the kings prevented their subjects from participating in the Samogitian expeditions, thus interfering with a legitimate crusade. Although the papal legates' investigations did not result in the condemnation of the Teutonic Order that the crusaders' enemies had expected, they provided modern historians with ample testimony to the cruelty of fourteenth-century warfare. Moreover, this cruelty was confirmed even by historians who wrote in praise of the crusade. In those days men boasted of their deeds in arms, even bloody deeds that made more tenderhearted contemporaries shake their heads in wonder.

✝

Principles of Frontier Warfare

The order's chroniclers did more than prove that war is terrible. Their descriptions of raids across the wilderness allow us to analyse the strategy which lay behind them. In general deepest winter and high summer were the best seasons for campaigning; during the rest of the year mud could be a major problem. February, June, and November were favourite months for Christian raids – in February the frozen rivers could be used as highways; June provided a period of warm weather before the first harvest; and in November the militia was free from agricultural work and the snow was not yet too deep for infantry. The chroniclers lavishly praised native knights for their deeds during these years. Few crusaders were coming from Germany, and the native Prussians and Livonians who replaced them were enthusiastic warriors, fighting for the love of battle, glory, and worldly advancement.

The expeditions were well organised. Unable to live off the land in the wilderness, raiders had to carry their supplies with them. Often they left their stores at a rendezvous site along the planned route of return, sometimes guarding them, sometimes burying them, and sometimes simply hiding them. Castles served as supply depots and resting places, and ships transported food and equipment when surprise was not important.

The Teutonic Knights knew many paths into Samogitia. They collected descriptions of routes used by merchants and raiders, giving the names of the men who had gone that way, the number of days' march for each stage of the journey, and other useful information. Once the raiders crossed the wilderness, they knew exactly what to do. The general practice was to divide the army into striking forces, each small unit plundering a designated area all day and meeting at a pre-determined location forward of the dispersal point, where camp would be pitched. A strong detachment would be kept in this central location to protect the booty and supplies and as a reserve force ready to assist against any threat which might appear. Since one day's raiding would generally suffice to ravage any small district, the army moved each day to a new location, proceeding in a zigzag pattern, often varying the march by going straight forward, or even returning to ravage a district again. They followed whatever route seemed best suited for catching the defenders by surprise, either before they could go into hiding or as they emerged from concealment. Sometimes small forces were sent ahead with the intention of retreating hurriedly and leading pursuers into an ambush by the main party. This instilled such caution among defenders that occasionally very small parties were able to make daring raids deep into the heart of the enemy countryside and escape unharmed. Each campaign was thoroughly planned, and as time passed new variations were added to the general theme. Christian and pagan alike employed the same tactics because they were the only ones available, and both adhered to a strategy of exhausting the enemy by attacking agricultural production and commerce.

✠

The Death of King Vytenis

Vytenis did not allow the crusaders free run of his country or of Samogitia. He was a skilful and determined warrior who had capable vassals in his service, and all hated their Christian foes. One vassal, David of Gardinas, first appeared in the crusader chronicles in 1314. The foremost pagan warrior of his generation, he was castellan of the second most important fortress in the country, Gardinas (Vilnius being the most important). What happened to his predecessor, the chamberlain, is unknown. David's first exploit was to destroy supplies left by Heinrich von Plötzke during a daring September raid into south-eastern Lithuania, far behind Vilnius. Killing the guards, burning the foodstuffs, and stealing 500 horses, David presented the grand commander with a terrible dilemma. When Heinrich reached the empty underground laager, he realised that the enemy was undoubtedly lying in wait somewhere along his way home. Doubting that his hungry forces could fight their way through an ambush, Heinrich made a 500-mile detour around the danger. Some of his men dug for roots, others ate their starving horses, and many died in their tracks. Those who escaped were exhausted from their ordeal, and many were too ill to return to duty quickly. Without any fighting, David of Gardinas had almost destroyed an entire army.

In time the grand masters realised that it was much easier to take crusaders up the Nemunas River than through the many swamps and streams of the wilderness. On the great river the grand masters could effectively employ their technological advantages – ships which could carry troops and supplies, castles which could protect strategic points and serve as bases for raids and major offensives, and missile weapons. Moreover, the Nemunas and its tributaries led directly into the Lithuanian heartland, while Lithuanians coming downstream were diverted toward the bogs along the Kurland bay. The grand masters built impressive castles along the wide river, first at Ragnit, close to the river's many mouths and protecting Samland from attack, then farther upstream, at Christmemel and Welun.

In August 1315 Samogitians slipped up to Ragnit unnoticed and were upon the walls before the alarm was given. The startled garrison hurried into the keep, a strong tower that demonstrated the engineering superiority of the Westerners. A crusader keep was tall enough to serve as a lookout and almost impossible to assault directly. The entrance was hardly more than a door high above the ground, reached by a narrow staircase and solidly barred from within. The base had no entrances or windows and could have a solid stone wall six metres thick. Any approach to the foot of the keep, any attempt to undermine it, was greeted with a barrage of heavy stones thrown from twenty metres or so above, or by a shower of crossbow shafts. Even wounded and exhausted men could defend such a post for several days, and since the garrison had a field of fire over the entire castle no enemy army could hold the castle against a relief force as long as the keep remained untaken. The Samogitians did not even try to assault Ragnit's keep. They were satisfied with ravaging and burning the fields that were ready for harvesting.

Six weeks later Vytenis appeared at Christmemel. He set up two hurling machines and brought up a multitude of Rus'ian archers. He put the remainder of his men to work cutting wood and stacking it in dry places whence it could be carried easily to the moat. His plan was to pile so much wood and brush around the castle that when fire was set to it, the heat would crack the walls and the smoke would suffocate the garrison.

As soon as the grand master heard this news he summoned his forces. Although he could not begin his march until his army was fully assembled, he sent ten knights and 150 men ahead on ships. Vytenis, having foreseen this occurrence, prevented their reaching the castle. The best the crusaders could do was to harass the besiegers, exchanging volleys of arrows and hoping to slow their work. On the seventeenth day of the siege the relief army approached. Vytenis was not ready yet for a general assault, but since he had only this one chance to take Christmemel before the grand master was upon him he gave the order to fill the moat with wood and straw, then to set fire to it. Thousands of men rushed toward the castle, their arms filled with wood. His archers fired thousands of arrows at the ramparts in an effort to drive the defenders from the wall or at least hinder their shots at the infantry. The garrison, however, was well protected behind crenellations; they fired their crossbows as rapidly as they could, striking down so many Lithuanians that Vytenis ordered the attack stopped. Burning his siege machines, he led his army in retreat.

This was the last time the crusaders heard of Vytenis. No one knows what happened to him. Legend has it that he died when struck by lightning, but that seems to be a mistranslation of the name of his successor, Gediminas. So little is known of the genealogies of the Lithuanian rulers that historians believed for centuries that Gediminas was Vytenis' son, whereas it appears that they were brothers. Was Vytenis killed by his brother? Or was that story a later effort to stain Gediminas' reputation? Was Vytenis killed at the siege of Christmemel? If so, the Teutonic Knights did not realise it and report on it, which they would certainly have done. Vytenis was a great man, an authentic national hero. Perhaps it is no coincidence that the first Lithuanian coins bore the symbol of a mounted rider called Vytis. The religious significance of that figure could well have been augmented by a canting reference to the great prince.

✝

Western Crusaders Arrive

Karl von Trier, having relieved Christmemel, was unwilling to dismiss his army without accomplishing something even more notable. He sent back much of his force, probably with great fanfare, to persuade enemy scouts that he had returned home; but he retained 6,000 men, then sent them by night farther up the river to Welun. The surprise there was complete. As the natives hurried from the village to the citadel, the Christians pursued them, slaughtering many of the fugitives. The crusaders made no effort to assault the central fortress but set fire to the houses and retreated.

Welun was the bulwark of the Samogitian defence system. The grand master was not ready to besiege it, but hardly a year passed without his men burning the suburbs. If he could not capture Welun immediately, he would wear down the people little by little, destroying their homes and fields, knowing that the grand prince was incapable of providing them food and additional garrison forces year after year.

In 1316 the first Western crusaders arrived. These Rhenish pilgrims (as they called themselves) had been recruited by Karl von Trier on a visit to Germany. From this time on, crusaders came ever more frequently to Prussia on what they called *Reisen* (journeys), a medieval euphemism for a military venture. The participants of this expedition were later able to relate that they had killed 200 pagans at the cost of fifty men. That boast was less important than the number of squires who became knights at the end of the expedition. The ceremony of dubbing knights became a popular part of each crusading expedition, with the honour performed by the most prominent visiting lord as soon as each candidate performed some deed of valour. Moreover, the grand master invited the most valiant warriors to sit at a table of honour modelled after King Arthur's Round Table, and awarded distinctions to the most outstanding knights.

✠

Prince Gediminas

While the crusaders were indulging in chivalric ceremonies in the Samogitian forests, the new grand prince of Lithuania was expanding his influence east and south. Like his predecessors, Gediminas understood that while Rus'ian princes, nobles, and burghers wanted an Orthodox ruler, some would accept any Christian ruler, and in the end all of them would settle for any overlord who could protect them against the Tatar khan who ruled the steppes of southern Russia. For three-quarters of a century Tatar khans had ruled over Rus', allowing only a modicum of independence even to the princes on the outskirts of their empire, Novgorod and Pskov in the north, Galicia and Volhynia in the west. Now the power of the khan was weakening, and Rus'ian princes and cities saw an opportunity to escape his terrible servitude. As each prince considered rebellion, he cautiously looked about for protection, for Tatar fury was notorious. A misjudgement could bring about a retaliation that few boyars or burghers would live to describe, that few would want to live to remember. Although some nearby Rus'ians had submitted to Vytenis, others did not look for salvation from Gediminas because he was an old antagonist whose armies had often ravaged their lands. The princes of Galicia and Volhynia sought aid first from the pope, then from Poland and Hungary. Since the Teutonic Knights were old allies, they even approached Karl von Trier. However, no Western ruler was ready to send a large force to the steppes, least of all the Teutonic Knights. The Rus'ians turned to Gediminas almost as a last resort. As it happened, it was a brilliant resolution of a complex problem. The Westerners were really too far away, had other pressing concerns, and were demanding a church union on Roman terms. The Byzantines and Balkan states were far too weak. Gediminas was relatively close by, was ready to give full attention to Rus'ian problems, and was tolerant in matters of religion.

As Gediminas proved that he could protect his clients, the trickle of men coming to him became a torrent. Gediminas often allowed the Rus'ian boyars to retain their offices and always permitted them to live by their traditional laws and customs. He especially respected the Russian Orthodox Church and its leaders; they, in turn, urged their people to be loyal to him. Gediminas used this augmentation of his power to make the conflict in Samogitia more equal than it had been. Even so, Gediminas' ability to resist the crusaders grew only slowly. He was not able to pour Rus'ian warriors suddenly into the war zone along the Nemunas. Even much later the overwhelming majority of his cavalry and foot were Lithuanians and only occasionally did he bring large numbers of Rus'ians to the west. It was more important that he could provide his nobles and boyars with appointments in his army, so that even if their lands were ravaged by crusaders, they did not have to choose between surrender and starvation. Now they could serve honourably as professional soldiers (often as officials or in garrisons of Rus'ian cities) where they could acquire the experience and military equipment which would make them equal to their Western opponents.

Soon Gediminas could sign his letters 'King of the Lithuanians and many Rus'ians'. He put his brothers Fedor (Theodoric) and Varnys (Woini) to rule over Kiev and Polotsk and his son Algirdas (Olgierd) over Vitebsk. Later he put David of Gardinas in Pskov, where he could harass the Livonian Order. He won over some Rus'ian princes through marriage alliances: he took the heiress of Vitebsk to wife himself and gave his daughter Maria to the prince of Tver. Later he expanded his net of alliances to include Moscow, Galicia, Masovia, and the kingdom of Poland.*

---

* An excellent account is S.C. Rowell, *Lithuania Ascending: A Pagan Empire within East-Central Europe* (Cambridge University Press, 1994).

Realising that his military technology was inferior to that of the crusaders, Gediminas sought to attract merchants and artisans from the West, men who knew how to make or acquire the equipment he needed. His contacts with German merchants in Riga were especially important. Those burghers, still fighting the Livonian Order, were eager to enlarge their trade and to strengthen any enemy of the Teutonic Knights. Their sole hesitation came from their desire to defend and extend the Christian faith. Furthermore, if they allied themselves with a pagan monarch against crusaders, violating a strongly held religious code, they would undermine their standing with the pope and emperor, and among other Hanseatic merchants and those nobles whose subjects purchased Livonian products. However, the archbishop of Riga told the merchants that they were not harming Christendom by their actions. Franciscan friars at Gediminas' court in Vilnius further assured them that the Lithuanians were ready for conversion, if only the crusaders would cease their attacks. The Franciscans were Gediminas' most fervent partisans, and they spread stories of his eager desire to become a Christian. This prospect, however dim it was, was an argument that the Rigans could use effectively to justify an informal alliance with the Lithuanian grand duke.

In actuality, there was almost no chance that Gediminas would join the Roman Church, but he allowed the Western visitors to fantasise all they wished. His toleration of the Eastern Church was vital to keeping the loyalty of his Rus'ian subjects and the Lithuanians expected him to remain pagan. Gediminas was interested in creating an empire which included both Roman and Rus'ian churches as well as pagans. Religious tolerance of any kind was incomprehensible to the crusaders. Freedom of religion meant freedom to err and freedom to persuade others to err. The Teutonic Knights had been taught to smash evil-doers over the head, and they could not learn to tolerate religious practices which would condemn masses of people to hellfire. For them this kind of tolerance was surely the greatest evil imaginable.

✛

The Crusader Response

The crusade was fundamentally a means of advancing Christendom, an ideal many nationalities could understand and share; it expressed religious concepts perfectly suited to the contemporary mind. The crusade was also a means of enlarging the territories of the Teutonic Knights, who represented the papacy and the Church at large as well as themselves. They justified holy war as the only way to pacify and Christianise pagans. That had been done successfully in Prussia and Livonia, it was being done with Moslems in Spain and Portugal. The kings of Poland and Hungary used the same reasoning for warring against Tatars and Turks – what was good for them as well as for Christendom was doubly right, doubly justifying the cost in blood and treasure.

What all late medieval crusades had in common was that they were popular struggles of Western Europeans against dangerous enemies on the borders of Christendom. There was an aura of romanticism connected with these crusades that the nineteenth-century public was able to grasp, but which eludes the modern mind.*

Similarly, medieval men and women were upset by the mere existence of pagans on their frontier, even the existence of non-Christians who were peaceful and tolerant. They feared the magic and superstition of the pagan priests, believed that their charms and incantations were effective, and looked upon war against such manifestations of devil-worship as a holy project. Nor were Eastern Christians pleased at having pagan neighbours – like the Tatars, Baltic pagans were not peaceful.

The Lithuanians saw no need to justify their raids into Christian lands to gather cattle and people for sale. The slave trade down the great rivers to Byzantium and the Moslem world was ancient. The Vikings had begun it, local peoples continued it, and Tatars would perpetuate it until the reign of Peter the Great. In addition, Lithuanian boyars were beginning to emulate their neighbours in establishing large estates based on grain production and serfdom. It was impolitic to subject local labour to such debasement, and unnecessary as long as they could round up experienced workers in Poland, Prussia, and Livonia. Christians did not frown on slavery in principle, they simply insisted that one had to limit the practice to enslaving non-Christians. In effect, Lithuanian pagans had it backward! And the crusaders were determined to put a stop to that.

The order's critics – including Paulus Vladimiri, the fifteenth-century Polish scholar who demanded that the Council of Constance declare the crusade un-Christian – never defended paganism *per se*. Assertions of the moral and intellectual superiority of paganism are a modern phenomenon, often associated with beliefs in the healing power of crystals and herbs, radical feminism, and nature worship, but only rarely with sorcery and voodoo, as medieval men and women would have done. Nor were Eastern Christians friendlier or more understanding of paganism than was the West; there was, in fact, that same mixture of revulsion and fascination that one sees in Western texts, especially the Renaissance era historians.

* An exception is Harvard scholar Samuel Huntington, whose 1993 article 'Clash of Civilizations', in *Foreign Affairs*, has been widely discussed.

Lithuanians were not children of nature. The Gediminid princes and their boyars lived in a political and social environment far too sophisticated and complex for them to qualify as examples of Rousseau's noble savage, even at the end of the century, when several of them became Roman Catholics, they were newly baptised, and their armies contained numbers of Moslem, Orthodox, and pagan warriors. Few demonstrated much respect for the Western church. Through most of the fourteenth century the Gediminids were pagans, and they evidenced little more than contempt for foreign superstitions.

Crusaders were outraged by stories of attacks on churches, desecration of the host, and the murder of priests, monks, and nuns. It should not be forgotten that this was the era of the Black Death, of flagellation cults, of mass hysteria, of witch hunts, of pogroms, and of secret heresies. The pagans were among the few visible enemies that religious men could find to blame for their troubles. They were an obvious and dangerous foe of Church and state.

That allows us to differentiate to a certain degree the Samogitian crusade from the purely territorial aspirations of the Teutonic Order. The difference may seem difficult to establish, especially if one reads only modern historians, but the spiritual aspects of crusading were never forgotten. The order needed subjects who would provide food and labour, castles that would serve as convents and supply depots, and frontier posts where scouts could live safely and where troops could gather when raiders were reported or when raids into pagan lands were being organised; in addition, there were strategic lands, such as Samogitia, which were bases for raiding Prussia and Livonia. Nevertheless, if one looks only at those situations where the military order fiercely defended its territorial integrity, one will be misled. More often than they cared to remember, the Teutonic Knights granted truces to the pagans, permitted papal emissaries to influence policy, and trusted the word of Lithuanian princes. Such a generous attitude was not present at all times in equal quantity, of course. Experience creates cynicism, and the Teutonic Knights could be very cynical when well-meaning outsiders argued that the crusade should be suspended so that the idealists could talk to the pagans about conversions; suspiciously, except to these newcomers, the Lithuanian offers usually appeared just as the Teutonic Knights were about to win a significant advantage over them. Similarly, Polish demands for the surrender of West Prussia and Culm, usually part of a plan for general peace, were hardly likely to cause the crusading warrior-monks to open their hearts to pleas that they seek a peaceful rather than forced conversion. Nevertheless, hope and idealism were still present in the fourteenth century.

For practical minds, however, there seemed to be little choice in using force as the principal method of making the Gediminid dynasty consider conversion.

Pagans happily sent priests and missionaries into the other world as martyrs. They ignored or rejected papal efforts to win them over through diplomacy, offers of crowns, or the sending of friars. Moreover, they were militant warriors. No matter who first shoved whom, the Teutonic Knights found themselves defending their own borders against Samogitian and Lithuanian raids almost as often as they marched or sailed forth in pride and chivalric pomp, or sneaked across the wilderness for sudden and devastating raids. Crusading visitors from the West came in large numbers, spending their money freely and risking death because they believed they were defending Christendom.

The Samogitian *Reisen* were joined by Frenchmen, Englishmen, Scots, Czechs, Hungarians, Poles, and a few Italians. It was an international venture that appealed to individuals who were uncomfortable in an era of rapidly growing nationalism. The more that nationalism came to the surface in politics, in the Church, and in literature, the more popular became the few surviving aspects of internationalism. The crusade against paganism bound many characteristics of Western religion and secular life together in colourful ways – as sport, as war, as chivalric display, and as recognition of worthy achievement. The fourteenth century was an age that honoured accomplishments. For nobles who wanted to prove themselves by doing noble deeds, the crusading expeditions into Samogitia provided an almost universally approved means to demonstrate their valour, daring, and knightly worth. By mid-century this aspect of the crusade had become more prominent than the religious obligations. Slowly the expeditions became more secular, more chivalric, until the crusade suffered the fate of idealistic knighthood everywhere and became an arthritic anachronism.

There was some national identity in the crusade, of course: the Teutonic Knights were the German Order. As such, they had to represent the German nation of the Holy Roman Empire. While the grand masters were well aware of that obligation, and they understood how to exploit Germans' love for their land and language, they were not to allow that aspect of their identity to overshadow others; that became a serious problem only in the fifteenth century.

There were few alternatives in the fourteenth century for the expression of the crusading ideal; and those few were more difficult, dangerous, and expensive than the crusade from Prussia, not to mention their being more time-consuming. The Samogitian expeditions became popular two decades after the fall of the Holy Land. A notable coincidence. Twenty years had sufficed to persuade most men that plans for a new Mediterranean crusade were impractical. The crusading spirit had seemingly breathed its last, but the Teutonic Knights knew how to revive it by organising small expeditions (too small to have achieved anything against the Turks) and sending the participants home with stories of exciting victories over the enemies of the Cross. What had once been almost unco-ordinated Polish, Bohemian, and German expeditions became a pan-European venture.

Thus there was nothing odd in Henry of Derby coming to Prussia in January of 1352 and challenging Casimir of Poland to combat. Henry had brought an army to fight the pagans, but had been told that there could be no expedition because the king was making trouble over the boundary markings between Prussia and Poland. So he decided to put an end to this interference. His bravado may have helped hasten a compromise, but the English nobleman was delayed in reaching Königsberg in time to join the winter expedition.

Nor was there anything particularly unusual in Louis of Hungary sitting through an elaborate pagan ceremony in 1351, the sacrifice of a red bull to sanctify the agreement with the Lithuanian prince, Kęstutis (pronounced Kenstutis, 1297–1382), regarding the ransom of Kęstutis' brother, who had been taken prisoner by Casimir that summer. The Polish and Hungarian crusaders soon regretted their naive trust, because Kęstutis slipped away with his brother, then attacked the camp so fiercely that the Polish and Hungarian monarchs barely escaped with their lives, and Boleslas of Masovia was slain.

In 1352 Louis was wounded in fierce fighting in Volhynia, and Casimir mortgaged Dobrin to the Teutonic Order to raise money for his campaign against the Tatars. In short, the crusades in East Central Europe were more complex than simply campaigns of Teutonic Knights against pagans in Samogitia and Lithuania. They also included wars against Orthodox princes and Moslem Tatars; and not far from everyone's mind were the Turks, camped on the doorsteps of Constantinople.

The Teutonic Order publicised its holy mission in every way imaginable to the era. Its architecture, for example, emphasised the ways that military and religious obligations intertwined; and every detail underscored the order's solidity and power. They succeeded so well that we rarely think of the more important expeditions by Poles and Hungarians in Galicia, Volhynia, and Ukraine.

✠

Hopes of Lithuanian Conversion

Every so often the Lithuanian dukes offered to discuss their accepting Roman Christianity. This was not always due to the steadily increasing pressure of the crusaders from Prussia and Livonia, and certainly not to a fear that the crusaders would conquer Lithuania, even though that pressure was important in the dukes' calculations of profit and loss. It was to eliminate the annoyance of crusader attacks. The grand masters' offensives had long hindered the grand prince from responding to other threats and opportunities to the south. Gediminas, and later his sons, especially Algirdas (1296–1377) and Kęstutis, observed with great interest the declining fortunes of the Tatar Golden Horde, and they extended their power and influence over nearby Rus'ian states whenever possible. However, their efforts to occupy southern Rus' completely, especially Galicia, were contested after 1370 by the king of united Hungary and Poland, Louis the Great. Upon Gediminas' death Algirdas had taken the title of grand prince and responsibility for most Rus'ian affairs, while Kęstutis defended the eastern and northern frontiers. They were among the most gifted and inventive diplomats in medieval history, making the most of their lands' slender population and economic base. They were talented leaders in war as well, but they were too astute to take great risks. Whenever the odds were against them, they did not hesitate to retreat or seek a truce. This was most frustrating to the grand masters, who had learned through hard experience that Algirdas and Kęstutis would honour an agreement only as long as it was clearly in their best interest.

While it is true that most political leaders will back out of a treaty or understanding when violating their promises will bring sufficient benefits, few have pledged their word with as much cold-blooded forethought as these two brothers and their offspring. The grand masters found it most frustrating to have churchmen and other well-meaning individuals crying for them to stop the holy war because the Lithuanian rulers were saying that they were sincerely contemplating conversion to Roman Catholicism, but that the crusader attacks made such a move politically impossible. The Lithuanian rulers were so skilled at exploiting the Christians' desire to think well of their enemies that it eventually became difficult for the Teutonic Order to believe that the Gediminid dynasty was ever sincere, even later when conversion was clearly in the princes' interest. But that is a long and confusing story that contemporaries found even more difficult to follow than do modern historians, for whom it is no easy task.

At one point in the spring of 1361 it appeared that Kęstutis might be persuaded to undergo baptism. Algirdas and Kęstutis had led a large raiding party through Galindia into central Prussia at a time when English and Saxon crusaders were present in Samland. The marshal, whose base was at Königsberg, proposed to Thomas Spencer and the duke of Saxony that they all make a forced march across Prussia and catch the raiders before they could escape back into the wilderness. The crusaders enthusiastically assented. Indeed, they succeeded beyond their greatest hopes, catching the raiders completely by surprise, killing 130 of them and capturing Kęstutis.

Grand Master Winrich von Kniprode kept his prisoner in honourable captivity in Marienburg, far from any possible attempt at rescue. In mid-November, however, the sixty-five-year-old prince made a daring escape. Aided by a Lithuanian servant who worked in the castle, Kęstutis slipped out of his cell, slithered up a chimney, stole a white cloak and walked unrecognised across the courtyard until he found the grand master's horse saddled and waiting. Climbing aboard the steed, he rode out the gate unhindered. Kęstutis later abandoned the horse on the road east toward Lithuania and headed off south on foot toward Masovia, where his daughter was the duchess of Płock. He was soon home, making fierce war and mocking his enemies. Such feats made him beloved in western Lithuania and Samogitia.

Algirdas, meanwhile, was expanding to the east, defeating the Tatars in 1363 at the battle of Blue Waters near the Black Sea and occupying Kiev; in 1368 and 1370 he reached the Kremlin in Moscow.

The crisis of the wars came in February of 1370, when Algirdas and Kęstutis brought their Lithuanian and Rus'ian armies into Samland. Winrich von Kniprode reacted swiftly, summoning units from as far away as Culm and ordering them to march swiftly to join the marshal's army. Kęstutis was supervising the burning of farms and villages around Rudau when the crusader force approached. Recognising the banners of his opponents, he fled the field immediately. Algirdas, in contrast, ordered his men to hurry to a wooded hill where they could fight for their booty and prisoners. The ensuing combat was among the bloodiest in memory. By nightfall the Teutonic Knights had routed the last pagan resistance, bringing the total of slain foemen to a thousand, but at the cost of twenty-six knights and 100 men. Algirdas, as usual, escaped, but it was the last time he sent troops into Prussia.

After Algirdas' death in 1377, Kęstutis insisted that the many Lithuanian territorial dukes follow his instructions and thereby avoid working at cross purposes to one another, or even beginning a civil war. This reflected the complex reality of the loose Lithuanian system of governance – already some of the dynasty's numerous progeny had understood that there were insufficient lands to satisfy all their ambitions, and none of the princes was noted for patience and self-sacrifice; moreover, some of their Rus'ian possessions were beginning to seek independence – even seeking help from Moscow, whose prince saw himself as the natural leader of all the Rus'ian states. The Gediminid dynasty had always highly prized courage, initiative, and cunning; it never taught or practised the so-called 'Christian' virtues, not even those dukes who had converted to Orthodoxy; and its tradition of family solidarity worked well only when everyone was threatened by a foreign power. As the Polish chronicler, Długosz, put it: '*Neque enim inter barbaros tuta et sincera possunt durare foedera, inter quos verus ignoratur Deus: nulla quoque viget fides, nullum sacrosanctum insiurandum, nulla legitima religio.'* Translation: don't trust the pagans. Now it was payback time for encouraging those traits, unless Kęstutis could keep his numerous nephews and sons in line.

Kęstutis did not adopt the title grand prince, but he might as well have. Still, his policies angered Algirdas' eldest son by his second marriage, Jogaila, and his full brothers, who were already feuding with their half-brothers from Algirdas' first marriage. Jogaila (1354–1434) had a somewhat better claim on the title of grand prince than did the eldest half-brother, Andreas (1342–99), because – in a practice widely observed in the Middle Ages – sons inherited a claim to the office held by the father at the time of their birth. Thus, Andreas was merely the son of a duke, while Jogaila was the son of the grand prince. In addition, Algirdas had recognised the superior talents of his son by Juliana, his second wife; and Juliana had become a powerful figure in her own right after being widowed. Formerly excluded from influence over her sons' upbringing because she was an Orthodox Christian and Algirdas had insisted on his sons being reared as pagans, she was now willing to use every means available to advance the interests of her eldest son against those of her predecessor's offspring. To make him more acceptable to potential Rus'ian subjects, she persuaded him to be baptised as an Orthodox Christian.

For a moment, therefore, it seemed highly likely that the Gediminid family, long loyal to its pagan roots, would cast its lot with Orthodoxy. If that was the only way for the ambitious dukes to become rulers of Rus', few doubted that they would allow any religious or moral sentiment to hinder their clambering up the ladder of fortune.

Jogaila, however, was not content to rule those portions of his father's eastern lands that had been bequeathed to him. He was determined first to gather all the eastern lands into his hands. That meant eliminating Andreas, whose northern lands abutted the Livonian Order's territories. Then he would acquire Kęstutis' western territories. Once all Lithuania was under his control – ruled by those brothers and half-brothers he could trust – he would then resume the policy of expansion that had been so successful earlier in the century.

Grave marker at Holm, one of
the first two churches in
Livonia, showing a thirteenth-
century warrior with a kite-
shaped shield.

Charging German knights on an early thirteenth-century metal casket from the Cathedral Treasury, Aachen, Germany. All German kings were crowned in this church, after which they would proceed to their election as Holy Roman Emperor and the coronation.

A manuscript illustration of crusaders in combat against eastern warriors. The helmet of the commander later reappears in the movie Alexander Nevsky, but it should be noted that he does not wear the order's cloak. Also, the Russian troops bear coats of arms, which was not yet common for them.

Jousting knights. Note the pot helmets and the musicians. A fourteenth-century frieze in Marienburg castle in Prussia.

Below: Knights in combat from a capital in Marienburg castle. The coat of arms indicates that this is a secular knight. The lion rampant is a common devise, but many crusaders came from Meissen and Flanders, where this was used. Interestingly, Teutonic Knights did not joust – too secular and vainglorious.

Below left: Knights in combat, from a capital in Marienburg castle.

Below right: Knights jousting, victory going to the rider with the griffon coat of arms, a common motif. *Chansonnier Manesse*, from the fourteenth-century Manesse Liederhandschrift, Universitätsbibliothek Heidelberg.

Romantic drawing of the ruins of Doblen, a major castle in Kurland that protected the communications route to Prussia. Like most castles it was constructed on a natural rise where water obstacles increased attackers' difficulties in achieving surprise or prosecuting a siege.

Romantic drawing of the ruins of Wenden, the seat of the Livonian master in the Livonian Aa River valley.

Marienburg castle from the Nogat River, with the water gate at the left, then the grand master's residence, and finally the high castle with the Priests' Tower in the center of the fortress. There was little chance for a successful assault on the walls from the narrow beach, and generally the Teutonic Order's allies (Danzig and other commercial centers) guaranteed naval superiority.

Marienburg castle from the southeast. Successive lines of defense sheltered the high castle from attack, while the high tower provided the defending commander with a good view of enemy activity.

Marienburg castle walls and warehouse facade, showing the covered walkways that protected the garrison from rain and hostile arrows.

The great hall in Marienburg castle. Unfortunately, the nineteenth-century restorers told us more about their artistic tastes than about the medieval era. Still, the elegant vaulting of the ceiling remains impressive even after the restorations following World War II.

Marienburg castle's middle courtyard, as reconstructed after World War II. Every comfort was provided for the garrison and visitors so that they did not suffer from the long cold and wet winters.

Jan Matejko's sketch for his large scale painting of the Battle of Tannenburg (1878). Vytautas holds the viewers attention, while Jagiełło watches from a distant rise. In the left foreground Grandmaster Ulrich von Jungingen falls.

Werner Peiner: The Siege of Marienburg (1939). In this battle between the Teutonic Knights and the Poles beneath Marienburg castle, the Teutonic Knights are obviously winning; in reality, the Poles simply marched away.

The ruins of the great castle at Wenden, where the Livonian master usually resided. This was destroyed in the Livonian War by Ivan the Terrible.

Banners hanging inside Marienburg castle. The battle flags captured at Tannenburg were taken to Cracow and put on public display. These are faithful copies.

9

The Conversion of Lithuania

The Feud Among the Lithuanian Dukes

The death of Algirdas in 1377 had led to civil war among his many sons, several of whom saw themselves as his potential heir. The one with the best claim to rule his lands in eastern Lithuania was Andreas, his eldest son by his first wife. But the one to triumph was Jogaila, the eldest son by his second wife. Jogaila drove his rival into exile, then withstood his efforts to return in alliance with the Livonian Knights. Although successful in that war, Jogaila discovered that his eighty-year-old uncle, Kęstutis, now demanded that all members of the family defer to his decisions on everything. Jogaila was furious. He wanted to rule, and he was too impatient to wait for nature to take its course.

Jogaila soon thought of a way to triumph over Kęstutis, as well as to eliminate permanently the chance that Andreas could prevail militarily. Through his younger brother Skirgaila (Skirgiełło) he made a secret alliance with the hated Teutonic Knights, promising to become a Roman Christian at some future date, and then sent Skirgaila to speak to Louis the Great of Hungary, Wenceslas of Bohemia (who was Holy Roman emperor), and perhaps even to Pope Urban VI. The Western monarchs and prelates who met Skirgaila persuaded the aged grand master, Winrich von Kniprode, to drop his support of Andreas and make a secret alliance with Jogaila.

A consummate actor and brilliant schemer, Jogaila made Kęstutis' son Vytautas (1350–1430) his closest friend. As a result, when Kęstutis became suspicious of the crusaders' improved knowledge of his military plans and Jogaila's tendency to bring his troops onto the field just a little too slowly to trap the German armies, Jogaila had Vytautas to plead his case. Kęstutis was by no means persuaded, but he had his son's own wild nature to worry about

– Vytautas was at an age at which he should have been given lands and responsibilities of his own, but he still seemed unready. Kęstutis understood that an unsubstantiated accusation against Jogaila would only harden Vytautas' belief that his cousin and friend was being abused. Therefore Kęstutis made concessions to Jogaila in order to keep Vytautas at his side a little longer. There was so much he needed to teach him. Not just of military matters, but also of men. Of course, treason on Jogaila's scale could not be concealed forever – not in a society of nobles who were often bored, who worried greatly about status and rank, who lived in close quarters with little privacy, and who fed on gossip and intrigue.* Nor could the policy disagreements be reconciled. Jogaila wanted to concentrate on the east, moving further into Rus', even at the price of surrendering lands to the crusaders; Kęstutis disagreed totally.

When Jogaila realised that Kęstutis would not attempt to discipline him, he became ever more independent, arranging for the marriage of his sister Alexandra to a Masovian duke without asking permission, conducting joint military operations with the Livonian Order, and driving his half-brothers Andreas and Kaributas (1342?–99) from their lands. In 1381 Kęstutis ended the problem, he thought, by arresting Jogaila (and perhaps Jogaila's mother), assuming control of his lands, and adopting the title of grand prince. However, at Vytautas' urging he released Jogaila and allowed him to return to his possessions in the east.

In 1382 Kęstutis marched to Novgorod-Seversk to deal with Kaributas, who had organised another rebellion. Jogaila, seeing his opportunity to strike, hurried to Vilnius, called for his supporters to join him there, and, sending a message to the grand master to march into Lithuania with all speed, then besieged Kęstutis' island castle at Trakai. When Kęstutis and Vytautas arrived to lift the siege they found themselves trapped between Jogaila's forces and the crusader army. Jogaila invited Kęstutis and Vytautas to a discussion that, he intimated, would resolve their differences, and there seized them. He imprisoned them in the fortress at Krivias (Krewo), then allowed Skirgaila, perhaps at his mother's urging, to murder Kęstutis and assume responsibility for ruling the western lands; then he did away with Kęstutis' powerful and famously beautiful Samogitian wife, Birutė; lastly, he signed treaties with the new grand master, Conrad Zöllner von Rotenstein, promising to become a Christian within four years and ceding western Samogitia to the Teutonic Order as soon as the crusaders could conquer it.

Vytautas escaped from prison through a ruse: the short, slight, beardless

---

* Modern men and women are by no means above scheming and backbiting, but few modern states disintegrate when hereditary leaders change their allegiance.

prince donned his wife Anna's clothing after an overnight stay and was out of the castle before the exchange was noticed. By early November he had made his way to a sister who had married Duke Janusz of Masovia. However, he could not stay there – Jogaila was already on his trail. Soon Vytautas appeared before the grand master in Marienburg, offering to become a Roman Christian and to join him in war against the usurper. Vytautas was at least safe in Prussia, though he was in the hands of his father's enemies. Would Vytautas, like Kęstutis some years before, have to find some way to escape from the grand master's fortress? And if he did, where would he go?

Conrad Zöllner was uncertain as to the best policy to follow. He had little experience in diplomacy, and he had never met either Vytautas or Jogaila personally. The policy he eventually decided upon was too delicately balanced to remain upright long – he baptised Vytautas (under the name of his sponsor, Wigand) and his wife and daughter (both generously released by Jogaila), then established them in western Samogitia, to rule the pagans who had surrendered; however, he carefully kept Vytautas under close supervision and assured Jogaila that he would prevent Vytautas from causing any trouble to the Lithuanian grand duchy. Neither Vytautas nor Jogaila were amused.

When Vytautas had appeared in Samogitia numerous warriors had hurried to his side. As much as they hated his Christian allies, they hated the murderers of Kęstutis and Birutė more. To have their prince back, they willingly co-operated in removing the pagan priests and desecrating the holy woods. They assisted in building primitive castles along the Nemunas River, and when Jogaila and Skirgaila declared war on Vytautas they fought against them enthusiastically. Vytautas possessed all the virtues of a great pagan prince, and it did not matter to them that he was nominally a Christian. To paraphrase the Polish chronicler Długosz, Vytautas was of all of Gediminas' descendants the greatest in the manly virtues and, for the most part, honest, civil, and humane.

Długosz was prejudiced, of course, since he was the court historian of Jogaila's heirs, the Jagiellonian dynasty. Długosz was the most widely read chronicler of the era, partly because he was a good writer. His Latin was solid, his anecdotes pithy, and he understood how to move a good story along. But his subject was also very important – the rise of Poland from obscurity and confusion to regional hegemony. One of his major themes was the conversion of Jogaila. Another was the evil nature of the Teutonic Knights.

✠

Lithuania Becomes a Christian State

Jogaila did not become a Roman Catholic out of conviction. It was a business arrangement. For Lithuanian dukes, almost everything was business. Even Jogaila's great passion, hunting, was partly business.

Jogaila converted in order to marry the heiress to the Polish crown. She was the younger daughter of Louis the Great, who had ruled Hungary and Poland from 1370 to 1382. The nobles and clergy of Poland had chaffed during this unwelcome union, and after Louis' death they insisted that the kingdoms be separated again. The younger daughter, Jadwiga, who was originally awarded Hungary, ended up in Cracow after Polish patriots refused to accede to the arrangements to marry the elder sister to Sigismund of Luxemburg (1368–1437), who had just become duke of Brandenburg. Sigismund, the brother of the Holy Roman emperor, Wenceslas (1361–1414), was just too German.* However, that was the problem with Jadwiga's proposed groom as well. A minor Habsburg prince, without many lands or promise of more, he was still a German. Then, once the Polish nobles and clergy broke the engagement, they found the number of potential bridegrooms limited; as a result they turned to Jogaila, who responded favourably to the suggestion that he could become the real ruler of Poland if he were willing to make Lithuania a Christian state. Inquiries to Pope Urban VI received a favourable response. The Polish nobles and clergy were also attracted by the fact that Jogaila and they had a common enemy – the Teutonic Order.

Meanwhile, the Teutonic Knights had been making great headway in their invasions of the Lithuanian highlands. With Vytautas and the Samogitians as allies, armies of German, French, English, and Scottish crusaders were marching right into the heart of the country without the usual warning and opposition along the way.

Jogaila judged the situation astutely. He desperately needed peace in order to pursue the negotiations with Polish representatives at Krivias, and he understood that the only way that he could be sure of Vytautas' co-operation in Christianising Lithuania was to make up their quarrel. Assassination would not do, and military victory seemed unlikely. Swallowing his pride and overriding his brothers' claims on Kęstutis' inheritance, Jogaila made secret contact with Vytautas and offered him his ancestral lands back. In July

---

* The Hungarians objected to having Sigismund as their ruler, too, but he used his brother's Czech and German troops to repress the nobles' repeated uprisings.

of 1384, at Vytautas' command, the Samogitians revolted against the Teutonic Order, seizing most of the crusader castles in their land all at once; then Vytautas' and Jogaila's forces besieged those few fortresses which remained untaken. Once the campaign had been concluded successfully, however, Jogaila reneged on his promises, naming Skirgaila as ruler of the west, leaving his disappointed cousin only a few small territories south-east of Masovia. There was nothing Vytautas could do except pretend to be satisfied.

To the delight of most of Christendom, when the Treaty of Krivias was signed in 1385 word went out that the Lithuanians would soon be baptised and priests would hold services in the former lairs of the pagan gods. In February of 1386 Jogaila, some of his brothers, and Vytautas underwent a Roman Catholic baptismal service in Cracow, after which he married Jadwiga. Jogaila then brought a handful of Christian priests to Vilnius to begin the process of conversion. More impressive were the thousands of Polish palatines and knights who accompanied them. The archbishop of Gniezno, who had presided at the baptism, marriage, and coronation, named as bishop of Vilnius a Polish Franciscan and ordered a new cathedral erected on the site of the long-since demolished first cathedral. According to the inaccurately informed *Nikonian Chronicle*, the king tortured and executed two boyars who preferred to become Orthodox Christians. This seems unlikely, but the report suggests accurately what many Rus'ians thought about the 'German faith'.

Franciscans were the preferred religious order for dealing with pagans. They had long experience in Lithuania; moreover, they were well known for their toleration of non-Christians, sometimes even preferring them over Christians who refused to live by their own democratic, pacifist version of the Gospels' message. Their task was not to be an easy one. As late as 1389 the Samogitians tied the captured castellan of Memel on his steed, wearing full armour, piled brush around him, and burned him alive as a sacrifice to their gods.

As king, Jogaila was officially known as Ladislas, the allusion to Ladislas the Short being unmistakable except in the Lithuanian prince's great stature. Poles, however, called him Jagiełło - the Polish form of Jogaila – in order to distinguish him from the many Piast princes also named Ladislas. He had little time to worry about the Christianisation processs personally. His presence was required at the opposite end of the kingdom, in Moldavia and Wallachia. These border regions had belonged to Hungary, but Polish influence had grown there during the reign of Louis the Great. Kęstutis' impressive incursions into Galicia had demonstrated that the Hungarians could not defend their steppe outposts without Polish help; and the Turks appeared to be even more dangerous enemies than the Tatars and Lithuanians, so that Hungarians had to look to their southern frontier. After Louis' death, with the Hungarian and Polish kingdoms separated, the Moldavians made themselves independent and began raising tariffs on goods transported over the new trade route between the Black Sea and Poland. Jagiełło's task was to stabilise the situation in Galicia (rather easily done, given the turmoil in Hungary and his own control of Lithuanian policy) and then extend Polish control over Moldavia and Wallachia. These tasks he accomplished before the end of 1387, though papal mediation was necessary to prevent war between Poland and Hungary. Fortunately for Jagiełło, since his hold on Polish loyalties was still very weak, Sigismund of Hungary was too busy dealing with his unruly nobles and Turkish attacks to do anything more than think about some future revenge on the Poles; Sigismund was keeping track, however. Awkwardly, his responsibilities were taking him too far south for him to do anything about the increasingly violent quarrels between Skirgaila and Vytautas, other than to warn them that, unless they could find some way to get along, he would have to remove one of them.

✠

Civil War in Lithuania

By spring of 1389 the escalating dispute between the Lithuanian dukes had gone beyond endurance; as Skirgaila said to Vytautas at one encounter, 'beware of me as I of you'. Soon thereafter Vytautas contacted Conrad Zöllner through two captive knights, Marquard von Salzbach and the Count of Rheineck, offering hostages (his brother Žygimantas and Žygimantas' son, Michael; his sister, Ringailė; his wife, Anna, and daughter, Sophia; and about a hundred others), a promise to bring all the Lithuanians into the Roman Church, and an alliance against Poland. Marquard spoke to the grand master, who remained sceptical about Vytautas' sincerity. When Vytautas heard this, he sent a second delegation led by Ivan of Galschan, Anna's brother, to inform the grand master that Skirgaila had learned of the earlier talks, that the governor of Vilnius was now on the alert, and that Jagiełło's youngest brother, Svidrigailo (1370–1452), had declared war on Vytautas. As almost his last action, Conrad Zöllner agreed to a new alliance with Vytautas and sent an army to invest Vilnius on his behalf. The attack was not successful, but in the three years to follow crusader armies marched with Vytautas throughout western Lithuania, achieving victory after victory. The new grand master, Conrad von Wallenrode, allowed Vytautas no contact with Lithuanians except in the presence of

Lithuanian-speaking knights. Marquard von Salzbach was foremost among these, thanks to his friendship with Vytautas, but von Wallenrode needed his talent, advice, and chivalric example too much to assign him full-time duty as Vytautas' companion.

Jagiełło was becoming desperate. His brothers had proven themselves either incompetent or untrustworthy; and their subjects, even the Samogitians, were willing to forgive Vytautas even his new alliance with the enemy. The king could rely only on Poles to hold Lithuania for him – as governor of Vilnius from 1390 to 1392 he appointed Jan Oleśnicki, a military officer from Cracow whose one-year-old son Zbigniew was to become one of the greatest figures in Polish history through his long association with the new king. As a temporary policy, this was working, but the king could see that native Lithuanians were unhappy. Something had to be done.

To make matters worse, the Hungarian king, Sigismund, was strengthening the position of the Teutonic Order in Masovia. In the spring of 1391 his palatine, Ladislas of Oppeln, mortgaged a castle near Thorn to the grand master, a key fortress protecting Duke Ladislas' lands in Dobrin and Kujavia that King Louis had given him in pawn several years earlier for loans and services. Jagiełło reacted angrily, attacking Duke Ladislas' lands, but the Teutonic Knights came down in overwhelming numbers to drive the Polish forces away. The question was then raised as to whether the Teutonic Order might purchase Ladislas' lands outright; other negotiations began in May of 1392 for the Teutonic Order to purchase the Neumark from Sigismund of Hungary. Conrad von Wallenrode was unwilling to purchase real estate with such cloudy titles – that was not consistent 'with God, Honour, or Justice' – but he wanted to do what he could for the king and queen of Hungary and for the duke of Oppeln. In late July he paid 50,000 Hungarian *Gulden* to Duke Ladislas, who gave him Dobrin to hold as pawn against repayment. This was immediately upon the heels of an agreement by which the grand master had purchased the rights to Zlatoria, near the Neumark, for 6,632 *Gulden*. Those agreements, though perfectly legitimate by traditional medieval standards, were direct challenges to the developing Polish concept of national sovereignty.

It would not be amiss to believe that Sigismund was working out a plot to dismember the Polish kingdom, taking the most important, southern parts for himself, while rewarding his fellow conspirators handsomely (if perhaps only temporarily) with the less valuable northern territories. Given this circumstance, and the fact that Sigismund was prone to talking too much, we can easily understand why the Poles were becoming paranoid about their national survival. What Poland needed was a ruler as slippery and unscrupulous as Sigismund. Slowly they came to realise that they had exactly that, that their monarch had married the kind of man who could outdo every contemporary in cunning and diplomatic duplicity – Jagiełło. The only question was, was he working for Polish interests, for Lithuanian, or only for his own?

Jagiełło was certainly not going to tell anyone anything other than what he wanted them to believe. In contrast to most of his countrymen, he was quiet and introspective, even dour. He drank no alcohol and ate very little. He had no enthusiasm for music or art, though he kept Rus'ian musicians at his court, and his sexual appetite was exceedingly moderate. His one passion was hunting, and his greatest enjoyment was listening to the nightingales in the forest. He was fortunate in possessing one of the greatest forests in all the world, one so extensive and forbidding that it has not completely disappeared even today. It was then filled with deer, European bison, and the vanishing aurochs, and Jagiełło was perfectly happy in its deepest and most inaccessible glens.

Jadwiga, for her part, was glad to have her uncouth husband off in the woods. She was a devout Christian, who was persuaded to abandon her young Habsburg lover only by churchmen's pleas to consider the lost souls of what could be her future subjects. Her greatest pleasures were church services and good deeds, her most feared moments were court entertainments and marital duties. She took an active part in politics, especially in dealing with the grand master, whose friendship she came to value. She was not quite clear herself what her husband's plans were. She did not know Lithuanian or Russian, and his Polish was still rudimentary; moreover, Jagiełło was not talkative.

✠

More Civil War in Lithuania

The questions that the Poles were asking about Jagiełło were exactly the ones that the Lithuanians were asking, too. As Jagiełło spent more and more of his time in Poland, his Lithuanian subjects gave their hearts increasingly to his rival. Vytautas held the lesser title of great prince, but he had been responsible for Lithuanian resistance to the crusader armies and hence had been able to make a reputation for himself as a valiant and straightforward man, a characterisation that Jagiełło could never hope for. Jagiełło and Vytautas mistrusted one another, and neither could forget the circumstances of Kęstutis' death. When Vytautas went over to the Teutonic Order in 1389, Jagiełło appointed Skirgaila, the duke of Kiev, to administer western Lithuania, Vytautas' lands; and he sent other brothers to participate in the coming war. None could win the love of their subjects as Vytautas had done, and some came over to the crusaders' side just to fight for him.

In the summer of 1390 Vytautas led crusaders from Prussia before the walls of Vilnius, where they were joined by the Livonian Knights. English bowmen, led by the future king of England, Henry Bolingbroke, demonstrated their customary efficiency in slaughtering vast numbers of enemies, Lithuanian, Rus'ian, and Polish. Vytautas lost a brother in the fighting, as did Jagiełło. Eventually the siege became a war of engineers, and after five weeks the weather turned bad. The crusaders reluctantly broke off their daily attacks and nightly revels and retreated to Königsberg, where they started the rounds of entertainment anew.

Although Poles were engaged in the war in Lithuania, the Teutonic Knights remained at peace with the kingdom of Poland. Neither side had any desire to start a general war, and Jadwiga absolutely forbade discussions of hostilities. The Teutonic Knights did not want to be distracted, Sigismund of Hungary was planning a major crusade against the Turks, and Poles rightly feared that the war would be fought in their lands – moreover, they suspected that they might well get the worst of the fighting. The reputation of the Teutonic Knights had grown since the last time Poles had entered the field against them, and as of yet few Poles trusted Jagiełło's motives or his military skill.

✠

The Tatar Complication

Meanwhile news from the steppe was fascinating listeners in Rus' and at the Polish court. Since 1385 Tokhtamysh, the Tatar khan, had been warding off as best he could the advance of Timur's (Tamberlane's) forces from Turkestan, but in 1391 he was crushed in a great battle, barely escaping the field with a handful of followers. He fled to Lithuania to ask for refuge and assistance. It appeared that Lithuania and Poland, in an alliance with Tokhtamysh, could drive Timur away and become the masters of the western steppe and more Rus'ian states. To do this, Jagiełło and his brothers would need peace with the Teutonic Knights, perhaps even their aid. How were they to achieve this? Jagiełło knew what the price would be – Lithuania to Vytautas and Samogitia to the Teutonic Order – but he was ready to pay it.

Jagiełło understood that he had better chances of making war on the steppe than his grandfather had possessed. For him it would not be the traditional struggle of swordsmen, spearmen, and archers. Innovation in warfare was changing the traditional strategies and tactics. The introduction of cannon had made many of the older fortresses obsolete – one of the reasons for the extensive recent rebuilding of the Prussian and Livonian castles – and temporarily gave the offensive an advantage over the defensive. The weapons were unwieldy and often unreliable, but under the right circumstances they were powerful. Their main use was in sieges, since they could shatter tall thin walls more effectively than stone-hurling machines had ever done and they were easier to erect and service than the bulky catapults. Mounted on defensive works, they could inflict fearsome casualities on attackers; in the field, they could kill at a greater distance than arrows, and their noise and smoke frightened horses and men alike.

Jagiełło had seen the effects of this new firepower personally. He knew that the constant influx of foreign crusaders who told the grand master about new weapons had resulted in the Teutonic Knights emphasising firepower – not only cannon, but also more archers. Even so, the grand masters' technological advantages were not as great as they had been in the past, and they were only temporary. The Lithuanians could now obtain the latest weapons through Poland – Cracow was actually closer to Italy, the industrial and technological centre of Europe, than to Livonia – and, consequently, the former pagans were never far behind the crusaders.

✙

Crusader Sieges of Vilnius

For the time being, such considerations were only dreams. Daytime plans had to concentrate on turning back the crusader advance up the Nemunas River. Jagiełło's brothers wanted heavier cannons to oppose the Teutonic Knights' new weapons, but since gun carriages did not exist yet the heavy weapons could only be transported by water. Because the Teutonic Knights controlled the lower reaches of the Nemunas River, the only route from Poland to Lithuania was from the Vistula up the Bug River to the Narew, then up that river's tributaries until close to streams that led down to the Nemunas at Gardinas. Cannon could be dragged over a short portage, or perhaps even transported the entire way over the many bodies of water in the Masurian Lake district. Not unexpectedly, the Teutonic Knights sought to block this route by building forts in the wilderness north of the Narew. This presented some complications, because that land belonged to the Masovian dukes, but it did hinder Jagiełło's efforts to send assistance to his brothers. The wilderness had been unoccupied since the withdrawal of the Sudovians to the east, and empty of all humans other than raiding parties from Prussia, Lithuania, and Masovia. But technically it was still Masovian.

Meanwhile the war had become even more brutal than before. The Teutonic Knights decapitated any Poles captured in the Lithuanian forts – they accused them of apostasy and aiding pagans – and the crusader raids into Samogitia met so little resistance that they were little more than man-hunts. In reprisal the Samogitians occasionally sacrificed prisoners to their gods, burning knights alive, tied to their mounts in full armour over a giant pyre, or shooting them full of arrows while bound to a sacred tree. Even so, the war was not continuous. Despite the desperate nature of the fighting, there were truces and sudden changes in alliances; and nothing disturbed the universal love of hunting, for which special truces were arranged.

Although Vytautas was a crusader ally, as he saw his ancestral lands being destroyed he began to look for an alternative means of returning to power in Vilnius. Intellectually, he understood that it was most logical to join forces with his cousin, but Vytautas was a passionate man, not always ruled by his mind. Besides, he had not forgotten Jagiełło's past treacheries and, well-aware of assassination plots, he surrounded himself with Tatar bodyguards. Consequently Vytautas was an emotional pendulum, swinging from one side to the other, forced to seek help from someone, but not liking any of the available allies. The Teutonic Knights took a cynical but philosophical view of this, as one chronicler stated: 'Pagans rarely do what is right, as the broken treaties of Vytautas and his relatives prove'.

Still, when he considered the situation rationally Vytautas saw his present alliance with the Teutonic Order as a losing strategy. Victory under such circumstances would make him an impoverished ruler, hated by his own people and dependent upon the goodwill of the grand master. He may have sent a message to Jagiełło, somehow evading the order's efforts to watch over his every move; if so, it was undoubtedly vague, the kind which would do no harm if discovered. Or perhaps Jagiełło merely sensed that the time was ripe to make his cousin a proposal. All that is known for certain is that in early August 1392 Jagiełło sent Bishop Henryk of Płock to Prussia as his emissary. This rather unpriestly Piast prince-bishop was related by marriage to the king's sister, Alexandra of Masovia. Henryk used the opportunity provided by confession to inform Vytautas of his master's propositions. Vytautas, under the pretext of allowing his wife to make a visit home, told Anna to negotiate with Jagiełło; he also managed to secure the release of many hostages who had been kept in honourable captivity in scattered fortresses. Then he gave his sister in marriage to Bishop Henryk and dismissed the English crusaders who had just arrived to join another invasion of Lithuania. He thus eliminated from the game the most dangerous bowmen in Europe, warriors who had been so effective in recent battles with Jagiełło's subjects.

Vytautas plotted his betrayal carefully, arranging for the Samogitian warriors stationed in the crusader castles entrusted to him to kill or capture the Germans in the garrisons. After this had succeeded, he sent Lithuanian armies on widely separated fronts into Prussia and Livonia and overwhelmed what forces the Teutonic Knights still had in Samogitia. Vytautas' return to Lithuania was greeted with wild enthusiasm. Every Samogitian appreciated his courage and cunning, contrasted his genial personality with Jagiełło's vengeful brothers, and understood that the series of military disasters was likely now at an end; and the highlanders were happy to see the reign of foreigners – Poles – at an end.

It was a year before Grand Master Wallenrode was able to take his revenge. In January of 1393 he struck at Gardinas, employing Dutch and French knights. This threatened to cut the major communication route between Masovia and Vilnius, effectively isolating Lithuania. Vytautas and Jagiełło appealed to the papal legate to arrange for peace talks, which did in fact take place in Thorn in the summer. After ten days, however, Wallenrode became ill and left the conference. A short while later he died.

The new grand master, Conrad von Jungingen, was a decisive leader of far-reaching plans and far-reaching vision. Regional peace could be achieved, he believed, by a decisive victory in Vilnius, the one location that Vytautas and Jagiełło had to defend with all their might.

Already collecting in Prussia in the waning days of 1393 was a great army of French and German crusaders, among whom was a body of Burgundian archers (perhaps English mercenaries) whose concentrated firepower had the potential to savage the pagans quite as badly as they had mauled French armies in recent years. The crusaders began their march up the Nemunas in January 1394, relying on the thick ice to serve as a highway into the Lithuanian heartland. Vytautas attempted to halt the crusader march early on, but he barely escaped death under the first barrage of his enemies' missile weapons, and his army was badly routed. The Lithuanian stand turned into a hurried retreat before the 400 advancing crusader knights and their thousands of sergeants and infantry.

Vytautas received a reinforcement from Poland, a strong contingent of knights, to join the 15,000 mounted warriors under his command, but their numbers were insufficient to stop the advance of the now much-feared archers into the heart of his country. The crusaders passed through forests, swamps, and open fields, evading ambushes, to reach Vilnius, where Vytautas was joined by his Rus'ian troops. The grand prince fought a desperate engagement, giving and taking heavy losses until his Rus'ian wing fled and was followed by one Lithuanian unit after the other. At last, he, too, had to retreat, and again he barely escaped the field alive. While Vytautas sought to rally his scattered and demoralised forces at a safe distance, the Teutonic Knights settled down to besiege his capital, a place they knew well from 1390. They made new plans to celebrate the conversion of the Lithuanians, this time assured by their arms that the baptismal ceremony would take place properly – a true conversion, not the ambiguous promises of Jagiełło and Vytautas, whose Christian names were used only in formal documents. What further proof, the crusaders asked, did anyone need that their allegiance to Rome was very thin?

On the eighth day of the siege the Livonian master arrived to reinforce the crusader host. He was welcomed heartily, for now the crusaders could surround the entire city, contain the sorties from the fortress, and make a determined assault on the wall at its weakest point. The Livonian forces were sent to the river front, where they built two bridges, then rode across the river to plunder the countryside. In this foraging they lost fifty men (only three of them German and only one a knight, indicating that a large native contingent was present) while killing and capturing 'innumerable' Lithuanians. Nevertheless, the siege did not go well. After another week of fighting, the firing posts that the engineers had built for the archers, the siege towers, and the bridges were destroyed by an inferno that the garrison set during a sortie. Nevertheless, the crusaders had some successes – their artillery had brought down a stone tower and set fire to various wooden fortifications. Soon afterward, however, the Lithuanians set a tower in the crusader camp ablaze, which not only caused extensive casualties among the French but destroyed most of the supplies, so that the crusaders would be unable to remain at Vilnius as long as planned. The grand master allowed the war of engineers to continue four more days, but it was obvious that the Lithuanians could destroy new siege works almost as fast as the crusaders could build them. An assault would require more time to prepare than the army could be kept fed by its remaining supplies. Also, Vytautas had been regrouping his scattered forces. Scouts were reporting that he would soon be coming to relieve the city. This meant that the crusaders would have to fight on two fronts – an unattractive prospect.

The leaders of the crusader armies met, discussed their situation, and reluctantly agreed to abandon the siege. The grand master sent the Livonian forces home first, then moved west himself, harassed by Lithuanians cutting down trees across the road, fortifying the river crossings, and laying ambushes in the woods. The Prussian force alternately negotiated and fought its way along the route away from Vilnius, then abruptly changed direction and marched through Samogitia, thereby avoiding Vytautas' army and the obstacles he had erected.

The expedition had been one of the most memorable enterprises of the medieval era – the siege of an enemy capital with knights and military specialists drawn from all of Europe – and a chivalric exploit worthy of any land; but the capture of the greatest city in Lithuania was beyond the ability of the crusaders. The war continued, with the Teutonic Order striking up the Nemunas River and ravaging the Samogitian settlements; they were far from attempting another invasion of the highlands, farther yet from Jagiełło's capital. The Lithuanians remained on the defensive, biding their time. They had no reason to risk everything on a pitched battle, no reason to carry the war back into Prussia. Not yet, at least.

✝

Peace

By the end of 1393 Vytautas was master of Lithuania. He had driven all Jagiełło's brothers from the land, and when his forces won a major battle in 1394, crushing the Volhynian, Galician, and Moldavian dukes, Jagiełło completely abandoned his brothers to their fate: Kaributas went into exile in Cracow; the Moldavian ruler also fled to Cracow, where he was imprisoned; Skirgaila died in Kiev in 1396, probably poisoned; and Svidrigailo fought for the Teutonic Order briefly before achieving a reconciliation. The former bishop, Henryk, died, unmourned, of poison.

Jagiełło retained the title of supreme prince, and Vytautas was satisfied with the lesser title of great prince until his very last days.* But as time passed, so real authority passed into the hands of Vytautas.

Meanwhile the crusader raids into Lithuania continued. Not only were the Prussian forces constantly in Samogitia, but so too was the black and white banner of the Livonian master – a black centre stripe horizontally flanked by white, with contrasting triangular tails fluttering behind. The last raid into Samogitia came in the winter of 1398, when the crusaders took 700 prisoners and 650 horses, and killed many people; they had surprised the defenders by entering the country during changeable weather, a gamble that had rarely proven worth the risk before, but paid high returns when successful. Vytautas did not retaliate. He was campaigning in southern Rus', longing for an end to the troublesome northern war that was hindering his

---

* In 1429 Vytautas sought to be crowned king of Lithuania, an honour cleverly offered by Sigismund, but his ambition was frustrated by Jagiełło, who arranged for the crown and other regalia to be stolen. The aged Vytautas was riding incredible distances through winter weather to prevent the coronation from being cancelled when his horse slipped and he was fatally injured.

chances for success on the steppe. Only his promise to Jagiełło stood in the way of making peace. Of course, promises were not serious obstacles to Vytautas.

Vytautas had an excuse to refuse obedience to Polish orders soon after-ward, when Jadwiga (who – not Jagiełło – was legally *rex* of Poland) demanded a tax from the Lithuanians, a tax that Vytautas' boyars had no desire to pay. The royal demand was not unreasonable. Vytautas had depended on Polish aid to defend Samogitia, and Polish nobles and clergy were asking why they had to bear all the costs, while the Lithuanians paid nothing. The Poles probably reasoned that Vytautas had no choice, and that no matter how much he protested, in the end he would make his subjects pay.

This presumed reasoning underestimated Vytautas. The grand prince was not fixated on Samogitia. Instead, he was studying the situation on the steppe. In the process of driving Jagiełło's brothers from their lands in south-ern Rus', Vytautas had confirmed suspicions that the Tatar hold on the region had weakened. Moreover, his popularity among his people would be seriously undermined if he appeared to be a mere Polish puppet.

Vytautas understood that if he did not pay the tax he would have to sue for peace with at least one enemy. Better the Teutonic Order than the Tatars, he reasoned, for it was against the weakened Tatars that he saw the best prospects of territorial expansion. In contrast to the potential conquest of the steppe, he could at best fight a defensive war against the Teutonic Knights. Peace with the grand master, of course, could be had only at a price – Samogitia. Fortunately for Vytautas, Jagiełło was caught up in the dream of driving the Tatars from the steppe too, removing them forever as a threat to his Polish and Lithuanian frontiers; and his Polish subjects, who had lived for generations in fear of the Tatars, agreed. It helped that Jadwiga knew the grand master personally and liked him; she had always wanted peace with Prussia and had encouraged the many inconclusive meetings with the grand master's representatives in the past. Now it appeared that there was the like-lihood of a breakthrough in the negotiation process.

Peace talks with the Teutonic Order culminated in September 1398 in the Treaty of Sallinwerder, which surrendered Samogitia to the Germans. Vytautas and Jagiełło led their armies to Kaunas, where the last pagans of Samogitia surrendered to the Teutonic Order. The Samogitians growled, but they understood that they could not fight without the grand prince of Lithuania and the prince-consort of Poland. Besides, they had been under crusader control before, and it had not lasted.

The next year, in the summer of 1399, a great army of Lithuanians, Rus'ians, Tatars, Poles, and Teutonic Knights rode out onto the steppe to challenge Timur's domination there. The result was another military disaster.* Had Vytautas been successful, the history of the Teutonic Order would have taken a new and more exotic turn than anyone had previously imagined. But even defeat on the steppe did not mean a return to the old ways. In the years to come some Teutonic Knights would accompany Vytautas against Rus'ian foes as far away as Moscow, and others would board ships to destroy a pirate stronghold on the island of Gotland.

It appeared that the crusade was at an end. The Teutonic Order had achieved its goal, the Christianisation of most pagans and the conquest of the rest. The Teutonic Knights still welcomed a handful of crusaders to assist in garrisoning their castles in Samogitia, but the crusade was essentially over by 1400.

Interestingly, the greatest complaints against the Teutonic Order came from those churchmen who were unhappy that the grand master was not forcing his new subjects to undergo baptism immediately. Conrad von Jungingen was instead pursuing a policy of economic development, and creating from the many petty Lithuanian boyars a smaller, dependable ruling class. He assumed, probably correctly, that in the course of time, this would result in the voluntary conversion of these stubborn woodsmen.

Vytautas believed that too. He secretly encouraged the Samogitians to hold out. He would soon be coming to free them again.

---

* Timur did not follow up his victory. Instead, he turned on the Ottoman Turks, beginning a two-year campaign that culminated in smashing their army at Angora in 1402. This left him master of Central Asia, the Golden Horde, Persia, and parts of India and Asia Minor.

10

The Battle of Tannenberg

Background

Two conflicts formed the bookends, so to say, of the fourteenth century in Prussia. The first, which began in the first decade of the century, was the order's acquisition of West Prussia, originally known as Pomerellia. This was a vital territory in several senses: its eastern border was the Vistula River, so that any hostile power possessing Pomerellia could interrupt the vital traffic up and down stream; its people and warriors were an important resource for the Prussian economy (especially the city of Danzig) and the order's war machine; and French, Burgundian, and German crusaders were able to travel to Prussia safely via Brandenburg, Neumark, and Pomerellia whenever the preferred route across Great Poland was closed. The Polish kings and the Polish Church, however, viewed the acquisition of Pomerellia by war and purchase as nothing less than theft. As far as they were concerned, no matter what Pomerellia's past or ethnic composition was, it was a Polish land, as the payment of Peter's Pence to the pope proved – no German state paid this tax, but the Polish lands did; and the patriots missed no opportunity to bemoan the loss of this province.

The second conflict, which concluded at the very end of the century, was over Samogitia. The Teutonic Knights saw this territory partly as a land bridge to Livonia that would permit year-round communication with their northern possessions, and partly as the heart of pagan resistance to conversion. Lithuanian grand princes, whose authority was seldom recognised by the Samogitians, fought hard to retain it as a part of their national patrimony.

Surprisingly, the Teutonic Knights had managed to make peace both with Poland (the Peace of Kalish, 1343) and Lithuania (the Peace of Sallinwerder, 1398). Two Lithuanians, Jagiełło of Poland and Vytautas of Lithuania, even assisted in ending Samogitian resistance to the order in return for its aid in expeditions against Moscow and the Tatars.

This era of co-operation came to an end in 1409, after an insurrection in Samogitia. The Teutonic Knights had reasons to believe that Vytautas had encouraged the rebels, and that behind Vytautas was the sly hand of Jagiełło. Their usually cautious diplomacy, however, was now in the hands of a brash new grand master, Ulrich von Jungingen, who was not only relatively young but seemed to believe that his military order had lost sight of its original purpose – to fight pagans. By that he understood Samogitians and their allies, not distant Rus'ians, Tatars, pirates, or Turks. He saw the immediate enemies right at hand: Poland and Lithuania.

The grand master's haughty demands that the Poles and Lithuanians cease providing aid to the Samogitian rebels provoked cries for war in both nations. But it was not yet clear that hotheads in Poland would move to action the more cautious mass of nobles and clergy who remained in awe of the Teutonic Knights' military reputation.

✠

The Changing Balance of Power

The membership of the Teutonic Knights, and especially the grand master's council, were confident of their ability to intimidate Polish nobles, Lithuanian boyars, and the prelates of both nations, no matter that the patriotic ire of powerful groups had been raised by Grand Master Ulrich's actions in 1409. They believed that the Polish and Lithuanian rulers had too many distractions to make common cause against them; moreover, they believed too that Vytautas and Jagiełło mistrusted one another too much to co-operate militarily – everyone knew the story of their feud's origin and their many subsequent reconciliations and falling-outs – and their nobles and churchmen were, like their counterparts in the West, difficult to lead. Also, since Jagiełło and Vytautas had never yet tried to bring their armies into the heart of Prussia, it seemed unlikely that they would do more than launch attacks at widely separated points, probably in Samogitia and West Prussia, perhaps Culm. The grand master could meet these attacks by using local resources defensively against the less dangerous threats and concentrating his mobile forces against the main army, which would probably invade West Prussia.

In addition, everyone was aware that Jagiełło and Vytautas had a permanent problem to their east, where Tatars were always a danger, and to the south, where Sigismund could raise levies in his Hungarian, Bohemian, and

Silesian lands and invade Poland at short notice. Lastly, almost every German knight believed that Polish nobles might be willing to fight in defence of their homeland but would be reluctant to approve raising troops for offensive warfare; it was axiomatic that the Polish prelates and knights would talk bravely but nevertheless refuse to approve funds for war or to authorise calling out the feudal levy. That miscalculation was founded on a well-proven rule, that the Poles had long mistrusted Jagiełło almost as much as did Vytautas and the Teutonic Order. However, time changes all things, and Jagiełło's relationship with his subjects had changed over the decade he had been king; they had learned to trust him more; they had become accustomed to him. He may not have produced a son yet, but there was a daughter, significantly named Jadwiga for her mother, who would inherit the throne some day. The Poles were more confident now that Jagiełło was their king, not simply a Lithuanian prince out for the main chance.

This changed attitude displayed itself in December 1409, when Nicholas Traba, a future archbishop of Gniezno, took part in the secret meeting of Jagiełło and Vytautas at Brest to make plans for war. Their subsequent diplomatic offensive won Duke Johan of Masovia as an ally, though not Duke Ziemowit IV, who remained neutral, nor the dukes of Pomerania, who became allies of the Teutonic Order. Most importantly, the people of Poland and Lithuania were prepared psychologically for the great conflict to come.

Even those few Germans who thought that Jagiełło might fight did not expect a great battle to come about as a result of the bluster, the embargo, or the grand master's raid into Masovia and Great Poland. First of all, large battles were a rare phenomenon – the risks were too great and the financial rewards too few, especially when compared to the security of raiding lands defended only by half-armed peasants or demanding ransom from burghers. Secondly, except for sporadic conflicts such as that in 1409 there had been peace between Poland and Prussia for seven decades now, and since the Samogitian issue had been resolved in the Treaties of Sallinwerder (1398) and Racianz (1404), why should there be war with Lithuania? Few living Germans or Prussians could remember the last significant Polish or Lithuanian invasion. A border raid from Great Poland or on some less well-protected frontier area of East Prussia was likely, after which another truce would be signed. On the principal issue, Samogitia, surely the Lithuanians in 1410, like the Poles in 1409, would back down?

Similarly, it was unlikely that the grand master would invade Poland again. Once the Poles had reinforced their border fortresses the grand master could not expect another series of easy victories without considerable help from crusaders; and it was unlikely that large numbers of volunteers would come to Prussia to participate in the invasion of a

Christian kingdom, though a good number of German and Bohemian mercenaries would travel east if financial incentives were added to the usual chivalric attractions. An invasion of Lithuania was completely out of the question; no grand master had ever sent a major force east unless he was certain that the Poles would refrain from raiding Prussia as soon as the garrisons rode into the wilderness – and such co-operation was very doubtful now. Lastly, the issues at stake did not seem to be of sufficient importance for any ruler to justify the risk of hazarding a pitched battle. That was the reason that, although the rival popes in Rome and Avignon and the rival emperors, Wenceslas of Bohemia and Ruprecht of the Palatinate, took some notice of the escalating tension throughout 1409 and 1410, their efforts at reconciliation were minimal; extraordinary measures did not seem merited for a distant conflict over inconsequential lands and personal vanities.

Western Europeans took little notice of Prussia because they had much more important concerns of their own to deal with – the Council of Pisa, which was supposed to end the Great Schism in the Church,* but which seemed to be doing little more than complicate an already difficult situation; the continuing northward advance of the Turks, who were marching out of the Balkans into the Steiermark and Croatia to threaten the lands of the Cilly family (who were related by marriage to both King Jagiełło and King Sigismund of Hungary) and thus open the way across the Alpine mountain barriers into Austria and Italy; and the war between Burgundy and France, which occupied so many families that had once sent crusaders to Prussia. Yet a great battle did occur on 15 July 1410, on a field between the villages of Tannenberg and Grunwald (Grünfelde).

This battle at Tannenberg/Grunwald/Żalgris – as Germans, Poles, and Lithuanians respectively call it – has assumed a prominence that exaggerates its real significance. The history of north central Europe was not suddenly transformed by this one battle. Changes in the balance of power were well under way before the battle was fought, and those changes were so fundamental that one can hardly imagine a greatly different world today if the battle had not taken place. The kingdom of Poland was already on the rise, and the day of the military orders had passed. It is not likely that the Teutonic Knights could have maintained political or military equality with

---

* The French supported the Avignon pope, the English and many Germans the Roman pope, and the Council of Pisa provided a third candidate for universal recognition. The situation in Germany became somewhat clearer after the death of Ruprecht of the Rhine. Germans, despairing of King Wenceslas ever amounting to anything, began to discuss whether his brother, Sigismund of Hungary, would be an effective Holy Roman emperor. Sigismund linked his candidacy with efforts to resolve the problems of the Church.

a nation as populous, creative, wealthy, and energetic as Poland; moreover, since Poland was a multi-ethnic state and this was the fifteenth century, not the twenty-first, there would have been few, if any, changes in the ethnic composition of Prussia had those lands come into the immediate posses- sion of the Polish crown. Within a year of the great battle the Teutonic Knights were able to defend themselves again and expel the Poles and Lithuanians from their territories. Nevertheless, the battle was so costly to the order in men and material that subsequent grand masters were never again able to regain the power or prestige their predecessors had enjoyed. For the Teutonic Knights the road led downhill from that day on, until the Thirteen Years' War (1453–66) brought complete disaster. Therefore, although the battle of Tannenberg may not be the decisive moment in the history of medieval Prussia, it was the start of a rapid and progressively steeper decline.

In the final analysis, Tannenberg was important because it was a highly dramatic event that lent itself to endless retelling, and, rightly or wrongly, the fortunes of entire peoples could be easily related to it.

✠

Political Manoeuvring

Not even the participants had anticipated anything like the battle that did occur. Although there had been bad feelings between the grand masters and the Lithuanian cousins for decades, the military conflict that began in August 1409 was not beyond a compromise settlement. There was international pressure applied by the popes individually to arrange just such a compromise peace, so that Christendom could stand united in its efforts to restore unity in the Church and drive back the Turks from the borders of Austria and Hungary, or at least stem their raids to collect slaves and booty.

Foremost of the secular rulers seeking to forestall the conflict was Wenceslas of Bohemia. Though widely repudiated as Holy Roman emperor by his German subjects, he sent representatives in 1409 to mediate the quarrel. They brought Ulrich von Jungingen and King Jagiełło together on 4 October for five days of talks that resulted in a truce until St John's Day (24 June) the following year. This sign of reconciliation made many hope that further compromises could be reached. The most important article in the truce agreement authorised Wenceslas to propose fair terms for a per- manent peace settlement. His proposal was to be presented before Lent, a date that allowed additional negotiations to take place before the truce expired. The critical months, however, were those before Lent, when Ulrich von Jungingen and Jagiełło each sought to sway the notoriously fickle monarch in his own favour.*

The grand master had a short history of the Samogitian crusade prepared, a document that depicted the Lithuanians as undependable turncoats who had violated their promises to the Poles in 1386 and to the Germans in 1398; moreover, it claimed that those Lithuanians who were indeed Christians were, in fact, members of the heretic Russian Orthodox faith, and that the Samogitians were complete pagans who had not allowed a single baptism in the past five years. Not relying on letters alone, the grand master sent an imposing delegation to Hungary. Those representatives signed an alliance with King Sigismund in December and agreed to pay him 40,000 *Gulden* for his assistance. Sigismund, in turn, honoured his guests by asking them to be godfathers to his newly born daughter, Elisabeth. From Hungary the delegates went to Bohemia to present final arguments before Wenceslas rendered his decision on 8 February 1410.

The core of the Bohemian peace proposal was to return to the *status quo ante bellum*. Those were hardly terms likely to please Vytautas and Jagiełło, especially since the Lithuanian complaints were ignored and the Poles were admonished to abstain from any and all aid to the Samogitian 'non-Christians'. Wenceslas warned that he would attack whichever party refused to honour the treaty he proposed – a conventional threat without much substance to it. The Teutonic Knights had won a total victory, right down to confirmation of their right to possess West Prussia and the Neumark. In fact it was too thorough a victory, too one-sided. There was never any possibility of persuading the king of Poland to accept the mediator's terms.

The time for the order's celebration was short. Polish diplomats remained in Prague for a month, arguing vainly that the terms of the peace treaty were unfair, until Wenceslas finally lost his temper and threatened to make war on Poland himself. The Poles departed, certain that war with the Teutonic Knights, at least, would follow; perhaps there would be a gigantic conflict with all their western neighbours as well. Jagiełło, who read Wenceslas' personality more accurately, was less intimidated: he rejected all proposals for further negotiations, and when Wenceslas summoned him to a conference in Breslau in May, he left the emperor and the Teutonic Knights waiting in vain for Polish representatives, who had already announced that they would not come.

---

* Historians remember Wenceslas mainly for his drunkenness. Britons and Americans remember him for the Christmas carol dating from the marriage of his daughter to King Richard II, 'Good King Wenceslas'. Czechs remember him for throwing the archbishop of Prague from Charles Bridge to drown.

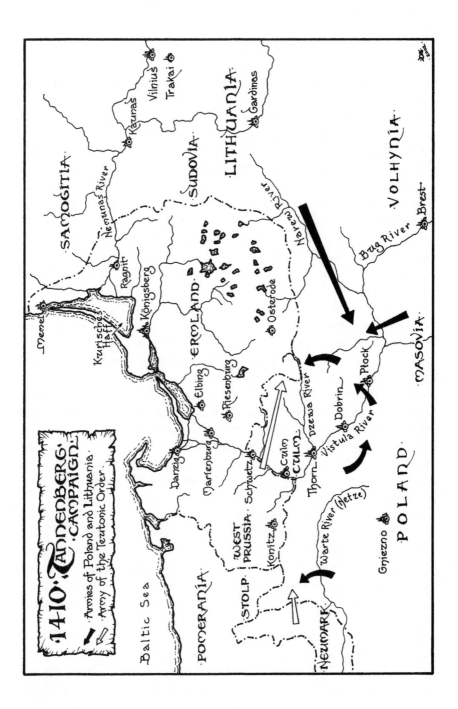

1410 TANNENBERG CAMPAIGN

Armies of Poland and Lithuania.
Army of the Teutonic Order.

Baltic Sea

POMERANIA

STOLP.

WEST PRUSSIA.

Schwetz

Konitz

Danzig

Marienburg

Elbing

Riesenburg

Königsberg

Ragnit

Kurisches Haff

Memel

SAMOGITIA

Nemunas River

Kaunas

Vilnius

Trakai

SUDOVIA

Gardinas

LITHUANIA

VOLHYNIA

Brest

Bug River

ERMLAND

Osterode

Narew River

MASOVIA

Plock

Dobrin

Vistula River

Drewenz River

Thorn

Culm CULM

Warte River (Netze)

NEUMARK

Gniezno

POLAND

✠

The Raising of Armies

The armies began to gather. When ready, Jagiełło summoned Vytautas to join him in Masovia. Until recently that had required a journey through a dense, swampy wilderness. However, thanks to the opening of the trade route along the Narew River it was now possible for Vytautas to bring his men to the desired location near Płock without undue difficulties. The bulk of the royal forces remained on the western bank of the Vistula, but Jagiełło sent Polish knights to the other bank to hold the fords for Vytautas, and more troops were coming in daily. By mid-June the king had at his disposal a force of more than 30,000 cavalry and infantry (18,000 Polish knights and squires, with a few thousand foot soldiers; some Bohemian and Moravian mercenaries; 11,000 Lithuanian, Rus'ian, and Tatar cavalry, a formidable contingent from Moldavia led by its prince, Alexander the Good, and some Samogitians).

Grand Master Ulrich had raised a huge force too, perhaps 20,000 strong. Since Jungingen had allowed the Livonian master to conclude a truce with Vytautas, however, none of those excellent knights were able to join him; in any case, the northern knights were not enthusiastic about the war, and although the Livonian master sent word to Vytautas immediately that the truce would expire at the end of the grace period, he would not send troops to Prussia or attack Lithuania's vulnerable northern lands until that time had passed. Moreover, since Jungingen could raise only about 10,000 cavalry in Prussia the rest of his warriors were 'pilgrims' and mercenaries. Sigismund had sent two prominent nobles with 200 knights, and Wenceslas had allowed the grand master to hire a large number of his famed Bohemian warriors.

The numbers for both armies are very inexact, with estimates varying from half the totals given above to almost astronomical figures. In all cases, however, the proportion of troops in the armies remained about the same: three to two in favour of the Polish king and the Lithuanian grand prince. But the grand master had a compensating advantage in equipment and organisation, and especially in having nearby fortresses for supplies and refuge; and since, as far as he knew, the enemy forces had not yet joined, he believed that he could fight them one at a time. A few of Jagiełło's and Vytautas' commanders had served together in earlier campaigns, some against the Tatars, some against the crusaders; nevertheless, their army was composed of troops so diverse that maintaining cohesion would be difficult. Jungingen had a larger number of disciplined knights who were accustomed to fighting as units, but he also had levies of secular knights and crusaders who were prey to fits of enthusiasm and panic; he was also fighting on the defensive, better able to fall back on prepared positions and more informed about roads, tracks, and what obstacles were passable. The odds were fairly nearly equal.

An order chronicler, an anonymous contemporary continuing the earlier work by Johann von Posilge, described the preliminaries of the battle in vivid detail, thereby giving useful insights into the attitude the crusaders held toward their opponents:

[King Jagiełło] gathered the Tatars, Russians, Lithuanians, and Samogitians against Christendom . . . So the king met with the non-Christians and with Vytautas, who came through Masovia to aid him, and with the duchess . . . [T]here was so large an army that it is impossible to describe, and it crossed from Płock toward the land of Prussia. At Thorn were the important counts of Gora and Stiborzie, whom the king of Hungary had sent especially to Prussia to negotiate the issues and controversies between the order and Poland; but they could do nothing about the matter and finally departed from the king, who followed his evil and divisive will to injure Christendom. He was not satisfied with the evil men of the pagans and Poles, but he had hired many mercenaries from Bohemia, Moravia, and all kinds of knights and men-at-arms, who against all honour and goodness and honesty went with heathendom against the Christians to ravage the lands of Prussia.

One hardly expects a balanced judgement from chroniclers, but the accusations of hiring mercenaries certainly strikes the modern reader as odd, since the Teutonic Knights were doing the same thing. Men of the Middle Ages, like many today, hated passionately, often acted impulsively, and reasoned irrationally. Yet they were capable of behaving very logically too. The leaders of the armies soon gave proof that they were men of their era, acting as they did alternately with cool reason and hot temper. Reason predominated at the outset of the campaign.

The Hungarian count palatine and the voivode of Transylvania mentioned in the passage above returned south hurriedly to collect troops on the southern border of Poland. Their threat was unconvincing, however; consequently they had no effect on the campaign at all. Sigismund, as was his wont, had promised more than he was willing to deliver; he did nothing beyond allowing the grand master to hire mercenaries, though he was in northern Hungary at the time and could have raised a large force quickly.

✠

The Invasion of Prussia

The strategies of the two commanders contrasted greatly. The grand master divided his forces in the traditional manner between East and West Prussia, awaiting invasions at widely scattered points and relying on his scouts to determine the greatest threats, his intention being to concentrate his forces quickly wherever necessary to drive back the invaders. Jagiełło, however, planned to concentrate the Lithuanian and Polish armies into one huge body, an unusual tactic. Although adopted from time to time in the Hundred Years' War, it was more common among the Mongols and Turks – enemies the Poles and Lithuanians had fought often. The Teutonic Knights did the same during their *Reisen* into Samogitia, but those had been much smaller armies.

In this phase of the campaign Jagiełło's generalship was exemplary. As soon as he heard that Vytautas had crossed the Narew River he ordered his men to build a 450-metre pontoon bridge over the Vistula River. Within three days he had brought the main royal host to the east bank, then dismantled the bridge for future use. By 30 June his men had joined Vytautas. On 2 July the entire force began to move north. The king had thus far cleverly avoided the grand master's efforts to block his way north and even kept his crossing of the Vistula a secret until the imperial peace envoys informed Jungingen. Even then the grand master failed to credit the report, so sure was he that the main attack would come on the west bank of the Vistula and be conducted by only the Polish forces.

When Jungingen obtained confirmation of the envoys' story he hurriedly crossed the great river with his army and sought a place where he could intercept the enemy in the southern forest and lake region, before Lithuanian and Polish foragers could fan out among the rich villages of the settled areas in the river valleys. His plan was still purely defensive – to use his enemies' numbers against them, anticipating that they would exhaust their food and fodder more swiftly than his own well-supplied forces. The foe had not yet trod Prussian ground.

The grand master had left 3,000 men under Heinrich von Plauen at Schwetz (Swiecie) on the Vistula, to protect West Prussia from a surprise invasion in case the Poles managed to elude him again and then strike down-river into the richest parts of Prussia before he could cross the river again. Plauen was a respected but minor officer, suitable for a responsible defensive post but not seen as a battlefield leader. Jungingen wanted to have his most valuable officers with him, to offer sound advice and provide examples of wisdom, courage, and chivalry. Jungingen was relatively young, and a bit hot-headed, but all his training advised him to err on the side of caution until battle was joined. Daring was a virtue in the face of the enemy, but not before.

Jagiełło, too, was a careful general. Throughout his entire career he had avoided risks. No story exists of his ever having put his life in danger or led horsemen in a wild charge against a formidable enemy. Yet neither was there the slightest hint of cowardice. Societal norms were changing. Everyone acknowledged the responsibility of the commander to remain alive; everyone accepted the fact that the commander should guide the fortunes of his army rather than seek fame in personal combat.

Consequently it was no surprise that the king's advance toward enemy territory was slow. His caution was understandable. After all, he could not be certain that his ruse had worked; and he had great respect for Jungingen's military skills. Without doubt, he worried that he would stumble into an ambush and give the crossbearers their greatest victory ever. He must have been half-relieved when his scouts reported that the crusaders had taken up a defensive position at a crossing of the Dzewa (Drewenz, Drweça) River. At least he knew where Jungingen was, waiting at the Masovian border. On the other hand, the news that the grand master's position was very strong could not have been welcome.

So far each commander had moved cautiously toward the other. Jagiełło and Jungingen alike feared simple tactical errors, such as being caught by nightfall far from a suitable camping place, or having to pass through areas suitable for ambush or blockade; in addition, they had to provide protection for their transport, reserve horses, and herds of cattle. Although each commander was experienced in directing men in war, these armies were larger than either had brought into battle previously, and the larger the forces, the more danger there was of error, of misunderstanding orders, and of panic.

Judged by those criteria, both commanders deserve high marks for bringing their armies into striking distance of each other without having made serious blunders. Both armies were well-supplied, ready to fight, and confident of a good chance for victory; the officers all knew their opponents well, were familiar with the countryside and the weather, and in full command of the available technology. The resemblance of some formations to armed mobs was offset by martial traditions, individual unit drill, and widespread experience in local wars. Neither army was handicapped by dissensions in command, quarrels among units, unusual prevalence of illness, or excessive anxiety about the impending combat – these problems existed, but they were probably shared equally and were not serious enough to merit mention in contemporary accounts. In short, there were no excuses for failure.

For the Teutonic Knights, each commander, each officer, each knight was as ready for combat as could reasonably be expected. All that remained uncertain was how the battle would begin, how individuals would react, and how the affair would unfold – for those are unknowns always present in warfare. Though many individuals had participated in raids and sieges, few had personal experience in a pitched battle between large armies. Some crusaders may have gained sad experience at Nicopolis in 1396,[*] and some of their opponents may have survived Vytautas' 1399 disaster on the Vorskla in the Ukraine against the Tatars, but those would be the only ones who knew what to expect when tens of thousands of combatants came together for a few minutes of intense struggle. Only they knew first-hand that warfare on this scale was chaos beyond imagination, with commanders unable to contact more than a few units, with movement limited by the sheer numbers of men and animals on the field, with the senses overwhelmed by noise, smoke from fires and cannon, and dust stirred up by the horses, the body's natural dehydration worsened by excitement-induced thirst, and exhaustion from stress and exertion. This led to an irrational eagerness for any escape from the tension – either flight or immersion in combat. Aside from that small number of experienced knights there was only the practice field and small-scale warfare in Samogitia, the campaign in Gotland,[†] and the 1409 invasion of Poland. Those provided good military experience, but there had not been a set-piece combat between the Teutonic Knights and the Lithuanians for forty years, or between the Teutonic Knights and the Poles for almost eighty. Throughout all of Europe, in fact, there had been many campaigns, but few battles. For both veterans and neophytes there was consolation in storytelling, boasting, prayer, and drinking.

The Lithuanians were more experienced, but only in the more open warfare on the steppes and in the forests of Rus'. Riding small horses and wearing light Rus'ian armour, they were not well equipped for close combat with Western knights on large chargers, but they were equal to their enemy in pride and their confidence in their commander. Memory of Vytautas' disaster on the Vorskla had been dimmed by subsequent victorious campaigns against Smolensk, Pskov, Novgorod, and Moscow. Between 1406 and 1408 Vytautas had led armies against his son-in-law, Basil of Moscow, three times, once reaching the Kremlin and at last forcing him to accept a peace treaty

---

[*] French and Hungarian crusaders were massacred by the Turks because they had lacked battlefield discipline. It was an experience that made Sigismund of Hungary extremely cautious for the rest of his long career.

[†] On behalf of the Prussian merchants and the Hanseatic League, the Teutonic Knights had destroyed a major pirate base at Visby, then held the island for several years against Danish efforts to retake it.

that restored the 1399 frontiers. Vytautas' strength was in his cavalry's ability to go across country that defensive forces might consider impassable; his weakness was that lightly-equipped horsemen could not survive a charge by heavy warhorses bearing well-armoured knights – he counted on his Tatar scouts to prevent such an event happening by surprise.

The mounted Polish forces were more numerous and better equipped for a pitched battle with the Germans, but they lacked confidence in their ability to stand up to the Teutonic Knights. The contemporary Polish historian Długosz complained about their unreliability, their lust for booty, and their tendency to panic. Most Polish knights – at least 75% – sacrificed armour for speed and endurance, but they were not as 'oriental' as the Lithuanians. In this they hardly differed from the majority of the order's forces, light cavalry suitable to local conditions. Of the rest, many Polish knights wore plate armour and preferred the crossbow to the spear, just as did many of the Teutonic Knights' heavy cavalry. The weakness lay in training and experience: many Polish knights were weekend warriors, landlords and young men; they were non-professionals who knew that they were up against the best trained and equipped troops in Christendom. Although some of them had served under the king previously, he seems to have drawn more troops from the north for this campaign than from the south; and it was the southern knights who had served with him in Galicia and Sandomir. Jagiełło could have called up more knights, but he could not have found room for them at the campsites, much less fed them. The masses of almost untrained peasant militia were much easier to manage; their noble lords could assume they would feed themselves and they could sleep outside no matter what the weather was. While the peasants' usefulness in battle was small – at best they could divert the enemy for a short while, allowing the cavalry time to regroup or to retreat – they were good at pillaging the countryside, thereby helping feed the army, and the smoke of villages they set afire might confuse the enemy as to where the main strength of the royal host lay.

The size of Jagiełło's and Vytautas' armies must have created serious problems for the rear columns. By the time thousands of horses had ridden along the roads, the mud in low-lying places must have been positively liquid, making marching difficult and pulling carts almost impossible; moreover, the larger any body of men and the more exhausted they became the more likely they were to give in to inexplicable panic. Scouting reports were unreliable; there were too many woods, streams, and enemy patrols. Nevertheless, the king, no matter how exhausted, nervous, or unsure he and his military advisors might be, had to avoid giving any impression of indecisiveness or fear; he had to appear calm at all times. Jagiełło's dour personality lent itself to this role. A non-drinker, he was sober at all times, and his demeanour was that of total self-control. His love of hunting had prepared him well for the hours on horseback and feeling at home in the deepest woods; he would have regarded the lightly inhabited forests of Dobrin and Płock as tame stuff indeed. Vytautas was the perfect foil; he was the energetic and inspirational leader who was everywhere at once, at home among warriors and disdainful of supposed hardships. No common soldier could complain that their commanders did not understand the warrior's life or the dangers of the forest, or that they did not share the tribulations of life on the march.

This need to appear to be in command was itself a danger – any army on the march can be held up at a ford or a narrow place between lakes and swamps, even if no enemy is present. The commander has to give some order, any order, even if it's only 'sit down', rather than seem to be unable to make a decision. Such circumstances, compounded by exhaustion, thirst, or anxiety, often resulted in hurriedly issued orders to attack or retreat that the men are unable to carry out effectively. In short, circumstances might limit the royal options to bad ones, and the perceived need for haste might cause the king to select the worst of those available. Jagiełło was certainly aware of all this, for he was an experienced campaigner. However, for many years his strength had lain in persuading his foes to retreat ahead of overwhelming numbers, or in besieging strongholds; his goal had always been to prepare the way for diplomacy. Now he was leading a gigantic army to a confrontation with a hitherto invincible foe, to fight, if the enemy commander so chose, a pitched battle in hostile territory.

Jagiełło seemed to have been checked at the Dzewa River before he could cross into Prussia. He was unwilling to attempt to force a crossing at the only nearby ford in the face of a strongly-entrenched enemy; he would not find it easy to move eastward and upstream – while the headwaters of the Dzewa presented no significant obstacle to his advance, the countryside there had once been thickly forested, and important remnants of the ancient wilderness still remained. Most importantly, although the Teutonic Knights had used the century of peace to establish many settlements in the rolling countryside, the roads connecting the villages were narrow and winding. There were too many hills and swamps for roads to proceed from point to point, and strangers could easily lose their sense of direction in the dense woods. The villagers were fleeing into fortified refuges or the forest. Although many of the inhabitants spoke Polish (immigrants not being subject to linguistic tests in those days), they were loyal to the Teutonic Order, and none wanted to fall into the hands of Vytautas' flying squadrons – especially not the terrifying Tatars – which were trying to locate the defensive forces and find a way around them. Making peasants give information or serve as guides was part of warfare. Burning villages marked the progress of the scouting units.

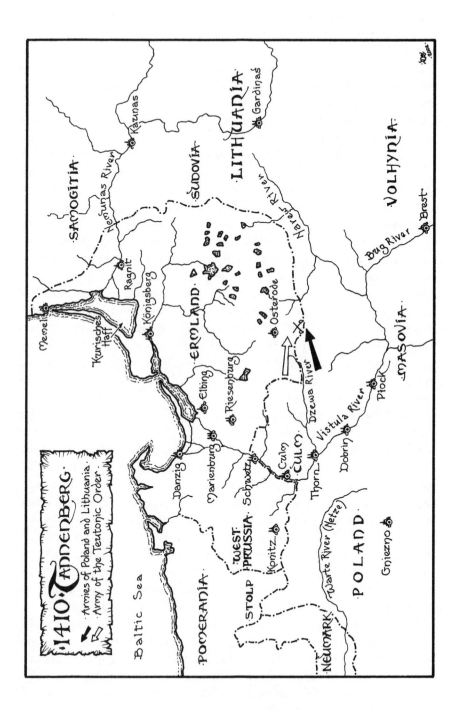

1410 TANNENBERG

→ : Armies of Poland and Lithuania
⇨ : Army of the Teutonic Order

SAMOGITIA

LITHUANIA

SUDOVIA

VOLHYNIA

ERMLAND

MASOVIA

POLAND

WEST PRUSSIA

POMERANIA

STOLP

NEUMARK

Baltic Sea

Nemunas River

Narev River

Bug River

Dzewa River

Vistula River

Warte River (Netze)

Kaunas

Gardinas

Brest

Memel

Ragnit

Königsberg

Kurisches Haff

Osterode

Plock

Elbing

Riesenburg

Dobrin

Danzig

Marienburg

Schwetz

Culm

CULM

Thorn

Konitz

Gniezno

Though this could hardly have been seen easily by the two armies confronting one another at the ford, they might well have been aware of the rising columns of smoke.

However, terrorising the countryside, burning, and pillaging was a far cry from the battle tactics that the Poles had become accustomed to; the long era of peace had softened the sensibilities of these amateur warriors. Polish knights were soon complaining to Jagiełło about their allies' behaviour – Tatars hauling women into their tents and then raping them repeatedly, killing peasants who spoke Polish, treating captives inhumanely – until the king finally ordered the prisoners released and admonished the steppe horsemen to avoid such cruel practices in the future. This restraint was not in his best interests – the king's best hope for making Jungingen weaken his position was to wreak such destruction on nearby rural communities that the grand master would feel compelled to send troops to protect them. However, within a short time Jagiełło and Vytautas saw that Jungingen was too good a commander to disperse his forces at such a critical moment.

The king must have been frustrated, yet he was unwilling either to allow his campaign to end from empty bellies or send his men to be slaughtered on some obscure river bank. While it was not clear that he could move eastward through the woods and swamps and around the incredibly complicated system of lakes without being easily blocked by the grand master, then forced to fight at a disadvantage, that seemed his only hope. This was, after all, the grand master's home ground, and surely the Teutonic Knights would have seen to the building of some roads. If so, however, why were they not using them now to harass the Polish rear?

Jungingen, for his part, does not seem to have worried about a Polish flanking manoeuvre. Teutonic Knights from nearby convents had hunted for recreation in these woods; hence they were familiar with every village, field, and forest; they knew well how the many long, narrow, twisting lakes would limit the options available to invading armies. Polish and Lithuanian scouts had been active for days, looking for paths through the surrounding woods, and they had yet to find one. The assurance of such local residents as had undoubtedly agreed to act as guides and scouts for the Teutonic Knights, that the roads were not suitable for the use of any large army, may have given Jungingen more confidence in his superior strategic position than was warranted.

This confidence was misplaced, however. When the Lithuanian scouts reported that they had found some roads leading toward Osterode that could be used – if the army moved before the Germans learned what was planned – the king and grand prince acted on the information quickly.

Jagiełło consulted with his inner council, then gave orders to prepare for a secret, swift march eastward and north around Jungingen's fortified position. He assigned each unit its place in the order of march and instructed everyone to obey the two guides who knew the country. The royal trumpeter would give the signals in the morning; until then no one was to make any movement or noise that might betray his plans prematurely. Unless his army could get a start of many hours, the stratagem was hopeless. Meanwhile, he sent a herald to make another effort at a peaceful settlement of the matter. Quite likely this was a deceptive manoeuvre to persuade the grand master that the king was in a desperate situation, but it might also have been a *pro forma* means of persuading the peace commissioners that he was truly desirous of ending the war without further bloodshed. It is hard to imagine what terms Jungingen might have considered acceptable in this situation, but the grand master nevertheless called a meeting of his officers; with one exception, they preferred war to further negotiations.

Jagiełło's actions may well have increased the grand master's overconfidence in the superiority of his situation. Certainly, when Jungingen's scouts saw the Polish camp empty, they assumed that the king was withdrawing. The Germans crossed the river on swiftly erected pontoon bridges and set out in pursuit, knowing that there is nothing easier to destroy than an army on the retreat. However, when the scouts saw that the Poles and Lithuanians were moving north-east in two columns, working their way in a wide arc around their flank, Jungingen had to reconsider his plans. If his men continued following the enemy units, they would not be able to stop Vytautas' Tatars from torching countless villages; worse, they might find themselves trailing the enemy through deep forests or fall into an ambush at some ford with nothing but desolated lands and wilderness at their rear. Therefore the grand master changed the direction of his advance in order to get ahead of the enemy columns. In fact the speed at which Jungingen's army moved almost caused it to overshoot the Polish and Lithuanian line of march. Meanwhile, the Polish scouts had completely lost contact with the Germans and were surprised when they found Jungingen once again blocking the roads north.

Jagiełło, in luring the German forces east, away from their strong fortresses in Culm, was moving his own army far from safe refuges, too; moreover, he had divided his forces, sending the Lithuanians east and north of the road used by the Poles. Should the grand master somehow attack his forces by surprise, especially before they could reunite, Jagiełło might suffer an irreversible disaster. Because many Poles still considered him a Lithuanian under the skin, Jagiełło was placing his crown at risk in seeking battle under such conditions. This was something that Ulrich von Jungingen surely understood – a victory over the Polish and Lithuanian armies could ruin his order's ancient enemies now and forever.

What the grand master did not understand was the need to remain calm and rational. When scouts reported to him that the invaders had gone as far as Gilgenberg and had burned the city, inflicting indescribable outrages on the citizens, Jungingen's temper flared. No more positional warfare – he would march on the foe by night and attack by surprise at dawn. When the grand master set his army in motion he was taking a risk that he could have avoided. The best-informed German chronicler, Posilge, described the recent movements of the two armies thus:

> The grand master with his forces and the guests and mercenaries rode against the king to the border near Drewenz, near Kauernik, and the two armies camped opposite one another. Because the king of Poland did not dare cross the Drewenz, he went toward Gilgenberg and took that city and burned it, and they struck dead young and old and with the heathens committed so many murders as was unholy, dishonouring maidens, women, and churches, cutting off their breasts and torturing them, and driving them off to serfdom. Also the heathens committed great blasphemies on the sacraments; whenever they came into the churches they ground the host in their hands and threw it under their feet, and in that way committed their insults. Their great blasphemies and insults went to the hearts of the grand master, the whole order, and to all the knights and men-at-arms among the guests; and they rode with righteous indignation against the king from Lubov to Tannenberg, to the village in the district of Osterode, and came upon the king without warning, having come in great haste fifteen miles by daybreak on the 15th of July. And when they could see the enemy, they formed their ranks and held the enemy in sight for more than three hours. The king meanwhile sent the heathens out to skirmish, but the Poles were altogether unready. If they had attacked the king immediately they would have won honour and booty, but that, unfortunately, did not happen; they wanted to call him out to fight chivalrously with them. The marshal sent the king two unsheathed swords with the heralds.

Such were the movements of the two armies. Jungingen had managed to bring his forces against the Poles and Lithuanians without warning, a considerable feat for any era. Then he wasted his advantage, letting the sleepless soldiers stand in battle order without food or drink until the enemy was ready. After that, he had his men dig camouflaged pits to trap the charging Polish cavalry, then ordered a withdrawal from that line so that the royal forces in the woods could have room to deploy in two lines in the open field against him. As a result, not only were his pits now part of the Polish defensive line, but his powerful artillery was now stationed at a place where it was ineffective; moreover, his infantry was standing where it was difficult to provide proper support for the massed bodies of knights. Even considering that the grand master could hardly expect the Polish knights to charge unless they had room to line up their units, this was poor generalship. Jungingen's troops were tired, wet from a morning shower, hungry, and undoubtedly becoming nervous. Moreover, the day was unusually warm, and the men were not accustomed to heat. Nevertheless, Jungingen had a good chance of prevailing if only he could persuade the king to commit his troops to battle first, allowing the experienced knights the opportunity for one of their long-practised counter-strokes. The grand master's pride, arrogance, and rashness were partly balanced by his courage and skill in battle – and he had a large force behind him. The masses of knights in the huge formations masked the poor placement of his supporting troops and gave him confidence in a total victory.

The sight of the armies forming their lines of battle was something that no participant ever forgot: the grand master's elite corps of white-clad knights around his large white banner with the black cross, the colourful flags of the castellans and bishops; Jagieło's crowned white eagle on a red field; the archbishop of Gniezno's white cross on a red field; the castellan of Cracow's crowned bear; the Polish marshal's lion-head breathing fire against a blue background; the Lithuanians' white knight (Vytis) on a white horse; and the geometric symbol for Vilnius. The serried ranks of the infantry and bowmen paraded into place, accompanied by music; the artillery was dragged to whatever slight rise might give the cannon a better field of fire. Messengers rode back and forth, ordering units to make small changes in their stations, and officers encouraged their men to stand valiantly and fight bravely.

One cannot ignore the role contemporary values played in this contest. The grand master wasted his advantages by not attacking promptly, then delaying longer in order to send the chivalric challenge for battle – two swords. The king was meanwhile purportedly hearing masses, ignoring the requests by his commanders for instructions. Jagieło had displayed excellent generalship in bringing his forces into the field, even considering the slowness of his advance after slipping away from the ford so cleverly; now he, too, seemed to let events run their course without his direction. Perhaps the king was using the religious services to delay the beginning of the battle, knowing that the German knights and horses would tire from wearing heavy armour; perhaps he was waiting for reinforcements; and perhaps he was paralysed by exhaustion and indecision. Historians' arguments about this point will never be fully resolved. Perhaps genuine piety persuaded him that time spent in prayer was the most important activity he could undertake at that moment.

Conventional religious practices were generally considered more important than cool-headed strategic or tactical decisions. 'God's will be done.' His opponent, Jungingen, took time for prayer too. The German troops began singing their anthem, *Christ ist erstanden* (Christ is Risen). Meanwhile, the Polish and Lithuanian troops chanted their battle-song, *Bogu rodzica dzewica* (Virgin Mother of God).

✠

The Combat

The knights with the two swords arrogantly presented them for the king's use and Vytautas', challenging them to come and fight. The king responded calmly, dismissed the heralds, then gave the signal for the battle to begin. While the Poles advanced in reasonably disciplined order, singing their anthem, the Lithuanians charged wildly and scattered the lightly armed units opposite them. Then the contending forces hammered away at one another for about an hour. Beyond this, there is little agreement in the various accounts. Apparently the Poles did not commit their major units, because the Germans remained on the defensive, awaiting an opportunity to charge ruthlessly into the rear of some retreating formation or gap in the lines.

The battle of Tannenberg is still being refought by historians today. Although the outline of the combat is very clear, German, Polish, and Lithuanian historians are not in agreement about the various actions which occurred during the battle, or even where the fighting took place on the broad field. The memorial chapel and mass graves have been located by archaeologists, but since some of those might indicate the slaughtered prisoners and wounded who perished over the following few days, there is no agreement even as to where the armies lined up. This much is agreed upon: the visiting crusaders were stationed on the left opposite the Lithuanians, presumably because they would be more motivated to fight against Tatar pagans than Polish Christians, but perhaps just because that was the most convenient posting; the Teutonic Knights held the centre and right of the line, opposite the Poles and their mercenaries.

The most important description of the battle is that of Jan Długosz, the Polish court historian. It is brief and tends to glorify the Polish contribution to the victory at the expense of the Lithuanian. In sum, he wrote that one wing of the 'crossbearers' defeated the horsemen under Vytautas after fierce fighting. Although Vytautas and the Smolensk regiments remained on the field, the Tatars fled, followed by many Lithuanians and Rus'ians. The German crusaders, seeing the wild flight of the enemy, assumed they had won a victory and left their positions to pursue them. This left a gap in the order's lines. The Poles, meanwhile, had been holding their own against the Teutonic Knights. Now, seeing their opportunity, they pressed harder, and came in through the gap created on the left when the crusaders broke ranks to pursue the Tatars; soon the Polish knights had put the main battle force of the Teutonic Knights in great difficulty.

This generally accepted understanding of the battle has been modified significantly by a recently discovered letter written in 1413 by a well-informed noble or mercenary captain. Its finger-wagging admonition to keep the ranks of the knights firmly in hand supports an alternate version of the combat given by less well-known chroniclers, that a small number of crusaders attached to the Teutonic Knights had fallen for a tactical ruse by the Lithuanians, a feigned retreat that led pursuers into a trap sprung by Polish knights waiting on the flank. The Lithuanians and Poles then drove into the disordered lines and rolled up the crusader formation.

Jungingen, seeing the disaster unfolding, should probably have sounded the retreat. Nothing of the kind entered his mind, however. His hot blood raging, he gathered together all the knights he could into a wedge formation and charged directly for a slight height where he supposed the king would be found; certainly, he could see the royal banner flying there and a large number of heavily-armed knights. Jungingen did not lack the courage to stake everything on this one charge – he knew that the warhorses would be too exhausted to bear his men from the field if the attack failed. Perhaps he hoped that his charge, coming at a somewhat unexpected angle, would find the Polish forces insufficiently disciplined to change their formation quickly enough to meet him. He was wrong. Vytautas, seen at the centre of Matjeko's painting, had seemingly been everywhere at once on his wing of the battlefield, performing fantastic and courageous feats; he now hurried over to the royal position with his men, perhaps to urge the king to reinforce the main battle lines with his reserves. In any case, Jungingen's advance fell just short of the royal bodyguard. In vain, he yelled 'Retreat!' Surrounded and exhausted, Jungingen perished with a multitude of his best men. The rest of the cavalry, seeing him fall, fled in disorder. Panic quickly spread through the German ranks. The light cavalry from Culm seem to have led the flight. The Polish knights, once they had destroyed the main battle force, turned on the disordered surviving units as they tried to escape down the narrow roads and chewed them up one after another. The rearmost German knights were hindered in their terrified flight by the tangled units ahead of them. Unable to get past the masses of men, horses, and wagons, unable to fight effectively against an enemy coming up from behind, all they could do was to try to surrender or die fighting against hopeless odds. The crusaders on the victorious left wing came back booty-laden only to fall into the hands of those who held the battlefield. This was Długosz's account of the battle; it quickly became the accepted story. Even the Germans agreed with Długosz, perhaps because he credited the Teutonic Knights with at least a partial victory, a rout of the pagan wing of the great army.

Polish historians emphasise royal generalship. They describe Jagiełło's determination to participate in the combat personally, how the royal banner was brought to earth at one point, and how the king was saved from injury only by the last-moment intervention of Zbigniew Oleśnicki, the royal secretary, when a knight from Meissen, Luppold von Köckritz, charged directly for him. Mythology did not hesitate to turn this incident into a personal combat between Jagiełło and Jungingen. In short, according to Polish patriotic scholarship, Polish intelligence, courage, gallantry, and self-sacrifice had won the day.

Lithuanian historians disagree sharply with this interpretation of events. They insist that Vytautas' men had made a tactical retreat, one common to warfare on the steppe, a ruse that tricked the crusaders from Germany into breaking ranks and dashing into an ambush. They regard the presence of Vytautas and the units from Smolensk fighting in the ranks of the victors during the decisive period of combat as proof that the main Lithuanian forces did not run away, but only lured the Germans into disordering their forces so badly that the way was open for the Polish attack. Credit for the victory should go to the grand prince, who inspired the tactics, who exhausted horse after horse in his relentless direction of the cavalry units, first on the right wing, then at the height of the fighting in the centre, when he brought the reinforcements that repelled Jungingen's charge; not to his rival, Jagiełło, who was practically useless during the entire combat, unable to give commands or to inspire by personal example.

Modern scholars, despite new archaeological information and newly discovered archival material, have not come to complete agreement as to what transpired. Everyone agrees that Jungingen made mistakes in bringing his army onto the field of battle; everyone agrees that Jungingen and Vytautas were brave warriors who risked their lives in desperate combat; almost everyone agrees that Jagiełło, for one reason or another, chose to remain where everyone could see him, by his tent on the hill, and that the decisive moment of battle was when the crusaders' attack on that position failed. All but the Lithuanians are practically unanimous in agreeing that a feigned retreat by an entire army was difficult and risky, although it was a common tactic for small units everywhere in Europe; also, if the retreat was a ruse, why was there no ambush of the pursuing forces? Or was there? More likely, the flight of the Lithuanian wing of the army was not planned. Jagiełło was, if anything, a cautious commander, and he would have understood that the retreat of an entire wing of his army would have been a disaster if the victorious crusaders had maintained discipline and charged with their full force into the gap left by the fleeing horsemen, then smashed into the flank of the royal forces. On the other hand, the forest at the rear of the Polish line, which would have hindered a retreat, may have shielded the central Polish battle formation from view or from an effective attack from the flank or rear. Because everyone agrees that the Teutonic Knights' defeat resulted from the ill-disciplined pursuit of the Lithuanian forces, the dispute about the motivation of the Lithuanian units cannot be resolved to universal satisfaction: either there was a strategic retreat on the part of a significant fraction of Vytautas' forces or those Lithuanians, Rus'ians, and Tatars had been driven from the field in defeat.

From the standpoint of observers at a distance of almost six centuries, the important fact is that the grand master's lines were left in disarray, a situation that the Polish and Lithuanian units led by Vytautas exploited. Those scholars who put faith in the possibility of a ruse tend to inquire how many Tatars were in Vytautas' levy, as if only steppe warriors could perform such a manoeuvre. Unfortunately, no contemporary source gives us more information about numbers than did Długosz, and not all scholars agree even upon the composition of the Polish and Lithuanian armies. But no matter. The Tatar contingent was not large, and it does not seem to have done any harm to its pursuers. Nor does it matter – the result was the same: the disruption of the German lines on the left wing led to a subsequent victory in the centre by the Polish forces. The Lithuanians had hitherto borne the brunt of the fighting, as the casualty figures substantiate, and they were still contributing significant pressure on the foe's disintegrating lines.

The grand master must have considered ordering a retreat and rejected it; Jungingen's decision to gamble everything on a massive charge at the royal tent might have been the best choice available. A chaotic retreat through the forest might have led to as complete a defeat as the army in fact suffered; and surely there would have been criticism that the grand master had missed his best chance to obtain a total victory over an enemy who was equally exhausted, certainly somewhat disorganised, and perhaps ready to collapse. Already thousands of Poles and Lithuanians had fallen in combat; some units had broken, and others were wavering. Had, by chance or skill, an arrow, spear, or sword brought down the king or great prince, the day would have belonged to Jungingen.

The total losses were almost beyond contemporary calculation: the oldest and also the lowest estimate was that 8,000 men died on each side. For the Teutonic Knights that meant that at least half the armed men perished.

Thousands more became prisoners. Most of the order's troops taken captive were put to the sword; only secular knights and officers were held for ransom. The dazed survivors gathered later, exhausted, wounded, and often without equipment, in the nearest cities and castles.

Jagiełło and Vytautas, for their part, were in no position to hurry with their armies into Prussia. Even though victorious, their losses had been heavy. The troops were fatigued; the horses were exhausted. The Lithuanians had fought for many hours, and the Poles had suffered, too, from the lack of sleep and drink, the tension of waiting, and the draining excitement of pitched battle. When the Germans fled, the Poles and Lithuanians had followed them for ten miles, cutting down those they overtook, and driving others into the swamps and forests to perish. When the victorious horsemen returned to camp they needed rest. Those with the most stamina went in search of booty, returning much later as exhausted as those who had been unable to move a foot from the battlefield. Meanwhile, the foot soldiers had been busy on the battlefield, gathering weapons, money, jewellery, and clothing, finishing off the wounded, slaughtering the lower-class prisoners, and burying the dead in mass graves. The Poles and Lithuanians needed a short pause to rest and to celebrate, possibly to pray, and to care for wounded and fallen comrades. Tatars and irregular troops rushed ahead to rob, rape, kill, and burn, starting panics that would hinder the organisation of regional defence.

There was no further effective resistance. The Teutonic Knights had lost so many castellans and advocates, so many knights, and so many militia units, that defences could not be manned. Those who survived had taken refuge wherever they could, often far from their assigned posts. The highest-ranking leaders had fallen almost to a man: the grand master, the marshal, the grand commander, the treasurer, and 200 knights. Marquard von Salzbach, the order's expert on Lithuanian affairs and a former friend of Vytautas, was apparently taken prisoner by Jagiełło's men, then beheaded by the grand prince. He had refused to be properly humble and submissive. Arrogant and proud to the end, unrepentant about having taunted Vytautas about his mother's virtue, he and his companions had anticipated being treated in a manner befitting their status; nevertheless, when their fate was clear there is no indication that their courage flagged. They had understood from the beginning that there was no good in being Jagiełło's and Vytautas' *former* friends.

Some contemporaries believed that Tannenberg was a disaster to the crusading cause comparable to Nicopolis, but most simply marvelled at the huge losses in men, horses, and equipment. As the continuation of Posilge's chronicle said: 'The army, both cavalry and infantry, was routed completely,

losing lives, goods, and honour, and the number slain was beyond number-
ing. May God have pity on them.'

That the defeat was so total and so final was hard for contemporaries to
grasp. The news spread to courts where old men remembered the exploits
of their youth in Lithuania – in Germany and France the disaster could
hardly be believed; to bishops and burghers in Livonia, who were not sure
whether to rejoice or mourn; to wives and families in Poland and Lithuania,
who both exulted in their rulers' exploits and gave thanks for the safety of
husbands, brothers, and friends; to neighbouring rulers who may have
hoped for another outcome of the war, one in which perhaps all the armies
would have gone down in defeat together. Everyone demanded more information, and especially an explanation of how the Teutonic Knights could
have suffered such an unexpected disaster. The responses were varied. The
Teutonic Knights talked about treason, the numbers of the enemy host, and
unfortunate tactics; the Poles were satisfied with courage, skill at arms, good
generalship, and God's favour.

The propagandists of the order worked hard to persuade contemporaries
that the disaster was not as bad as it appeared, that it was the work of the devil
through his agents, the pagans and schismatics – and most of all, that it was the
fault of *the Saracens*. Moreover, they argued that now more than ever crusaders
were needed in Prussia to continue God's work. The Polish propagandists
laboured, too, to present their interpretation of events, but they did not have
the long-term contacts which had been developed in many crusading *Reisen*.
Their praise of Jagiełło and his knights tended to awaken more sympathy for
the hard-pressed order than was good for Polish interests. After the first impact
of the news was absorbed by the European courts, after the first months of
difficulty had passed, interpretations favoured by the order tended to prevail.

The modern reader, looking back on almost six centuries of events that
dwarf the battle of Tannenberg without driving it from the public mind,
hardly knows how to understand the negative attitudes toward the Teutonic
Knights. Comparisons to Wilhelmine Germany of 1914 and to Hitler are
unworthy of comment, though Germans of those generations thought of
their acts as deeds of national revenge for the battle in 1410. In the context
of twentieth-century events one is tempted to say that contemporaries of
Tannenberg were right, that there is a divine justice operating in the world.
In concluding that the Teutonic Knights had paid the price for having lived
by the sword and swaggered in a world of pride, contemporaries found that
Biblical admonitions came easily to mind: Tannenberg was God's punishment for the Teutonic Order's outrageous conduct. Pride had risen too high
– Jungingen personified his order's universally acknowledged tendency to
arrogance and anger – and a fall had to follow.

The deficiencies of this method of justifying past events (*Weltgeschichte als Weltgericht*) should be obvious: if victory in battle reflects God's will, then the Tatar domination of the steppe and the harassment of Polish and Lithuanian borderlands is also a reflection of divine justice; God punishes kings by sacrificing many thousands of innocent lives. Good Old Testament theology, but hard to fit into a New Testament framework. It is best that we do not tarry long in either the shadowy realm of pop psychology or dark religious nationalism, but move back into the somewhat better-lit world of chronicles and correspondence.

Conflicting views of modern historians about the battle of Tannenberg and its aftermath make for interesting if confused reading. One could summarise them roughly by saying that until the 1960s each interpretation reflected national interests more than fact. Since then, historians have become both more polite and less certain of their inability to err. Archaeology is beginning to shed light on the battlefield, giving promise that problems left by the literary sources may be more fully resolved. Political issues in Germany and Poland that seemed to depend on every imaginable historical justification have disappeared with the political parties that sponsored them, so that at last a quiet discussion about the past is possible. Most importantly, since the fall of Communism German and Polish historians have come to respect each other sufficiently to give real attention to one another's ideas. There is, indeed, reason to hope that some day we may come to a better and more general agreement as to what really happened at Tannenberg and what it really signified.

11

The Long Decline and the End in the Baltic

The Aftermath of Tannenberg

When Jagiełło's forces had rested three days from the exhaustion of battle and the pursuit, he ordered them to move north. There was no hurry. The king was never one to rush. Still, he did not allow himself to be diverted by opportunities to occupy towns and castles that could be easily taken, but headed straight for Marienburg at a deliberate pace. If Jagiełło could make himself master of that great fortress, he would be well placed to occupy the rest of Prussia. Already secular knights and burghers were coming to him, declaring their willingness to live as Polish subjects if their former rights and privileges were guaranteed. Garrisons of castles, often not having orders to fight or sufficient men to defend the walls, were surrendering; castellans who urged resistance, as at Osterode, Christburg, Elbing, Thorn, and Culm, were expelled by burghers who then surrendered the cities. There seemed no point in resisting the inevitable. Even the bishops of Ermland, Culm, Pomesania, and Samland hurried to Jagiełło to acknowledge him as their lord. Lesser men, overcome by the depressing spirit of defeatism, followed their example. Jagiełło's chancery was hard-pressed to issue documents defining each new vassal's rights and obligations.

The king sent his men out to find the body of Ulrich von Jungingen and take it to Osterode for burial; later the fallen grand master's corpse was brought to Marienburg to lie with his predecessors in St Anne's Chapel.

✠

Heinrich von Plauen

Jagiełło and Vytautas were enjoying a triumph of which they had hardly dared dream. Their grandfather had once claimed the Alle River – which more or less marked the boundary between the settled lands along the coast and the wilderness to the south-east – as the Lithuanian frontier. Vytautas now seemed to be in a position to claim all the lands east of the Vistula. Jagiełło was ready to make good the ancient Polish claims to Culm and West Prussia. However, even as they were celebrating their brief moment of joy there appeared among the Teutonic Knights the only member of this generation whose leadership and tenacity could be compared to theirs: Heinrich von Plauen. Nothing in his past had indicated that Plauen would ever be more than a simple castellan, but he was one of those men who rise suddenly above themselves in moments of crisis. Born forty years earlier in the Vogtland, a small territory between Thuringia and Saxony, he had first come to Prussia as a crusader. Impressed by the warrior-monks, he had taken the vows of poverty, chastity, obedience, and war against the enemies of the Church. His noble birth had guaranteed him a position of rank, and long service had earned him promotion to command at the castle of Schwetz, a well-manned observation post on the west bank of the Vistula north of Culm for the defence of the West Prussian frontier against raiders.

When Plauen learned of the magnitude of the order's defeat, he alone of all the surviving castellans assumed responsibility beyond what had been assigned to him: he ordered his 3,000 troops to Marienburg, to garrison the fortress there before the Polish army could arrive. Nothing else mattered. If Jagiełło wished to divert his efforts to Schwetz and capture it, so be it. Plauen's duty, as he saw it, was to save Prussia. That meant defending Marienburg, not worrying about minor castles.

All Plauen's training and experience ran against this assumption of authority. The Teutonic Knights prided themselves in their unconditional obedience, and it was not immediately clear whether or not a more prominent officer had escaped the battlefield. However, in this situation obedience was a principle that cut with the flat side of the sword: it had turned out officers who did not exceed instructions without long reflection; no one made independent decisions. In the Teutonic Order one rarely had to hurry; there was time to discuss matters fully, to consult a council or an assembly of commanders, and to come to a common understanding. Even the most self-assured grand masters consulted the membership about military decisions. Now there was no time for that, and the traditions of the

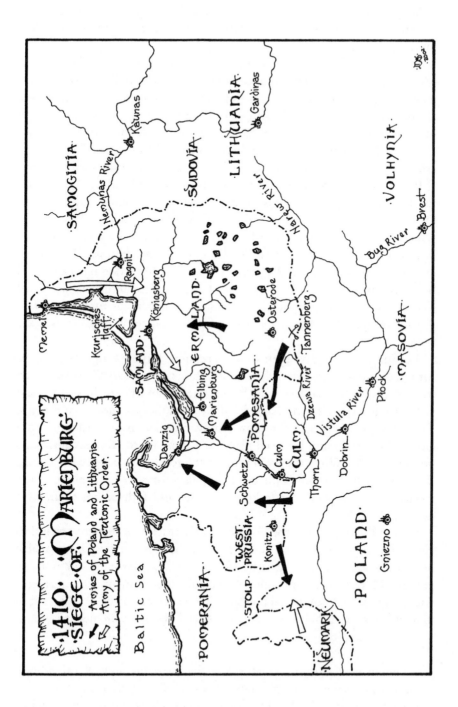

·1410· 'SIEGE·OF·'MARIENBURG·

⇨ Armies of Poland and Lithuania.
⇨ Army of the Teutonic Order.

Baltic Sea

POMERANIA·

·STOLP· ·WEST·PRUSSIA·

NEUMARK·

·POLAND·

Gniezno

Konitz

Schwetz

Dobrin

Thorn

CULM·

Culm

Danzig

SAMLAND

Elbing

Marienburg

ERMLAND·

Osterode

POMESANIA·

Dzewa River

Tannenberg

Vistula River

Płock

·MASOVIA·

Memel

Kurisches Haff

Königsberg

Ragnit

Neman River

Nemunas River

SAMOGITIA·

Kaunas

SUDOVIA·

LITHUANIA·

Gardinas

Narew River

Bug River

Brest

VOLHYNIA·

military order paralysed all the surviving officers save one; the rest were awaiting orders or seeking an opportunity to talk with others about formulating a plan of action.

Heinrich von Plauen began to give orders: to commanders of threatened castles, 'Resist!'; to Danzig sailors, 'Come to Marienburg!'; to the Livonian master, 'Send troops as quickly as possible!'; to the German master, 'Raise mercenary troops and send them east!' Such was the Prussian tradition of obedience that his orders were carried out. A miracle that should not have occurred did. Resistance stiffened everywhere; when the first Polish scouts arrived at Marienburg, they found defenders lining the walls, ready to fight.

Plauen gathered men from every possible place. He had the small garrison of Marienburg, his own men from Schwetz, the 'ships' children' from Danzig, some secular knights, and the militia of Marienburg. That the last was ready to assist is witness to Plauen's personality: among his first commands was one to burn the city and suburbs to the ground. This act of destruction prevented the Poles and Lithuanians from finding shelter and stores, eliminated demands that Plauen attempt to defend the city walls, and cleared the ground in front of the castle. It was perhaps more important morally in indicating how far the commander was ready to go to save the castle.

The surviving knights, their secular brethren, and the burghers began to stir out of their shock. After the first Polish scouts withdrew, Plauen's men stocked the castle's larders with bread, cheese, and beer, drove pigs and cattle inside the walls, and hauled fodder from the storehouses and fields. They brought guns into position, removed remaining obstructions to a clear field of fire, and discussed plans for defending the fortress against all possible attacks. When the main units of the royal army arrived on 25 July, the garrison had already gathered in supplies for a siege of eight to ten weeks. That was food and fodder the Poles and Lithuanians themselves needed.

Vital to the defence of the fortress was Heinrich von Plauen's spirit. His genius for improvisation, his desire for victory, together with an insatiable lust for revenge, spread to the garrison. Those character traits had probably prevented his advancement earlier – a volatile temperament and impatience with incompetence are not appreciated in a peacetime army. At this critical moment, however, they were exactly the qualities that were needed.

He wrote to Germany:

To all princes, barons, knights and men-at-arms and all other loyal Christians, whomever this letter reaches. We brother Heinrich von Plauen, castellan of Schwetz, acting in the place of the Grand Master of

the Teutonic Order in Prussia, notify you that the King of Poland and
Duke Vytautas with a great force and with Saracen infidels have besieged
Marienburg. In this siege truly all the Order's forces and power are being
engaged. Therefore, we ask you illustrious and noble lords, to allow your
subjects who wish to assist and defend us for the love of Christ and all of
Christendom either for salvation or money, to come to our aid as quickly
as possible so that we can drive them away.

Plauen's call for help against the 'Saracens' may have been hyperbolic (though
some Tatars were Moslems), but it touched a nerve of anti-Polish sentiment
and stirred the German master into action. Knights began moving toward
the Neumark, where the former advocate of Samogitia, Michael
Küchmeister, still had a considerable force intact, and officers hurriedly sent
out notices that the Teutonic Order was willing to hire any mercenary who
would report for duty immediately.

Jagiełło had hoped that Marienburg would capitulate quickly.
Demoralised troops elsewhere were surrendering at the least threat. Those
at Marienburg, he persuaded himself, would surely do the same. However,
when the garrison, unexpectedly, did not capitulate, the king had only
unsatisfactory alternatives to choose from. He was unwilling to attempt an
assault on the high walls, and retreat would be an admission of defeat.
So he ordered his army to begin siege operations in the hope that the
defenders would lose hope; the combination of fear of death and hope of
surviving was a powerful inducement to surrender on terms. However,
Jagiełło quickly learned that he did not have sufficient troops to press an
attack on a fortress as large and well designed as Marienburg and simultaneously send troops to other cities to demand their surrender; nor had he
ordered his own siege guns sent down the Vistula in time to use them now.
The longer his forces remained before Marienburg, the more time the
Teutonic Knights had to organise their defences elsewhere. The royal
victor cannot be blamed greatly for his miscalculation (what would historians have said if he had not tried for the jugular vein?), but his siege tactics
failed. Polish troops hammered away at the walls for eight weeks with
catapults and cannon taken from nearby castles. Lithuanian foragers
burned and ravaged the countryside, sparing only those regions where the
burghers and nobles hastened to provide them with cannons and powder,
food and drink. Tatar raiders struck throughout Prussia, proving to everyone's satisfaction that their reputation for savagery was well deserved.
Polish forces moved into West Prussia, capturing many small castles which
had been left without garrisons: Schwetz, Mewe, Dirschau, Tuchel,
Bütow, and Konitz. But the vital centres of Prussia, Königsberg and

Marienburg, remained untouched. Dysentery broke out among the Lithuanian forces (too much delicate food), and finally Vytautas announced that he was taking his men home. However, Jagieło was determined to remain until he had taken the castle and captured its commander. He refused offers of a truce, demanding the prior surrender of Marienburg. He was sure that just a little more perseverance would be sufficient for total victory.

Meanwhile, help had started on its way to Prussia. The Livonian army came to Königsberg, relieving troops there for use elsewhere. This helped counter accusations about 'the Livonian treason', for having honoured the truce with Vytautas rather than having harassed his lands and forced him to divert troops to frontier defence. From the west, Hungarian and German mercenaries hurried to the Neumark, where they were formed into an army by Michael Küchmeister. This officer had been inactive till now, too concerned about the loyalty of the nobility to risk an engagement against Polish forces, but in August he ordered his small army against an equal number of Poles, routed them, and captured the opposing commander. Then he marched east, recapturing city after city. By the end of September Küchmeister had cleared West Prussia of hostile forces.

At that point Jagieło was unable to maintain the siege any longer. Marienburg was impregnable if the garrison did not lose its nerve; and Plauen saw to it that the hastily assembled troops retained their will to fight. Moreover, the garrison was encouraged by the withdrawal of the Lithuanian forces and the news of victories elsewhere. Therefore, even though supplies were dwindling, they took heart in the good news and in the knowledge that the order's Hanseatic allies controlled the rivers. In the meantime, Jagieło's knights were pressing him to go home – the time that they were required to render military service had long since expired. He was running out of supplies, and disease had broken out among his troops. In the end, Jagieło had no choice but to acknowledge that the defence still had a great advantage over the offence; a brick fortress surrounded by water defences could be taken only after a lengthy siege, and perhaps even then only when luck or treason tipped the odds. Jagieło did not have the time or the resources for a longer siege at this juncture, and he would not have them in the future.

After eight weeks, on 19 September the king gave the command to withdraw. He had built a stronghold at Stuhm, just south of Marienburg, fortifying it strongly, garrisoning it with his best men, and then filling it with all the food and fodder that could be collected from the countryside. Afterward he ordered his men to burn all the fields and barns in the vicinity to make it more difficult for the Teutonic Knights to collect food for a siege. By holding a fortress in the heart of Prussia, he hoped to keep the pressure on his enemies and to give encouragement and protection to the nobles and burghers who had surrendered to him. On his way home he stopped at the shrine of St Dorothea in Marienwerder to pray. Jagiełło was now at all times a devout Christian. In addition to personal piety, which he wanted no one to doubt because of his pagan and Orthodox past, he had to demonstrate that surrounding himself with Orthodox and Moslem troops was purely business.

As the Polish forces retreated, history repeated itself. Almost two centuries before, as Prussia was conquered by armies of crusaders from Poland and Germany, it was the Poles who did much of the fighting, but the Teutonic Knights who eventually came into possession of the lands because, then as now, there were too few Polish knights willing to stay in Prussia and defend it for the king. The Teutonic Knights had the greater endurance. In the same manner they now survived the disaster at Tannenberg.

Plauen gave orders to pursue the retreating army. The Livonian forces moved first, besieging Elbing and compelling the citizens to surrender, then moving south into Culm and regaining most of the cities there. The castellan of Ragnit, whose troops had been watching Samogitia during the battle of Tannenberg, moved through central Prussia to Osterode, capturing the castles one by one and expelling the last of the Poles from the order's territories. By the end of October Plauen had recovered every town except Thorn, Nessau, Rehden, and Strasburg – all located right on the border. Even Stuhm had surrendered after three weeks, the garrison abandoning their castle in return for free passage to Poland with all their possessions. The worst was over. Plauen had saved his order in its most desperate moment. His courage and determination had sparked a similar commitment from others, and he had turned the broken survivors of a military disaster from beaten men into warriors. He did not believe that one battle would be decisive for the history of his organisation, and he inspired many to share his vision of ultimate victory.

Aid from the West came surprisingly quickly as well. Sigismund declared war on Jagiełło and sent more troops to the border of southern Poland to pin down knights who might join Jagiełło's army. Sigismund wanted the Teutonic Knights to remain a threat to Poland's northern provinces and be able to aid him in the future; it was in this spirit that he had earlier agreed with Ulrich von Jungingen that neither would make peace without consulting the other. Ambitious to become emperor, he wanted to present himself to German princes as a firm defender of German institutions and German lands. Therefore, exceeding any legitimate authority – as was appropriate for a true leader in crisis situations – he called the electors together in Frankfurt am Main and urged them to send help to Prussia immediately. Most of this was show, however. Sigismund's real interest was in being elected German king, the first step to becoming emperor.

The most effective help came from Bohemia. This was surprising, because King Wenceslas had not originally shown much interest in saving the Teutonic Knights: although news of Tannenberg had arrived in Prague within a week, he had done nothing. That was typical of Wenceslas, who was often inebriated when decisions had to be made, and even when sober was not particularly interested in work. It was only after the order's representative shrewdly lavished gifts on the royal mistresses, then promised payments to impecunious lords and mercenaries, and finally suggested to the king a proposal that would make Prussia subordinate to Bohemia, that the monarch acted. Wenceslas was suddenly willing not only to allow his subjects to campaign in Prussia, but he loaned the order's diplomat more than 8,000 Marks to pay them.

The Prussian state was saved. Except for the loss of lives and property, both of which were considered replaceable in the long term, the Teutonic Order did not seem to have suffered greatly. Prestige was damaged, of course, but Heinrich von Plauen had recovered most of the castles and driven the enemy beyond the frontiers. Later generations of historians have seen the battle as an incurable wound from which the order later bled to death. In October of 1410 that would have been considered an unlikely future for the Teutonic Knights.

✠

Significance of the Battle of Tannenberg

The next battleground was over public opinion. Heinrich von Plauen sought to explain to nobles in Germany and France, to Sigismund, to Wenceslas, and to the three prelates who claimed the title of pope, what had happened in Tannenberg. He needed a plausible story which could counteract the propaganda already cleverly disseminated by Jagiełło's diplomats. Plauen's story had to explain the defeat without compromising either the honour of his knights or suggesting that a future victory was unlikely. Thus he could not say that the Poles were better warriors, or better led, or even that their numbers were too great. He chose to say that the Teutonic Knights had been stabbed in the back (a tale that found an echo after 1918, with even less logic) by a group of secular knights of Polish ancestry; he accused the members of the Lizard League* of lowering their banners and fleeing, thereby causing a

---

* A fraternal/chivalrous order of knights in Culm. 'Lizard' meant dragon.

panic in the crusader ranks. Jungingen, he said, had died bravely trying to reverse the consequences of this treason. Thus was born a conspiracy theory that poisoned German historiography until 1945.

For some important monarchs and churchmen, the lesson of Tannenberg was often all too clear. It was the long-awaited opportunity to extort money and favours from the proud knights of the Teutonic Order. The opportunistic Wenceslas, who had demonstrated his fickleness over the decades, proved once again that he blew with the winds of politics; nor was Sigismund more reliable. Both supported the grand master as long as he poured money into their coffers. But Plauen's money was not inexhaustible. Therefore he found himself in the unenviable position of raising additional revenues from lands and cities which had been recently ravaged by invaders. At first he received considerable co-operation, partly because many people wished to avoid further suspicion of treason, partly because people understood that Plauen could expect no effective help from abroad unless the money continued to flow. But that could not last; people cannot give what they do not have.

Plauen had much to do. Now that he had driven the Polish and Lithuanian armies from Prussia, he had to reorganise the shattered economy, restore the depleted ranks of the order, appoint new officers, and persuade the important rulers of Europe that the Teutonic Knights were still a power to be reckoned with. If he could win a military victory he could achieve all these goals and eliminate his need to buy friendship. However, that victory would be hard to achieve, because his immediate subordinates were persuaded that Prussia needed a period of peace in which to reorganise.

Plauen ordered his forces to assemble in West Prussia for an invasion of Poland, but during a bout of illness he was overthrown by his staff and arrested. The conspirators hurriedly called a grand chapter together, intimidated the representatives, and elected Küchmeister grand master with instructions to discharge the mercenaries and negotiate with the Polish king for a permanent peace. This policy was a mistake. The war the conspirators had attempted to forestall soon overwhelmed them. Küchmeister's clumsy efforts at clever and deceitful diplomacy were easily turned aside by Jagiełło, who, having disarmed his foes, then hammered them into submission. The terms of the Treaty of Melno (1422) were much harsher than what Jagiełło had offered Plauen. Tannenberg had not been immediately fatal, but the need to maintain large numbers of mercenaries ready for combat eventually eroded the financial resources that had sustained the war machine through the decades. The road to the future, for the Teutonic Knights, led downhill.

✚

A Century of Decline

What happened to the Teutonic Order after the defeat at Tannenberg? Certainly there is far more to the decline of a state than being worn down by overwhelming forces; more than the personal failure of leading personalities; and more than the simple operation of the law of inertia. Internally there were problems that can be traced directly to the military disaster at Tannenberg.

Firstly, at a critical and chaotic moment many local officers who might never have earned promotion had been forced to take control of administrative operations which previously had been directed from the centre of the Prussian state; visitations ceased, and in the course of time officers who had become used to acting independently came to resent orders from Marienburg which limited their autonomy. It hardly needs saying that the officers of the next critical years were either aged or very young or newly arrived in Prussia. Factions began to rise, often based around regional origins – Bavarians and Austrians were suspicious of Rhinelanders, and vice versa. The authority of the grand masters was undermined by successful revolts, so that the castellans and advocates felt justified in resisting even the most minor reforms aimed at reasserting the grand masters' control over the convents. No longer could the knights boast of rendering obedience without question, for that combination of mock humility and chest thumping no longer had any substance.

Secondly, religious reform became an obsession. In an era that believed that God judged organisations and states for the moral shortcomings of the people and their leaders, it was logical for the Teutonic Knights to conclude that the defeats at Tannenberg and after were punishments for their failure to live up to their vows of poverty, chastity, and obedience. Many modern readers may find that bizarre, except for the obvious impact of allowing the good life of hunting and drinking to interfere with one's duties, to neglect training for battle, or to harden hearts so excessively that one's subjects seek the first opportunity to change rulers. There is no indication that this was true before 1410. Visitors considered Prussia a model state. Pride was the deadly sin of the pre-Tannenberg knights. The complaints about misgovernment began to heap up later, as hard-pressed castellans and advocates collected emergency taxes year after year, squeezed the citizenry for extraordinary services, and haughtily rejected cries for justice and mercy.

Thirdly, a state in decline rarely governs well. The Teutonic Order was no exception, and monastic reform was essentially irrelevant to that collection of problems. Perhaps more prayer and a greater emphasis on chastity will result in treating one's subjects better, but the connection is not easily demonstrated. When one compares the Teutonic Knights to contemporary ecclesiastics, can one say that the officers were extraordinarily sinful? Or that they were more arrogant or oppressive than neighbouring secular rulers?

The grand masters were, without exception until the last to rule in Prussia (Albrecht von Hohenzollern), true to their monastic oaths, even pious, devout, and puritanical. Of course, their example alone was insufficient to keep the officers and men within the narrow bounds prescribed by the rules, but there must have been a substantial majority of the membership who agreed with their efforts to enforce the rules; after all, the knights, priests, and sergeants at the general chapters elected one reforming grand master after another. While the chivalric trappings of the Teutonic Knights had long been more prominently displayed than in the typical monastic foundation, the Roman Catholic Church has never found pomp and ceremony completely incompatible with its religious functions; today, even the most resolutely Protestant visitor can be impressed by a papal mass in the Vatican. The medieval era put a much greater emphasis on processions, celebrations, and public prayer – one can hardly imagine a modern head of state ordering the entire population to pray for the success of its diplomats, then attending lengthy services day after day, and the public voluntarily doing the same.

The real problem was the grand masters issuing edicts they could not enforce or which were irrelevant to the problems the castellans and advocates had to deal with. It was not that the convents were overrun with women and other secular creatures, but the uniformity and discipline that had once been the pride of the order was gone. When military disasters followed hard upon one another's heels, the officers had a difficult time keeping men and mercenaries in order. As drink and minor luxuries became commonplace, morale sank under public ridicule and criticism. The religious community was on the defensive, unable to prevail by force of arms or by exhortation. The answer to the problem of discipline was peace, a restoration of the financial health of the country, and finding a new military task which would keep the knights busy and spiritually satisfied.

Fourthly, the number of knights was declining. The population of Europe was recovering only slowly from the plague, and there were fewer unemployed younger sons of minor nobility seeking a religious vocation. Even more importantly, the prestige of the order sank too low to attract good recruits. That was not the disaster it would have been a century earlier, thanks to changes in military tactics which made knights less useful than mercenaries, but it was still hard on morale. The most successful fifteenth-century armies were composed of mercenary soldiers, men in the prime of life hired for short periods, then dismissed. Such armies had proven their ability to defeat levies of horsemen, mobs of peasant infantry, and ageing knights who had once been formidable warriors. Moreover, the soldiers (in German *Sold* means pay) were willing to campaign as long as necessary, as long as the pay lasted. Mercenaries had already become common in Prussia; now they were indispensable. The handful of friar-knights now served only as officers, supervising the hired troops, the levies, and the military specialists such as cannoneers, engineers, and quartermasters. Since money was in short supply, the grand masters preferred to spend it on mercenaries and equipment rather than on noble horsemen. The knights sensed that their role was changing, and not all of them were pleased. Few of them fitted easily either into the form prescribed by practices common 250 years earlier or those necessary for the future.

Fifthly, more money was needed than ever before. Consequently the merchant oligarchy in the cities and the knights in the countryside understood how important they were becoming, and they resented the obligations imposed by the order – especially military service and taxes – and the limitations they placed on their role in the supervision of justice and the formulation of foreign policy. As long as their mercantile interests were defended against competitors and pirates, the cities did not complain too loudly; but after Tannenberg they were giving out more and more money for less and less protection. At the least they wanted a voice in foreign affairs. The nobles felt the same way. One by one the grand masters had to give way to those protesters until finally there was the choice either of giving the Prussian League full participation in the government via some type of assembly or of attempting to suppress the cities and secular nobles. In 1454 Grand Master Erlichshausen decided to fight, with disastrous results.

These main causes of internal decline do not explain fully the reasons why Prussia fell so low. For that it is necessary to look beyond the narrow horizons of the Baltic, to the greater problems besetting all Europe at that time.

First of all, the grand masters' loss of authority was not a uniquely local problem. The inability of the head of state to exercise power was seen in the Holy Roman Empire, the Roman Catholic Church, the kingdom of Poland, the Grand Duchy of Lithuania, and the united kingdoms in Scandinavia. Everywhere the lower orders challenged the right of their betters to give orders; everywhere, at every level, individuals and groups attempted to strip power from those above them and gather it into their own hands. Pictorial expressions of the Wheel of Fortune illustrate each ruler's problem: the monarch sits atop a loosely fastened wheel, hands filled with orb and sceptre, wearing a tall crown and draped in expensive robes; but the balance is delicate, and the slightest wisp of air disturbs the equilibrium; how easily and swiftly one is thrown from the heights to utter despair and humiliation!

Secondly, crusading goals had changed. As long as the Lithuanians, even the Samogitians, had remained pagan, there was still a religious justification for the crusade led by the Teutonic Order. However, once Jogaila had become Ladislas Jagiełło of Poland and Vytautas had been baptised and had sent delegates to Constance to proclaim all Samogitia to be Christian, it became increasingly difficult for the grand masters' representatives to persuade European knights that the operations in Lithuania were crusades, that war against Poland was justified, and that they should volunteer their services and contribute their wealth to such ventures. The procurators certainly found it ever more difficult to persuade the popes with the traditional arguments.

The principal danger to Christendom was now clearly in the Balkans. The Turks were on the move, or seemed to be – they might have been more interested in rounding up slaves and cattle than in acquiring new provinces, but that was hardly a comfort for those who fell into their hands. The Islamic gains in the late fourteenth century frightened traditional supporters of the crusading movement, who were unable to prevent their possessions in Greece from being overwhelmed and who already foresaw the fall of ancient Christian kingdoms south of Hungary. The great crusade of 1396, which was supposed to reverse that momentum, ended in disaster at Nicopolis; how much the French crusaders' fatal contempt for their adversaries was a result of their experiences in Samogitia can only be guessed, for the Lithuanians were renowned as good warriors, in their own forests and swamps equal to any in Europe, and very nearly a match for the Tatars. Yet the crusaders had repeatedly bested them. Surely that was proof that Western crusaders could whip the Turks and their local Slavic allies? Alas, no. After Nicopolis, the French sent no further major expeditions to Prussia. They left the northern crusades to the Germans, who were now led by the chastened organiser of the Nicopolis venture, Sigismund, king of Hungary and later Holy Roman emperor, whose sole interest in crusading (inasmuch as he could manage to concentrate on any one matter) was to guard against the Turkish menace and crush the Hussite rebels in Bohemia.* He had little sympathy for the border wars of the Teutonic Order except as a means of applying pressure on Jagiełło, with whom he was contending for control of Silesia and Bohemia.

---

* The Hussites can be considered early Protestants, since they emphasised communion in both kinds (bread and wine for the congregation) and hymns and sermons in the local language. But they were also Czech nationalists who resented the German domination of Bohemia. The Teutonic Knights supplied many knights to Sigismund's efforts to crush them, but they were almost always beaten badly.

A third danger was heresy. The Hussites in Bohemia not only defended themselves against Sigismund's armies of German and Hungarian 'crusaders', but they went on the offensive. The Teutonic Knights suffered damage to their properties in Germany and Prussia, reaping all the problems of defeat without any of the rewards expected for their efforts. Between the Turks and the Hussite heretics, the crusading energies of Central Europe were exhausted. There were none left to be used against Christian peoples in Lithuania and Poland.

Fourthly, there was an attitude of depression among the general population, a feeling that one's endeavours would lead only to failure, that even the best success was transitory and vain. Johan Huizinga called that era 'the Waning of the Middle Ages' and compared it to the senility of old age. Certainly there were fewer nobles now who were willing to abandon their comfortable lives for a religious vocation, fewer who were willing to travel far to 'journey' into the cold Samogitian wilderness. Talk replaced action, show superseded performance. What was the use in any case? Was there really much hope of accomplishing anything? The world was doubtful, suspicious, cynical. If anything should be done, it should be done against the Turks. But even there, God seemed to be on the other side.

Chivalry was not dead, of course, and chivalry was the motor that had long propelled the Samogitian crusade. But chivalry had overheated: the parts had melted together, and now nothing moved. In those aspects of it that remained, chivalry was an expensive form of display which only the greatest lords could afford. It was now priced beyond the reach of those nobles who had accompanied the territorial princes to Prussia; and no prince wished to compete with Albrecht of Austria, whose outlay in 1377 had bordered on the fantastic. Also, the Teutonic Knights lacked the money to entertain on the new scale of lavishness. What had been wealth in the fourteenth century was poverty in the fifteenth, and the grand masters could not even attain the old scale. No one wanted to travel on a tourist class crusade, and few could afford to go first class.

In short, crusading was no longer enjoyable. The extravagance of activity, the delight in adventure, and the search for fame that were the hallmarks of fourteenth-century chivalry were gone. The Samogitian *Reisen* had combined the excitement of the hunt, the danger of warfare, and the adventure of travel with a brilliance of display and entertainment that no one else could match. Now the crusaders could not raid Lithuania to chase down villagers, nor did they dare offer open battle. They could not even provide the chivalric spectacle that was the vogue from Burgundy to Italy. Nor could any other crusade provide a substitute. Consequently potential crusaders stayed home and talked of the old glories.

The decline of Prussia as a state was beyond the control of the grand masters. Not even the German convents of the order cared much. Although they, too, talked much and gave frequent advice, they did not provide warriors, crusaders, or money – and without those, what use was advice? Their new endeavour was to support the emperor in his ventures. The fact was that the crusade from Prussia was over. The Teutonic Knights had outlived their usefulness there. All that remained was to demonstrate this fact.

✠

The Thirteen Years' War

In 1449 a grand chapter elected Louis von Erlichshausen as grand master. A man eager to force the issue of Prussian unity to a decision, Erlichshausen believed that the order's problem was not the lack of means, but the lack of will. Correctly sensing that the Prussian League was his principal challenge at the moment, he followed the example of the most successful German princes of the era by attempting to curb, hopefully crush, its most influential members. In this he was not only supported, but pressured by important officers to act even more decisively. Erlichshausen had been offended not only by the protesters' tone and the demand that he end the emergency taxes on commerce, but by their insistence that he send his Italian-trained lawyers out of the assembly so that he could not turn to them for advice. Erlichshausen knew the League's weak point was its lack of legal standing; and therefore he sent a young lawyer, Laurentius Blumenau – a Danzig-born patrician who had studied in Italy – to speak to Emperor Friedrich III (1440–93) and Pope Nicholas V (1447–55) about the crisis. The bishop of Ermland was the decisive voice in this; he had been among those advisors who had most strongly recommended striking down the League, but his advice had been repeatedly rejected by the previous grand master, Louis' brother Conrad von Erlichshausen; now his advice led three cardinals to send a papal legate, the Portuguese bishop Louis de Silves, to Prussia in late 1450.

Equally involved in the dispute was Cardinal Nicholas von Cusa, bishop of Brixen, whose reputation as diplomat and scholar made his a powerful voice in German politics. His extensive correspondence with the grand master contained advice that the order took seriously.

The order's procurator (the lawyer who represented the grand master at the papal curia), the highly capable Jodokus von Hohenstein, argued that the League was a 'conspiracy' designed to destroy the Teutonic Order. This was a tactic which did not even win universal support inside the order's membership. The juristic foundation of his argument was sound, but the timing was not. The grand master could have waited for a moment when his enemies were weak or divided, but waiting was not in Erlichshausen's personality. He moved quickly and confidently, hoping perhaps to overawe the opposition by sheer force of character. Clearly, the influence of Blumenau was important in reinforcing his existing tendency to disdain his less nobly-born and less educated opponents.

The grand master and his advisors were also very much aware of Danzig's current estrangement from Lübeck over English competition and piracy (activities which were essentially interchangeable at this time). Danzig was ready to compromise, Lübeck was not. If ever there was a moment that the grand master could challenge the merchants in Danzig, this was it.

Louis von Erlichshausen was doubtless encouraged to believe that he could intimidate his opponents. He had just enjoyed a great success in Livonia: Heidenreich Vincke von Overberg had died in June 1450, bringing to an end the most contentious era in the order's history, the civil war between the Westphalian knights and the Rhinelanders. Years earlier Vincke had led the Westphalian party to a bloodless victory over their opponents, then made peace with Lithuania. When the grand master had ordered him to keep the pressure on the enemy, the Livonian master had begun to work together with the German convents to limit the grand master's authority; this, in effect, would decentralise the order, allowing each region to concentrate on local concerns. With Vincke off the scene, Erlichshausen was able to begin returning the Rhinelanders to more nearly equal status with the Westphalians. The new master, Johann von Mengede, though a Westphalian, agreed with the grand master that the Prussian League had to be crushed – the parallel with the hated Livonian Confederation was too obvious to be missed.

Within a short time Erlichshausen and Blumenau frightened the members of the Prussian League, who came to believe that the lawyer's pompous declarations were a true guide to the grand master's future actions against their freedom and property. The secular nobles, gentry, and burghers began making plans to defend themselves.

Erlichshausen mistook his opponents in thinking that they would accept a papal or imperial ruling as the last word in the dispute. In permitting Blumenau to ask the pope and emperor whether the Prussian League was a legal body or not, he was too clever by half. Of course, the pope and emperor assigned lawyers the task of consulting the charters of the order. The lawyers made prompt, clear answers: the League was illegal and must dissolve itself. That in itself achieved nothing except to warn the cities and nobles to beware of lawyers, especially clever ones like Blumenau, who was able to persuade papal and imperial officials that the League's expensively obtained forged documents were, in fact, not genuine. The League's high-powered lawyer was overmatched by the grand master's. Blumenau could dig into the order's extensive archive and come up with whatever document the experts needed, and the League's lawyers could not.

It was not long before this dispute came to the attention of Aeneas Silvius Piccolomini, the papal legate to the imperial court. Piccolomini could remember one evening years ago at the Council of Basel, when he listened entranced to a missionary's stories about life in Lithuania and the problems caused by the Teutonic Knights' activities; he had more recently been working closely with the legate Louis of Silvius. Piccolomini was a many-sided individual. He was without question the most spectacular scholar in the Church, a figure whose masterful rhetoric and elevated style of composition was transforming the ways that every aspiring lawyer wanted to speak and every chancery official sought to write Latin. As the 'Apostle of Humanism to the Germans', his determined efforts to impress the 'barbarians' made as many enemies as friends – he was either unaware that his mail would be opened and his devastating analyses of politicians' abilities and his opponents' foibles would be read, or he did not care. His ability to shift his point of view according to the needs of the moment outraged the 'simple, honest' Germans, who quickly concluded that he was a shifty Italian, not to be trusted in any way. (Stereotypes are no modern invention.)

Piccolomini's job was a difficult one. He gave high priority to preventing another church council from being called. The papacy was weak enough as it was without having to go through the Basel experience again.[*] Christendom needed leadership, not feuds. Therefore, Piccolomini did not see another Church council as being in anybody's interest. Reforms had to be made, of course, but those should be traditional ones, such as freeing churches and monasteries from the control of local families; but that was not a programme likely to be welcomed by the minor princes of Germany. In the end, he argued, the papacy had to have an income in order to be an effective force in international affairs; and, in principle, the more income a pope had, the better he would be able to support the crusading movement, the less he could be intimidated by secular rulers, and the more justice he could bring to society.

A second task was to preserve the powers of those very princes who were stripping the Church and the empire of their most important resources. Piccolomini worried about leagues of cities and knights (like the Prussian

---

[*] The churchmen, unhappy at papal reluctance to turn the Church into a more representative body, refused to dissolve the council when ordered to go home. Instead, they declared the pope deposed and elected an anti-pope. It took years to restore unity.

League) which were becoming more powerful than any one prince. If the princes were made impotent, the Holy Roman Empire would become totally impotent; without strong princes, Christendom would be too weak to protect itself. Piccolomini saw no way to make a parliamentary government effective nor any way to put some backbone into the Habsburg emperor, Friedrich III.

A third assignment was to persuade the emperor, the kings of Hungary and Poland, and the princes to support a crusade against the Turks. Belgrade had been attacked in 1451, but had been saved by John Capistrano; Constantinople had obviously been targeted, and when that great city was besieged in 1453 Piccolomini's duty was to arrange a general peace in East Central Europe so that Germans, Hungarians, and Poles could march together to its rescue. Resolving the Prussian dispute was suddenly Piccolomini's highest priority.

Justice, alas, often moves slowly. Constantinople had already fallen before the Prussian matter could be argued at the imperial court. Delays were caused by someone waylaying the League's representatives and stealing their papers, and by the Polish ambassador warning that his monarch, Casimir, would not participate in the crusade if any 'outsiders' interfered in the Prussian matter – this provoked shouted threats from the German princes. The most Piccolomini could do was to seek to delay a decision. As much as he detested urban leagues, he did not want a war now.

Piccolomini's letter to Cardinal Oleśnicki, the power behind the throne in Poland, in October 1453 illustrates well the manner in which he attempted to cajole, persuade, and intimidate his listeners and readers into going along with his wishes. His epistle was a masterpiece of eloquence, classical citations, wisdom, flattery ('I am fully aware of the many ecclesiastical responsibilities of your office which involve not only yourself but the king, and that after him you by virtue of your rank as cardinal are the second most important man in Poland. I am also aware that decrees are not passed without your approval, that higher courts seek your opinion, and that plans for war and peace are not made without consulting you.'), self-flattery, irony, and chastisement of Polish efforts to seize the thrones of Hungary and Bohemia. By the time he concluded, his letter had, as Piccolomini put it, become a book – but the power of his style made it certain that the letter would be read by a far larger audience than the august bishop of Cracow would have liked.

Piccolomini's speech to the *Reichstag* was among his greatest orations. As reported in his history, *de Pruthenorum origine*, he had said: 'This quarrel, most high Caesar, seems to me neither small nor contemptible . . . It is not the fields of Arpinas or Tusculanus that are contested, but great provinces which are desired by a powerful king.' He concluded with a denunciation of warfare in general, citing the proverb 'Laws are mute when kings speak'. His advice was, as usual, rejected. In January of 1454 the emperor ruled against the Prussian League. Now it remained to the grand master to figure out some way to enforce the decision – without conceding the secondary point in the imperial ruling, that the Teutonic Order's Prussian possessions were a part of the Holy Roman Empire. The German convents were willing to make any concession necessary to save the order, especially if the concession resulted in an increase in the German master's influence. The grand master, however, was not willing to abdicate his sovereignty or authority. Nor was Friedrich III going to do anything that might involve him in a war. His path to success lay on the marriage bed (*Bella gerant alii, tu felix Austria nube*: 'Others wage war, but you, happy Austria, marry') and he had only recently taken a wife.

As for Piccolomini's hopes of organising a crusade to recover Constantinople, he was close to success when Pope Nicholas V died; thereupon nothing could be done until the papal election, because the new pope might wish to pursue different policies or have different priorities. As a result, even though the new pope, Calixtus III (1455–8), was so determined to revive the crusading spirit that he made Piccolomini cardinal in order for him to have the necessary rank to override resistance, Christendom had lost a year.

✠

The War

The members of the Prussian League, aware that they could not resist the Teutonic Order militarily if they gave the grand master time to raise an army, ended the litigation in February by delivering him a letter of secession: they withdrew their allegiance to Prussia and turned to the king of Poland. Their written justification echoed the most extreme statements of Polish sovereignty over Prussia. Naturally, King Casimir (1447–92) welcomed their action, although he was neither ready nor eager to go to war on their behalf at that moment.

The challenge by the estates took everyone by surprise. The grand master, who had been arming for war but was not yet ready, found that he was not able to fight everywhere at once. The castles in Elbing, Danzig, and Thorn fell immediately, then were either fully or partially destroyed.

Nothing remained of the walls or buildings in Elbing and Danzig, and only the mighty Danzker was left in Thorn – that toilet facility was the only reminder that the order had once ruled there! Soon every important post in West Prussia except Marienburg, Stuhm, and Konitz was in the hands of the rebels. Slowly the grand master's officers recruited mercenaries in Saxony, Meissen, Austria, Bohemia, and Silesia – all the eastern duchies of the empire – until he had a force of 15,000 troops.

Such a state of affairs sixty years earlier would have brought pagan Samogitians into the countryside, fifty years ago Islamic Tatars. Now all of Lithuania was Christian and united with Poland. There was no vengeful prince eager to humble his proud enemies, urged on by rabidly anti-German nobles and clergy. Quite the contrary. At the head of the Polish state was Casimir, a quiet man whose principal difficulty was in persuading his independent-minded nobles and clergy to adopt any type of foreign policy, even one directed toward defending the country against an obvious threat from the Turks. Instead of worrying about the southern and eastern frontiers, however, the nobles were alarmed that the conquest of Prussia could provide their king not only with more of the resources needed to drive back the Islamic armies, but also enhance his ability to dominate the Polish clergy and nobles. These groups feared that any authority which could make royal armies effective in war could also be misused in peacetime. Therefore there was little rejoicing in the diet about the success of the royalist forces in Prussia.

The king chose to support the Prussian rebels despite the diet's lack of enthusiasm. To his delight and surprise, the uninterrupted string of victories seemed to indicate that the destruction of the Teutonic Order would be cheap, quick, and total. Casimir hurried north to claim the credit, riding through Prussia in a triumphal procession, cheered by the inhabitants of city and countryside, welcomed by mayors and nobles. The end of the Teutonic Knights as a territorial power seemed assured, a matter of days rather than months.

The Prussian League settled down to a siege of Marienburg, while royal levies watched Konitz. The only danger was the arrival of relief troops from the west, because the German master had recruited Bohemian mercenaries. Those were the finest troops in Europe at the time, still enjoying the prestige won in the Hussite wars, wars they had fought to a standstill against the Holy Roman Empire and the Church. Even so, Casimir felt confident that his feudal levy from Great Poland could overpower these mercenaries as they crossed into Prussia. He was mistaken. The castellan at Konitz was another Plauen – Heinrich Reuss von Plauen, a future grand master. When Plauen saw the two armies engaged in battle below his fortress, he sallied out and struck the Polish host in the rear. Caught between the two forces, the Polish knighthood was cut to pieces and the king barely escaped being captured. It did not take a genius to imagine what kind of peace settlement Louis von Erlichshausen could have extracted from Poland in return for Casimir's release. The dream of such an event had sustained the Teutonic Knights' persistence for decades now, and it had come so close to becoming reality.

As it was, the battle was far from decisive. What might have been the end of an unnecessary conflict became the beginning of the terrible Thirteen Years' War. For lack of money the Polish king was unable to raise new troops; the diet would not vote sufficient funds to hire mercenaries and his nobles refused to serve in any expedition long enough to deal his enemies a fatal blow. The Prussian League, led by Danzig, made up the difference by taxing itself far more heavily than the grand master would ever have dared attempt, but the League's efforts, too, seemed totally in vain. Battlefield success eluded them.

The war dissolved into a series of local feuds, many of which cannot be easily fitted into a sensible party alignment. The knights of the order won some minor engagements, lost several border castles, watched helplessly from the ramparts as various mercenary forces plundered the countryside without regard for the peasantry's allegiance, and slowly bled to death in numerous insignificant combats. The League's navy (three vessels from Danzig) beat a much larger Livonian-Danish fleet in August 1457 near the island of Bornholm in a night-time engagement. Although Denmark pulled out of the war, the Danzig merchants were otherwise unable to profit from the victory.

Although the League's revenue measures drove some members back to the Teutonic Knights and provoked the lesser guilds in several cities to attempt revolts, Louis von Erlichshausen was unable to profit from the situation. He could not command his mercenaries effectively because he could not pay them, and his financial circumstances hardly allowed him to promise tax relief as an incentive to switch sides. As a temporary measure he pawned his cities and fortresses to his mercenaries, even Marienburg, while he pressed his remaining subjects for more money.

Erlichshausen's surrender of Marienburg proved to be a disastrous mistake, second only to that of beginning the war itself. The mercenaries had no interest in the situation other than that their salaries be paid, and their concern with money grew more intense the longer they remained unpaid. The grand master was able to make only partial payments, and his later successes – the recapture of the town of Marienburg and risings in the League's cities – moved the mercenaries not in the least. Rather, they believed the League was winning the war. The merchant oligarchies in the smaller Prussian towns, supported by troops sent from Danzig, bloodily repressed lower-class movements which had temporarily threatened their regimes; and the king helped in Culm and other border provinces. Consequently the mercenaries felt confident in pressing the grand master for more money. In February of 1457 Erlichshausen had to bow to their demands for a temporary settlement – another partial payment, with permission for the mercenaries to sell the pawned fortresses to the highest bidder in case he failed to raise the remainder of the fantastic sum. Of course, he was unable to raise the money when it came due.

It was at that moment that the Danzig merchants displayed their financial strength. Casimir lacked the funds to pay his mercenaries, and most members of the Prussian League had suffered too greatly from the disruption of trade to raise the sum those troops demanded. But Danzig could raise money and did. Despite the declaration of war by Denmark, whose monarch had hoped to weaken the Hanseatic League, Danzig's trade had prospered. Not without sacrifices, however, and not without difficulty; but the money was collected. That effort secured the destruction of Erlichshausen's plans and assured the victorious position of Danzig atop the ruins of the grand master's state. Casimir granted privileges to Danzig which made it dominant in local politics and trade; in return, the merchant oligarchy presented the king the keys to impregnable fortresses. Louis von Erlichshausen was ingloriously evicted from his quarters in Marienburg, taken prisoner to Konitz, and told he would be turned over to the king; Blumenau, who had attempted to persuade the mercenaries that their actions were 'against God, against justice, and against Holy Scripture', had been mugged and thrown out of the castle. At the last moment the grand master escaped and made his way to Königsberg. That fortress, far from the reach of the Prussian League and its fleet, was thereafter the grand master's residence. The war continued.

This seemed like the appropriate moment for Cardinal Piccolomini to re-enter the fray. The immediate matter at hand was the impending demise of the bishop of Ermland, a loyal supporter of the grand master. If the Prussian League could arrange for the election of a friendly man as his successor, the balance of power might well be tipped. There were three canons living in Danzig, six living in exile in Silesia, and seven held prisoner by the grand master (an action which had brought upon him a papal excommunication). When the grand master heard that the Silesian canons were proposing that the bishop retire from his bankrupt diocese on a pension in order to permit the election of a Polish underchancellor, he sent the Ermland cantor, Bartholmaus Liebenwald, to Rome to speak with Piccolomini. Liebenwald had not returned farther than Silesia when the news arrived that the bishop was dead. Sharing the cardinal's advice to elect as bishop a powerful personality known both to the pope and the emperor, not the minor figures proposed by the League and the grand master, Liebenwald suggested that the rump chapter elect Piccolomini himself. The six canons agreed, and sent Liebenwald back to Rome to announce their choice to Pope Calixtus III.

Within days the pope confirmed Piccolomini's election and gave him full authority to arrange matters there and in the region as he wished. Whatever was necessary to restore peace, the pope promised his fullest co-operation. Of course, Piccolomini could not go to Prussia in person. He had much too much to do in Rome, and the pope was not in good health. Instead, he gave detailed instructions to Liebenwald, named him episcopal vicar, and gave him full authority to negotiate, to raise armies, and to collect taxes. He wrote sweet letters to the Polish king, urging Casimir to send a representative to Rome to negotiate a peace. The monarch was not pleased, nor was he co-operative. So Piccolomini raised the stakes.

The death of the bishop of Culm gave Piccolomini his opportunity. The bishop of Ermland had been a dependable supporter of the Prussian League – in fact, a key member of the leadership. When a Polish candidate for the Culm bishopric appeared in Rome, then the grand master's candidate, Piccolomini spoke on behalf of the former, only to have the pope refer the matter to a jurist, who told Piccolomini to choose between the candidates. Confusion abounded. Just what was the wily Italian up to? The confusion was doubled when he refused a sizeable bribe. What was the world coming to when you couldn't even trust an Italian (and a churchman, to boot) to take a bribe?

Speculation was rife. Would Piccolomini demand the payment of Peter's Pence in West Prussia? That speculation diminished only when his efforts to bring the parties together in Prague failed. Then, in August 1458, Piccolomini became Pope Pius II. No longer did he have the time, nor the physical strength, for efforts to bring the candidates, the royal representatives, the League's lawyers, and the grand master's procurator together again for peace talks. Pius II retained the *pro forma* title of bishop of Ermland, rejected renewed efforts at bribery, and sent an administrator north to manage the diocese and to work toward a peace settlement. That administrator was first the grand master's ally, then neutral, and finally a supporter of the League. His military role in the conflict was insignificant, but from that time forth Ermland was an independent territory, freed from the direct domination of either grand master or king. The truce he arranged from October 1458 to July 1459 failed to lead to concrete results, but there was no serious fighting until the end of 1461.

Piccolomini was an unusual figure for a man of letters. First a reformer; then a diplomat and author; at the end he was a crusader. However, his efforts to organise European resistance to the Turkish advance were a mirror image of his failure in Prussia. The Holy Roman emperor, Friedrich III, was more interested in taking Hungary from Matthias Corvinus (1458–90) than in fighting in the Balkans, so that the successful defence of Belgrade in 1456 had resulted only in a temporary respite, not a rollback of Ottoman gains; and when Jan Hunyady died during the siege, the Christians lost an irreplaceable general. Furthermore, the French were offended by the pope's Italian policies, the Italian cities were too absorbed in their own affairs to look abroad, and even Rome itself was in constant turmoil. In 1464, after four years of preparation, Pius II managed to gather together a small, ill-disciplined force, which he led south to meet the Venetian fleet and be transported across the Adriatic Sea to the Balkans. However, the ill, gout-ridden pontiff died before any of his unruly troops could board ship. He was succeeded by a pope, Paul II (1464–71), who could not speak proper Latin but who understood politics. Determined to expunge the Hussite heresy, he was very displeased with Gregor von Heimburg, lawyer for Georg of Podiebrady (1458–71), the pro-Hussite king of Bohemia. Since Heimburg was also representing the Teutonic Order, the pope automatically favoured the grand master's enemies. Thus the proud papacy of Pius II, the epitome of Renaissance Humanism, began its descent into its pre-Reformation squalor. Papal interest in the North was henceforth confined largely to the return on financial assets. But money was hard to come by.

Since not even Danzig could pay all the mercenaries now, the Prussian League had to release many of its hired troops. Dismissing the soldiers of fortune, however, did not remove them from the country – it simply turned them loose on the peasantry. As the ragged soldiers ravaged the countryside, sometimes they acknowledged being in the service of one side or the other, sometimes not. They were joined by bands of impoverished peasants originally raised to defend harvests and villages, but who now went from region to region seeking food and shelter, not begging, but as armed units, taking what they needed through threats or force. It was a war of all against all, with pity, loyalty, and morality long forgotten.

The town of Marienburg temporarily came back into the possession of the order, betrayed by a Bohemian mercenary commander; but it was lost again, after a year's siege, to hunger. The grand master had no money to hire a relief force, and he had no ships available to carry grain from Livonia to the beleaguered garrison. The revenge of the victors was gruesome and uncommonly severe – execution for the officers of the order's mercenaries.

Despite these setbacks, both emperor and pope encouraged the order to fight on. Pius II had even used his ecclesiastical weapons against the League and the king of Poland – placing them under the interdict – but to no avail. The Polish king ignored the pope's demands as complacently as any grand master had ever dared; and the rebellious German nobles and burghers were equally as capable of ignoring papal edicts. The war spread to include all Scandinavia and the Hanseatic cities, to involve Poland and Hussite Bohemia, and the ambitions of the emperor, but in Prussia it remained essentially a civil conflict; Polish troops were often but a minor factor in the warfare. Casimir was unable to raise taxes or call out the general levy without the consent of the diet, and the nobles were reluctant to see the king successful in Prussia. Oleśnicki had returned from the Council of Basel in 1451 to denounce the royal policies. His death in 1455 had not ended clerical opposition to the crown, since Casimir was determined to control the appointment of ecclesiastical officials; in contrast, the church-men thought that it would be more appropriate for them to appoint the king.

The Lithuanian contribution to the war was to tie down the troops of the Livonian Order. In 1454 the Council of Lords, having negotiated with the Teutonic Knights for an alliance, coerced Casimir into rendering the long-delayed oath to protect Lithuanian rights, then into returning Volhynia to the grand duchy. Afterward they let him fight the war on his own. Casimir could obtain the money to hire mercenaries only by offering concessions to the Polish diet; this was a major step toward establishing the powers of the chamber of deputies as equal to those of the senate (the royal council).

At the end of 1461 the grand master raised a body of mercenaries in Germany which, in spite of its small numbers, seemed capable of sweeping his exhausted enemy from the field. The only major battle of the war resulted, fought in September 1462 between two diminutive forces. The grand master's army advanced out of Culm, where a base had been estab-lished with great effort. The League forces came out of Danzig, the main-stay of the rebel coalition and the only city able to pay any mercenaries. Actually, both armies were ragtag assemblages of city levies, dispossessed farmers, unruly mercenaries, and a handful of knights. The units of the Prussian League proved to be the least weak. Employing the difficult tactic of fighting behind a wagon-fort, they destroyed the grand master's forces, occupied a number of castles and towns, and threw Erlichshausen back to his last refuges. In the autumn of 1463 the Prussian League's navy destroyed the order's fleet.

It was time for peace talks but not yet for a peace agreement; for that both sides had to become even more exhausted. Almost everyone who was anyone offered to mediate the dispute. Pope Paul II and the Hanseatic League made the most determined efforts, and finally, in 1466, a papal legate arranged a settlement. Only repeated reverses and the inability to hire more troops persuaded Erlichshausen to accept the harsh terms.

✠

The Second Peace of Thorn 1466

The peace treaty provided for West Prussia and Culm to be 'returned' to the king of Poland and for Ermland to become independent. Marienburg, Elbing, and Christburg also went to Poland. This collection of lands was henceforth known as Royal Prussia. Moreover, the order promised to abandon its ties to the Holy Roman Empire, become a fief of the Polish crown, and accept up to half of its members from Polish subjects. The incompleteness of the victory was a disappointment to those who had hoped to uproot the grand master's state altogether, but it was a realistic settlement that reflected battle lines that neither side seemed capable of changing significantly no matter how long they fought. Poles could take heart from having at last come into possession of long-disputed territories, and they anticipated that the division of Prussia would leave their ancient enemies too weak to make trouble again. The Prussian League, however, did not see the legal situation in exactly that way: Prussians, even those now under Polish sovereignty, still continued to think of themselves as belonging to one country.

The formal ceremonies disguised all this. Erlichshausen went to Casimir and swore to uphold the peace. Of course, he had no intention of honouring the full terms of the agreement. He did not offer homage as required, arguing that he was restrained by his prior commitments to the pope and the emperor, neither of whom would allow their rights to be infringed in this matter. The papacy quickly supported him in this by declaring the treaty void, a violation of papal charters and harmful to the interests of the Church. The tie of the military order to the papacy again came to supersede secular bonds, to present the Polish king with seemingly insoluble problems in disposing of this troublesome neighbour even after he had won near total military victory. Nor were there any Polish knights who had an interest in joining the Teutonic Order. That provision of the treaty was a dead letter from the beginning.

Despite official rejection of the peace terms, there was nothing to prevent them from being implemented at a later date (homage was finally rendered in 1478, though it was strictly personal, obligating the grand master alone, and not his order or its lands), and certainly there was no reason for the war to begin again. The most important provisions – the territorial concessions to Poland and the independence of the Prussian League – were *fait accompli*. The other provisions were comparatively minor. Casimir had obtained the grand master's submission once, and that would not be forgotten. The precedent had been set.

The grand master moved his residence to Königsberg, taking the marshal's quarters. This was accomplished without difficulty since the marshal was in Polish captivity, but there were expensive changes necessary for the castle to serve as the seat of a grand master and his court. Königsberg was not Marienburg, but it was still impressive. Perhaps the change in residence should be seen as symbolic of the grand master's general loss of status and authority. His castellans and advocates took possession of the most important estates and incomes, leaving him with insufficient income to perform his statutory duties. Power devolved into the hands of the marshal, Heinrich Reuss von Plauen, who was elected grand master in 1469. Plauen was able to continue the reorganisation of the order's administration for only one year. Upon his death, he was succeeded by a cautious but more traditional grand master, Heinrich Reffle von Richtenberg, whose hope was to restore the prosperity of the land and to end the complicated internal quarrels. However, he could not reach those goals with the slender resources at his command; the selfish interests of the castellans and advocates blocked every effort at reform now and later.

The Thirteen Years' War had made radical changes in Prussia. By 1466 the estates were no longer complaining about the order's misrule in matters such as taxation or devaluation of the coinage. Those abuses seemed laughable in retrospect. The noble and burgher estates had won only one significant advantage out of all their struggles – control of their local governments – which they used to suppress the guildsmen and labourers so as to increase their profits to the point that they could pay the few self-imposed taxes and exactions more easily. In East Prussia there was a new land-owning class composed of former mercenaries, who had been paid with fiefs taken from secular knights who had perished and from estates of the Teutonic Order. These mercenaries replaced many of the native knights, and from them descended many of the Junker families of Prussia. Future grand masters would know better than to embark on ambitious projects in support of Livonia or imperial efforts in the Balkans, to challenge the Prussian estates or the king of Poland, or even their own membership. The Teutonic Order was marking time, without even much of an idea of what to do if an opportunity presented itself.

Poland, in contrast, had reached the sea. It had taken lands claimed by the crown since the thirteenth century – Culm, Pomerellia, Danzig – and extended its reach onto lands beyond those: to Stolp and Pomerania. For a short period Casimir had the opportunity to lay a new foundation for royal authority, basing it on the cities and gentry. That policy had achieved military and political victories in Prussia. That he did not extend this to the cities and gentry throughout Poland was a long-term mistake. He had entered into the Thirteen Years' War against the wishes of the magnates and the Church. (In 1454 Oleśnicki had counselled accepting the concessions the grand master had been willing to make at that time; he had foreseen the stubborn resistance that the well-fortified grand master could offer.) Having achieved peace in Prussia, the king's interests turned to dynastic politics. To that goal he sacrificed the possibility of internal reforms and his temporary ascendancy over those who would limit royal authority.

For much of the next fifty years the grand masters were impoverished vassals of the Polish kings. Technically their allegiances were divided, but practically there was nothing that they could do. Any effort to change their situation would result in swift cries of outrage from the cities and vassals, opposition from important officers, and rebukes from one or another of their lords. As the fifteenth century came to a close, however, the knights noticed that a number of German princes seemed to have discovered ways to increase their authority over their subjects, foster industry and commerce, and then tax the profits. The knights began to discuss means by which their order might do the same in Prussia. It is worth noting that those same secular reformers were also the swiftest to seize upon the popular demands for reforms in the Church, reforms that ultimately led to the Reformation.

✠

Dissolution and Rebirth

The thunderstorm that the Reformation represented struck Prussia, Lithuania, and Poland one after the other. The Roman Catholic Church in Poland, beset by German demands for reforms, Lithuanian resentment of Polish domination, Uniate desires for more autonomy, Orthodox hatred, and its own parishioners' fears of each of these foreign peoples, was hard-pressed to find adequate responses. Moreover, the papacy saw East Central Europe as an unimportant backwater, one which could be ignored while the Church concentrated on preserving the physical liberty of the pope in Rome from local families, preventing either Spanish or French domination over Italy, and assisting the Holy Roman emperor in re-establishing the authority of the Church over Lutheran dissidents in Germany. How the papacy could assist the young emperor, Charles V (1519–56), in crushing his various enemies – which now included an ever-more aggressive Turkish sultan – without at the same time making him so powerful as to endanger the pope's own independence was a conundrum which was never resolved satisfactorily. Similarly, it could find no way to help the Polish king until the Counter-Reformation, when the Jesuits came to Cracow and Vilnius.

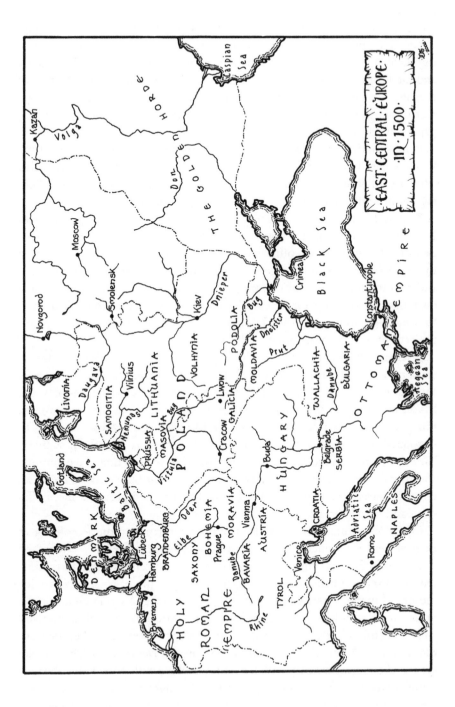

EAST · CENTRAL · EUROPE · IN · 1500 ·

But this is to move the story along too swiftly. The Reformation did not come all at once, nor did contemporaries instantly recognise in its beginnings what it later became. In East Central Europe as elsewhere the forerunner of the Reformation was the spread of Renaissance culture among the nobility and intellectuals. The centres of the New Latin that marked the adoption of Renaissance ideas and attitudes were always the chanceries – that of the king, first of all, then those of the bishops; and as the model for all, that of the papacy. In Germany the princes vied with proud cities and ambitious prelates in demonstrating their support of the new art, literature, and manners of the Renaissance. Founding and fostering universities was even more irrefutable evidence of intellectual superiority in an age which appreciated the bold façade more than perhaps any other in European history.

Saxony led the way in applying the imaginative yet logical processes of Renaissance thought to government. Humanistically trained scholars, despising the noble-born office-holders and their inefficient ways, proposed to receptive princes ways of centralising authority, raising greater revenues, and encouraging trade and commerce. So successful had the Saxon princes been that the Teutonic Order had elected the physical weakling Friedrich of Saxony as grand master in the hope that he could work the same magic on the economy and government of Prussia.

Friedrich did what he could, which was insufficient to reverse the downward trend of the order's fortunes, but he did prepare the way for reforms such as those which would be proposed in a few years by a professor at the Saxon university at Wittenberg – Martin Luther. On the whole, however, this grand master's role was indirect: Friedrich encouraged the bishops to introduce humanists into their cathedral chapters and give them as free a hand as practical to reorganise the administration so as to improve economic and moral life in their dioceses; Friedrich also hired humanists to create an effective bureaucracy on the Saxon model that would permit a more efficient and more just government.

Friedrich's humanists – first Paul Watt, his former tutor, a professor at Leipzig; and subsequently Dietrich von Werthern, a lawyer – established new offices, thereby eliminating ageing knights from important administrative posts; consolidated convents, appropriating some of their incomes for the grand master's use; eliminated the practice whereby one estate or the other could veto legislation; redefined court procedure and etiquette; and lastly, in ruthless bureaucratic warfare, drove their conservative enemies from the country. When the German master died, Friedrich's brother, Duke Georg of Saxony, came up with a plan for dealing with potentially obstructionist successors by abolishing the office. As might have been anticipated, the idea found little support in the Holy Roman Empire. The new German master organised opposition to changes in the traditional practices, and Friedrich's visits to Germany in 1504 and 1507 led only to a clarification of the issues, not a resolution of them.

Foreign policy was similarly militant. One war scare followed another, with blame for the tensions shared by all sides. The Teutonic Order made no great secret of its ambitions to be freed of all obligations to the Polish crown, to recover its lost territories, and even to become a great power again. In return, the king and his advisors began to discuss means of eliminating the hated order altogether, if possible; at the least to humble its notorious pride. The king, however, was well aware that Duke Georg, whose armies could easily cross Silesia into the Polish heartland, was ready to protect his brother. (Much later Augustus the Strong of Saxony demonstrated the closeness of the two lands.) Furthermore, war in the north of Poland would not go unnoticed by the king's neighbours. But what really kept the two parties from going beyond burning villages and stealing cattle was the immense cost of warfare. Neither king nor grand master could afford to raise an army; the king could not persuade the diet to levy war taxes, because the representatives did not want royal authority increased, lest he emulate those German lords the Teutonic Order so admired.

The demise of Grand Master Friedrich in late 1510 again presented an opportunity to consider new ideas at the 'national' level. One suggestion, made principally by Polish nobles and clerics, was for the election of the Polish king as grand master. They would have welcomed a celibate monarchy, because that would have guaranteed the elective nature of their kingdom. The king, in fact, was willing to consider this proposal for his descendants, provided he could get a papal exemption for himself to marry! The Teutonic Knights, however, had their own candidate already selected: Albrecht of Hohenzollern-Ansbach (1490–1568). The family was one of the most important in Germany, but it was hardly wealthy enough to endow eight sons with a suitable living. The order's interests and the Hohenzollerns' coincided perfectly.

Obtaining universal approval of the order's choice was not easy, although the young man was related to the king of Poland and the king of Bohemia and Hungary, and had excellent connections to the Empire and Church. The approval of the convents in Germany and Livonia was obtained – there was no proper election – and in 1511 Albrecht was made a member of the order and installed as grand master on the same day. He immediately received moral and political support from the Emperor Maximilian (1493–1519), who urged him to attend the *Reichstag* and other imperial gatherings and, by the way, to give more attention to imperial wishes. In their meeting in Nuremberg in early 1512, Albrecht explained that before he could give his oath to the emperor he had to be freed from his obligations to the king of Poland. Forbidden by the emperor to render homage to the Polish king, he immediately adopted the internal and foreign policies of his predecessor – to reverse the provisions of the two treaties of Thorn by any means possible – but he introduced an entirely different personal life style.

Albrecht had been forthright about his lack of interest in a life without sex, but the members had hastily explained that while ordinary knights and priests had to follow the rules carefully, the grand master was a prominent noble and high official who was exempt from petty requirements. All that he had to sacrifice was marriage, they said, since the vow was celibacy, not chastity. Surely, if popes could live openly with their women, and cardinals and archbishops flaunt their mistresses in public, a great German prince, twenty-one years of age and reared for a secular life, could be excused for not playing the role of a lowly friar?

Albrecht saw more clearly than many of his contemporaries that the future belonged to those princes who could take control of their territories, suppress contentious nobles and unco-operative assemblies, encourage trade and industry, tax the increased prosperity of their subjects, and then hire professional armies for a rational yet daring foreign policy that could take advantage of opportunities when they appeared. He was, in short, among the first of the absolutist princes, more able to exploit his opportunities because the Teutonic Order had already made discipline and order a state tradition – at least, it honoured discipline and order, though those ideals had fallen low since the glorious days of the fourteenth century; although recent grand masters had reduced the strife inside the membership and reasserted control over their officers, they had lacked the means to do more than stage impressive parades and public ceremonies of a mixed ecclesiastical and chivalric nature. Without question, the elaborate costumes of the officers and knights, the bishops and their canons, the abbots with their friars and monks, the burghers with their guilds, and the mounted knights with their troops, made for first-class spectacle. But there was a difference between spectacle and power, and what separated Albrecht from many contemporaries is that, as time passed, he learned how to discern the difference.

The young prince's plans involved great patience, first to make the necessary reforms so as to increase his power, and second to await the opportunities to exercise this power. At first he relied on the 'Iron Bishop' of Pomesania, Hiob, one of the great humanists of the era, whose respect for tradition and moderation was not lost on the Polish monarch and his prelates. In 1515, however, Albrecht came under the influence of Dietrich von Schönberg, a charismatic young charlatan who specialised in mathematics, astronomy, and astrology. The young grand master, always alert to the latest cultural trends, became an enthusiastic listener to his favourite's astrological predictions. He also became Schönberg's companion on immoral nocturnal adventures. Freed finally from the company of priests and elderly pious knights, Albrecht proved himself an accomplished student of libertine life, at least of such as Königsberg had to offer. Schönberg also persuaded him that the time had arrived to interject himself into foreign affairs, to use Prussia's strategic position in the rear of Lithuania now that the Polish monarch, Sigismund I (1506–48), was about to go to war with Basil III (1505–33) of Russia. Schönberg travelled to Moscow, returning with a treaty promising financial support for an army sufficient in size to tie down Polish troops or even inflict devastating defeats on them; Schönberg then used his considerable rhetorical skills to confuse the Prussian assembly and whip up a war fever among the representatives – he outlined in graphic detail Polish plans (mostly fictitious, the rest exaggerated, but with just enough truth to be plausible) to require that half the knights in the order be Poles and to introduce a tyrannical government on the Polish model, with the inevitable result of seeing poverty and serfdom spread into the yet relatively prosperous provinces of Prussia. The townspeople and knights of Prussia were not complete fools, but their knowledge of the damage that Polish nobles and prelates were doing to their country made them susceptible to the grossest propaganda and racial prejudice.

Such activities could not be kept secret from King Sigismund, nor did Albrecht want them to be. Only when universally recognised as the man who could tip the balance between the great powers could Albrecht make the kind of demands that would restore to his order the lands and authority it had possessed eleven decades earlier. That obviously required a different kind of ruler than those whose piety and loyalty had led them to obey orders from past Holy Roman emperors which had led the military order into one disaster after another. Albrecht was probably not more intelligent than his predecessors; he may not even have been more devious; certainly he did not work harder, at least not when he was young. What he had was a kind of presence, an understanding that he stood above tradition and customary rules. His knights were awed by his birth and breeding – that finely developed air of authority, the assumption that one has the right to make judgements and give orders, and the posture and tone of voice that make inferiors aware that they are in the presence of one of their betters. Certainly no previous grand master would have considered holding a tournament, much less participated in it personally, but Albrecht staged one in Königsberg in 1518 and not only jousted but joined in the melee.

While the adventurous policies of the new grand master made him important in the considerations of high diplomacy, it was an impractical programme. As long as there was no war, Albrecht could strut about as a great figure, impressing the German master with his plans and plans for plans; but when it actually came to war between Poland-Lithuania and Moscow in 1519, he learned that the promised Russian subsidies would not come and therefore he could not pay his troops. Imperial help was likewise absent; Maximilian was rather more interested in Polish help for his own ventures than in rescuing the grand master. As a result of Albrecht's political miscalculations, every effort to escape from his problems made his situation more precarious. Königsberg's fortifications indeed repelled the Polish assaults at the last minute, and much of the ground lost in the opening months of the war was recovered, but all his hopes rested ultimately on a great army raised by the German master and brought to the frontier. Eighteen hundred horsemen and 8,000 foot soldiers passed through Brandenburg to Danzig. There, however, the mercenaries waited in vain for the grand master and his money. Albrecht was unable to appear: Polish garrisons blocked the crossings of the Vistula, and Danzig warships patrolled the seas; moreover, he had too little money to pay the army. Ultimately, the mercenaries went home, undoubtedly spreading the word about the grand master's unreliability as a paymaster.

If Sigismund had not been occupied in the south, that would have been the end of Albrecht, but in fact the king had only a small force that he could send to Prussia. This was insufficient to hold the order's troops in check long. The grand master's forces ravaged Royal Prussia, reconquered the Neumark, and worried about the appearance of Polish troops. When the Poles came at last, they brought with them Tatars, Bohemian mercenaries, and good artillery; but their numbers were insufficient to capture Albrecht's fortresses. Nevertheless, the grand master, knowing that all would be lost if a larger enemy force came north, seeing that he now possessed but few subjects who had not been robbed of the means to provide food for his troops and pay taxes, willingly signed a truce at the end of 1520. Schönberg left for Germany, to die in the battle of Pavia (1525), fighting for Emperor Charles V; he was unable to spin a magic web over the emperor as he had Albrecht – Charles V had too many problems already with the Turks, the French, and the Protestants to seek a confrontation with the Polish monarch over the distant and unimportant province of Prussia.

The end of Roman Catholicism in East Prussia came as no surprise. During Albrecht's 1522 visit to Nuremberg to plead in vain for money from the princes of the Holy Roman Empire, it was clear that he had been visibly affected by Lutheran teachings. In early 1523 Martin Luther had directed one of his major statements 'to the lords of the Teutonic Knights, that they avoid false chastity'. It was not hard to make inroads among the membership. The knights, and there were fewer of them now, had been reared in a

Germany seething with unrest over church corruption. They understood the issues involved in Luther's protests, and they were unhappy with the lack of morality at the papal curia. Moreover, they understood corruption – Pope Clement VII's appointment of one absentee bishop to office in Pomerellia and nomination of a relative for the post brought that issue forcefully home. Albrecht, perhaps aware of the public mood and certainly personally concerned about ecclesiastical corruption, took steps to prepare the members of his order for reform proposals: during the Christmas holiday of 1523, while the grand master was still in Germany, he allowed Lutheran preachers to deliver sermons at his court in Königsberg.

This was not hypocrisy. The once brash young prince had learned piety through harsh experience. His youthful sins had led not only him to disaster, but also his innocent subjects. Albrecht had apparently decided to devote the rest of his life to atoning for his early foolishness and indiscretion. Unlike repentant men of an earlier generation, however, he never contemplated withdrawing into a cloister for prayer and penitence. This Renaissance-era prince instead reflected on the choices available to him, and he selected a hard one: the correction of the basic flaw in his order's status that had condemned Prussia to a century of foreign invasion and civil conflict, its awkward mixture of secular and clerical duties that made it something more than a religious order and something less than a sovereign state.

The grand master quietly sought to discover what response neighbouring princes would make if he followed Luther's advice, as many northern German bishops were doing, and secularised his Prussian lands. Already during his absence Protestant ministers had carried through the essentials of the Protestant reforms: they had introduced the German language into the worship services, had begun the singing of hymns, and had abolished pilgrimages and the veneration of saints. It was a very practical reform, one based on the general unhappiness with current church conditions but without methodological or theological justifications. Those came later. As the monks, nuns, and priests renounced their vows of celibacy, rumours inevitably began to circulate that the grand master, too, was planning to lay aside his vows, marry, and make himself the head of a secular state. The rumours concentrated on the scandal of the grand master leaving the clerical state and contracting a marriage.

Surprisingly, there was little outrage. The pope and the emperor, of course, warned him against such a course, and his Brandenburg relatives did not approve, but the knights in Prussia and the cities and nobles favoured it decisively and the king of Poland allowed himself to approve it. Secularisation resolved two pressing problems at once: confiscation of the remaining ecclesiastical properties made money available to pay the grand master's debts, and the way was open to incorporate East Prussia into the Polish kingdom, thereby establishing a peaceful and mutually unthreatening relationship with the monarch. On 10 April 1525, Duke Albrecht took the oath of allegiance in Cracow, a scene immortalised on one of the greatest Polish canvases by the nineteenth-century nationalist painter, Jan Matejko.

East Prussia was not absorbed into the Polish state even to the minimal extent that West Prussia had been. The duke maintained his own army, currency, assembly, and a more or less independent foreign policy. The administrative system changed hardly at all, and the former laws remained in force. A few titles were revised. It was the introduction of Lutheran reforms that had the most profound results.

In 1526 Albrecht entered the 'true chastity of marriage' with Dorothea, the eldest daughter of Friedrich of Denmark (1523–33). The Danes specialised in providing spouses to the German states along the Baltic; East Prussia completed the collection of regional alliances. This provided Albrecht with a powerful protector and a number of well-placed brothers- and sisters-in-law. Friedrich was also the most important Lutheran ruler of the time.

The uproar in Catholic Germany was as loud and denunciatory as the applause in Protestant Germany, but in Prussia all was quiet. The handful of knights who were too old or unprepared to assume the demands of secular knighthood or who still kept faith with the old belief went to the German master in Mergentheim, who distributed them among his convents and hospitals. Those who remained in Prussia were given fiefs or offices; a few married and founded families, becoming a part of that Junker class for which Brandenburg-Prussia was later famous. However, on the whole, the noble class changed little in its composition. What changed was the nobles' authority over the serfs, which grew considerably once East Prussia was a secular state. However, the nobles and burghers failed to acquire the political influence they had anticipated obtaining according to the Treaty of Cracow. The Great Peasant Revolt of 1525 was the free farmers' reaction to rumours that they would be reduced to serfdom by their new lords. Albrecht suppressed the rising easily, but the event undermined the self-confidence of the nobles and gentry so greatly that they looked to the duke for leadership in this and all other matters.

Duke Albrecht of Prussia soon abandoned his efforts to be named a prince of the empire, thus assuring himself of imperial forgiveness and giving him the protection of the Holy Roman Empire against excessive demands by the Polish king in the future. However, Charles V had been too far away, in Spain, or too busy with Luther and the Turks, to give careful consideration to such a minor matter while there was still time. In 1526, however, having seen what happened in East Prussia because he had failed to act, the emperor granted that status to the Livonian master and his possessions. In 1530 Charles named the German master to be the new grand master; henceforth the Teutonic Order was expected to serve the Habsburg dynasty's political programme.

Royal Prussia was not affected by the secularisation of East Prussia's government, except, of course, in that Protestant ideas circulated from town to town more easily. Potentially, the people already considered themselves an autonomous German-speaking part of the Polish kingdom with the right to make independent decisions on religion. The townsfolk welcomed both the prospect of peace and the spread of the Lutheran reforms. Not only did the way to a spiritual and cultural reunification of Prussia seem to have opened, but also another means of asserting the authority of the commercial classes and gentry over the ecclesiastical figures who were the nominal rulers of many cities and much of the countryside.

Many who might have objected to the reforms found themselves muted by the even more appalling prospect of the peasant revolt. The rising of peasants here and there in Prussia during 1525 in imitation of the Great Peasant Revolt in Germany was a sobering warning that there were worse changes possible than those associated with cleaning up long-festering problems in the local churches and monasteries. The 1526 uprising in Danzig further demonstrated that unrest had spread to the lower classes in the towns. This was not a time for the upper classes to quarrel over religion – live and let live was the only practical policy.

Albrecht did not consider himself a rebel or disrupter of church unity. Years later he was still continuing his correspondence with Rome and honouring the pope as the head of the Church. The formal separation came later, as one inevitable step of many. The nature of the transformation of Prussia would be easy to exaggerate; in 1525 Protestantism was a reform advocated and welcomed by many devout Roman Catholics who saw no practical alternative. Within a year Sigismund could congratulate himself on his foresight. Louis Jagiellon of Hungary (1516–26) fell in the battle of Mohács and the Turks occupied most of his kingdom. The deceased boy king left the remnants of Hungary and his claims to other kingdoms to the Habsburg, Friedrich of Austria, who later became emperor. With Poland now besieged by strong enemies on the east (Moscow), the south (the Turks), and the west (the Habsburgs), it was fortunate that Sigismund had at least relieved himself of worries about the north.

The emperor, meanwhile, had the extensive resources of the Teutonic Order in Germany to use in his wars against the Turks. There would be no distractions by northern affairs. In short, everyone seemed to benefit from the secularisation of the Prussians lands. This assessment was not universal, of course, and anyone who suggested that the Prussian example should be applied to Livonia could count on a hot dispute.

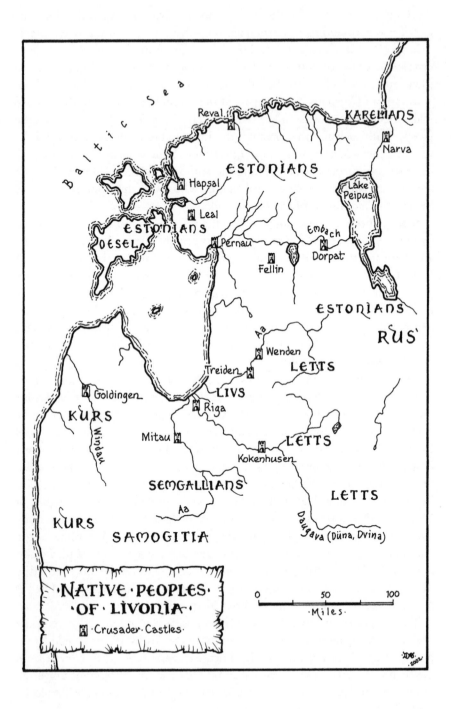

Baltic Sea

KARELIANS

Reval

ESTONIANS

Narva

Hapsal

Lake
Peipus

Leal

ESTONIANS

OESEL

Embach

Pernau

Dorpat

Fellin

ESTONIANS

RUS'

Aa

Wenden

Treiden

LETTS

LIVS

Goldingen

Riga

KURS

Mitau

LETTS

Windau

Kokenhusen

SEMGALLIANS

LETTS

Aa

KURS

SAMOGITIA

Daugava (Düna, Dvina)

·NATIVE·PEOPLES·
·OF·LIVONIA·

0   50   100

·Miles·

⚑·Crusader·Castles·

12

The End in Livonia

Livonia and Prussia had grown apart during the Thirteen Years' War. Erlichshausen's desperate need for money had caused him to look northward, but he succeeded only in provoking the Livonian Knights to limit his authority over them and their lands in every way. By 1473 the Teutonic Knights consisted of three autonomous regions – Prussia, Germany, and Livonia – connected only by a common heritage and occasional common interests. This meant that when wars came to Livonia, the Livonian Order was on its own.

The victories of Wolter von Plettenberg (Livonian master 1494–1535) over Ivan III (the Great, 1462–1505), the grand duke of Moscow, at the beginning of the 1500s had brought five decades of peace to Livonia. Peace with neighbours, that is. Internal problems were present in abundance. But Wolter managed to keep even those within acceptable bounds, and his influence persisted long after his death at an advanced age in 1535. Unfortunately for his successors, the tide of history was running against them. First and foremost, the Livonian Order no longer governed the region more or less alone, but shared power with the Livonian Confederation, a body which was capable of regulating the coinage, passing common laws for commerce and crime, debating significant issues and unifying public opinion, but lacked an executive branch which could devise an effective foreign policy or unite the region's military forces under one command. Secondly, the Livonian Order remained a small Roman Catholic organisation in a fiercely Protestant region. Not only were the Scandinavian kingdoms and the duchy of Prussia Lutheran, but so were most of the burghers in the Livonian cities and some of the nobles in the countryside; Protestant offshoots were even strong in Lithuania, and the kings of Poland looked favourably upon the spread of Protestantism in rival lands, assuming more or less correctly that citizens who dared think independently about religion would make trouble for their secular rulers too. Thirdly, several areas formerly important for recruiting knights, especially Lower Saxony and Holstein, were now Protestant; only Westphalia, which had remained Roman Catholic, provided knights for service in the Baltic, and only a few knights could be recruited locally. To a certain degree the insufficiency in recruits was offset by hiring mercenaries. But money had to be raised to pay the mercenaries, and this was best done by increasing grain exports. The question was, how to do this? The answer was to reduce the native population to serfdom and require them to labour on the order's estates.*

It is often mistakenly assumed that the crusaders had reduced the native population to serfdom immediately after the conquest in the thirteenth century. In fact, most natives were free taxpayers into the fifteenth century, when a number of developments began the process of changing their status into servitude. Perhaps most important in this social revolution was the natives' declining usefulness in warfare. As long as hostile armies were penetrating into the country, as was common in the thirteenth and fourteenth centuries, the Livonian master had to rely on the local militias to assist in garrisoning the castles and fighting in pitched battles; but once the Livonian Order managed to build an effective defensive system the militiamen's function changed, to building fortifications and carting supplies. Next most important was the development of a cash economy. The natives never had much money, and their standard of living was miserably low. Even so, their grain contributions had always been calculated in cash equivalents, payments they often had to borrow to fulfil in years of poor harvests; as they sank into debt, they lost their former protected legal status. In addition, prisoners-of-war were commonly settled on estates as serfs. As the number of free farmers dwindled it was impossible to attract them into border regions whenever Russian or Lithuanian armies carried away the work force. As a result, the owners of the estates tended to replace the lost free peasants with serfs. It is also quite likely that landless sons of free farmers accepted work on the terms of serfs, while retaining their free status; in the course of time these either intermarried with serfs or 'slipped' down to their level.

By the early 1550s members of the Livonian Order were openly discussing their options. The one mentioned most often was to convert to

---

* Most peasants in Central Europe were poor. There were degrees of poverty, of course, but those reflected more than the condition of servitude. Climate, weather, war, disease, and price fluctuations were important too. Livonia was far to the north, with poor soil and a short growing season. Moreover, the loss of personal freedom was occurring throughout the region at this time – in Poland, Lithuania, and Russia. In contrast, serfdom was disappearing in the West.

Protestantism, divide up the order's lands among the officers and knights, and make the kinds of reforms in the economy and education that were needed to provide the revenues necessary for national defence. This suggestion brought stalwart Roman Catholic knights almost to apoplexy, causing them to warn direly that this would cost them dearly with the Holy Roman emperor and the electors. Eventually, the decision by the Rigan canons to make a Protestant the assistant and heir of the aged archbishop led to a brief, almost bloodless civil war. The Roman Catholic faction prevailed, more or less, then not long afterward Wilhelm von Fürstenburg became master of the Livonian Order. Most observers interpreted these as Roman Catholic victories, but since the military unpreparedness of the Livonian Confederation had been fully displayed for all neighbours to observe, the triumphs meant little.[*]

The problems of Livonia meant little to rulers to the west and south. Denmark and Sweden were too interested in fighting one another to disperse military resources to the east; the king of Poland could never have persuaded his nobles and clerics to authorise spending money to extend his authority to the north – against all evidence they saw the king as a potential tyrant, and they wanted to keep him as weak as practical with the needs of national defence.

The new ruler to the east, however, was of a different mind. Ivan IV (1533–84) of Russia was not yet known as 'the Terrible', but he was already considered a ruthless monarch with an enormous appetite for more land. Grand duke of Moscow, he took the title of tsar after crushing important Tatar khans to his south and east, thereby expanding his empire almost to the Black Sea; thereafter many Tatars reluctantly served in his armies, while those still beyond his control, mainly in the Crimea, dreamed of defeating him yet and resurrecting the long-lost prestige of the Golden Horde. Ivan had also won over Lithuanian lords from Poland, and he was acquiring new military equipment and expertise as fast as he could find someone to sell it. Later generations of historians would credit him with wanting to conquer the Baltic coastline in order to open trade to the West. More realistically, he just enjoyed taking lands from his neighbours, much as he luxuriated in devising imaginative new ways of humiliating his domestic enemies before murdering them.

Ivan's method of dividing the Livonian rulers was to combine threats with

---

[*] Even knights who preferred Roman Catholicism could see that the need for church reform was pressing, and since the Council of Trent had not yet been called there was general despair that the papacy would begin to deal with the Church's most pressing problems. Worse, no one could see how conservative ecclesiastical reforms in Germany would help Livonia politically.

offers of peace. When the truce negotiated by Wolter von Plettenberg expired, Ivan agreed to renew it only on the condition that the Livonians began to pay ancient taxes and tributes. No living person had ever heard of such taxes and tributes, and certainly the Livonian Order had never paid any. The issue was not so clear in Dorpat, however. There the bishop and the burghers had always stood somewhat aloof, asserting their independence from the Livonian master and even the archbishops of Riga. In the past, they conceded, they had paid some rents to Novgorod and Pskov for swamplands used by beekeepers and hunters, and they might be willing to do so again, if the price was reasonable.

That was all the encouragement Ivan needed to press the point. He offered a bargain. He would settle for an annual payment of 1,000 *Talers* and the back taxes, a mere 40,000 *Talers*. Since this lump sum was the equivalent of 10,000 oxen, the Livonian ambassadors tried to persuade him to reduce the sum until he finally tired of the game and raided their quarters to seize the moneys they said they had brought with them. But the pleasure he had anticipated would come from handling the coins turned into bitter anger when he learned that the Livonians had not brought a schilling with them.

Neither party had been perfectly honest. The tsar was claiming tribute payments from the twelfth century, before the arrival of the crusaders, and claiming it over regions no Rus'ian prince had ever collected payments from. On the other hand, the Livonians were hoping to evade making any payments at all, expecting that the Holy Roman emperor would declare any treaties they signed null and void. Also, there were indications that the king of Poland, Sigismund Augustus (1548–72), might come to the Livonians' aid. The tsar decided to make a pre-emptive strike, to occupy Livonia while the Polish king was still busy in the south.

In late 1557 the tsar ordered his soldiers and militia to assemble for a long and dangerous winter march to the coast. When the Livonian Confederation received reports that Russian forces had filed out of Moscow, marching through the snow toward the north-west, it ordered a mobilisation.

The campaign was very different from that a half-century earlier. The Livonian cities raised 60,000 *Talers* to pay for the cost of a short war, but Master Wilhelm von Fürstenburg decided against meeting the enemy in the field as Wolter von Plettenberg had done. The reputation of the Russian troops and artillery, victors in numerous recent engagements with the Tatars, contrasted too strongly with the unpreparedness of his own forces. The sad performance of the troops and officers in the brief civil war, and the consequent financial crisis, suggested that Livonia was far from ready for a serious fight. The master's unwillingness to seek a decisive battle precluded the possibility of a short war.

Baltic Sea

Reval   Tolsburg

ESTONIA   Narva

Hapsal   Wesenberg   Neuschloss

Weissenstein

Sonnenburg   Wiek   Oberpahlen

OESEL   Pernau   Fellin   Dorpat

Ermes   Pskov

Windau   Wolmar   Marienburg

Kandau   Wenden   Trikaten   Marienhausen

Goldingen   Segewold

COURLAND   Riga   LIVONIA   Ludsen

Mitau   Ascheraden

Grobin   Bauske   Kokenhausen   Rositen

Selburg

Düna

Dünaburg

·1557 ~ 1563·

0   50   100

·Miles·

The Germans were numerous enough to fight, if collected in one body and led to war, but the defensive strategy caused them to be scattered; consequently they were outnumbered wherever the Russians chose to attack. The nobles, who formed the main cavalry force, were hesitant to fight pitched battles that would leave their numbers depleted and their families and fiefs without protection. The citizen militias were not trained for field service. The mercenaries wanted to live to spend their wages. Nobody wanted to arm the peasants. In short, the will to fight was lacking, and Fürstenburg was unable to make the members of the Confederation serve against their wishes. The plan adopted was to defend the fortified cities and castles, use the small forces available to harass the invaders, and hope that the Russian supply system would break down during bad weather and cause the tsar to order a retreat. In early 1558 Ivan's armies marched through the lands of Dorpat without encountering resistance, plundering as they went, then assembled before Narva and began a siege. The Tatar general prevented the German relief army from approaching the city, and on 12 May the Russian artillery opened fire. The defences were strong and might have held firm if an accidental fire had not broken out. Soon the city was burning, and, as the citizens herded their wives and children into the citadel, the Russians stormed the walls. After the sack had ended and the fierce passions of the tsar's Russian and Tatar troops had cooled, Ivan's general accepted the surrender of the castle in return for the free withdrawal of the garrison and the people who had taken refuge there. Thus Ivan captured the key to Estonia and trade up the Narva River toward Pskov and Dorpat. With that Ivan IV could have been satisfied, because the Livonians were ready to agree to almost any terms short of surrender, but his appetite was only whetted.

Master Wilhelm called a meeting of his castellans and advocates to discuss the situation. At the end of the meeting the decision was hardly courageous: they sent the tsar 40,000 *Talers* as the required tribute. Ivan showed much greater spirit: he sent it back. Then he ordered a march on Dorpat.

The Livonians now began to organise in earnest – much too late. In June of 1558 the estates of the Confederation met in Dorpat to discuss their next steps. They sent to Denmark for help – although King Christian had already said that he could not provide troops; they authorised Reval to blockade Narva against ships trying to trade there; and they asked Sweden for a loan of 200,000 *Talers* and mercenaries. Despite their desperation, however, they did not acquiesce to the demand of the Polish monarch that he be given Riga as compensation for his help. In July, however, Dorpat surrendered to Russian besiegers after only token resistance. Since Dorpat should have held out for a considerable time, but didn't, morale sank everywhere. The delegates to the Confederation wrote to Poland and effectively accepted the royal conditions for providing military assistance. At the same time the Livonian Knights chose Gotthard Kettler, the castellan of Fellin, to 'share' Fürstenburg's duties.

Kettler was an adherent of Protestant ideas. Although originally a Roman Catholic, like all recruits into the order, he had been stationed in Germany for a few years. There he had seen possibilities for reforming the military order that he longed to put into practice. Upon his return to Livonia he became identified with that faction wishing to imitate the Prussian branch of the order, to secularise the state, divide up its lands among the members, and become landed nobles. This minority faction had been temporarily suppressed by Wilhelm von Fürstenburg, but now it revived, its numbers swelled by the failure of the master's policies. As it became obvious that the Livonian Order could not perform its military role properly, demands for reform rose; and the reform that was called for was that espoused by Gotthard Kettler, who almost alone of all the castellans was able to achieve minor victories against the marauding Russian cavalry forces. His courage and initiative in the field were equalled by his restraint, and willingness to work within the old framework of the order until a consensus was achieved.

Most Livonians were giving up all thought of defending themselves alone. The nobles and castellans stood paralysed by the atrocities committed on their unresisting subjects; the burghers were appalled by the behaviour of the Hanseatic League, which not only failed to send aid but took advantage of Reval's troubles to bypass the port rather than unload their cargo for subsequent shipment to Russia; and the churchmen were hawking their dioceses to German and Scandinavian dynasties, hoping to escape their situation with a profit. The members of the Livonian Order hardly did better. The castellan of Wesenburg proved himself more competent at chasing willing women than chasing away Russians; he abandoned the strongest and best-stocked fortress in Estonia and fled to Reval. That the castle did not fall to the Russians was due solely to the initiative of a young warrior who garrisoned it with the few men who followed him. The castellan of Reval sent to the Danish monarch to come and take possession of the province. Only because King Christian died suddenly did Estonia not return to Danish ownership. When no troops arrived the citizens of Reval concluded that they would have to defend themselves, and they set to work, building new fortifications against the powerful siege train of the enemy. Their old walls would not have withstood a serious bombardment, but Ivan gave them the time to get ready. Having exhausted his men and his supplies, the tsar left garrisons to hold Narva and Dorpat, then withdrew back into Russia with his men, a vast number of prisoners, and an incredible amount of booty. The diocese of Dorpat never recovered: the last bishop died in Russian captivity and was not replaced.

The Russian army renewed its advance in January 1559, this time strik-ing from Dorpat through the rolling countryside of central Livonia to Riga, then past that well-fortified city into Semgallia and Kurland. There it cap-tured ill-prepared fortresses one after the other. The Tatars reinforced their traditional reputation for cruelty, but the Russian troops who had beaten the Tatars and made them serve the tsar were almost equally feared.

Readers of the chronicles may well doubt whether the Russians were as cruel in these years as later, or as horrible as the retelling of the story fixed them in popular memory. No doubt the atrocities seemed crueller because Livonia had been at peace so long, but at that time Ivan was still making a sincere if clumsy effort to win over German lords and native peasants. This would change later, as Ivan's periodic bouts of insanity were combined with his promotion of ambitious but frightened newcomers to office, newcom-ers who understood that the tsar would not accept excuses for any failure. Ivan's 'secret police' used terror against the tsar's enemies at home, and terror against his opponents abroad.

Nor were the Russians the only threat to life and property. Unpaid mer-cenaries and outlaws roamed the countryside. Soon enough Livonians would learn to protect themselves against all soldiers – hideouts would be dug in the woods, girls and young children would be kept out of the way, and the men would defend every fortified church and manor to the utmost; they especially had to prevent marauding irregulars from having their will, for such troops were always worse than organised army units. In the future, when the scum of all Europe appeared in one or another of the armies that operated in Livonia, people learned how to avoid or survive the sacking, plundering, and mistreatment that Germans, Lithuanians, Poles, Swedes, Danes, English, Scots, Dutch, and even more exotic adventurers practised on the civilian population. Even so, the memory of the first years of horror was not erased. The Russians were saddled with a reputation for barbarity that served splendidly as war propaganda for both sides – by the Russians to cow their enemies, and by the Livonians to win help from abroad and to encourage their subjects to fight to the last against the Muscovites.

That the Russians were hardly without human feelings is proven by their careful administration of conquered districts and their practice of confirm-ing landholders and merchants in their former rights and possessions. Also, at the very height of his success, in March 1559, Ivan IV suddenly and unex-pectedly granted a truce to his enemies. Through this he hoped to obtain a peaceful surrender and settlement of terms by which Livonia would be governed.

The reason for halting the Muscovite advance seems to have been the impending intervention of Danes, Swedes, Poles, and Lithuanians into the

Livonian War, but most of all an invasion by the Crimean Tatars. Apparently the tsar hoped to secure his gains in the north by negotiation, to balance the intervening powers against one another, and keep them all away while he sent his own army south. He was mistaken in this. The northern powers were indeed jealous of one another, but not one monarch was willing to withdraw his hand from the booty that lay before him, and each was eager to get his share before the others gobbled it up. Ivan's gesture cost him six months, months in which he could have occupied most of Livonia, months during which his opponents secured footholds in the country and raised troops to send into the fighting.

In September of 1559 the Livonian Order forced Wilhelm von Fürstenburg to resign his office. Kettler, with authority now in his hands alone, was delayed in secularising his order only by the military crisis. He had already signed a treaty with Sigismund Augustus at Vilnius that made Livonia south of the Daugava a Polish protectorate. At this same time the bishop of Oesel sold his lands to Magnus of Holstein, the younger brother of the king of Denmark. Magnus was soon in Moscow pursuing a policy of his own that involved marriage into the tsar's family and the creation of a mockable, impotent state grossly subservient to Russia. The Swedes came into the war in June of 1561, when Reval and the nobility of Harrien, Wierland, and Jerwen gave homage to King Eric. The era of German rule was coming to an end, but no one could predict what would succeed it. Not even the foreign powers now intervening in the war were able to do much at first, as the Russian summer offensive of 1560 swept over the land.

The Livonian Knights had, in fact, developed an effective strategy for dealing with the Russian invaders. In the beginning they had attempted to bring infantry and artillery to bear on raiding parties, but they could not catch Tatar horsemen; when confronted by overwhelming numbers of infantry and cavalry, they retreated into stout fortresses. These tactics left the countryside extremely vulnerable to raiders. Out of necessity Kettler now improvised cavalry tactics that could limit the damage that Russian horsemen could do. Relying on the superior knowledge of the land and the ability to fall back on the castles, they were aggressive in harassing the enemy wherever they found him. This prevented the Russians from spreading out to loot and burn, thus restricting their ability to live off the land and offering some protection to the Livonian peasants. In addition, Kettler persuaded the Lithuanians to defend the southern lands and allowed the Swedes to hold the north. Concentrating his remaining forces, Kettler promoted able commanders whose youth and daring were breathing new spirit into the army. Alas for his fortunes, luck was not with them, as this passage from a contemporary chronicle describes:

On August 2 thirty horsemen went out to forage some seventeen miles from the camp. They spotted five hundred Russians on the other side of a stream. Both sides were so close that each opened fire. One Russian was killed and the rest retreated across a hay field back toward the main body. Eighteen Germans turned back and twelve were left to pursue the enemy. As soon as the latter saw this main force they, too, turned back and made for camp, but they lost some men. The first group brought word of what had happened and the landmarshal . . . set out with three hundred horsemen, intending to engage the five hundred Russians. (They had not received word that there were any more than this. In fact, there were forty thousand.) They first attacked the enemy pickets and drove them back onto the main group. The Germans followed in hot pursuit and were surrounded by the enemy, all escape cut off. Guns and sabres were used in close combat, but the larger group wore down the smaller and many Germans were slain. Those who had remained in camp and had not taken part in the battle fled through the marshes and forests, each as best he could. This defeat took place . . . ten miles from Ermes. So many of the Russians were slain that it took fourteen wagons to bring them to [a] manor where the bodies were burned. The German casualties, killed and captured, were two hundred and sixty-one.

The battle at Ermes was a fatal defeat. The numbers lost were not great, but the fallen knights were the flower of the Livonian Order. Everyone then realised that the end was approaching for the traditional government and way of life. Despite the confusion, the defeats, and the feeling that resistance was hopeless, the Livonian Knights had stayed in the field, harassed the enemy foragers, and defended their most important castles against attack. The extensive correspondence between the master and his castellans and advocates shows that the efficient organisation did not break down completely. Troops were still moved from one threatened point to another, and supplies were collected and distributed with a minimum of difficulty; but the knights were now too few and too old, the number of mercenaries both too large to pay with the reduced incomes and too small to be successful in pitched battle, and the financial condition of the treasury pitiful. The correspondence with foreign princes was staggering in its volume. Gotthard Kettler tried desperately to raise money and troops from the Holy Roman Empire, and to keep the neighbouring princes from dividing the country among themselves, but he had little success in any of these projects. Although Kettler may have plotted from the beginning to subvert the rule of his order and to make himself a landed prince, it is proper that he be given credit for these efforts to save the Livonian Knights and their possessions, and to pass down that inheritance intact to one ruler.

Still, there was little that Kettler could do to prolong the existence of his military order. Once his field army had been routed, Kettler could not defend the castles effectively. Many brothers went into an imprisonment that ended in the streets of Moscow, their heads bashed in or cut off when they collapsed in exhaustion during the victory parade. The great fortress at Fellin, with all its stores, weapons, and the treasury, was lost when the mercenaries demanded that the commander accept a tsarist offer of surrender; Fürstenburg, who had wanted to fight to the death, was carried away to Moscow to spend the rest of his life in comfortable captivity. Ivan hoped that Fürstenburg would be able to persuade other Livonians to accept him as their lord, with the landed vassals ruling Livonia according to their ancient traditions, their only obligations to the tsar being taxes and military service; and he promised merchants access to the Russian market. A few nobles and burghers did come over to the tsar, but most of those did so only after being captured and given no other reasonable choice. Far more believed the gory stories of Ivan's atrocities that were giving him the name 'the Terrible'; as far as they were concerned, tsarist promises meant less than examples of tsarist tyranny. Better, they believed, to try any expedient that gave some promise of surviving the crisis. Soon after this Kettler began secret talks aimed at the dissolution of the order on terms that would make him duke of such regions as could be saved from the Russians.

There were a few brothers who protested handing over the castles, one after the other, to Polish garrisons, but they could not suggest means by which the Livonian Knights could hold the fortresses alone. Only by concentrating the troops who remained and borrowing heavily to pay mercenaries could they even hold Kurland; and Kettler found that difficult because his royal patron was becoming reluctant to loan him anything more.

The Livonian Order was technically still in existence, although most of the brethren were now dead or missing. They had found too late effective tactics for countering the Russian numbers. Now the ranks of their knights were too thin, and the good commanders had fallen in battle. No army can expect to fight without suffering an occasional setback, and if the strategy involves daring tactics, the number of defeats must necessarily be higher. The one defeat at Ermes had wiped out the most effective cavalry unit. Most survivors were now ready to give over the fight to others. The ensuing power vacuum drew the outsiders right into the country.

The sense of panic that followed the crushing defeat at Ermes and the fall of the great fortress at Fellin in the centre of the country was observed carefully by the Estonians, that sturdy people which had never reconciled itself to the crusaders' domination. The memory of earlier insurrections which had failed miserably had taught caution, but now those whose courage and initiative had not been crushed saw that the time had come – if it ever could come – when it might be possible for them to throw out their oppressors. They were unused to arms, having been deprived of weapons for generations, but in 1559 the Livonian Knights had raised units of native infantry, equipped them with swords, spears, and shields, and used them to support the small bodies of mercenaries and feudal cavalry trying to contain the Russian marauders provisioning the besiegers of Reval; eventually the Russians abandoned their attack and retreated. These sturdy peasants then came to realise that if they fought for the Russians instead of against them, they could become independent again – or at least free of German rule. The tsar encouraged them to rebel, reminding them how he had welcomed everyone, even German nobles, who had come over to him at the beginning and rewarded them for their service and loyalty; he listened to the Estonians' advice, employed them as scouts and spies, and sent them into the German-occupied regions to spread his propaganda among those who would listen. In the occupied regions he ordered his officials to provide the peasants with seed grain, to help rebuild their homes, and to keep the troops from marauding and plundering. In contrast, the Germans were extorting extraordinary taxes to pay the cost of the war and drafting every available man for military service, for transporting supplies and equipment, or for working on fortifications.

By the autumn of 1560 the Estonians had concluded that German rule was so weak that no serious resistance could be expected if they were to rebel, seize the forts and castles, and call on the tsar for help. No great preparation would be needed; in fact, efforts to plan ahead might alert the nobility to their danger. It would only be necessary to hold out with primitive weapons and daring until well-trained Russian troops could arrive. The chronicler Russow reported:

> In the autumn, as the situation in the country was so awkward, an alarm went out that the peasants in Harrien and Wiek had risen against the nobility because the nobles had imposed heavy taxes and rents upon them and made them perform difficult service, and nevertheless had not been able to protect them in the time of need, but left them to the Muscovites without resistance. Therefore, they thought that they did not need to obey the nobles any more or perform any services, but they wanted to be free from them or annihilate and root out the nobility altogether. And so they went ahead with their plans and destroyed some manors, and whatever noble they caught they slew and killed.

The number of rebel Estonians under arms was not large – about 4,000 – and they were poorly equipped, with no supplies or fortresses to fall back upon;

but they threatened to spread social revolution throughout Livonia, thereby bringing a sudden end to three-and-a-half centuries of German hegemony. Gotthard Kettler took the situation seriously, writing to the Polish king for help and committing the rest of the country so completely to the crown that it meant the practical end of the rule of the Livonian Knights there.

The rising was of short duration. The peasants lacked good leaders, proper arms, proper training, and the discipline that comes only with experience. They drove away their German officers and elected leaders – some chosen according to ancient tribal practices and decorated with the traditional pagan symbols of office – but these were no match for the professionals who had come from the West.

Credit for subduing the rebellion must go to the Danish commander in Wiek, Christopher von Münchhausen. Despite having but a small body of mercenaries, he ordered the handful of episcopal vassals to serve as his cavalry, rounded up the nearby Estonian peasantry to serve as foot soldiers against their rebel brethren, and then proceeded to trick the insurrectionary leader into thinking that the approaching army was another group of revolutionaries coming to join him. He caught the rebels by surprise, routed them, and captured their leader; then he quickly moved against hostile units elsewhere and dispersed them. As the few surviving rebels escaped to join the Russians, German nobles reappeared to take brutal revenge on guilty or suspect individuals and communities.

The German nobles were not content to return to the pre-war situation, but insisted on subjecting all peasants to serfdom. They had wished to do this for decades, but had not dared to violate law and custom wantonly. Now there was no one to stop them; and, in the years to come, the Polish, Danish, and Swedish monarchs agreed to sacrifice the few remaining rights of the peasantry in order to keep the unsteady loyalty of these nobles. Although the military worth of the feudal cavalry was very doubtful at the onset of the war, at length the Baltic barons became doughty warriors whose knowledge of the land, its customs, its traditions, and its languages made them indispensable to anyone who hoped to hold and administer the territories.

For the peasantry the failed rising was an unmitigated disaster. Even many of the free farmers were reduced to a state of near-slavery, subject to the wilful brutality and exploitation of a class of warrior-knights who were not required to exercise the caution of their ancestors in dealing with their subjects. In addition, the peasants suffered through years of war in which they lost more property and lives than any other group. First Russian armies came through, then Swedish or Polish forces, and finally the robbers who took advantage of the disorder. The peasants were taxed, burned out, murdered, raped, driven away from their ancestral homes, stripped of all means of self-defence, and left to suffer the ravages of marauders, famine, and disease. When the two decades of war ended, those who survived counted themselves lucky. Then the nobles – who now included many newly-arrived Swedish and Polish mercenary captains and royal favourites – organised a new administration to tax and exploit the peasants more effectively and brutally than ever before.

By the autumn of 1561 there was practically no place outside Kurland which remained in the hands of the Livonian Order. The castle of Sonnenburg on Oesel, which was being eyed by Duke Magnus, was the only fortress that Kettler could still offer to the Polish king; and if he waited much longer, until that was lost too, then it would be unlikely that he could bargain for a duchy in Kurland. Already he had committed the southern lands to the king so thoroughly that he would be fortunate to salvage anything for himself and those few surviving knights and administrators who were willing to serve as landed vassals. In September he sent the castellan of Riga to negotiate on his behalf and for the archbishop of Riga in Königsberg.

The ambassador left us a memoir that describes the short negotiations that brought an end to the Livonian Order. He arrived in Königsberg on a Saturday afternoon, found his lodgings, and rested. The next morning he attended worship service, had a short breakfast with two scholars sent by Duke Albrecht of Prussia, then was summoned to an audience with his royal majesty. Sigismund Augustus did not have business on his mind, however; he only wanted more company for lunch. So the ambassador sat down at a round table with the king, a few nobles, and an observer from Sweden. The fare was good and the wine worth commending. After the meal there was light conversation, during which Duke Albrecht arranged for the ambassador to meet with the chief Polish officials who would conduct the negotiations. That meeting was strictly business, filled with knowledgeable and critical discussions of vital details, and lasting until three in the morning. The next day a Polish official came to the ambassador's lodgings for lunch to discuss some of the more important points confidentially; and they came to a general agreement on the questions of succession, use of the German language, the retention of traditional rights and privileges, religious liberty, and the status of Livonia within the Holy Roman Empire. The next morning the ambassador met with the duke's representatives, who had little to say other than good wishes – because Albrecht had hopes of inheriting the new duchy should Kettler die without heirs, and he did not want his officials to say anything which might harm his chances. At lunch all the principal negotiators met again, at which time the Polish representative passed the ambassador a note asking for an urgent and secret meeting. Soon afterward he and the ambassador agreed upon all the basic points, including the method of announcing the agreement to the world.

The details are too tedious to repeat, but they indicate the care with which both sides entered into the agreement. On 28 November 1561 the Livonian Knights were secularised; and on 5 March 1562 Master Kettler informed the world of this. Thenceforth he was Duke Gotthard of Kurland, and the Livonian Order ceased to exist.

The two decades of war that followed can be divided into three periods. The first was the Seven Years' War (1563–70), a conflict principally between Denmark and Sweden that ended after the Swedish nobility deposed their insane monarch and adopted a policy more favourable to Poland, after which Danish influence declined and the two remaining Western powers, Sweden and Poland, joined to face the tsar. Next was an equally long period, 1570–8, during which Ivan IV almost expelled his opponents from the region, until at last everyone joined together to resist him. Ivan was his own worst enemy, executing his generals and terrorising his own nobles and citizens, so that any gains made by the Russian and Tatar generals were accomplished in spite of the tsar rather than because of him. Of course, it was not possible for him to provide sufficient troops both for the Livonian theatre and to throw back the Crimean Tatar assaults; he correctly chose to give priority to the Tatar threat (and by eliminating them as a major military force he made possible subsequent Russian advances to the south). Finally, there were the three years following 1578, when Stefan Batory, the newly elected Polish monarch, resolved the problems with the Turks that had kept him busy on Poland's southern frontiers. Leading his experienced troops north, the great general-king routed the Russian armies out of Livonia and reconquered parts of Rus' that had formerly belonged to the Lithuanian state. The Swedes joined in this offensive, occupying Estonia and the Russian coastline up to the mouth of the Neva River. In 1582, Ivan IV, bankrupt, exhausted, and mentally ill, admitted defeat and signed a peace treaty that left Livonia in Western hands for another century.

For Sweden and Poland this was not a happy development. The war had drawn them into a distant region, drained them of men and treasure, and given them grounds for future quarrels.

For Russia it meant another century of weakness and isolation; the country was deprived of those European contacts that could balance the Asiatic influences on its culture and politics. The frustrated tsar died soon thereafter, leaving his country in a shambles. For Livonia it was the beginning of centuries of conflict, centuries when the country went from being an important if isolated part of Western Europe to a minor province of Eastern Europe. Soon Livonia would be practically forgotten, a footnote in the careers of great men.

✠

The Turkish Wars

Coin collectors are aware that the Teutonic Knights survived into the seventeenth century, because the beautiful Talers produced in this period properly bring high prices. But historians lose interest once the military role of the grand masters is reduced to providing a handful of troops to Habsburg operations on the distant Balkan front.

This is understandable, but unfortunate. The Turks first attacked Vienna in 1529 and raided almost annually along the frontier until the final siege of Vienna in 1689. The principal reason that the Turks could not advance farther north was weather: by the time that grass was high enough to feed the horses of an army marching out of Istanbul, the Turkish commanders were already counting the days necessary to cross the Balkans and proceed up the Danube; once at the Austrian or Polish frontiers, the Turks had only a few weeks left for campaigning before they had to start their return journey. If the Christians could delay an operation at all, it would frustrate the Turkish efforts to round up cattle, horses and slaves. Thus, the seemingly obscure struggles to capture border castles were of vital importance.

Troops raised by the German, Bohemian and Austrian convents were involved in many of these campaigns. Only the commanders were members of the military order – the fighting units were mercenaries. This part of the Teutonic Order's history is little known, but it deserves closer study because these campaigns illuminate the military problems of the Habsburg dynasty and also the confrontation of Serbs (Orthodox Christians who were Turkish subjects) and the Croatians (Roman Catholics who were Habsburg loyalists).

This era came to an end when Napoleon secularized the German possessions of many religious orders, among them the estates of the Teutonic Knights.

One unfortunate characteristic of this era, from the modern point of view, was the escalating arrogance of the order's members. Men of the Middle Ages would not have understood this. Arrogance was part and parcel of the average noble's personality – it may have caused the lower classes to hate its 'betters', but it guaranteed instant respect and obedience. The Teutonic Knights had always exhibited their share of arrogance, but, as the order evolved from a military organisation with large numbers of ordinary knights to a clique of well-born nobles, they began to lose contact not only with good manners, but also with reality. As lands were lost, the officers made demands for the return of those possessions that were inversely proportional to their ability to govern or defend them. Arrogance may have been universal, but the Teutonic Knights turned it into an art form.

13

Summary

There had still been a future for the Teutonic Order once the crusading era had fully run its course. Several futures, in fact, since the organisation had disintegrated into three distinct parts in 1525. But that fate was not preordained; it merely came about.

The secularised members of the Teutonic Order in Prussia gave up all efforts to continue their former crusading and religious functions. Albrecht von Hohenzollern-Ansbach adopted the Lutheran teaching and secularised the state. Those who wished to remain friar-knights withdrew to Germany to discuss impossible plans to conquer Prussia and reinstall Roman Catholicism. Perhaps the best hope for the military order to continue its crusading tradition had been Polish proposals to resettle them on the Turkish frontier, using the order's German resources to support a small but efficient army. Those proposals had all been rejected as a result of pride and stubbornness, combined with hatred of the Polish king, a justified suspicion of his motives, and a fear of defeat in the Balkans. In any case, the Polish offers had not been altogether fair and honest: Prussia was to be surrendered for new, unsettled, danger-filled territories. The knights saw this as trickery, a none-too-subtle means of killing them off and seizing their lands. They gave the crusade against the Turks but feeble support. Perhaps nothing demonstrates better the moral bankruptcy of the traditions of the Teutonic Knights in their last days in Prussia, and the amorality of their enemies too, than the mock negotiations to move the order to the Balkans.

Grand Master Johann von Tiefen did command a Prussian force on one last crusade, a miserably botched invasion of Moldava led by the Polish king in 1497. The aged grand master died of illness and exhaustion during the harrowing retreat.

The Livonian Knights survived longer and better than their Prussian brethren. There were those who should have known better who accused the knights of being lazy, drunken, womanising cowards. A more accurate assessment is that a Roman Catholic military-religious order found it impossible to recruit knights and men-at-arms from its traditional North German homeland, which was now Protestant, and Livonia did not produce enough noble sons to fill the ranks.* Nor did the order have the money to maintain a large mercenary army in peacetime, the power to persuade the independent-minded estates of the Livonian Confederation to tax themselves, or the ability to force on the estates common plans in wartime. Lastly, it could no longer count on reinforcements from Prussia in moments of emergency. Unable to stand up to the numerous well-armed, well-trained, experienced troops sent by Ivan the Terrible, the Livonian Order went down fighting, defending Lutheran and Roman Catholic subjects alike from an insane Russian Orthodox tsar.

Into the vacuum came Poland-Lithuania, Sweden, and Russia. None was particularly interested in acquiring the Baltic coastline, but all were determined that the others would not get it either. Therefore, though each new mega-state had more important problems – Sweden with Denmark, Poland-Lithuania with the Turks, Russia with the Tatars – all would be drawn into war over the pitiful remains of the mini-empire of the Livonian Order.

The German Order (*Deutscher Orden*, a more accurate name than Teutonic Knights) continued its military and religious role in the Holy Roman Empire for almost another three centuries, serving in imperial armies against Turkish sultans, French kings, and Protestant princes. Most members were Roman Catholics, but in accordance with the Augsburg Treaty of 1555 they had to share the faith of the rulers in the Protestant and Reformed parts of Germany; hence some members of the order were Protestants. It had a distinguished and varied career. The Teutonic Knights of this era were a baroque organisation that contrasted strongly with the Gothic order of medieval Prussia. Hardly a region of south Germany does not boast of a palatial residence that was formerly the seat of a local castellan. Their time eventually expired, too, and Napoleon abolished the German Order along with many other relics of bygone times.

The German Order was revived twice after Napoleon's fall, first as a private order for the Habsburg family, then as a religious order after 1929. Small churches and hospitals continue to operate under its auspices today. These are missions which go back to the order's foundation at Acre in 1189

---

* Almost no knights had ever been recruited in Prussia or Livonia, lest they find ways to foster the interests of their secular relatives. This policy was relaxed in Livonia in the fifteenth century, but even there the few recruits were usually from families recently brought east from Westphalia by relatives who held high office and could promise them swift advancement.

– caring for the sick, the aged, and the troubled. That aspect of the order had been important throughout the Middle Ages too. Hardly a middle-sized town in Germany was without a hospital, church, or convent which street names commemorate today. By serving local needs, the order kept alive the memories and traditions of the past.

Today the German Order provides priests for German-speaking communities in non-German-speaking countries, particularly in Italy and Slovenia. In this it has returned to another major aspect of its original mission, the spiritual care of Germans who were being neglected by other orders.

This later history suggests that it had not been necessary for the Teutonic Knights in Prussia to see themselves solely as a territorial state. It is understandable that they did so – looking back to their expulsion from Transylvania, the loss of the Holy Land, the destruction of the Templars, and the jealousy of Ladislas the Short – but it is less understandable that they forgot their primary duty to serve as crusaders. The crusade had once been a matter separate from the state, so that they could discuss the conversion of Mindaugas' Lithuanians without first conquering his lands; it was sufficient to be present at his coronation. Unfortunately, the acquisition of West Prussia and Danzig had changed the Poles from traditional allies to mortal enemies, so that the Teutonic Knights came to see further territorial conquests as the best means of protecting themselves. Once they had convinced themselves that they would be safe only if they held onto all of Prussia – and Samogitia as well, to secure the land route to Livonia – they were doomed. Changing times found them petrified in old ideas.

Samogitia was lost at Tannenberg in 1410, a fact that the order acknowledged, more or less, in the Treaty of Melno in 1422; but the knights deluded themselves for many years that the crusading tradition could still be revived. Worse, they came to believe that little else could be done until the order had taken revenge for the defeats at Tannenberg and after; the ancient belief that one could not be both a vassal and honourable came to be the ghost at the banquet that spoiled every occasion for celebration. That collection of self-deceptions became the evil spirits of the order. They made a radical break with the past impossible.

In sum, what happened after the battle of Tannenberg was a lengthy and often unplanned reorientation of the Teutonic Order from its commitment to an outdated crusade to other endeavours. That was painful and cost the order heavily. The future was partly determined by the men ruling at the time, partly by events beyond their control. History makes its own rules; men play their games within those bounds. The Teutonic Knights had mastered the possibilities during the fourteenth century and had prospered. When history introduced new challenges and the order failed to meet them satisfactorily, the Teutonic Knights shattered into three parts. Two of those,

Prussia and Livonia, vanished in the sixteenth century. The third evolved, ultimately finding a small but useful niche in the vast edifice of modern Roman Catholic orders and activities.

What remained of the order's political heritage was that of a powerful symbolism. Lithuanians and Poles remembered the evil deeds attributed to the crusaders vividly, and Germans tended to remember only the crusaders' glorious victories.

There should be no misunderstanding of this circumstance, for it relates to modern history rather than to medieval. Poland and Lithuania disappeared as states in the eighteenth century, while Germany became a more eastward-looking power which could associate its traditions and aspirations with medieval Prussia. That circumstance has caused subsequent generations to view the medieval crusades in Eastern Europe (and the other eastward migrations by Germans, Jews, and Poles known as the *Drang nach Osten*) as first a stage of German imperialism, then as a forerunner of Nazism. Historians must share more than a small burden of the guilt for that overly simplified misreading of history, more than even that borne by the history-makers themselves, because they should know better the consequences of their actions. Medieval history is filled with atrocities and cruelties, yet it is not right to perpetuate mutual hatreds. Just as the English and French have largely forgiven one another for the many misdeeds of the Hundred Years' War, so, too, must the descendants of the aggressors and victims do the same, if for no other reason than because it is impossible to say that either side was purely aggressor or purely victim.

A first step is to see that historians do not describe the crusading movement only as a selfish seizure of land belonging to innocent peoples, but as an aspect of both larger and local events. The larger scene must include the interplay of differing religious beliefs, the expansion of peoples, dynasties, and trade, and great personalities; the local should include geography, past interactions of peoples, their desires for glory, revenge and booty, and the accidents of life and death to major and seemingly minor political figures. Misunderstandings, too, should be included – though these can be exaggerated: Christians may not have known much about the Golden Horde, but not understanding what the Tatars wanted was not the problem. History is more than victimisation, more than heroic posturing. More, alas, than any historian can write. But one must do what one can. Above all, we should remember that historians who simplify the complexity of the past too much do a disservice to future generations who must live with the impressions their work makes on readers.[*]

---

[*] Readers may wish to consult: William Urban, 'Rethinking the Crusades', *Perspectives* (the newsletter of the American Historical Association) 36/7, October 1998, pp.25–9; and 'Victims of the Baltic Crusade', *Journal of Baltic Studies* 29/3, Autumn 1998, pp.195–212. The latter was awarded the Vitols Prize of the AABS for best article published in the *JBS* that year.

Appendices

Appendix A

Major Figures in the History of the Teutonic Order

Hermann Balk The first master in Prussia, 1230–9, and Livonian master 1237–9. Probably a former canon of the Hildesheim church, he may have joined the Teutonic Knights in Acre in 1189. He died in 1239/40.

Louis von Erlichshausen Grand Master 1450–67. His efforts to suppress the Prussian estates representing burghers, vassals, and gentry led to the Thirteen Years' War. The Peace of Thorn, 1466, ended the order's last hopes at recovering its lost importance.

Siegfried von Feuchtwangen Grand Master 1303–11. He moved his residence from Venice to Marienburg, thus establishing the Prussian crusade as the order's primary duty.

Albrecht von Hohenzollern-Ansbach The last grand master in Prussia, 1511–25. He introduced Lutheran reforms, secularised the order's domains, married, and became the duke of Prussia, 1525–68.

Conrad von Jungingen Grand Master 1393–1407. His military and diplomatic skill led to the victorious conclusion of the Samogitian Wars. The Treaty of Sallinwerder, 1398, brought peace with Poland and Lithuania and guaranteed his order possession of Samogitia, thus securing the overland route to Livonia.

Ulrich von Jungingen Grand Master 1408–10. His defeat and death at the battle of Tannenberg marked the end of the order's era of greatness.

Winrich von Kniprode Grand Master 1352–82. His genial personality and instinctive sense of etiquette won the order firm friends among the highest nobility of Germany, France, and England. Under his supervision the Teutonic Order became famous for its chivalry and courtesy.

Michael Küchmeister Advocate of Samogitia, Grand Master 1414–22. Fearing that Heinrich von Plauen's policies would lead to another military disaster, he led the high officers in a coup-d'état, after which everything went wrong. The First Peace of Thorn, 1422, was the true beginning of the order's downhill course.

Poppo von Osterna Prussian master 1237 and 1241–4, Grand Master 1253–7. From a prominent family in the Nuremberg region, it must have come as a surprise that he separated from his wife to join a military order (she entered a nunnery). Poppo guided the order through its most difficult crisis, the war against Sventopełk of Pomerellia and the Prussian pagans.

Heinrich von Plauen Grand Master 1410–13. His heroic efforts in saving Prussia from the armies of Poland and Lithuania almost resulted in restoring the order's power and prestige.

Hermann von Salza Grand Master 1210–39. Friend and confidant of popes and emperors, he presided over the order's rise to prominence in the Holy Land and sent knights to Transylvania, Prussia, and Livonia.

Anno von Sangershausen Livonian master 1254–6, Grand Master 1257–74. He governed through the critical years following the 1259–60 defeats by the Samogitians and the subsequent revolts in Prussia and Livonia.

Conrad von Thüringen (Thuringia). Although grand master for only a year, 1239–40, he was the first important noble to join the order. Henceforth it became easier to recruit knights and ask for pious donations of money and lands.

Appendix B

The Grand Masters to 1525

Heinrich Walpot	1198–1200
Otto von Kerpen	1200–1208
Heinrich Bart	1209–1210?

Hermann von Salza	1210–1239
Conrad von Thüringen	1239–1240
Gerhard von Malberg	1241–1244
Heinrich von Hohenlohe	1244–1249
Gunther von Wullersleben	1249–1253
Poppo von Osterna	1253–1257
Anno von Sangershausen	1257–1274
Hartmann von Heldrungen	1274–1283
Burchard von Schwanden	1283–1290
Conrad von Feuchtwangen	1291–1297
Gottfried von Hohenlohe	1297–1303
Siegfried von Feuchtwangen	1303–1311
Karl von Trier	1311–1324
Werner von Orslen	1324–1331
Luther von Braunschweig	1331–1335
Dietrich von Altenburg	1335–1341
Ludolf König	1341–1345
Heinrich Dusemer	1345–1351
Winrich von Kniprode	1352–1382
Conrad Zöllner von Rothenstein	1382–1390
Conrad von Wallenrode	1390–1393
Conrad von Jungingen	1393–1407
Ulrich von Jungingen	1408–1410
Heinrich von Plauen	1410–1413
Michael Küchmeister	1414–1422
Paul von Russdorf	1422–1441
Conrad von Erlichshausen	1441–1449
Louis (Ludwig) von Erlichshausen	1450–1467
Heinrich Reuß von Plauen	1469–1470
Heinrich von Richtenberg	1470–1477
Martin Truchseß von Wetzhausen	1477–1489
Johann von Tiefen	1489–1497
Friedrich von Sachsen	1498–1510
Albrecht von Hohenzollern	1511–1525

Bibliography

The literature pertaining to the Teutonic Knights is extensive. The time and vast area covered by the crusades of the military order, and the employment of its history for propaganda and political ends, tend to give this literature a mosaic quality. Most of the books and articles are in German or Polish, but the number of books in English has, fortunately, increased dramatically in recent years.

Original Sources in Translation

The Chronicle of Henry of Livonia, translated by James A. Brundage. University of Wisconsin Press, Madison, 1961. The *Chronicle* is a lively, intelligent account of the period 1180–1227. Apparently written for the benefit of William of Modena, the papal legate who arrived in Riga in 1225, it is more thorough and more reflective than all but a very few mediaeval chronicles.

Chronicle of Novgorod, translated by Robert Michell and Nevil Forbes. Camden third series vol.25, London, 1914. Much less useful than the foregoing, and uneven in quality. Unfortunately, the editors mix together the texts of several editions of this indispensable account of the early history of an important Russian state.

The Hypatian Codex, Part Two: The Galician-Volhynian Chronicle, annotated translation by George A. Perfecky. Fink, München, 1973 (Harvard Series in Ukrainian Studies, 16, III). A somewhat dense and frustrating text with fascinating anecdotes. Essential for thirteenth-century Lithuania and Poland.

The Livonian Rhymed Chronicle, translated by Jerry C. Smith and William Urban. New and expanded 2nd edition, Lithuanian Research and Studies Center (LRSC), Chicago, 2001. An indispensable narrative for the second half of the thirteenth century: naïve, lively, informative.

The Annals of Jan Długosz, English abridgement by Maurice Michael. IM Publications, Chichester, 1997. Fails to catch the spirit of the prose of this knowledgeable Polish Renaissance author, but provides the basic story.

Johannes Renner's Livonian History 1556–1561, translated by Jerry C. Smith and William Urban, with Ward Jones. Edwin Mellen, Lewiston, Queenston, Lampeter, 1997. A well-informed chronicle of the last days of the Livonian Order.

The Chronicle of Balthasar Russow & Forthright Rebuttal by Elert Kruse & Errors and Mistakes of Balthasar Russow by Heinrich Tisenhausen, translated by Jerry

C. Smith, Juergen Eichhoff and William Urban. Baltic Studies Center, Madison, 1988. The best contemporary Livonian history.

Secondary Sources in English

These are the best. Some well-known works have been omitted because their only worth is for propaganda in disputes now long forgotten or for providing the authors' income.

Barber, Malcolm, ed. *The Military Orders, vol.1: Fighting for the Faith and Caring for the Sick.* Variorum (Ashgate), Brookfield, 1994.

Burleigh, Michael. *Prussian Society and the German Order: An Aristocratic Corporation in Crisis c.1410–1460.* Cambridge University Press, Cambridge, 1984.

Christiansen, Eric, *The Northern Crusades: The Baltic and the Catholic Frontier, 1100–1525.* Cambridge, 1998.

Davies, Norman. *God's Playground: A History of Poland in two volumes.* Columbia, New York, 1982.

Evans, Geoffrey. *Tannenberg 1410:1914.* Hamish Hamilton, London, 1970.

Jasienica, Pawel (translated by Alexander Jordan). *Jagiellonian Poland.* American Institute of Polish Culture, Miami, 1978.

Knoll, Paul. *The Rise of the Polish Monarchy: Piast Poland in East Central Europe, 1320–1370.* University of Chicago Press, Chicago and London, 1972.

Murray, Alan V., ed. *Crusade and Conversion on the Baltic Frontier 1150–1500.* Ashgate, Aldershot, 2001.

Nicholson, Helen, ed. *The Military Orders, vol.2: Welfare and Warfare.* Ashgate, Aldershot, Brookfield, Singapore and Sidney, 1998.

— *Templars, Hospitallers and Teutonic Knights: Images of the Military Orders, 1128–1291.* Leicester University Press and St Martin's, Leicester, London and New York, 1993.

Nicolle, David. *Lake Peipus 1242: The Battle on the Ice.* Osprey, London, 1996.

Rowell, Stephen C. *Lithuania Ascending: A Pagan Empire within East-Central Europe, 1294–1345.* Cambridge University Press, Cambridge, 1994.

Turnbull, Stephen. *Crusader Castles of the Teutonic Knights, vol.1: The Red Brick Castles of Prussia;* and *vol.2: The Stone Castles of Livonia.* Reed, London, forthcoming 2003/2004.

— *Tannenberg 1410.* Reed, London, forthcoming 2003/2004.

Urban, William. *The Baltic Crusade.* 2nd edition, LRSC, Chicago, 1994.

— *The Prussian Crusade.* 2nd edition, LRSC, Chicago, 2000.

— *The Samogitian Crusade.* LRSC, Chicago, 1989.

— *Tannenberg and After: Poland, Lithuania and the Teutonic Order in Search of Immortality.* Revised edition, LRSC, Chicago, 2002.

Four books deserve special notice for their outstanding illustrations:

Arnold, Udo, ed. *800 Jahre Deutscher Orden*. Bertelsman, Gütersloh/Munich, 1990. (Catalogue of the exhibition in the German National Museum in Nürnberg in co-operation with the Internationale Historische Kommission zur Erforschung des Deutschen Ordens.)

Benninghoven, Friedrich, ed. *Unter Kreuz und Adler: der Deutsche Orden im Mittelalter*. Hase & Koehler, Mainz, 1990. (Catalogue of the exhibition of the Geheimes Staatsarchiv Preussischer Kulturbesitz, Berlin.)

Kulnyt, Birut, ed. *Lietuvos Istorijos Paminklai* (Monuments of Lithuanian History). Mintis, Vilnius, 1990.

Roesdahl, Else, and Wilson, David, eds. *From Viking to Crusader: Scandinavia and Europe 800–1200*. Rizzoli, New York, 1992.

Original Sources

Nineteenth-century German and Polish scholars produced several very important critical editions and collected works. The most important are listed below. See commentary on http://www.rrz.uni-hamburg.de/Landesforschung/Quellen.htm.

Scriptores Rerum Livonicarum. Sammlung der Wichtigsten Chroniken und Geschichtsdenkmale von Liv-, Ehst-, und Kurland, edited by A. Hansen. 2 vols. E. Frantzen, Riga and Leipzig, 1853. Carefully edited chronicles which are available elsewhere in more modern editions.

Scriptores Rerum Prussicarum, edited by Theodore Hirsch and others. 6 vols. S. Hirzel, Leipzig, 1861–74; Frankfurt, 1965. Contains the chronicles of the Teutonic Order.

Heinrici Chronicon Livoniae, edited by Leonid Arbusow and Albert Bauer. 2nd edition, Hahnsche, Hannover, 1955. The standard scholarly edition.

Livländische Reimchronik, edited by Leo Mayer. Georg Olms, Hildesheim, 1963 (reprint of 1876 edition). The principal account of the period 1227–90.

Preussische Urkundenbuch. Hartung, Königsberg, 1882–; Elwert, Marburg/Lahn, 1955–. Also: http://www.phil.uni-erlangen.de/~plges/quellen/pub/4frame.html. The collected documents of the Teutonic Order.

Liv-, Est-. und Kurländische Urkundenbuch, edited by Friedrich Georg von Bunge. 12 vols. H. Laakman, Reval, 1853–9; Riga and Moscow, 1867–1910. The collected documents of the Livonian Order.

Das Zeugenverhör des Franciscus de Moliano (1312), edited by August Seraphim. Thomas Oppermann, Königsberg, 1912. A transcript of the inquiry by the papal legate into the feud between Riga and the Teutonic Knights. Often incautiously mined for snappy quotes.

Lites ac Res gestae inter Polonos Ordineque Cruciferorum. 3 vols. Kónicke, Poznań, 1892. The papal legates' hearings into the Teutonic Knights' misdeeds in Poland. Also often used naively.

Monumenta Poloniae Historica. 6 vols. Gravenhagen, 1893; Państwowe Wydawnictwo Naukowe, Warsaw, 1961. Contains the minor chronicles.

Johannis Długossi, Historiae Polonicae in Opera Omnia, edited by Alexander Przezdziecki. CZAS, Cracow, 1876–8. The most important source for mediaeval Polish history.

Secondary Accounts

Books on the crusading order in German and Polish are numerous, and the number of articles is almost beyond counting. The most important are:

Arnold, Udo, ed. *Die Hochmeister des Deutschen Ordens 1190–1994.* Elwert, Marburg, 1998. (*Quellen und Studien zur Geschichte des Deutschen Ordens,* 6.)

Benninghoven, Friedrich. *Der Orden der Schwertbrüder.* Böhlau, Köln-Graz, 1965.

Biskup, Marian, and Labuda, Gerard. *Dzieje Zakonu Krzyżackiego w Prusach: Gospodarka–Społeczeństwo–Panstwo–Idelogia.* Morskie, Gdańsk, 1986.

Boockmann, Harmut. *Der Deutsche Orden: Zwölf Kapitel aus seiner Geschichte.* Beck, München, 1981. The most easily read overview.

Ekdahl, Sven. *Die Schlacht bei Tannenberg 1410, Quellenkritische Untersuchungen, vol.1: Einführung und Quellenunterlage.* Duncker und Humblot, Berlin, 1982. Highly recommended.

Górski, Karol. *L'Ordine Teutonico, alle Origini dello Stato Prussiano.* Einaudi, Turin, 1971.

Jučas, Mečislovas. *Žalgiro mūšis.* 2nd edition, Baltos Lankos, Vilnius, 1999.

Kuczyński, Stefan. *Spór o Grunwald.* MON, Warsaw, 1972.

Labuda, Gerard, ed. *Historia Pomorza, vol.1* (in two parts): *do roku 1466.* Wydawnictwo Poznańskie, Poznań, 1972.

Lowmiański, Henryk. *Studia nad Dziejami Wielkiego Ksi stwa Litewskiego.* UaM, Poznań, 1983.

Murawski, Klaus Eberhard. *Zwischen Tannenberg und Thorn: Die Geschichte des Deutschen Ordens unter dem Hochmeister Konrad von Erlichshausen 1441–1449.* Wissenschaftlicher Verlag, Göttingen, 1953. (*Göttinger Bausteine zur Geschichtswissenschaft,* 10–11.)

Schumacher, Bruno. *Geschichte Ost- und Westpreussens.* 6th edition, Holner, Würzburg, 1977.

Tumler, P. Martin. *Der Deutsche Orden: Werden, Wachsen und Wirkung bis 1400.* Panorama, Wien, 1955.

Index